Gallery of

Best

Resumes

for

People Without a Four-Year Degree

A Special Collection of Quality Resumes by
Professional Resume Writers

SECOND EDITION

by David F. Noble

Gallery of Best Resumes for People Without a Four-Year Degree, Second Edition
A Special Collection of Quality Resumes by Professional Resume Writers
Originally published as *Gallery of Best Resumes for Two-Year Degree Graduates*

© 1990, 2000 by David F. Noble

Published by JIST Works, an imprint of JIST Publishing, Inc.
8902 Otis Avenue
Indianapolis, IN 46216-1033
Phone: 800-648-JIST   Fax: 800-JIST-FAX   E-mail: editorial@jist.com

Visit our Web site at http://www.jist.com for more information on JIST, free job search information and book chapters, and ordering information on our many products!

Other books by David F. Noble:

Gallery of Best Cover Letters
Gallery of Best Resumes
Professional Resumes for Executives, Managers, and Other Administrators
Professional Resumes for Accounting, Tax, Finance, and Law
Using WordPerfect in Your Job Search

Quantity discounts are available for JIST books. Please call our Sales Department at 1-800-648-5478 for a free catalog and more information.

Proofreader: Veda Dickerson
Interior Designer: Debbie Berman
Cover Designer: designLab, Seattle
Page Layout: Debbie Berman

Printed in the United States of America.

03 02 01 00   9 8 7 6 5 4 3 2 1

ISBN: 1-56370-736-5

In memory of my brother,
Maynard A. Noble (1929-1995),
and to Peggy, Ron, Chris, and Wendy,
who made him rich with their loving care

Acknowledgments

To all those who helped to make possible this updated and renamed Gallery for people without a four-year degree, I would like to acknowledge my appreciation. I am most indebted to all the professional resume writers who sent me updated versions of their work for inclusion in this book. These writers took the time on short notice to supply updated copies and new documents to fit the new title of the book.

If you need assistance with your resume or cover letter, please consult the List of Contributors at the back of this book for a professional writer located in your area.

I want to express my gratitude to Bob Grilliot for suggesting the inclusion of resumes for people without four-year degrees, and to Barb Ruess and Michael Cunningham for agreeing to a doable schedule. Debbie Berman's work is again top-notch, and it was a pleasure to work with Veda Dickerson as proofreader.

Contents

Acknowledgments v

Introduction 1

Why a Gallery for People Without a Four-Year Degree? 1

How This Book Is Organized 2
This useful "idea book" of best resumes for people without a four-year degree has three parts: Resume Writing Tips; a Gallery of 229 resumes written by 79 professional writers; and an Exhibit of 30 cover letters, together with tips for polishing cover letters. With this book, you not only have a treasury of quality resumes and cover letters but also learn how to view them as superior models for your own resumes and cover letters.

Who This Book Is For 4

What This Book Can Do for You 4
This collection of professionally written resumes shows you how to play up your skills and work experience in your own resume to be more competitive as a job applicant in the current job market.

Part 1: Best Resume Tips 5

Best Resume Tips at a Glance 6

Best Resume Writing Tips 7

Best Resume Writing Strategies 8

Best Resume Design and Layout Tips 9

Best Resume Writing Style Tips 14

Part 2: The Gallery of Professional Resumes 17

The Gallery at a Glance 18

How to Use the Gallery 19

Resumes Grouped by Occupational Fields

Accounting/Finance Resumes 21
Administrative Support Resumes 31
Communications Resumes 43

Computer Technology Resumes 55

Customer Service Resumes 73

Design Resumes 87

Education and Training Resumes 99

Engineering and Technology Resumes 105

Environment Resumes 153

Health Care Resumes 165

Hospitality Resumes 207

Human Resources Resumes 225

Law Enforcement and Criminal Justice Resumes 235

Legal Support Resumes 245

Maintenance Resumes 251

Management Resumes 257

Military-to-Civilian Transition Resumes 297

Sales and Marketing Resumes 309

Social Service Resumes 343

Part 3: Best Cover Letter Tips

.... 349

Best Cover Tips at a Glance 350

Best Cover Letter Writing Tips

.... 351

Myths about Cover Letters

.... 351

Tips for Polishing Cover Letters

.... 352

A quality resume can make a great impression, but it can be ruined
quickly by a poorly written cover letter. This section shows you how to
eliminate common errors in cover letters. It amounts to a *crash writing
course* that you won't find in any other resume book. After you read the
following sections, you will be better able to write and polish any letters
you create for your job search.

Using Good Strategies for Letters 352

Using Pronouns Correctly 353

Using Verb Forms Correctly 354

Using Punctuation Correctly 355

Using Words Correctly 358

Exhibit of Cover Letters

.... 360

Appendix: List of Contributors

.... 391

Occupation Index

.... 403

Features Index

.... 405

Introduction

Like the *Gallery of Best Resumes*, the *Gallery of Best Resumes for People Without a Four-Year Degree* is a collection of quality resumes from professional resume writers, each with individual views about resumes and resume writing. Unlike many resume books whose selections "look the same," this book contains resumes that look different because they are representations of *real* resumes prepared by different professionals for actual job searchers throughout the country. (Certain information on the resumes has been fictionalized by the writers to protect, where necessary, each client's right to privacy.) Even when several resumes from the same writer appear in the book, most of these resumes are different because the writer has customized each resume according to the background information and career goals of the client for whom the resume was prepared.

Instead of assuming that "one resume style fits all," the writers featured here believe that a client's past experiences and next job target should determine the resume's type, design, and content. The use of *Best* in the book's title reflects this approach to resume making. The resumes are not "best" because they are ideal types for you to copy, but because resume writers have interacted with clients to fashion resumes that seemed best for each client's situation at the time.

This book features resumes from writers who share several important qualities: good listening skills, a sense of what details are appropriate for a particular resume, and flexibility in selecting and arranging the resume's sections. By "hearing between" a client's statements, the perceptive resume writer can detect what kind of job the client really wants. The writer then chooses the information that will best represent the client for the job being sought. Finally, the writer decides on the best arrangement of the information, from the most important to the least important, for that job. With the help of this book, you can create this kind of resume yourself.

Most of the writers of the resumes in this Gallery are members of either the Professional Association of Résumé Writers (PARW) or the National Résumé Writers Association (NRWA). Some of the writers belong to both organizations. Those who have CPRW certification, for Certified Professional Résumé Writer, received this designation from PARW after they studied specific course materials and demonstrated proficiency in an examination. Those who have NCRW certification, for National Certified Résumé Writer, received this designation from NRWA after a different course of study and a different examination. Some of the writers are currently not members of either organization but are either past members or professional writers in Indiana, Michigan, and Ohio who were invited by the author to submit works for possible selection for the first edition of this Gallery (*Gallery of Best Resumes for Two-Year Degree Graduates*). For contact information about PARW and NRWA, see their listings at the end of the Appendix (List of Contributors).

Why a Gallery for People Without a Four-Year Degree?

First of all, it should be made clear that people without a four-year degree are not people without education or who go to college for a couple of years, grow tired of studying, drop out of college, and get a job. This stereotypical misconception is refuted by almost every resume in this Gallery. People without a four-year degree comprise diverse kinds of individuals including those, such as paralegals, who took courses of a particular curriculum to work in a specialized field; those who got a two-year degree as a step toward getting a bachelor's degree; those who were job changers—people in transition—who acquired a two-year degree and possibly additional certification(s) to move to a field of new opportunity; those who had to interrupt their education for various reasons; those who had to work for economic reasons rather than study; and those who took different paths (military training, technical education, and so on) to their current occupation.

People without a four-year degree have special resume needs. Compared to traditional four-year students, who may have more campus activities and less full-time work experience to report on a resume, people without a four-year degree may have more full-time work experience to report. This means that Skills and Achievements will tend to be highlighted first and Education put last in their resumes. The converse will be true for traditional four-year degree job candidates.

People without a four-year degree also need resumes that will help them compete successfully for jobs of employers who traditionally prefer workers with four-year and higher degrees. This Gallery showcases resumes that have helped people without a four-year degree to compete successfully for better jobs in today's job market.

How This Book Is Organized

Gallery of Best Resumes for People Without a Four-Year Degree consists of three parts. Part 1, "Best Resume Tips," presents resume writing strategies, design and layout tips, and resume writing style tips for making resumes visually impressive. Many of these strategies and tips were suggested by the resume writers who contributed resumes to *Gallery of Best Resumes* (Indianapolis: JIST Works, 1984). From time to time, a reference is given to one or more Gallery resumes that illustrate the strategy or tip.

Part 2 is the Gallery itself, containing 229 resumes from 79 professional resume writers. The location of 20 of these writers has become unknown since the first edition of this Gallery. Some of these writers have retired, and several have changed careers. Included also are a few "before" resumes from clients so that you can see how the writers improved these resumes.

Resume writers commonly distinguish between chronological resumes and functional (or skills) resumes. A *chronological resume* is a photo—a snapshot history of what you did and when you did it. A *functional resume* is a painting—an interpretive sketch of what you can do for a future employer. A third kind of resume, known as a *combination resume*, is a mix of recalled history and self-assessment. Besides recollecting "the facts," a combination resume contains self-interpretation and is therefore more like dramatic history than news coverage. A chronological resume and a functional resume are not always that different; often, all that is needed for a functional resume to qualify as a combination resume is the inclusion of some dates, such as those for positions held. All three kinds of resumes are illustrated in the Gallery.

The resumes in the Gallery are presented in the following occupational categories:

Accounting/Finance

Administrative Support

Communications

Computer Technology

Customer Service

Design

Education and Training

Engineering and Technology

Environment

Health Care

Hospitality

Human Resources

Law Enforcement and Criminal Justice

Legal Support

Maintenance

Management

Military-to-Civilian Transition

Sales and Marketing

Social Service

Within each category, the resumes are generally arranged from the simple to the complex. Most of the resumes are one page, but a number of them are two pages. A few are more than two pages.

The Gallery offers a wide range of resumes whose features you can use in creating and improving your own resumes. Notice the plural. An important premise of an active job search is that you will not have just one "perfect" resume for all potential employers, but different versions of your resume for different interviews. The Gallery is therefore not a showroom where you say, "I'll take that one," alter it with your information, and then duplicate your version 200 times. It is a valuable resource of design ideas, expressions, and organizational patterns that can help make your own resume a "best resume" for your next interview.

Creating multiple *versions* of a resume may seem difficult, but it is easy to do if you have (or have access to) a personal computer and a laser printer or some other kind of printer that can produce quality output. You will also need word processing, desktop publishing, or resume software. If you don't have a computer or a friend who does, most professional resume writers have the hardware and software, and they can make your resume look like those in the Gallery. See the List of Contributors in the Appendix for the names, addresses, phone numbers, and e-mail addresses of the professional writers whose works are featured in this book. A local fast-print shop can make your resume look good, but you will probably not get there the kind of advice and service the professional resume writer provides. Of course, if all you have is a typewriter without memory, you can still produce versions of your resume, but you will need to retype the resume for each new version.

Part 3, "Best Cover Letter Tips," contains a discussion of some myths about cover letters, plus tips for polishing cover letters. Much of the advice offered here applies also to writing resumes. Included in this part is an exhibit of 30 cover letters. Most of these letters accompanied resumes that appear in the Gallery.

The List of Contributors in the Appendix is arranged alphabetically by state and city. Although most of these resume writers work with local clients, some of the writers work with clients by phone from anywhere in the United States.

You can use the Occupation Index to look up resumes by the current or most recent job title. This index, however, should not replace careful examination of all of the resumes. Too many resumes for some other occupation may have features adaptable to your own occupation. Limiting your search to the Occupation Index may cause you to miss some valuable examples. You can use the Features Index to find resumes that contain representative resume sections that may be important to you and your resume needs.

Who This Book Is For

Anyone who wants ideas for creating or improving a resume can benefit from this book. It is especially useful for active job seekers—those who understand the difference between active and passive job searching. A *passive* job seeker waits until jobs are advertised and then mails copies of the same resume, along with a standard cover letter, to a number of Help Wanted ads. An *active* job seeker believes that a resume should be modified for a specific job target *after* having talked in person or by phone to a prospective interviewer *before* a job is announced. To schedule such an interview is to penetrate the "hidden job market." Active job seekers can find in the Gallery's focused resumes a wealth of strategies for targeting a resume for a particular interview. The section "How to Use the Gallery" at the beginning of Part 2 shows you how to do this.

Besides the active job seeker, any unemployed person who wants to create a more competitive resume or update an old one should find this book helpful. It shows the kinds of resumes that professional resume writers are writing, and it showcases resumes for job seekers with particular needs.

What This Book Can Do for You

Besides providing you with a treasury of quality resumes whose features you can use in your own resumes, this book can help transform your thinking about resumes. If you think that there is one "best" way to create a resume, this book will help you learn how to shape a resume that is best for you as you try to get an interview with a particular person for a specific job.

If you have been told that resumes should be only one page long, the examples of multiple-page resumes in the Gallery will help you see how to distribute information effectively across two or more pages. If you believe that the way to update a resume is to add your latest work experiences to your last resume, this book will show you how to rearrange your resume so that you can highlight the most important information about your experience and skills.

After you have studied "Best Resume Tips" in Part 1, examined the professionally written resumes in the Gallery in Part 2, and reviewed "Tips for Polishing Cover Letters" in Part 3, you should be able to create your own resumes and cover letters worthy of inclusion in any gallery of best resumes.

P·A·R·T
1

Best
Resume Tips

Best Resume Tips at a Glance

Best Resume Writing Tips 7

    Best Resume Writing Strategies 8

    Best Resume Design and Layout Tips 10

    Best Resume Writing Style Tips... 14

Best Resume Writing Tips

In a passive job search, you rely on your resume to do most of the work for you. An eye-catching resume that stands out above all the others may be your best shot at getting noticed by a prospective employer. If your resume is only average and looks like most of the others in the pile, the chances are great that you won't be noticed and called for an interview. If you want to be singled out because of your resume, it should be somewhere between spectacular and award-winning.

In an active job search, however, your resume complements your efforts at being known to a prospective employer *before* that person receives it. For this reason, you can rely less on your resume for getting someone's attention. Nevertheless, your resume has an important role in an active job search that may include the following activities:

- Talking to relatives, friends, and other acquaintances to meet people who can hire you before a job is available

- Contacting employers directly, using the *Yellow Pages* to identify types of organizations that could use a person with your skills

- Creating phone scripts to speak with the person who is most likely to hire someone with your background and skills

- Walking into a business in person to talk directly to the one who is most likely to hire someone like you

- Using a schedule to keep track of your appointments and callbacks

- Working at least 25 hours a week to search for a job

When you are this active in searching for a job, the quality of your resume confirms the quality of your efforts to get to know the person who might hire you, as well as your worth to the company whose workforce you want to join. An eye-catching resume makes it easier for you to sell yourself directly to a prospective employer. If your resume is mediocre or conspicuously flawed, it will work against you and may undo all of your good efforts in searching for a job.

The following list offers ideas for making resumes visually impressive. Many of the ideas are for making resumes pleasing to the eye, but a number of the ideas are strategies to use in resumes for special cases. Other ideas are for eliminating common writing mistakes and stylistic weaknesses.

A number of the ideas came from comments of professional resume writers who submitted resumes for *Gallery of Best Resumes* (Indianapolis: JIST Works, 1994). The name of the writer appears in brackets. Resumes in *Gallery of Best Resumes for People Without a Four-Year Degree* that illustrate these ideas are referenced by resume number.

Some of these ideas can be used with any equipment, from a manual typewriter to a sophisticated computer with desktop publishing software. Other ideas make sense only if you have a computer system with word processing or desktop publishing. Even if you don't have a computer, take some time to read all of the ideas. Then, if you decide to use the services of a professional resume writer, you will be better informed about what the writer can do for you in producing your resume.

Best Resume Writing Strategies

1. **Although many resume books say that you should spell out the name of the state in your address at the top of the resume, consider using the postal abbreviation instead.** The reason is simple: it's an address. Anyone wanting to contact you by mail will probably refer to your name and address on the resume. If they appear there as they should on an envelope, the writer or typist can simply copy the information you supply. If you spell out the name of your state in full, the writer will have to "translate" the name of the state to its postal abbreviation.

   Not everyone knows all the postal abbreviations, and some abbreviations are easily confused. For example, those for Alabama (AL), Alaska (AK), American Samoa (AS), Arizona (AZ), and Arkansas (AR) are easy to mix up. You can prevent confusion and delay simply by using the correct postal abbreviation. As resumes become more "scannable," the use of postal abbreviations in addresses will become a requirement.

   If you decide to use postal abbreviations in addresses, make certain that you do not add a period after the abbreviations, even before ZIP codes. This applies also to postal abbreviations in the addresses of references, if provided.

   Do not, however, use the state postal abbreviation when you are indicating only the city and state (not the mailing address) of a school you attended or a business where you worked. In these cases, it makes sense to write out the name of the state in full.

2. **Adopt a sensible form for phone numbers and then use it consistently.** Do this in your resume and in all of the documents you use in your job search. Some forms for phone numbers make more sense than others. Compare the following forms:

123-4567	This form is best for a resume circulated locally, within a region where all the phone numbers have the same area code.
(222) 123-4567	This form is best for a resume circulated in areas with different area codes.
222-123-4567	This form suggests that the area code should be dialed in all cases. But that won't be necessary for prospective employers whose area code is 222. This form should be avoided.
222/123-4567	This form is illogical and should be avoided also. The slash can mean an alternate option, as in ON/OFF. In a phone number, this meaning of a slash makes little sense.
1 (222) 123-4567	This form is long, and the digit 1 isn't necessary. Almost everyone will know that 1 should be used before the area code to dial a long-distance number.

222.123.4567   This form, which resembles a Web address, is becoming popular.

Note: For resumes directed to prospective employers *outside* the United States, be sure to include the correct international prefixes in all phone numbers so that you and your references can be reached easily by phone.

3. **Make your Objective statement focused, interesting, and unique so that it grabs the reader's attention.** If your Objective statement fails to do this, the reader might discard the resume without reading further. An Objective statement can be your first opportunity to sell yourself.

4. **In the Experience section, state achievements, not just duties or responsibilities.** Duties and responsibilities for a given position are often already known by the reader. Achievements, however, can be interesting. The reader probably considers life too short to be bored by lists of duties and responsibilities in a stack of resumes. See, for example, Resume 180.

5. **When skills and abilities are varied, group them according to categories for easier comprehension.** See, for example, Resume 16.

6. **To make your promotions stand out, list your work experiences chronologically, with the range of dates for each position.** [Beverly Baskin, Marlboro, New Jersey]

7. **Summarize your qualifications and work experiences to avoid having to repeat yourself in the job descriptions.** [Wendy A. Lowry, Erie, Pennsylvania]

8. **To appear less like a student and more like an experienced candidate for a specialized job, play down typical education information and play up any experiences related to your job objective.** Distinguish those experiences in a separate section apart from college/university experiences. Consider using the heading Leadership Experience. Instead of listing related courses (a section commonly found on resumes of graduating students), call attention to "areas of emphasis" that seem relevant to the targeted job. See, for example, Resumes 4, 8, 11, 35, and 36. [Alan D. Ferrell, Lafayette, Indiana]

9. **To diminish the negative impact of a gap in your employment, omit the dates of employment and consider listing employment in some order other than chronological.** [Carol Lawrence, Savannah, Georgia]

10. **Create a prominent Skills and Abilities section that draws together skills and abilities you have gained in previous work experience from different careers.** See, for example, Resumes 13 and 16. If you have worked for the same company over an entire career, use this section to showcase the skills and abilities you have acquired in different positions with that company. [Joseph DiGiorgio, Erie, Pennsylvania]

11. **Avoid using the archaic word *upon* in the References section.** The common statement "References available upon request" needs to be simplified, updated, or even deleted in resume writing. The word *upon* is one of the finest words of the 13th century, but it's a stuffy word on the eve of the next century. Usually, *on* will do for *upon*. Other possibilities are "References available by request" and "References available." Because most readers of resumes know that applicants can usually provide several reference letters, this statement is probably unnecessary. A reader who is seriously interested in you will ask about reference letters.

12. **Consider presenting a list of projects or detailed information in an addendum.** See, for example, Resumes 19, 57, and 89. [Carla Culp Coury, Glen Carbon, Illinois]. In the addendum, you might highlight your skills, including job-related and transferable skills. Use the addendum *after* an interview and include it with a thank-you note. [Gayle Bernstein, Indianapolis, Indiana]

Best Resume Design and Layout Tips

13. **Use quality paper correctly.** If you use quality watermarked paper for your resume, be sure to use the right side of the paper. To know which side is the right side, hold a blank sheet of paper up to a light source. If you can see a watermark and "read" it, the right side of the paper is facing you. This is the surface for typing or printing. If the watermark is unreadable or if any characters look backward, you are looking at the "underside" of a sheet of paper—the side that should be left blank if you use only one side of the sheet.

14. **Use adequate "white space."** A sheet of white paper with no words on it is impossible to read. Likewise, a sheet of white paper with words all over it is impossible to read. The goal is to have a comfortable mix of white space and words. If your resume has too many words and not enough white space, the resume looks cluttered and unfriendly. If it has too much white space and too few words, the resume looks skimpy and unimportant. Make certain that adequate white space exists between the main sections. For examples that display good use of white space, see Resumes 1, 35, 61, 62, 68, 70, 88, 101, 105, 139, and 165.

15. **Make the margins uniform in width and preferably no less than an inch.** Margins are part of the white space of a resume page. If the margins shrink below an inch, the page begins to have a "too much to read" look. An enemy of margins is the one-page rule. If you try to fit more than one page of information on a page, the first temptation is to shrink the margins to make room for the extra material. It is better to shrink the material by paring it down than to reduce the size of the left, right, top, and bottom margins. If you do your resume on a computer, lowering the point size of the type is one way to save the margins.

16. **Be consistent in your use of line spacing.** How you handle line spacing can tell the reader how good you are at details and how consistent you are in your use of them. If, near the beginning of your resume, you insert two line spaces (two hard returns in a word processing program) between two main sections, be sure to put two line spaces between main sections throughout the resume.

17. **Be consistent in your use of horizontal spacing.** If you usually put two character spaces after a period at the end of a sentence, make certain that you use two spaces consistently. The same is true for colons. If you put two spaces after colons, do so consistently.

Note that an em dash—a dash the width of the letter *m*—does not require spaces before or after it. No space should go between the *P* and *O* of P.O. Box. Only one space is needed between the postal abbreviation of a state and the ZIP code. You should insert a space between the first and second initials of a person's name, as in I. M. Jobseeker (not I.M. Jobseeker). These conventions have become widely adopted in English and business communications. If, however, you use other conventions, be sure to be consistent. In resumes, as in grammar, consistency is more important than conformity.

18. **Make certain that characters, lines, and images contrast well with the paper.** The quality of "ink" depends on the device used to type or print your resume. If you use a typewriter or a dot-matrix printer with a cloth ribbon, check that the ribbon is fresh enough to make a dark impression. If you use a typewriter or a printer with a carbon tape, make certain that your paper has a texture that allows the characters to adhere permanently. (For a test, send yourself a copy of your resume and see how it makes the trip through the mail.) If you use an inkjet or laser printer, check that the characters are sharp and clean, without ink smudges or traces of extra toner.

    After much use, a cloth ribbon in a typewriter or a daisywheel printer may cause some characters (especially *a*, *e*, *o*, *g*, and *p*) to look darker than others. The reason probably is that ink has collected in the characters on the type bars or print wheel. To fix this problem, use a toothbrush and a safe solvent to clean the type.

19. **Use vertical alignment in stacked text.** Resumes usually contain tabbed or indented text. Make certain that this "stacked" material is aligned vertically. Misalignment can ruin the appearance of a well-written resume. Try to set tabs or indents that control this text throughout a resume instead of having a mix of tab stops in different sections. If you use a word processor, make certain that you understand the difference between tabbed text and indented text, as in the following examples:

    Tabbed text: This text was tabbed over one tab stop before the writer started to write the sentence.

    Indented text: This text was indented once before the writer started to write the sentence.

    Note: In a number of word processing programs, the Indent command is useful for ensuring the correct vertical alignment of proportionally spaced, stacked text. After you issue the Indent command, lines of wrapped text are vertically aligned automatically until you terminate the command by pressing Enter.

20. **For the vertical alignment of dates, try left- or right-aligning the dates.** This technique is especially useful in chronological resumes and combination resumes. For examples of left-aligned dates, see Resumes 66, 74, 113, and 116. For right-aligned dates, look at Resumes 59, 63, 65, 71, and 166.

21. **Use as many pages as you need for portraying yourself adequately to a specific interviewer about a particular job.** Try to limit your resume to one page, but set the upper limit at four pages. No rule about the number of pages makes sense in all cases. The determining factors are a person's qualifications and experiences, the requirements of the job, and the interests and pet peeves of the interviewer. If you know that an interviewer refuses to look at a resume longer than a page, that says it all. You need to deliver a one-page resume if you want to get past the first gate. For examples of two-page resumes, see Resumes 6, 15, 21, 24, 25, 26, 49, 57, 61, and 65. For three-page resumes, look at Resumes 19 and 98.

22. **When you have letters of recommendation, use quotations from them as testimonials in the first column of a two-column format or somewhere else in the resume.** Devoting a whole column to the positive opinions of "external authorities" helps to make a resume convincing as well as impressive. See, for example, Resume 37. [Carla Culp Coury, Glen Carbon, Illinois]

23. **Unless you enlist the services of a professional printer or skilled desktop publisher, resist the temptation to use full justification for text.** The price that you pay for a straight right margin is uneven word spacing. Words may appear too close together on some lines and too spread out on others. Although the resume might look like typeset text, you lose readability. See also Tip 4 in Part 3 of this book.

24. **If you can choose a typeface for your resume, use a serif font for greater readability.** Serif fonts have little lines extending from the top, bottom, and end of a character. These fonts tend to be easier to read than sans serif (without serif) fonts, especially in low-light conditions. Compare the following font examples:

Serif	**Sans Serif**
Century Schoolbook	Gill Sans
Courier	Futura
Times New Roman	Helvetica

    Words like *minimum* and *abilities* are more readable in a serif font.

25. **If possible, avoid using monospaced type like this Courier type.** Courier was a standard of business communications during the 1960s and 1970s. Because of its widespread use, it is now considered "common." It also takes up a lot of space, so you can't pack as much information on a page with Courier type as you can with a proportionally spaced type like Times Roman.

26. **Think twice before using all uppercase letters in parts of your resume.** A common misconception is that uppercase letters are easier to read than lowercase letters. Actually, the ascenders and descenders of lowercase letters make them more distinguishable from each other and therefore more recognizable than uppercase letters. For a test, look at a string of uppercase letters and throw them gradually out of focus by squinting. The uppercase letters become a blur sooner than lowercase letters.

27. **Think twice about underlining some words in your resume.** Underlining defeats the purpose of serifs at the bottom of characters by blending with the serifs. In trying to emphasize words, you lose some visual clarity. This is especially true if you use underlining with uppercase letters in centered or side headings.

28. **If you have access to many fonts through word processing or desktop publishing, beware of becoming "font happy" and turning your resume into a font circus.** Frequent font changes can distract the reader adversely, AND SO CAN GAUDY DISPLAY TYPE.

29. **To make your resume stand out, consider using a nonstandard format with the headings in unconventional display type.** See, for example, Resume 70. When you compare this idea with the preceding idea, you can see that one of the basic rules of resume making is, "Anything goes." What is usually fitting for resumes for most prospective jobs is not always the most appropriate resume strategy for every job opportunity. [Nita Busby, Placentia, California]

30. **Be aware of the value differences of black type.** Some typefaces are light; others are dark. Notice the following lines:

    A quick brown fox jumps over the lazy dog.

    A quick brown fox jumps over the lazy dog.

Most typefaces fall somewhere in-between. With the variables of height, width, thickness, serifs, angles, curves, spacing, ink color, ink density, boldfacing, and typewriter double-striking, you can see that type offers an infinite range of values from light to dark. Try to make your resume more visually interesting by offering stronger contrasts between light type and dark type. See, for example, Resumes 1 and 150.

31. **Use italic characters carefully.** Whenever possible, use italic characters instead of underlining when you need to call attention to a word or phrase. You might consider using italic for duties or achievements, as in Resumes 6, 25, and 99. Think twice about using italic throughout your resume, however. The reason is that italic characters are less readable than normal characters.

32. **Use boldfacing to make different job experiences more evident.** See, for example, Resumes 58, 61, 63, 109, and 110. When a typewriter or dot-matrix printer is the only printing device available, try combining underlining with boldfacing to make different career experiences stand out. If the underlining impairs the readability of the boldfacing, use only boldfacing. [Robert Markman, Cedar Grove, New Jersey]

33. **If you use word processing or desktop publishing and have a suitable printer, use special characters to enhance the look of your resume.** For example, use enhanced quotations marks ("and") instead of their typewriter equivalents (" "). Use an em dash (—) instead of two hyphens (--) for a dash. To separate dates, try using an en dash (a dash the width of the letter *n*) instead of a hyphen, as in 1993–1994.

34. **Consider using shading creatively in a table.** See Resume 203.

35. **To call attention to an item in a list, use a bullet (•) or a box (□) instead of a hyphen (-).** Browse through the Gallery and notice how bullets are used effectively as attention getters.

36. **For variety, try using bullets of a different style, such as diamond (♦) bullets, rather than the usual round or square bullets.** Examples with diamonds are Resumes 25, 27, 40, 49, 57, 62, 89, 101, 137, and 188. For other kinds of "bullets," see Resumes 2, 15, 17, 19, 21, 41, 44, 46, 53, 55, 56, 57, 61, 64, 85, 87, 93, 97, 131, and 150. [Gerald Hosek, Chicago, Illinois]

37. **Make a bullet a little smaller than the lowercase letters that appear after it.** Disregard any ascenders or descenders on the letters. Compare the following bullet sizes:

    • Too small   ● Too large   • Better   • Just right

38. **When you use bullets, make certain that the bulleted items go beyond the superficial and contain information that employers really want to know.** Many short bulleted statements that say nothing special can affect the reader negatively. Brevity is not always the best strategy with bullets. For examples of substantial bulleted items, see Resume 101. [Melanie A. Noonan, West Paterson, New Jersey]

39. **When the amount of information justifies a longer resume, repeat a particular graphic, such as a filled square bullet (■) or a right-pointing arrow, to unify the entire resume.** See, for example, Resume 118.

40. **If possible, visually coordinate the resume and the cover letter with the same font treatment or graphic to catch the attention of the reader.** See,

for example, Resumes 23, 181, and 195 and Cover Letters 18, 14, and 4, respectively. [Michael Robertson, Alexandria, Louisiana]

41. **Try to make graphics match the subject of the resume.** See, for example, Resumes 44, 70, 79, 93, 116, 139, 170, and 206.

42. **Use a horizontal line to separate the name (or both the name and the address) from the rest of the resume.** If you browse through the Gallery, you can see many resumes that use horizontal lines this way. See, for example, Resumes 24, 25, 27, 30, 55, 60, 61, 62, 63, and 101.

43. **Use horizontal lines to separate the different sections of the resume.** See, for example, Resumes 6, 45, 56, 66, 80, 151, 170, and 202. See also Resumes 17, 49, and 110, whose lines are interrupted by the section headings.

44. **To call attention to a resume section or certain information, use horizontal lines to enclose it.** See, for example, Resumes 3, 12, 35, 38, 64, 94, 99, and 109. See also Resumes 10, 34, and 84 in which two or more sections are enclosed by horizontal lines.

45. **Change the thickness of part of a horizontal line to call attention to a section heading below the line.** See, for example, Resumes 24, 33, and 80.

46. **Use horizontal lines between sections and then vary the positions of the section headings along the lines.** See, for example, Resume 24.

47. **Use a vertical line (or lines) to spice up your resume.** See, for example, Resumes 105, 113, 168, 186, and 209. See also Resume 5 in which both vertical and horizontal lines are used.

48. **Use shaded boxes or headings to make a page visually more interesting.** See, for example, Resumes 147, 203, 217, and 222. Compare these boxes with the *shadow* boxes in Resumes 19, 123, and 166. Note the *shadow oval* in Resume 122.

Best Resume Writing Style Tips

49. **Check that words or phrases in lists are parallel.** For example, notice the bulleted items in the Professional Experience section of Resume 125. All the verbs, used for duties in the current job, are in the present tense. Notice also the list in the Profile section of Resume 210. Here all the entries begin with nouns.

50. **Use capital letters correctly.** Resumes usually contain many of the following:

    ■ Names of people, companies, organizations, government agencies, awards, and prizes

    ■ Titles of job positions and publications

    ■ References to academic fields (such as chemistry, English, and mathematics)

    ■ Geographic regions (such as the Midwest, the East, the state of California, and Oregon State)

Because of such words, resumes are mine fields for the misuse of uppercase letters. When you don't know whether a word should have an initial capital letter, don't guess. Consult a dictionary, a handbook on style, or some other authoritative source. Often a reference librarian can provide the information you need. If so, you are only a phone call away from an accurate answer.

51. **Check that capital letters and hyphens are used correctly in computer terms.** If you want to show in a Computer Experience section that you have used certain hardware and software, you may give the opposite impression if you don't use uppercase letters and hyphens correctly. Note the correct use of capitals and hyphens in the following names of hardware, software, and computer companies:

LaserJet III	Hewlett-Packard	dBASE
PageMaker	MS-DOS	Microsoft
WordPerfect	PC DOS	Microsoft Word
NetWare	PostScript	

The reason that many computer product names have an internal uppercase letter is for the sake of a trademark. A word with unusual spelling or capitalization is trademarkable. When you use the correct forms of these words, you are honoring trademarks and registered trademarks.

52. **Use all uppercase letters for most acronyms.** An *acronym* is a pronounceable word usually formed from the initial letters of the words in a compound term, or sometimes from multiple letters in those words. Note the following examples:

BASIC	Beginner's All-purpose Symbolic Instruction Code
COBOL	COmmon Business-Oriented Language
DOS	Disk Operating System
FORTRAN	FORmula TRANslator

An acronym like *radar* (radio detecting and ranging) has become so common that it is no longer all uppercase.

53. **Be aware that you may need to use a period with some abbreviations.** An *abbreviation* is a word shortened by removing the latter part of the word or by deleting some letters within the word. Here are some examples:

adj. for *adjective*	*amt.* for *amount*
adv. for *adverb*	*dept.* for *department*

Usually, you can't pronounce an abbreviation as a word. Sometimes, however, an abbreviation is a set of uppercase letters (without periods) that you can pronounce as letters. AFL-CIO, CBS, NFL, and YMCA are examples.

54. **Be sure to spell every word correctly.** A resume with just one misspelling is not impressive and may undermine all the hours you spent putting it together. Worse than that, one misspelling may be what the reader is looking for to screen you out, particularly if you are applying for a position that requires accuracy with words.

If you use word processing and have a spelling checker, you may be able to catch any misspellings. Be wary of spelling checkers, however. They can detect a misspelled word but cannot detect when you have inadvertently used a wrong word (*to* for *too*, for example). Be wary also of letting someone else check your resume. If the other person is not a good speller, you may not get any real help. The best authority is a good dictionary.

55. **For words that have a couple of correct spellings, use the preferred form.** This form is the one that appears first in a dictionary. For example, if you see the entry **trav·el·ing** *or* **trav·el·ling**, the first form (with one *l*) is the preferred spelling. If you make it a practice to use the preferred spelling, you will build consistency in your resumes and cover letters.

56. **Avoid British spellings.** These slip into American usage through books published in Great Britain. Note the following words:

British Spelling	American Spelling
acknowledgement	acknowledgment
centre	center
judgement	judgment
towards	toward

57. **Avoid hyphenating words with such prefixes as** *co-*, *micro-*, *mid-*, *mini-*, *multi-*, *non-*, *pre-*, *re-*, **and** *sub-*. Many people think that words with these prefixes should have a hyphen after the prefix, but most of these words should not. The following words are spelled correctly:

coauthor	microcomputer	minicomputer
coworker	midpoint	multicultural
cowriter	midway	multilevel
nondisclosure	prearrange	reenter
nonfunctional	prequalify	subdirectory

Note: If you look in a dictionary for a word with a prefix and can't find the word, look for the prefix itself in the dictionary. You might find there a small-print listing of a number of words that have the prefix.

58. **Be aware that compounds (combinations of words) present special problems for hyphenation.** Writers' handbooks and books on style do not always agree on how compounds should be hyphenated. Many compounds are evolving from *open* compounds to *hyphenated* compounds to *closed* compounds. In different dictionaries, you can therefore find the words *copy editor*, *copy-editor*, and *copyeditor*. No wonder the issue is confusing! Most style books do agree, however, that when some compounds appear as an adjective before a noun, the compound should be hyphenated. When the same compound appears after a noun, hyphenation is unnecessary. Compare the following two sentences:

> I scheduled well-attended conferences.
>
> The conferences I scheduled were well attended.

For detailed information about hyphenation, see a recent edition of *The Chicago Manual of Style*. You should be able to find a copy at a local library.

59. **Be sure to hyphenate so-called *permanent* hyphenated compounds.** Usually, you can find these by looking them up in a dictionary. You can spot them easily because they have a "long hyphen" (–) for visibility in the dictionary. Hyphenate these words (with a standard hyphen) wherever they appear, before or after a noun. Here are some examples:

all-important	self-employed
day-to-day	step-by-step
full-blown	time-consuming

2
P · A · R · T

The Gallery
of Professional Resumes

The Gallery at a Glance

How to Use the Gallery 19

Resumes Grouped by Occupational Fields

■ Accounting/Finance Resumes 21

■ Administrative Support Resumes 31

■ Communications Resumes 43

■ Computer Technology Resumes 55

■ Customer Service Resumes 73

■ Design Resumes 87

■ Education and Training Resumes 99

■ Engineering and Technology Resumes 105

■ Environment Resumes 153

■ Health Care Resumes 165

■ Hospitality Resumes 207

■ Human Resources Resumes 225

■ Law Enforcement and Criminal Justice Resumes 235

■ Legal Support Resumes 245

■ Maintenance Resumes 251

■ Management Resumes 257

■ Military-to-Civilian Transition Resumes 297

■ Sales and Marketing Resumes 309

■ Social Service Resumes 343

How to Use the Gallery

You can learn much from the Gallery just by browsing through it. To make the best use of this resource, however, read the following suggestions before you begin.

Look at the resumes in the category containing your field, related fields, or your target occupation. Use also the Occupation Index to do this. Notice what kinds of resumes other people have used to find similar jobs. Always remember, though, that your resume should not be "canned." It should not look just like someone else's resume but should reflect your own background, unique experiences, and goals.

Use the Gallery primarily as an "idea book." Even if you don't find a resume for your specific occupation or job, be sure to look at all the resumes for ideas you can borrow or adapt. You may be able to modify some of the sections or statements with information that applies to your own situation or job target.

Study the ways professional resume writers have formatted the names, addresses, and phone numbers of the subjects. In most instances, this information appears at the top of the first page of the resume. Look at type styles, size of type, and use of boldface. See whether the personal information is centered on lines, spread across a line, or located near the margin on one side of a page. Look for the use of horizontal lines to separate this information from the rest of the resume, or to separate the address and phone number from the person's name.

Look at each resume to see what section appears first after the personal information. Then compare those same sections across the Gallery. For example, look just at the resumes that have a Goal or an Objective statement as the first section. Compare the length, clarity, and use of words. Do these statements contain complete sentences, or one or more partial lines of thought? Are some statements better than others from your point of view? Do you see one or more Objective statements that come close to matching your own objective? After you have compared these statements, try expressing *in your own words* your goal or objective.

Repeat this "horizontal comparison" for each of the sections across the Gallery. Compare all of the Education sections, all of the Qualifications sections, and so on. As you make these comparisons, continue to note differences in length, the kinds of words and phrases used, and the effectiveness of the content. Jot down any ideas that might be true for you. Then put together similar sections for your own resume.

As you compare sections across the Gallery, pay special attention to the Career Highlights, Qualifications, and Experience sections. Notice how skills and accomplishments are worked into these sections. Skills and accomplishments are *variables* that you can select to put a certain "spin" on your resume as you pitch it toward a particular interviewer or job. Your observations here should be especially valuable for your own resume versions.

After you have examined the resumes "horizontally" (section by section), compare them "vertically" (design by design). To do this, you need to determine which resumes have the same sections in the same order, and then compare just those resumes. For example, look for resumes that have personal information at the top, an Objective statement, an Experience section, an Education section, and finally a line about references. (Notice that the section heads may differ slightly. Instead of the word *Experience*, you might find *Work Experience* or *Employment*.) When you examine the resumes in this way, you are looking at their *structural design*, which means the order in which the various sections appear. The same order can appear in resumes of different fields or jobs, so it is important to explore the whole Gallery and not limit your investigation to resumes in your field or related fields.

Developing a sense of resume structure is extremely important because it enables you to emphasize the most important information about yourself. A resume is a little like a newspaper article read quickly and usually discarded before the reader finishes. That is why the information in newspaper articles often dwindles in significance toward the end. For the same reason, the most important, attention-getting information about you should be at or near the top of your resume. What follows should appear in order of descending significance.

If you know that the reader will be more interested in your work experience than your education because you don't have a four-year degree, put your Experience section before your Education. If you know that the reader will be interested in your skills regardless of your education and work experience, put your Skills section at or near the beginning of your resume. In this way, you can help to ensure that anyone who reads only *part* of your resume will read the "best about you." Your hope is that this information will encourage the reader to read on to the end of the resume and, above all, take an interest in you.

Compare the resumes according to visual design features, such as the use of horizontal and vertical lines, borders, boxes, bullets, white space, graphics, and inverse type (light characters on a dark background). Use the Features Index for help here. Notice which resumes have more visual impact at first glance and which ones make no initial impression. Do some of the resumes seem more inviting to read than others? Which ones are less appealing because they have too much information, or too little? Which ones seem to have the right balance of information and white space?

After comparing the visual design features, choose the design ideas that might improve your own resume. You will want to be selective here and not try to work every design possibility into your resume. As in writing, "less is more" in resume making, especially when you integrate design features with content.

Accounting/Finance

Resumes at a Glance

RESUME NO.	LAST OR CURRENT OCCUPATION	GOAL	PAGE
1.	Customer Service Rep./Teller	Accounting position	23
2.	Service Manager	Accounting position	24
3.	Supervisor	Accounting position	25
4.	Warranty Administrator	Not specified	26
5.	Travel Expense Auditor/Accts. Receivable Clerk	Position in data entry or accounting	27
6.	Loan/Service Officer	Not specified	28
7.	Financial Consultant	Not specified	30

COLLEEN L. FISK
27 Wall Street
Lincoln, NE 00000
(000) 000-0000

OBJECTIVE: An entry-level accounting position.

EDUCATION: **A.S. with Honors in Accounting**   XXXX
Lincoln Community College, Lincoln, NE
• Dean's List all semesters: GPA 3.4

Courses:
Accounting I & II
Intermediate Accounting I & II
Managerial Accounting
Computer-Assisted Accounting
Microcomputer Business Applications
Business Law I & II

Computer Skills:
Lotus 1-2-3
MD-DOS
dBASE
WordPerfect

Business Program Graduate
Washington High School, Small Town, NE

EXPERIENCE:

Thrifty Savings Bank, Lincoln, NE
Fours years as Customer Service Representative/ Teller:
Opened and closed accounts, handled safe deposit and
mortgage invoices, processed checks, deposits, and
withdrawals, provided set up and secure access to safe
deposit boxes, resolved customer problems, etc. Balanced
teller drawer.

Shop Quick, Lincoln, NE
Three years as Produce Clerk.

**COMMUNITY
SERVICE:**

Parent Volunteer, Main Street School; Bridge Road Middle
School, Lincoln, NE

Volunteer Speaker, Junior Achievement, Small Town,
Nebraska School System. Spoke to 5th grade on starting a
business.

REFERENCES: Available upon request.

Functional. *Shel Horowitz, Northampton, Massachusetts*

A resume whose design you can comprehend at a glance because of side headings and use of
boldface. Ample white space offsets narrow top and bottom margins.

Jeffrey A. Gordon

5555 Willow Creek Circle
Anywhere, New York 55555

Telephone/Message:
(555) 000-0000

OBJECTIVE: Entry level *Accounting* position where excellent customer service, communication, and technical skills can be utilized.

HIGHLIGHTS OF QUALIFICATIONS:

- **Accounting Skills:** Familiar with basic accounting procedures including cash control. Experience in the use of Bedford Accounting software, Lotus 1-2-3, WordPerfect, PersonalWrite, Multiplan. Completed course work in Computerized Accounting, Income Tax, Cost Accounting, Accounting Principles I-III, Introduction to Spreadsheets.

- **Customer Service:** Ability to communicate effectively and establish excellent rapport with people at all levels. Handle all aspects of customer inquiries and complaints.

- **Personal Attributes:** Very accurate and detail-oriented individual with excellent communication skills. Works well independently and as a contributing team member. Analytical and problem solving abilities.

EDUCATION:

A.A.S. in Accounting, May 1994 - Honeywell Community College, Honeywell, NY
Certificate in Lotus 1-2-3, 1991 - Honeywell Development Center, Honeywell, NY
United States Navy Training Certificates, 1981/85 - Firefighting School; Magazine Sprinkler School; Electricity, Electronics & Hydraulics School; Basic Electricity & Electronics School; Intro to Motors and Generators; Intro to Electrical Conductors and Wiring Techniques.
Certificate in Electrical Trades, 1980 - Honeywell Trade School, Honeywell, NY
Graduate - Honeywell High School, Honeywell, NY

EXPERIENCE:

<u>Service Manager</u>, Honeywell Ski Village, Honeywell, NY   8/91 to xx/xx
Responsible for managing the service shop which includes daily operations, supervision of technicians, repairs, warranties, sales, ordering, and cash control. Closed store and experience with bank deposits. Handled extensive customer relations.

<u>Electrician</u>, Honeywell Manufacturing, Honeywell, NY   3/87 to 7/91
Performed electrical wiring on manufactured rail cars.

<u>Self-Employed Electrician</u>, Honeywell, NY   11/85 to 3/87
Handled all operational details for business specializing in residential and commercial wiring.

<u>Work Center Supervisor/Gunner's Mate</u>, United States Navy   6/76 to 4/85
Operated, repaired and maintained all electronic systems in the division. In charge of all sprinkler tests and damage control. Served aboard USS Whatever and USS Boat. Secret Security Clearance. Obtained an Honorable Discharge. Enlisted in U.S. Naval Reserves (4/85-4/91).

ACTIVITIES/INTERESTS:

- Supplemental Instruction Leader in Economics, Honeywell Community College (1992)
- Past Member of the Honeywell Exotic Bird Club
- Enjoy Skiing, Backpacking, and Kayaking

REFERENCES AVAILABLE UPON REQUEST

2

Combination. *Betty Geller, Elmira, New York*

A resume for an Electrician/Service Manager who went back to school to become an Accountant. Sections relevant to accounting appear first above technical experience.

KEITH M. DAIGLE

7 Hapworth Street	Winter, ME 04432	(555) 989-32

OBJECTIVE

Accounting position in a manufacturing environment.

SUMMARY OF QUALIFICATIONS

Analytical/mathematical aptitude employed in calculating labor costs, computing precise measurements and completing detailed reports for steel roofing projects

Commendable scholastic accomplishment demonstrated by earning a **3.8 GPA for Accounting** coursework and **3.79 GPA overall** in an Applied Business degree program

Leadership skills exhibited in making crew assignments, overseeing construction projects and serving as on-site problem solver

Telephone/personal **communication skills** used in thoroughly discussing projects with homeowners, contractors and maintenance supervisors to meet customer demands

Organizational talents utilized daily to prepare materials and organize resources, ensuring timely and successful project completion

Basic knowledge of **Quattro Pro** and **WordPerfect** from school and home computer usage

EDUCATION

A.S. Applied Business, DOVER COLLEGE, Summer, ME, Magna Cum Laude, May 1995

Coursework Related to Objective:
- ✓ Accounting I & II
- ✓ Business Finance
- ✓ Managerial Accounting
- ✓ Intermediate Accounting

WORK HISTORY

MACK ROOFING SPECIALISTS, Winter, ME Supervisor, Steel Roofing and Clerk, Sheet Metal Shop	1988 to present
DISCOUNT RETAILERS, Winter, ME Stock Clerk	1986 to 1987

3

Combination. *Elizabeth (Lisa) M. Carey, Waterville, Maine*

This resume emphasizes qualifications and skills relevant to the career goal of an accounting position. A Work History without accounting experience appears last.

AMY J. BALANCE, 2 Fanning Rd., Raynaud, MA 00000

(000) 000-0000

PROFILE

Versatile, detail-oriented accountant/bookkeeper working toward
accounting degree seeks challenging and rewarding position utilizing
eight years business experience...excellent interpersonal, communication and computer skills...well organized team worker...super-
visory experience.

WORK HISTORY

Dilbert's Car World, Ethol, MA,
Warranty Administrator   (9/94-Present)
Function as overseer of warranty claims, dealership's largest
receivables, from preparation and submission to maintenance of
status and resolution. Maintain files, manuals and bulletins.
Instruct other dealership personnel in current warranty policy
and procedures. Process 30-35 claims daily.

Bookkeeper   (5/92-9/94)
Performed full range of dealership bookkeeping needs, including
accounts receivable/payable, warranty claims, plus a variety of
schedules, and cost and sales analysis. Other duties as fill in
for switchboard, data entry, billing and reception.

Erect Construction Corp., Houton, NH
Secretary/Receptionist   (11/91-5/92)
Duties included maintenance of job cost spreadsheets.

Iacoca-cola Chrysler, Portsville, MA
Bookkeeper/Office Manager   (9/89-6/91)
Duties included bank deposits, accounts payable, payroll and taxes,
profit analysis of car sales, salesperson commission sheets,
warranty claims, bank/credit card reconciliations.

The Check-Out Companies, Inc., Peterson, NH
Bookkeeper   (7/87-9/89)
Functioned as full-charge bookkeeper utilizing computerized system
performing inventory, job cost and monthly bank reconciliations.

Raynaud Saab, Inc., Raynaud, MA
Bookkeeper   (8/86-7/87)

EDUCATION

Massachusetts Technical Institute, Beanville, MA
- A.S., Accounting Degree slated for December, 1995
- B.S., Accounting Degree slated for December, 1996

Courses completed in major: Elementary Accounting I, II,
Intermediate Accounting, Advanced Accounting I, II, Cost
Accounting, Microeconomics, Macroeconomics, Information
Systems Concepts, Finite Math, Statistics, Introduction to
Marketing. * GPA 3.1

Certificate, Lotus 1-2-3 - Generic Technical College, Oaks, NH

References Available on Request

4

Combination. *Stephen H. Mazurka, Exeter, New Hampshire*

Not everyone has access to a laser printer. This resume in Courier type has boldface and
underlining to emphasize important information. Note four-year degree work in progress.

DEBORAH JACKSON
12345 — 1ˢᵗ Avenue SW
Anytown, USA 99999
(555) 555-5555

OBJECTIVE:

A position in data entry and/or accounting where skills in spreadsheet development and troubleshooting can improve efficiency and enhance profitability.

PROFILE:

Results-oriented team member with 8 years' experience in data entry and accounting. Particularly skilled in creating new spreadsheets to improve efficiency and reduce costs. Strong mathematical aptitude. Knowledgeable and experienced in all facets of accounting functions, including:

- Accounts Receivable
- Accounts Payable
- Payroll

Well-versed in PC operations, word processing (Word and WordPerfect for Windows) and accounting software (Lotus 1-2-3, Excel, and Quattro Pro). Excited by the challenge of learning new technology and systems.

ACHIEVEMENTS:

- Audited expense reports for more than 100 employees.
- Audited 100 expense reports for one employee for 1991-1992 to resolve $3,500 balance discrepancy.
- Created procedures for entries on new software dealing with accounts receivable and order entry.
- Developed a new form for reporting travel expenses.
- Created a PC invoice for manual invoicing.
- Developed spreadsheet to reduce inventory control process time by up to 75%,
- Established user-friendly spreadsheet application methods allowing most personnel to operate with minimal training.
- Created year-to-year sales comparison spreadsheet to determine number and frequency of orders.

EXPERIENCE:

ABC CORPORATION, Anytown *Travel Expense Auditor/Accounts Receivable Clerk*	1993 to XXXX
O'BRIEN ELECTRIC CONSTRUCTION, INC., Anytown *Office Manager/Full-Charge Bookkeeper*	1990 to 1993
HOLSTEED, INC., Anytown *Accounts Receivable Clerk*	1989 to 1990
JUNIOR COLLEGE OF ANYTOWN, Anytown *Night School Education Assistant*	1987 to 1988

EDUCATION:

- A.A., Computer Applications Management, 194, 3.64 GPA
  Junior College of Anytown
  Received College's Certificate of Adaptability

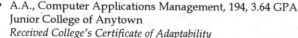

5

Combination. *Carole S. Barns, Woodinville, Washington*

A vertical line by the name, address, and phone number is an effective eye-catcher. Bullets before achievements in one place avoid redundant listing of them in Experience section.

JONATHAN D. ROBERTS

26518 Best Street
Anytown, MN 02369

email: jodrov@yahaa.net
(555) 555-1234

MANAGEMENT
BANKING / FINANCIAL ARENA

...Recognized for substantially increasing loan and mortgage portfolios...

High-profile professional with 12+ years experience in finance and banking. Reputation as a problem solver, with excellent communication, analytical and customer service skills. Instrumental in launching new divisions; personally responsible for increasing mortgage portfolio loans from $0 to $86 million in the first year. Demonstrated track record of consistently meeting short-and long-term corporate goals. Computer literate.

MAJOR STRENGTHS

• Financial Analysis	• Asset Management	• Commercial Credit
• Branch Operations	• Customer Service	• Consumer Loans
• Loan Administration	• Portfolio Management	• Secondary Markets

PROFESSIONAL EXPERIENCE

ANYTOWN BANK, New York, NY
Loan / Service Officer   1995 - Present
Recruited to expand branch operations. Hire, train and evaluate 15 staff. Oversee general office functions, site operation, inventory control, and financial reporting. Administered asset management functions, including direct control of $12 million portfolio. Responsible for monthly reconciliations / internal accounts. Conduct weekly customer service and technical training sessions.
• Recipient, Top Performance Award (1997)
• Highest Loan Closing Rate in Northeast Division (1995)
• Re-engineered sales / marketing functions resulting in higher loan closing rates

Administrative / Loan Assistant   1994 - 1995
Responsible for all support functions relating to the delivery of traditional and non-traditional products and services to target markets. High level customer service, outside professional and executive management contacts. Prepare loan packages and customer documents as requested. Cross-sell bank products.

BESTBANK, Queens, NY   1987 - 1994
Personal Banker Level III / Corporate Office (1994)
Personal Banker Level II / Branch 2 (1992-1994)
Personal Banker Level I / Office 2 (1987-1992)
Fast track promotion to Personal Banker Level III. One of two staff involved in the opening of a new branch. Opened and serviced new accounts; analyzed loan requests, completed loan packages, negotiated financing terms, and closed consumer loans and lines of credits. Trained new employees, worked with Branch Manager and other officers to develop new business.
• Rated "Superior" (1994)
• Exceeded sales and loan procurement quotas (2nd Quarter 1993; 4th Quarter 1993)
• Consistently met monthly Account Retention Forecasts and Quarterly Survey Goals
• Motivated team to achieve higher sales penetration through proactive marketing

FIRST NATIONAL BANK, New Park, NY
Loan Officer   1985 - 1987
Oversaw daily operations, including deposits, customer service, end-of-day proofing and personnel issues.
• Trained and instructed new personnel on banking procedures
• Developed and implemented detailed daily reporting forms; increased quality control and customer service rating 64%

6

Combination. *M. Carol Heider, Tampa, Florida*

Lines separating the main sections make them readily apparent. The two lines on page 1 in effect enclose a profile, which includes Major Strengths in columns. Being in columns, these

JONATHAN D. ROBERTS
Page 2

PROFESSIONAL EXPERIENCE (continued)

CITY FEDERAL, New York, NY
New Accounts Manager   1984 - 1985
Promoted to New Accounts Manager in 6 months.

COMPUTER SKILLS

Word 6.0, Excel, Lotus 1-2-3, PowerPoint

EDUCATION

BANKING INSTITUTE, New York, NY (Expected 2001)
Pursing Associate of Arts, Finance

Relevant Courses:
Mortgage Lending
Financial Accounting Methods
Business Planning
Marketing for Mortgages

ABC SCHOOLING, New York, NY (1997)
Excel

Seminars / Courses
Mortgage Loan Training
Managing Personal Cash Flow
Lending School
Strategic Planning
Sales Training

COMMUNITY / PROFESSIONAL ACTIVITIES

Business Banker's Association, member
Professional Financing Association, member
Walk for Health, volunteer

strengths can be easily replaced with other strengths for a different prospective employer. Grouping three positions for one employer ("BESTBANK") avoids repetition in the description of the duties for these three positions. Education without a four-year degree is put almost last.

Thomas P. Adams

2000 Sullivan Street
New York, New York 55555
Home: (212) 555-5555
Office: (212) 444-4444

SUMMARY

Aggressive, goal-oriented Financial Services professional, with considerable expertise in the sale of financial instruments to a varied retail base. Utilize excellent interpersonal, communication and presentation skills to develop and maintain strong account relationships. Possess excellent analytical and problem-solving skills.

EXPERIENCE

4/91 - Present

Dreyfus Service Corporation, New York, NY
Financial Consultant (8/94 - Present)
- Successfully developed a strong client base in the sale of mutual funds, variable annuities and brokerage services.
- Consistently rank in *Top 5* in sales, within region; reached ***110% of quota*** for the year, by August of 1995.
- Conduct in-depth consultations with prospective clients to assess needs and recommend appropriate financial products. Utilize computer analysis to develop investment plans, ie. college funds, retirement planning, etc...
- Closely monitor market trends, and performance of Dreyfus Family of Funds, to assist with the development of investment strategies.
- Research and resolve account problems, as warranted.
- Participate with the development of sales/marketing ideas.

Unit Specialist (11/93 - 7/94)
- Supervised 15-20 Account Representatives within the Outbound Program, which actively encouraged new accounts to expand their portfolio of investments.
- Trained staff in sales techniques; motivated representatives to meet monthly goals and objectives; and conducted one-on-one sessions to discuss individual progress.
- Accountable for meeting personal goals.
- Prepared weekly/monthly reports utilizing Dbase and Paradox.

Account Representative (4/91 - 10/93)
- Cross-sold various funds; maintained ongoing knowledge of over 80 mutual funds to properly service account base; tracked trends to assess performance of portfolios; and responded to inquiries and expedited processing of requests.

8/88 - 3/91

Meacham Surgical Supply Inc.
Service Manager
- Supervised and trained service technicians; assured the timely servicing of customer repairs; and prepared bi-annual reports concerning staff performance.
- Involved in the sale of new equipment.

EDUCATION

Nassau Community College
A.S. - Business Administration, 1990

LICENSES

- NASD Series 6, 7 & 63
- New York & New Jersey Life and Health Insurance

References Furnished Upon Request

Combination. *Judith Friedler, New York, New York*

Month/Year indicators for each position show that there was never a gap in this person's work experience since April, 1991. Bullets guide the eye down the page.

Administrative Support

Resumes at a Glance

RESUME NO.	LAST OR CURRENT OCCUPATION	GOAL	PAGE
8.	Customer Service Support Rep.	Not specified	33
9.	Administrative Secretary	Not specified	34
10.	Assistant to Director	Position using computing skills	35
11.	Legal Administrative Assistant	Administrative Assistant	36
12.	Secretary	Not specified	37
13.	General Office Clerk	Position in office support/ customer service	38
14.	Office Manager	Not specified	39
15.	Owner/Manager	Secretarial/Bookkeeping position	40
16.	Clerk/Bookkeeper	Clerical/Bookkeeping/Office support position	42

JOHN C. DESMOND
555 55th Street, Apt. 55 • New York, NY 55555
Residence (555) 555-5555 • Work (555) 555-5555

PROFILE

Administrative Assistant with excellent evaluations in diversified industries. Strong computer literary with a proven track record of mastering major computer applications in the completion of work assignments. Interact effectively with co-workers, customers and management. A highly motivated employee who is able to work creatively and diligently to achieve goals in a timely fashion.

WORK EXPERIENCE

LONDON BOOKMAKERS, INC.   New York, NY
Customer Service Support Representative   5/55 to Present

- Process all trade and mass market special rush orders from its worldwide offices, from initial request through follow-up on fulfillment.
- Investigate validity of large debt claims for 4 in-house customer representatives.

<u>Major Achievements</u>

- Of 26 persons in department, often chosen to complete time sensitive tasks.
- Selected by supervisor to assist in troubleshooting difficult accounts.
- *Officially* evaluated as: cooperative and easy to get along with, accurate in work assignments, and willing to assume greater responsibilities than required.
- Promoted to permanent full-time position from status as temporary worker.

BEST TEMPORARY SERVICES   New York, NY
Temporary Worker   5/55 - 5/55

- Completed various corporate assignments in a number of capacities including Administrative Assistant, Word Processor, Data Entry Operator and Receptionist.
- Consistently rated as excellent worker on customer feedback forms.

LEE GORDON & COMPANY (small clothing firm)   New York, NY
Administrative Assistant   5/55 - 5/55

- Interacted extensively with customers, sales force, warehouse and carriers.
- Utilized computer programs for scheduling, appointments and inventory.
- Coordinated shipping and verified shipping reports.
- Researched data for documents and manuscripts.

CITY AGENCY   New York, NY
Secretary/Customer Service   5/55 - 5/55

- Deemed by supervisor as punctual, conscientious worker who followed orders well.
- Processed material requisitions from all facilities in system.
- Resolved customer complaints regarding billing and shipping problems.

EINSTEIN'S HEAVY MACHINERY   New York, NY
Accounts Payable Clerk   5/55 - 5/55

- Performed data entry of company's purchase orders.
- Edited and printed packages for supervisor.
- Prepared and filed invoices and compiled payments.

EDUCATION

New York City Two Year College   New York, NY
Major: Accounting   5/55 - Present

New York City Business & Computer School   New York, NY
Certificate of Completion, Computer Operator Specialist/Accounting   5/55- 5/55
GPA: 4.0 on a 4.0 scale

SKILLS

Microsoft Works for Windows, Lotus 1-2-3, Dbase, WordPerfect 5.1,
Microsoft Word 6.1, Typing 65 wpm, Data entry with 10,000 keystrokes.

References furnished upon request.

8

Combination. *David Feurst, New York, New York*

Firm names and centered headings in all-uppercase letters, together with positions in bold italic, make the design of this sharp resume easy to comprehend at a glance.

JUDITH A. BURR

235 W. Thayer Ave. ◆ Bismarck, North Dakota 58501
(701) 255-3141

CAPABILITIES

- Knowledgeable in all clerical duties: typing, filing, dictaphone, research, IBM-PC and various computer software.
- Hire, train and supervise support personnel.
- Plan itineraries, luncheons, make travel and hotel arrangements.
- Customer and public relations skills.
- Conduct field surveys to ensure compliance of labor laws.
- Bookkeeping experience, including preparation of financial statements and reports.
- Performed various reception duties including the operation of an AT&T System 75 switchboard.

ACHIEVEMENTS

- Assumed responsibility of office in absence of supervisor.
- Acted as trouble shooter for six small loan offices.
- Personally administered all lending activities: credit decisions, budget planning, loan delinquencies, accounting and work plan scheduling.
- Assisted entrepreneurs with state labor regulations.
- Addressed questions on land descriptions for aerial applicators and beekeepers.
- Owner-operator of small business.
- Commercially wholesaled finished goods and supervised 75 students.

WORK HISTORY

North Dakota Office of Management & Budget - Administrative Secretary III

The North American Coal Corporation - Receptionist and Switchboard Operator

North Dakota Fifty-second Legislative Assembly - Stenographer

North Dakota Department of Agriculture - Liaison Officer

North Dakota Department of Labor - Compliance Inspector

North Dakota Fifty-first Legislative Assembly - Stenographer

McCarney's Ford Incorporated - Personal Secretary to President, and Car Clerk

Beneficial Finance Company - Business Woman's Manager

EDUCATION

Associate of Arts degree in Business Administration, Bismarck State College, Bismarck, ND

HONORS AND AWARDS

Member, Phi Theta Kappa Society.

REFERENCES AVAILABLE UPON REQUEST

9

Functional. *Claudia Stephenson, location unknown*

An older worker fearful of age discrimination. To discourage it, the writer omitted dates in the Work History and highlighted capabilities and achievements.

JaneAnn Troise

555 East Main Road
Elmira, NY 00000
000/000-0000

Objective: Position utilizing excellent word processing and computer skills, with opportunity for advancement to management.

Skills:
- Machine dictation (25-30 wpm)
- Keyboarding (65-72 wpm)
- Extensive experience with WordPerfect 5.1
- Knowledge of Lotus 1-2-3, dBase III Plus, DOS, Windows

Education: **State University of New York State College of Technology,** Elmira, NY
Associate Degree in Word Processing (May 1992)
Major coursework:
- Accounting
- Office Management
- Records Management
- Word Processing
- Document Processing
- Supervisory Management
- Business Communications
- Office Systems
- Microcomputers
- Transcription (Legal and Medical)
- Office Administration and Procedures

Experience: SUNY COLLEGE OF TECHNOLOGY, Elmira, NY
Student Accounts Department
<u>**Assistant to Director**</u> - Performed general office duties including letter composition, word processing (WordPerfect and Banner), filing, telephones, other duties as required. Completed forms on PELL grants for New York State. (1991-XXXX)

DEPARTMENT OF SOCIAL SERVICES, Anywhere, NY
<u>**Secretary**</u> - Recorded and transcribed meeting minutes. Routed assignments; kept running log of al clients and social worker assignments. Typed correspondence and performed other general office duties. (1989-1991)

PROJECT UNITY PROGRAM, Elmira, NY
<u>**Outreach Worker/Team Secretary**</u> - Assisted rural clients with medical, dental, family, and social problems. Worked in association with Department of Social Services (Child Protection Unit), Public Assistance (Food Stamp Divisions), Drug and Alcohol Abuse Program, and other agencies. Maintained 125+ clients. (1986-1989)

LABOR DEPARTMENT OUTREACH, Elmira, NY
Farm Labor Division
<u>**Office Manager**</u> - Acted as liaison between farmers and migrant workers. Maintained state and federal records pertaining to all aspects of migrant labor forces and their families. (1985-1986)

Activities:
- **WordPerfect 5.1 Tutor** - SUNY College of Technology.
- **Volunteer Emergency Dispatcher** - Elmira, NY Fire Department and Ambulance Corps.
- Enjoy walking, mountain bike riding, camping, reading, crocheting, painting.

References Available Upon Request

10

Combination. *Betty Geller, Elmira, New York*

A worker who went back to school. The resume shows first the Objective and the Skills and Education sections because they display best the person's new career interests.

CHRISTINE BUROSEK
380 Wellington Lane
Darien, Illinois XXXXX
(XXX) XXX-XXXX

OBJECTIVE
To secure an Administrative Assistant position in an interesting field which will challenge my abilities allowing me to fully utilize my communication, organizational, and problem solving skills.

PROFESSIONAL SKILLS
Knowledge of WordPerfect (DOS and Windows), MS Word, Lotus, Excel, Quicken, Simple Money bookkeeping program, and Reflex database program. Typing speed: 80 w.p.m.; experienced in dictaphone usage.

EXPERIENCE

SHAPIRO & LEMITZ, INC. (law firm); Chicago, Illinois   **October 1990 - Present**

Legal Administrative Assistant
- Interview clients, open files, draft petitions and letters, and file petitions at courthouse.
- Research legal issues and devise new angles to argue in court.
- Perform general bookkeeping functions; implemented computerized bookkeeping system.
- Verify accuracy of bills received and submit payment.
- Generate client bills, place collection calls, and file paperwork needed for litigation when necessary; automated firm's billing system.
- Compute employee withholdings and prepare paychecks; also prepare payroll and corporate tax returns.
- Independently manage office when partners are out of town (often for weeks at a time).

Law Journal Editor/Manager
- Draft and edit the firm's law journal, *Illinois Family Law Report*, keeping abreast of changes in laws.
- Develop marketing materials and solicit new subscriptions. Increased subscription base by 33%.
- Maintain and bill current subscription list. Discovered an efficient way to manage records in-house.
- Respond to inquiries from potential and current subscribers.

MILESTONE ANSWERING SERVICE, INC.; Bensenville, Illinois   **March 1988 - Present**

Supervisor   (June 1992 - Present)
- Promoted from Assistant Supervisor in July 1993.
- Maintain previous responsibilities while training and scheduling all operators, programming new accounts and making changes to existing accounts, and handling complaints and general office problems.
- Achievements include preserving several accounts, revamping training program, and reducing employee turnover.

Sr. Telereceptionist / Telereceptionist   (March 1988 - June 1992)
- Promoted to senior status in May 1990.
- Answered an average of 70 calls per hour, prioritizing emergency calls.
- Worked alone on third shift and independently devised solutions to problems.
- Trained new and existing operators.
- Implemented a customer service program which emphasized taking a proactive approach when resolving problems.
- "Employee of the Year" 1990 and 1991. "Operator of the Month" for a total of twelve months.
- Maintained perfect performance statistics for three years straight; only employee to achieve this.
- Earned an additional 25% of base pay for outstanding performance on the job.

EDUCATION
College of DuPage; Glen Ellyn, Illinois
Associate of Applied Science, June 1991   Consistent Dean's List recognition   G.P.A.: 3.7/4.0

Combination. *Georgia Veith, location unknown*

Although narrow margins reduce white space, they can keep a resume to one page. Put near the top are impressive skills and substantial responsibilities at a law firm.

LORETTA L. LIERHOST

3330 Independence Blvd., #926
Parma Heights, Ohio 44144
112 888.0085

PROFILE
Experienced, degreed professional with proven skills and abilities, and excellent communication with all levels of customers, colleagues and management.

SUMMARY OF QUALIFICATIONS

Time management skills; organizing and coordinating personal schedule and instructing and assisting others with their schedules.

Problem solving proficiency and decision making ability; able to draw from experience and knowledge, and apply to current situations in a timely manner.

Excellent computer awareness and software comprehension; competent in working with several current software applications.

Document composing, compiling and presentation; with superior grammar and comprehension of English language and vocabulary.

COMPUTER/EQUIPMENT/SKILLS

Windows	Ami Pro	WordPerfect	Freelance Graphics
Harvard Graphics	Lotus 1-2-3	Shorthand	Dictaphone

EMPLOYMENT

PROLAB, INCORPORATED   1962 to Present
International corporation that manufactures and markets cleaning supplies to [primarily] the food service industry.
Secretary to Area Manager/Assistant Vice President — *Sanford Heights, Missouri*
Secretary to District Manager — *Cincinnati, Ohio*
Secretary to Sr. Vice President — *Company Headquarters: St. Paul, Minnesota*
Secretary to District Manager — *St. Louis, Missouri*

- o Composed District Secretary Procedure Manual for two divisions, kept them updated
- o Trained District Secretaries in policies, procedures and methodologies; set up offices working closely with managers
- o Assisted with pilot programs for divisions, which eventually were established throughout the company
- o Coordinated and managed all aspects of three office moves; including office layout, purchasing equipment, deciding on phone system and implementing the use

EDUCATION

OAKLAND COLLEGE; Farmingham, Missouri — ***Associate Degree in Business Administration***
Business Technology Center – *Certificates of Completion in WordPerfect and Lotus 1-2-3*
Case Western Reserve University; Cleveland, Ohio – *Nursing Program Participant*

Also: 8 years volunteering at hospital in emergency room and patient care, and trained as Unit Tech

12

Combination. *Lorie Lebert, Novi, Michigan*

A thick horizontal line and a skills box of the same width call attention to each other visually.
A mix of different indents keeps this resume from appearing monotonous.

Janet M. Mirror
428 Main Street ▪ Elmira, NY 00000 ▪ (000) 000-5555 / 000-4444

OBJECTIVE
Position in Office Support / Customer Service

CAREER PROFILE
- Proven administrative, secretarial and general office experience.
- Strong background in all aspects of customer service and support.
- Knowledge of computers: Microsoft Word, PageMaker, File Maker.
- Outstanding typing skills (85 WPM); proficient in use of office equipment.
- Efficient and good natured; excellent reputation with all former employers.

SKILLS AND ABILITIES
- Provided administrative and secretarial support in various office environments.
- Provided secretarial support for Assistant Vice President as well as task groups and committees.
- Responsible for the organization and efficient processing of bulk mailings to customers.
- Utilized efficient and courteous customer service in both retail and business settings.
- Processed orders, entered and retrieved data using both PC's and mainframe computers.
- Facilitated spreadsheet and database management for Assistant VP of Marketing/Public Affairs.
- Coordinated provision of communications materials for all segments of the medical center.
- Gained exposure to all aspects of sales, marketing, promotion and public relations activities.
- Maintained accurate, up to date comprehensive and confidential files and records.
- Opened and routed mail to appropriate departments within the company.
- Coordinated and managed multiple priorities and projects on a timely basis.
- Answered busy telephones, directed and routed calls, and scheduled appointments.

WORK HISTORY

1993 - Present	General Office Clerk	Elmira Power Company, Elmira, NY
1989 - 1993	Receptionist/Clerk	James Company, Elmira, NY
1988 - 1989	Office Assistant	Temporary Services, Elmira, NY
1986 - 1988	Secretary	Elmira Health Services, Elmira, NY
1980 - 1986	Receptionist/Typist	Elmira Paper Company, Elmira, NY
1978 - 1979	Customer Service Clerk	Precision Company, Elmira, NY

EDUCATION
Elmira Community College, Elmira, NY
A.A.S., Secretarial Science - 1985

Precision Company, Elmira, NY
Various Customer Service Seminars

Elmira Health Services, Elmira, NY
Attended various Secretarial Seminars
Obtained JET Proofreading Certificate

13

Combination. *Betty Geller, Elmira, New York*

The applicant has no Work History gaps, suggesting a chronological resume, but functional Profile and Skills sections avoid redundancy in job descriptions.

SALLIE SMITH
234 Mt. Manor Court • White Lake, Michigan 48383 • 248.555.3696

ssmith@comcast.com

PROFESSIONAL OVERVIEW

PROFILE   Well-qualified professional office administrator. Experience in fast-paced environments that depend on efficiency and accuracy. Exceptionally dependable and competent. Self-starter with strong general business knowledge.

EXPERTISE   **Office Management** — Skilled at handling multiple responsibilities concurrently, extremely organized and efficient. Handles complex issues professionally.

Finance — Experience with accounts payable/receivable, invoicing, collections, payroll, commission reconciliation, billing, insurance claims, job costing, client credit checks, corporate audits, month-end reporting.

Human Resources — Manage benefits administration, employee testing and training, encouraging and mentoring. Good diplomat with excellent listening skills.

Customer Service — Well-developed interpersonal/customer relation skills; ability to communicate, relate, offer assistance, and handle stressful situations with competence. Extremely congenial and helpful.

Other — File for notice of commencements, furnishings, and claims of lien/foreclosure. Experience booking international export shipments, hazardous material handling, customs forms management. Handled product research, new item contracts, product return. Knowledge of diverse industries.

SKILLS   **Computer** — Windows 95, Microsoft Word/Excel/Access/PowerPoint, Peachtree Accounting, WordPerfect, industry-specific applications, E-mail, Internet.

EXPERIENCE

BUILT-RITE CONSTRUCTION   Livonia, Michigan
OFFICE MANAGER, xxxx-current
 Scope of responsibility encompasses the administration of all office concerns for large excavation corporation in southeastern Michigan.

SWEENEY & ASSOCIATES   Dearborn, Michigan
OFFICE ADMINISTRATOR/SUPERVISOR/SHIPPING MANAGER, xxxx-xx
 Responsibilities included support and interaction of health and beauty care products for national manufacturer and representative; interacted with national accounts.

FAMILY DENTAL SERVICES/PRIVATE DENTIST OFFICES   Garden City, Michigan
DENTAL ASSISTANT/RECEPTIONIST, xxxx-xx
 Chairside assistant for general, periodontal, pediatric, and endodontic dentistry. Managed customer service, appointments, billing, insurance, collection, accounts receivable, ordering.

EDUCATION/PROFESSIONAL DEVELOPMENT

COUNTY COMMUNITY COLLEGE   Livonia, Michigan
 Classes in Business, Mathematics, English, Marketing

COMPUSA: Numerous computer classes

CAMTEC – Construction Association of Michigan Training & Education Center: "Construction Accounting," "Getting Paid," "Lien Law and Payment Bonds," "Advanced Bookkeeping"

14

Combination. *Lorie Lebert, Novi, Michigan*

Information in the Professional Overview is grouped according to three criteria. Subtopics under Expertise make areas of expertise easy to spot. Boldfacing is used effectively.

Debbie K. Thomarr

0000 Worthington Avenue, Somewhere, Indiana 00000   ◇   **(812) 000-0000**

OBJECTIVE

Seeking challenging professional Secretarial/Bookkeeping career position; to contribute my extensive office management, communication, and accounting skills to benefit your organization.

QUALIFICATION SUMMARY

Eighteen years diverse experience in developing and sustaining highly successful business/Office management career. Expertise in management functions including administrative/secretarial, bookkeeping, marketing, promotions, and advertising. Computer skills: Lotus 1-2-3, ProWrite, Label Master.

PROFILE

Energetic, out-going, and high-spirited, yet sensitive and composed. Demonstrate effective listening skills. Open to new concepts, willing to compromise and do whatever necessary to achieve goals. Organized, deal with challenges effectively.

FASHION RETAIL EXPERIENCE

Owner/Manager. *Kid Drive*. Carland, Indiana: 0000-0000
Researched and co-developed business concept. Located, established, and managed highly successful Children's Retail Clothing Store. Formulated budget, maintained accurate records, and performed bookkeeping tasks. Tracked/controlled inventory and processed special orders. Prepared financial reports and tax records. Screened, hired, trained, evaluated and fired personnel.

◇ Successfully marketed store and developed advertising/sale campaigns.
◇ Utilized extensive and positive interpersonal relationship skills when interacting with customers and store personnel, promoting positive mediation and compromise procedures. Served effectively as a productive team member within three-year partnership before assuming full ownership.

OFFICE MANAGEMENT EXPERIENCE

Bookkeeper. *Klamer CPA Group*. Thisp, Illinois: 0000-0000 (Part-Time and Seasonal)
Assisted with office management duties. Performed seasonal tax preparation including computer record keeping.

Self-Employed Bookkeeper. Thisp, Illinois: 0000-0000 (Home Business)
Provided bookkeeping services to small business. Prepared quarterly tax reports.

15

Combination. *Colleen S. Jaracz, Vincennes, Indiana*

Larger font sizes, indented paragraphs, and adequate line spacing between sections help to make this resume two full pages. Boldfacing job positions helps them stand out.

Debbie K. Thomarr (Page Two)

OFFICE MANAGEMENT EXPERIENCE (Continued)

Office Manager/Head Bookkeeper. *Klamer CPA Group*: Indialantic, Florida: 0000-0000

✧ Set-up, organized, and implemented all office management procedures at newly opened office. Personnel manager, acquired, trained, scheduled, and assigned bookkeeping and secretarial duties of three staff members.

Life/Health Insurance Underwriter. *Gilded Insurance Company*.
Thisledown, Illinois: 0000-0000
Underwriting Department Clerk initially, promoted to **underwriter** after two months.
Reviewed medical information on insurance applications to determine coverage approval.

Administrative Secretary. *Eastern Illinois University*. Charleston, Illinois: 0000-0000
Performed receptionist and secretarial duties for the Head of the Health and Education Department and seven professors.

COMMUNITY AFFILIATIONS

Style Show Coordinator. Plan and coordinate style shows for various community organizations involving extensive planning and public relations responsibilities.
Teacher's Aide. *Vincennes School Corporation*. Tutored and assisted classroom teachers for eight years. Volunteered with book fairs and school registration procedures.

✧ **Chairman** for three years of the organizing committee for the school's annual auction fund-raiser which increased profit each year. Recruited and scheduled workers, personally visited approximately 175 area merchants to request merchandise donations. Set-up and ran auction, tracked bids and payments and performed secretarial duties associated with the project, including acknowledgments to participants.

✧ Served as **PTO Secretary** keeping records and minutes of all board and public meetings.
Church Offices including Sunday School Teacher, Bible School Director, and Church Treasurer. Utilized organizational skills involving scheduling, financial planning, promotions and public relations skills. As treasurer, tracked all bookkeeping, accounts payable, and tax records of all contributions.

EDUCATION/PROFESSIONAL SEMINARS

Olney Central College. Olney, Illinois: Associate in Applied Science Degree, (Medical, Secretarial)
Seminars on: Contract law, human anatomy and medical terminology, computer programs, bookkeeping, business management, and stress reduction in the work place.

Unusual bullets (✧) call attention to special accomplishments and positions held. The use of italic for the names of the places where the individual worked makes them more visible.

MARY A. HOMEMAKER

5555 East Main Circle	Elmira, NY 55555	(555) 111-0000

OBJECTIVE
Clerical/Bookkeeping/Office Support position.

SUMMARY OF QUALIFICATIONS
Outstanding math skills; enjoy working with figures.
Knowledge of clerical details, record and file maintenance.
Strong background in all aspects of customer service and support.
Excellent organizational, planning, interpersonal and communication skills.

SKILLS AND ABILITIES

Bookkeeping:
- Responsible for all accounts receivable and payable functions as auditor for
- hotel operation.
- Prepared daily, monthly, and yearly balance sheets for auditing purposes.
- Oversaw daily cash control, prepared bank and credit card deposits.
- Collected payments for customer billing and posted to general ledger.

Clerical:
- Posted all room, tax, valet, long-distance and restaurant charges to house guests' individual accounts.
- Prepared comprehensive housekeeping report for Head Housekeeper. Utilized computer to schedule reservations around the world for guests.

Customer Service:
- Handled customer inquiries and complaints in a professional manner.
- Adept at handling confrontational situations, resolving them appropriately.
- Communicated with guests and customers via switchboard operation.

Management:
- Scheduled, trained and supervised staff arriving for daily shift.
- Supervised and oversaw security of building, including physical plant.
- Oversaw all hotel operations and guest relations as management staff.

EXPERIENCE

Clerk/Bookkeeper	Elmira Conference Center	Elmira, New York
Desk Clerk	Happy Town Hotel	Elmira, New York
Secretary/Production Clerk	Elmira Manufacturing Company	Elmira, New York
Job Cost Clerk	Binghamton Mailing (Mail Order Dept.)	Binghamton, New York

EDUCATION/TRAINING
Business Administration Program - Purdue University Extension, Purdue, New York
Associate's Degree, Secretarial Science - Elmira Technical College, Elmira, New York
Graduate - Anywhere High School, Anywhere, New York

ACTIVITIES/INTERESTS
Volunteer: Travel & Tourism (Information Center), Anywhere County Chamber of Commerce;
   Anywhere Soup Kitchen, Anywhere, New York
Past Instructor of Quilting Program, James Human Resource Center, James, New York
Past Girl Scout Leader

REFERENCES AVAILABLE UPON REQUEST

16

Functional. *Betty Geller, Elmira, New York*

A resume for a displaced homemaker who returned to school. The functional format highlights qualifications (in pyramid layout) and skills grouped according to four categories.

Communications

Resumes at a Glance

RESUME NO.	LAST OR CURRENT OCCUPATION	GOAL	PAGE
17.	Newsletter Editor	Broadcast/Print communications position	45
18.	Account Executive, printing company	Not specified	46
19.	Owner of consulting firm	Not specified	48
20.	Auto Race Track Promoter	NASCAR Public Relations Specialist	51
21.	Pond Designer	Not specified	52
22.	Head Photographer/Sportswriter	Journalism/Sportswriting position	54

Yvonne R. Cosgrove

17-03 Sydney Terrace, Lakeland, NJ 55555
(000) 000-0000

CAREER FOCUS

To enter the world of broadcast or print communications with progressive responsibility in any areas involving:

✓ sales and administrative support
✓ editing or copywriting
✓ research or brainstorming to develop creative programming ideas
✓ coordination of program segments or production scheduling

THUMBNAIL SKETCH

✓ Prior varied experience, encompassing news reporting, editorial work, secretarial support and boutique management.
✓ Extremely people oriented, assertive and articulate, with an inherent talent to relate easily to diverse personalities and engage them in conversation.
✓ Attentive listener, exhibiting genuine enthusiasm and interest, inspiring others to freely and comfortably share information.
✓ Resourceful, thorough and inquisitive researcher who intuitively generates leads, extrapolates important information and develops creative story angles.
✓ Competent administrator who can handle multiple projects simultaneously in a self-motivated and organized manner.

BACKGROUND HIGHLIGHTS

1991 – Present   THE LAKELAND REPORTER, Wanaque, NJ
Editor of community newsletter distributed monthly to 700 families.

✓ Broadened computer skills while in a homebased situation by taking over entire responsibility for publication of a 20-page columned newsletter formerly produced by two people.
✓ With minimal guidance by association president and no prior experience on Apple Macintosh computer, quickly learned word processing, formatting and desktop publishing functions (Microsoft Word and Ready Set Go II program), combining text and graphics.
✓ Edited articles for grammatical accuracy and style.

1987 – 1991   THE VILLAGE COURIER, Franklin, NJ
Staff reporter for local newspaper that had a circulation of 52,400.

✓ Wrote front page human interest stories from personal interviews with political officials and leaders of benevolent organizations.
✓ Contributed to weekly articles and summarized proceedings of town council meetings.

1980 – 1987   BABBLING BROOK COUNTRY CLUB, Mt. Pocono, PA
Assistant manager of golf shop at private country club.

✓ As buyer of women's sportswear and accessories, met with manufacturers' sales representatives to select a collection of styles appropriate for the members of the club and their guests.
✓ Negotiated with vendors to resolve issues of shipment shortages, billing discrepancies and returns.
✓ Provided a personalized buying service for customers, resulting in substantial repeat business.

1977 – 1980   NATIONAL SANITATION SYSTEMS, Doylestown, PA
Secretary to three department managers.

ACADEMIC PREPARATION

1990   Ramapo College, Mahwah, NJ — A.A. degree in Media Communications

COMMUNITY SERVICE

✓ Active in the Lakeland Public Schools Parent-Teacher Organization.
✓ Chaired Committee for Elementary Grade Creative Writing Contest.

17

Combination. *Melanie A. Noonan, West Paterson, New Jersey*

Laser printing at 600 dpi (dots per inch) makes smaller print crisp and readable. Horizontal lines, check marks, job positions in boldface, and a casual font make this resume "classy."

OPTIONS GALORE
123 X Street • Anywhere, America 00000 • (000) 000-0000 • optionsgalore@aol.com

EXPERTISE

Sales / Technical Sales / Business Development / Account Retention
Commercial Printing Industry

Focus on aggressive new account development, relationship sales, technical/consultative sales, customer service. Provide on-site technology consulting.

Conduct active prospecting, identify leading prospects, build long-term partnerships with clientele, provide accurate proposals to include written specifications, project price and terms. Negotiate long-term contractual agreements and consistently follow up to reinforce interest, provide clarification, gain the competitive advantage and make the sale.

Technologies
Full web heat set, half web heat set, cold web, cold web newsprint, sheet-fed and digital printing (Indigo and Heidelberg)

HISTORY

YOUR PRINTING COMPANY, Anywhere, HI (2/95 - present)
half- and full-web commercial printer; plants in three states

Account Executive

- **Exceed sales quotas by 30+% yearly**
- **Personally generated $2,750,000+ in annual sales in 1999**

Sample projects:
Solicited a client to win approval for the redesign of its membership applications. Developed a customized, cost-effective, efficient program which enabled this public company to conduct targeted, select advertising campaigns. *Saved the client more than $250,000 annually.*

Developed an image library/archival system for magazine publications which dramatically elevated the quality and allowed the client to use these images generically throughout his stores and on the Internet. *Improved client's customer base, increased its product line and boosted total sales.*

Apprentice/Sales Training *one year*
Apprenticed and learned the technical aspects of each operation in the Estimating, Electronic Pre-press, Stripping, Plating, Pressroom and Bindery/Finishing Departments. Also spent two months accompanying the National Sales Manager on sales calls.

SOUND ADVICE, Anywhere, USA (1993-95)
25+ retail home theater and electronics stores; public company
Sales Associate, Electronics
- Highest Department Producer in two company-wide contests

EDUCATION
Business Administration, Ivy League Community College, Anywhere, USA (1992-94)

PROFESSIONAL AFFILIATIONS
Hawaii Direct Marketing Association; Advertising Federation of Honolulu; Direct Marketing Association

18

Combination. *Beverley Kagan, North Miami Beach, Florida*

In the Expertise section three slashes separate four areas of expertise in a title. In the History section bullets point to outstanding achievements. Italic also is used for achievements.

OPTIONS GALORE   Page 2

SELECTED SPECIALIZED TRAINING

Spent 1-3 months in each of the following departments (Your Printing Company):

Estimating
- Configured layouts for efficiency
- Estimated paper usage/waste
- Calculated manufacturing costs from press make-readies through bindery set-up and running

Electronic Pre-press
- Used software such as Quare, Cure and Freehand, while working with graphic designers
- CHEWER, COWER site, CHEWER and QUIRE NET communications
- IRIS and wax thermal proofing

Stripping
- Camera work to include line shots, making screens, developing film
- Exposing film
- Conventional stripping
- Burning blue lines
- Producing color keys and match prints
- Cower waterproofing

Plating
- Step and repeat

Pressroom
- Hanging plates
- Color Adjustment
- Registration

Bindery
- Folder and saddle stitching; Perfect binding; drilling, shrink-wrapping

Direct Mail Fulfillment
- Solo and marriage mail
- Simplex, duplex laser and ink jet personalization
- Credit card manufacturing
- Variable data/variable imaging
- One-to-one marketing

Additional courses/seminars
Mead Paper
Quare

A distinctive feature is a second page that is devoted to "selected specialized training." It is grouped by seven departments. Bullets point to training received in each department. Short statements provide white space and make the second page easy to read.

BEVERLEY DRAKE

120-B West 2nd Street
Oswego, New York 13126

555•343•1371
voice mail: 800•789•4369

> ▸ language proficiency
> ▸ solid planning, organizational, and
>   time management capabilities
> ▸ extensive computer background
> ▸ high work ethic and attention to detail
> ▸ strong problem resolution skills
> ▸ communication and interpersonal strengths

Writing, Editorial, and Desktop Publishing Support Services

9 yrs. as owner / manager of full-service business center providing computerized typesetting and laser printing; writing, editing, and proofreading; faxing; copying; binding; laminating; office supply sales. Marketable skills include:

▸ writing and editorial	▸ customer service	▸ planning and coordinating
▸ document and forms design	▸ marketing and advertising	▸ decisionmaking and goal setting
▸ records management	▸ accounting, payroll, purchasing	▸ human resources / job placement

ACCOMPLISHMENTS AND EXPERIENCE

Writing and Editorial
- forms design; writing of job descriptions, reports, press releases, and other materials
- author of over 20 business- and career-related articles published in newspapers and business newsletters
- write and set up job training and administrative policy manuals for various employers
- Certified Professional Resume Writer with 20 years experience preparing and critiquing career materials

Technology and Desktop Publishing Expertise
- working knowledge of DOS, Windows, WordPerfect, PC Tools, Quicken, 386Max, Check-It, virus programs
- troubleshoot computer, software, and peripheral problems; software installation
- information research and e-mail use via Internet and on-line services
- typeset and design business, personal, promotional, and marketing forms and documents
- negotiate with printers concerning customer specs and design work needed
- prepare camera-ready masters for print shop reproduction

Administrative and Business-Oriented
- set up business center from scratch (sold 1994); trained partner in small business management
- office support staffing and supervision for nursing home, university department, and business center
- trained office and nursing home administrative staff regarding policies and procedures
- set up simplified financial records and accounting system for own business

EDUCATION

A.A. degree—Virginia Intermont College, Bristol VA   (Phi Theta Kappa honors)
Yearly continuing education through conference seminars sponsored by international writing group
Various workshops—personnel, supervisory, purchasing, desktop publishing, marketing, job search

CERTIFICATIONS AND AFFILIATIONS

- Certified Professional Resume Writer (CPRW)   credentialed in 1993
- Professional Association of Resume Writers   1991 to present

19

Combination with an Addendum. *Beverley Drake, Rochester, Minnesota*

A professional resume writer's own resume. The intense black of the shadow box in the upper-right corner becomes a visual key for the bold black lines and headings in the resume.

EXPERIENCE HISTORY   **BEVERLEY DRAKE**

DRAKE CONSULTING, Oswego, NY   1994 to present
Owner of consulting firm with 3 main divisions: p.t.
- Alternative Professional Temp — quick, short-term office support
- CareerVision — resume and job search systems
- WordSmart — freelance writing, editorial, desktop publishing, and business services

PRECISELY YOURS BUSINESS SERVICES, INC. and RESUMES U.S.A., Oswego, NY   1985 to 1994
[Ex] Owner/Operator of 2 businesses set up from scratch   9 yrs.

STATE UNIVERSITY OF NEW YORK, College at Oswego, Oswego, NY
Technical Assistant to Director and Associate Director of Campus Life   temp p.t. / 12 wks.

OPERATION OSWEGO COUNTY, Oswego, NY (county's industrial development corp.)
Word Processor   temp p.t. / 5 mos.

METROPOLITAN WATER BOARD, Oswego, NY
Interim Secretary to Plant Manager   temp p.t. / 6 mos.

ITHACA GUN COMPANY, Ithaca, NY
Assistant to Director of Personnel; Executive Secretary to Vice President of Operations   temp / 4 mos.

BABCOCK INDUSTRIES, INC., Ithaca, NY
Executive Secretary to Controller   temp / 8 mos.

PRESBYTERIAN CHURCH, Oswego, NY (renamed Faith United Church)
Office Manager and Secretary to Pastor   p.t. / 2 yrs.

CORNELL UNIVERSITY, Ithaca, NY
Sr. Administrative Secretary to Dir. of Administrative Programming, Computer Services   2 yrs.
Sr. Administrative Secretary to Dean of The Graduate School   6 mo.
Sr. Administrative Secretary to Director of Cornell Plantations   4 mo.

RECONSTRUCTION HOME, Ithaca, NY (Skilled Nursing Facility)
Business Office Supervisor (promoted from Administrative Secretary and Account Clerk)   2 1/2 yrs.

ROBERT KIEFFER, M.D., Ithaca, NY
Office Manager, Medical Office Assistant / Secretary   2 yrs.

Continual work experience is expressed in years for only the top two positions on this
Experience History page. Because no position is in boldface, all jobs—even temporary ones—
seem equally important. All-uppercase characters make the workplace names stand out.

ARTICLES PUBLISHED   Beverley Drake, CPRW

DATE	TITLE	PUBLICATION
11//95	Secretaries, Take Charge: Sharp Secretaries as Managers in the Future Workplace	NASS Magazine
10/95	Did You Hear What Your Client DIDN't Say Today?	PARW Spotlight
9/95	Resumes As Critical Marketing Tools	PARW Spotlight
8/95	Need A Good Typist? Selecting the Right Person for Your Business or Personal Needs	NASS Magazine
8/95	Vision-Driven Resume Writing—Part II A Vision-driven Approach to Success	PARW Spotlight
7/95	Vision-Driven Resume Writing—Part I Are We Losing Our Identity as Resume Writers?	PARW Spotlight
10/94 1/25/93	Employment Terms—Usage and Effect On Job Search Strategy (reprint) Employment Terms Have Changed (original article)	PARW Spotlight The Oswego Observer
9/94 11/93	Resume Writing—Are You Selling Yourself? [excerpts from] Are You Selling Yourself Enough?	PARW Spotlight The Keyboard Connection
2/94 1/94	Watch Out ... Your Product May Become A Lost Leader (reprint) Watch Out ... Your Product May Become A Lost Leader (original article)	The Business Entrepreneur PARW Spotlight
7/93	High Prices Help More Than They Hurt	PARW Spotlight
5/3/93	The Game of Job Hunting	The Oswego Observer
3/8/93	Elements of A Good Resume	The Oswego Observer
12/7/92	December Grads Need Jobs: Resume Solutions for the '90s	The Oswego Observer
10/19/92	Who's Out There Doing Resumes?	The Oswego Observer
10/5/92	What's In A Word?	The Oswego Observer
10/92 8/17/92	Job Hunting, Then and Now (reprint) Job Hunting, Then and Now (original article)	PARW Spotlight The Oswego Observer
6/22/92	Create Job References Before You Need Them	The Oswego Observer
5/92	Job Searches and Career Planning—Only For Use By Women	PARW Spotlight
4/20/92	Defining Resume Objectives	The Oswego Observer
3/16/92	Psych Yourself Up For Success	The Oswego Observer

This page, an Addendum to the resume, is not attached to the resume but carried to interviews. The list of publications is arranged in descending chronological order. Boldfacing links the Addendum visually to the resume when all three pages are placed side by side.

Clay Cartman

"I trust Clay as I would trust a brother or son. He is of high moral character, his work ethic and industrious-ness is second to none, and he <u>always</u> thinks of others ahead of himself. He also exhibits an incredibly positive attitude at all times. - Jim McTolberts, A.D. (Basketball Coach)

Education

Ball State University. Muncie, IN: 1999-Present / Major: Public Relations
- ✦ Member of Public Relations Student Society of America ✦ Served on campaign project competition

Vincennes University. Vincennes, IN: 1997-1999 **Cum Laude - Associates Degree, Public Relations**
- ✦ Member of the Admissions Corp ✦ Alumni Office Student Intern

Profile

- ✦ Responsible problem solver, patient, good listening skills.
- ✦ Outgoing personality - positive, enjoy a challenge - persistent
- ✦ Honest, believe in complete integrity - to maintain highest degree of professional reputation for himself and his employer - committed.
- ✦ A gentleman in all respects.

Experience

16th Street Speedway. Indianapolis, IN: Summer Internship, 1999 (race nights only)
Responsible for all track promotions, pace car driver, post race celebrations, and all stage events including driver interviews, prize give-away's, special promotions, media releases and autograph signings.

Indianapolis Raceway Park. Indianapolis, IN: 1999 (oval race nights only)
Marketing/Promotions Volunteer. Assisted on marketing/promotion activities before, during and after races.

WOOO, WGOO, WOOO. Indianapolis, IN: 1999
Assisted with on-site promotions such as Red, White and Zoo at the Indianapolis Zoo and the Free State at the Indiana State Fair.

WEOO / WOOO (Emert Communications). Indianapolis, IN: Summer Internship, 1998
Contacted clients, communicated with Accounting Department, interacted with Sales and Programming Departments and distributed prizes and tickets to promotion winners. Efficiently performed general office tasks. Efficiently assisted in preparing and running promotions including: Riley Children's Hospital Telethon, Sky Concert, Indiana State Fair, and Circle Fest.

Affiliations

4-H Club (1991-1997) ✦ Chapter President: 1996/1997. ✦ Geranium program top salesman: 1994, 1996-1997.

Goal/Interest

I want to leave a positive impact wherever I work. My goal is to make a difference, and to enhance the reputa-tion of the company with which I am affiliated. My career goal is to eventually become involved in NASCAR – Open Wheel car racing as a Public Relations Specialist.

<u>Present Address</u>
22 Devengin Hall
Muncie, IN 47306
(812) 000-0000

<u>Home Address</u>
South County Road
Coatesville, IN 46121
(812) 000-0000

20

Combination. *Colleen S. Jaracz, Vincennes, Indiana*

Contact information is put at the bottom of the page to give the important testimonial prominence just below the lines after the name. The Goal appears last as a personal remark.

JOHN OUTLOOK   *A Mission To Make A Difference!*

1155 Hammond Drive #D-4260, Atlanta, GA 30328
(770) 393-3554

OBJECTIVE

To secure a responsible position leading to a progressive career path while utilizing
educational background and personal potential.

EDUCATION

A.A. Degree, Professional and Technical Communications
ROCHESTER INSTITUTE OF TECHNOLOGY, Rochester, NY

EXPERIENCE HIGHLIGHTS

Writing
- Wrote a wide range of stories, poetry, and newspaper articles for campus newspapers.
- Selected to serve a seven-month co-op as the Big Shanty Museum newsletter editor and
  wrote and edited numerous articles.
- Developed persuasive letters that turned-around public opinions.
- Wrote a campaign speech involving increased deaf awareness that was accepted by a
  governor candidate.

Camera Operations & Production
- Produced numerous creative documentaries and animated films.
- Shot video footage that was aired locally and nationally.

Photography
- Photographed special events and weddings and created final photo albums.
- Experimented with high speed photography and other equipment that accounted for
  excellent results and numerous clientele compliments.

Farming & Ranching
- Provided wildlife assistance and animal care at a nature center.
- Prepared a Jersey Calf for display and received the "Best Herdsman Award."

Fish Breeding & Pond Building
- Prepared 20-gallon tanks and breeded a wide range of fish including Sailfin Mollies.
- Constructed goldfish ponds and waterfalls for individual homeowners.
- Lobbied against abusive behavior of major animal authority leaders.

Miscellaneous Experience
- Painted houses and performed a wide range of landscaping work.
- Assisted in performances at the National Theatre of the Deaf.
- Interacted with customers, assisted in product selections, and provided courteous
  services.

PROFESSIONAL & PERSONAL PROFILE (Professionally assessed - separate career report provided upon request)
- Outgoing and friendly with close customer relations
- Punctual and dedicated with strong desire to outperform and succeed
- Detail-oriented and a team player with developed interpersonal abilities
- Creative thinker and a problem-solver
- Resourceful with a sense of mission to help others

1 of 2

21

Combination. *Terek A. Jabali, location unknown*

A distinctive touch is the slogan in the upper-right corner for a person of many talents.
Experience highlights are grouped according to six categories for easier reading.

JOHN OUTLOOK

Activities/Acknowledgments:
- Writer, Spring Hill College student newspaper
- Story/Poetry Writer, Berry College student magazine
- Camera person, Berry College
- Agriculture Club & Handicap Awareness Group, Berry College
- Marine Biology Club, Spring Hill College
- Berry College personality scholarship recipient

VOLUNTEER
- Chattahoochee Nature Center
- Tutor deaf children
- Newsletter Editor, Atlanta Hears, Atlanta, GA

LIMITATIONS
Limited hearing capacity (almost normal communication with hearing aid)

EMPLOYMENT HISTORY

SELF-EMPLOYED, San Francisco, CA
Pond Designer, 1993 - Present
TOM SCOTT MANNING PAINTING, San Francisco, CA
Painter's Assistant, 1985 - 1994
INGRAM MICRO, Atlanta, GA
Warehouse Assistant, 1994
DOCKTOR'S PET SHOP, San Francisco, CA
Sales Representative, 1987 - 1989
SELF-EMPLOYED, San Francisco, CA
Photographer/Camera Person, 1986 - 1989

The individual has been self-employed as a Pond Designer since 1993, but the Profile (at the end of the first page) and the Volunteer section show his interest in working with people. Horizontal lines call attention to the Experience Highlights and Employment History sections.

WILLIAM L. LOGGINS

207A Jericho Dr. ◆ Duncan, SC 00000   (000) 000-0000

Objective: An entry-level journalism position with a special interest in sports writing.

EDUCATION:

Bachelor of Liberal Arts, December 1995
Palmetto State, Duncan, SC
Major: Mass Communications with Media Emphasis
Full soccer scholarship
Member of Men's Soccer Team
Team was ranked in top 15 for 1993 and 1994 by the NCAA, Div. II Poll

Associate of Liberal Arts and Science, May 1992
Meredith County Community College, Mason, NJ
Full soccer scholarship
Member of Men's Soccer Team
Team was ranked 3rd and 5th for 1990 and 1991 respectively by the NJCAA

Athens High School, Athens, NJ
Diploma, June 1990
Member of Men's Varsity Soccer Team
Chosen to be an All-Section Player in the 10th - 12th grades. Traveled to Italy, France, and England with various soccer teams to play choice teams worldwide.

EXPERIENCE:

Communications: Palm State University Media Services
Head Photographer/Sportswriter (Palm State newspaper)
- Provided photographs; developed, printed and proofed photography.
- Furnished editorials and features.
- Produced, directed, filmed and edited orientation video of Lander's new physical training complex.
- Developed a working knowledge of video camera, linear editing and videotape recording equipment and basic audio operations.
- Experienced with 35MM cameras, B/W dark room process and enlargers.

Meredith County Community College
Sportswriter/Photographer (Meredith newspaper)
- Provided photographs and conducted interviews for editorial and feature articles.

Athletic: YMCA, Duncan, SC
Soccer Referee
- Refereed games for youth teams.

Mason Country Club, Mason, NJ
Assistant Pool Director
- Provided upkeep of pool/camp; managed and arranged work schedules for eight lifeguards.
Camp Lifeguard
- Taught swimming and diving to up to 40 youth participants at pool.

Palmore College Youth Sports Camp, Athens, NJ
Sports Instructor
- Taught soccer, baseball and swimming to 10 - 12-year old camp participants.

Special Olympics, Athens, NJ and Mason, NJ
Volunteer Coach

22

Functional. *Gwen P. Noffz, Greenwood, South Carolina*

A resume with just an Objective, an Education section, and an Experience section is usually chronological, but the absence of Experience dates makes the format functional.

Computer Technology

Resumes at a Glance

RESUME NO.	LAST OR CURRENT OCCUPATION	GOAL	PAGE
23.	Systems Programmer	Not specified	57
24.	Instructor/Consultant	Not specified	58
25.	MIS/Fan Operations, Chicago Bears	Not specified	60
26.	Owner/Manager	Specialist in computer support services	62
27.	Computer Operations and Systems Professional	Not specified	64
28.	Warehouse Worker	Position in computer data analysis/service	65
29.	Lead Technician	Network/Computer services	66
30.	MIS Coordinator/TQL Coordinator	Not specified	67
31.	Engineering Technician	Not specified	68
32.	Front End Manager, Market	Not specified	69
33.	Computer Services Technician	Not specified	70
34.	Computer Systems Manager	Not specified	71
35.	Not specified	Computer electronics position	72

Glen L. Holt

1902 Coachman's Trail • South Bend, Indiana 46637
(219) 243-0296

Objective: *Systems Programmer*

Profile

Individual with six years experience in PC based computer programming. Quick learner; able to identify and apply problem solving skills with expediency. Dependable, willing to go the extra mile to finish the task. Enjoy interacting with customers; good listener. Possess excellent verbal and written communication skills.

Areas of Expertise

- *Dos/Windows Applications*
- *Real Time RF Data Collection*
- *Custom Programming*
- *Delphi*
- *Touchscreen Application*
- *Bar Coding*
- *Clipper, C*
- *Toledo Scales*
- *Interfacing*

Professional Experience

TECHNICAL SKILLS
- Install, service and repair new and existing PC equipment and peripherals
- Create, write, and install specialty programs for business and personal use
- Write documentation and user manuals; maintain records of individual software projects
- Interface other software packages for complete customization

Accomplishments
- Designed shipping system to represent company requirements; then modified the program to fit other clients
- Created and designed chemical batching system software for NISCO a major supplier to the automotive industry
- Wrote process management system for manufacturing company requiring exact tolerances

CUSTOMER SERVICE
- Meet with clients, in-house and on-site, to determine their individual requirements
- Design and specialize system to client specification; troubleshoot through telephone communication
- Supply technicial training and support for existing software packages as well as our own systems
- Write shell for various clients which expands functionality of off-the-shelf software
- Act as liaison with customers and sales managers

CLIENT LIST
- Performed services at various businesses some of which included:
  - *Bayer*
  - *Essex, Ft. Wayne*
  - *Bethlehem Steel*
  - *National Standard*
  - *Uniroyal*
  - *Dodge*

Education

1996 *Associate Degree in Computer Science* • PURDUE UNIVERSITY, West Lafayette, Indiana

Work History

1993-Present	*Systems Programmer*	COMPUTER SOFTWARE COMPANY • South Bend, Indiana
1992-1993	*Assistant Manager*	HOT & NOW • Ft. Wayne, Indiana
1991-1992	*Sound System Setup*	PURDUE UNIVERSITY • West Lafayette, Indiana

23

Combination. *Patricia Strefling, Niles, Michigan*

Larger font size for the individual's name and the section headings makes this information stand out. If you look down the center of the page, you can size up the resume quickly.

Bruce Saburn

2803 Lyndon Avenue ◆ Wilmington, North Carolina 28405
(910) 123-4567 Home ◆ (910) 123-7654 Fax
Saburn@Wilmington.Net

PROFILE

✓ More than 13 years experience as a technical trainer/instructor with strong knowledge in software and technical training.
✓ Dynamic presentation skills.
✓ Strong ability to translate technical information making it more easily understood by nontechnical audiences.

EXPERIENCE

Technical Training Overview
- Excellent oral communication and presentation skills.
- Experienced with accelerated learning techniques.
- Development of courses based on needs analysis.
- Preparation of lesson plans and other course documents.
- Strong technical writing skills.

Software Training Capabilities
- Ability to learn new software applications quickly through self-study of documentation.
- Working knowledge of computer hardware architecture and peripheral interfacing.
- Provide training on-site or off-site.
- Currently capable of teaching the following courses:

Word Processing
WordPerfect (through 6.1 Win/6.0a DOS) - Introduction, Intermediate & Advanced
Microsoft Word 6.0 - Introduction, Intermediate & Advanced

Databases
Microsoft Access - Introduction, Intermediate & Advanced
Paradox - Introduction

Spreadsheets
Excel - Introduction, Intermediate & Advanced
Lotus 1-2-3 rev. 5 - Introduction & Intermediate
Quattro Pro (Windows & DOS) - Introduction

Other Courses
PowerPoint	Harvard Graphics
Freelance	ACT!
Internet	DOS and Hard Disk Management
Basic Computer Use (DOS & Windows)	

24

Combination. *Sandy Adcox Saburn, Wilmington, North Carolina*

A resume based on a design by Pat Kendall of Aloha, Oregon (see Resume 91 in *Gallery of Best Resumes*). Lines thickened over staggered heads are novel and create interest.

Bruce Saburn

EMPLOYMENT HISTORY

Instructor/Consultant   March 1995 to Present
COMPUTER TRAINING & CONSULTING, Wilmington, NC

Specialist-Technical Training   September 1981 to December 1994
Chemistry Technician   May 1977 to September 1981
CP&L - BRUNSWICK NUCLEAR PLANT, Southport, NC

TRAINING & CERTIFICATIONS

Kepner-Tregoe Certified - Analytic Troubleshooting (ATS)
CP&L - Certified Instructor

EDUCATION

A.A.S. - Computer/Electronic Engineering Technology   May 1995
A.A.S. - Chemistry   May 1977
CAPE FEAR COMMUNITY COLLEGE, Wilmington, NC

REFERENCES

And teaching demonstration provided upon request

With a background in technical training, the individual wanted to transfer his skills to a computer-related field. The expanded Experience section resembles a summary of skills. Nice touches are the staggered, flush-right, contact information lines and the check mark bullets.

LAWRENCE M. RIVERA

723 Schmidt Boulevard • Chicago, Illinois 00000
(312) 555-5555

COMPUTER PROFESSIONAL

TECHNICAL PROFILE:

IBM-PC'S ♦ COMPATIBLES ♦ PCI MAINFRAME ♦ PCS MAINFRAME ♦ SELECT MAINFRAME
UPS MAINFRAME ♦ WINDOWS ♦ WORD ♦ ACT ♦ EXCEL ♦ FOX PRO
CRYSTAL REPORTS ♦ ACCESS ♦ COMMENCE ♦ PHOTOSTYLER

AREAS of SKILL & EXPERTISE:

- Strong computer operations abilities including: backups and disaster recovery; additional experience in enhancing and upgrading systems.
- Keen ability to fully utilize PC and mainframe systems to meet needs and provide business solutions.
- Excellent communication skills - easily interacts with departmental staff to determine specific application needs and utilize information to program/develop software to meet operating specifications.
- Learns new systems and software readily; strong desire to expand computer knowledge and apply it to improving business/departmental performance.
- Develop and administer computer training programs - instruct new and existing staff on new software applications.
- Additional experience includes staff management and leadership; possesses outstanding customer service abilities.

MAJOR PROJECTS & ACCOMPLISHMENTS:

♦ Utilizing Access (PC environment), programmed a relational database for the Chicago Bears - program is utilized to cross-reference radio broadcasting data by variables. This program also allows for the generation of legal contracts for advertisers and performs billing functions.
♦ Created numerous databases utilizing Fox Pro and Access that greatly improved the compilation and retrieval of data.
♦ Provides upper management with the technical assistance necessary to develop programs to efficiently and accurately track sales responses to specific marketing programs.
♦ At Jersey City Medical, coordinated Geriatrics department start-up; selected computer system, performed staff training and administered policies to ensure adherence to grant rules.

PROFESSIONAL EXPERIENCE:

CHICAGO BEARS • Chicago, IL   1994-Present

MIS/Fan Operations
Assists in maintaining systems utilized for various fan/client operations including ticketing, billing, marketing, customer service, etc. Manipulates data to provide upper management with client related reports. Develops various databases and programs specific to user/department applications. Utilizes system to research and resolve client difficulties.

25

Combination. *Alesia Benedict, Rochelle Park, New Jersey*

An aggressive resume (with page borders, horizontal lines, italic heads, and diamond bullets) to help a two-year degree graduate compete successfully against four-year graduates.

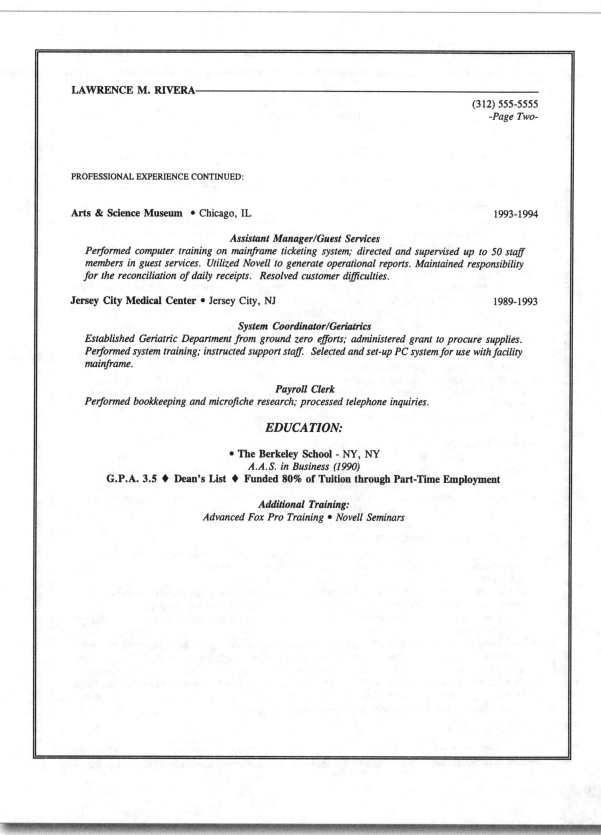

LAWRENCE M. RIVERA————————————————————————

(312) 555-5555
-Page Two-

PROFESSIONAL EXPERIENCE CONTINUED:

Arts & Science Museum • Chicago, IL   1993-1994

Assistant Manager/Guest Services

Performed computer training on mainframe ticketing system; directed and supervised up to 50 staff members in guest services. Utilized Novell to generate operational reports. Maintained responsibility for the reconciliation of daily receipts. Resolved customer difficulties.

Jersey City Medical Center • Jersey City, NJ   1989-1993

System Coordinator/Geriatrics

Established Geriatric Department from ground zero efforts; administered grant to procure supplies. Performed system training; instructed support staff. Selected and set-up PC system for use with facility mainframe.

Payroll Clerk

Performed bookkeeping and microfiche research; processed telephone inquiries.

EDUCATION:

• **The Berkeley School** - NY, NY
A.A.S. in Business (1990)
G.P.A. 3.5 ◆ **Dean's List** ◆ **Funded 80% of Tuition through Part-Time Employment**

Additional Training:
Advanced Fox Pro Training • *Novell Seminars*

Notice how the resume is made interesting by type changes: all caps in the Profile, normal text in the Skill section, boldface for the Projects section, and italic in the Experience section. Bullets alternate between filled circles and filled diamonds.

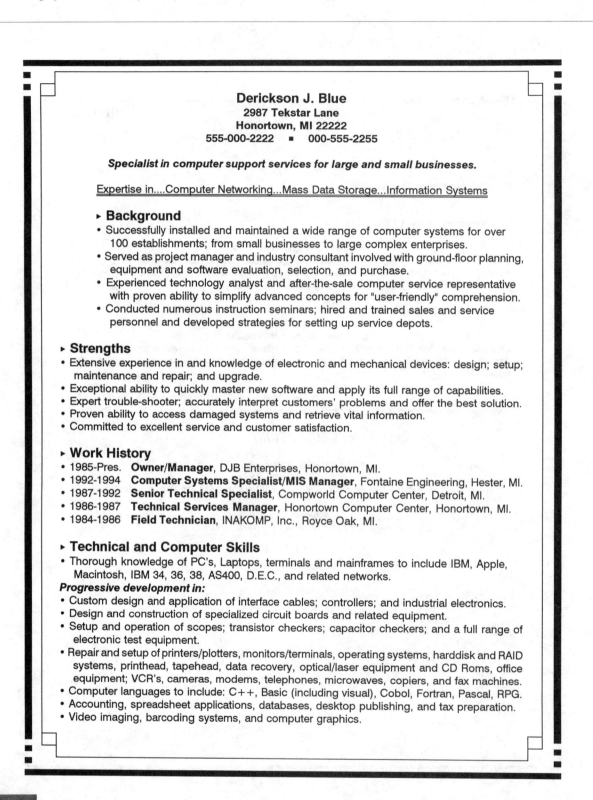

Derickson J. Blue
2987 Tekstar Lane
Honortown, MI 22222
555-000-2222 ▪ 000-555-2255

Specialist in computer support services for large and small businesses.

Expertise in....Computer Networking...Mass Data Storage...Information Systems

▸ Background

- Successfully installed and maintained a wide range of computer systems for over 100 establishments; from small businesses to large complex enterprises.
- Served as project manager and industry consultant involved with ground-floor planning, equipment and software evaluation, selection, and purchase.
- Experienced technology analyst and after-the-sale computer service representative with proven ability to simplify advanced concepts for "user-friendly" comprehension.
- Conducted numerous instruction seminars; hired and trained sales and service personnel and developed strategies for setting up service depots.

▸ Strengths

- Extensive experience in and knowledge of electronic and mechanical devices: design; setup; maintenance and repair; and upgrade.
- Exceptional ability to quickly master new software and apply its full range of capabilities.
- Expert trouble-shooter; accurately interpret customers' problems and offer the best solution.
- Proven ability to access damaged systems and retrieve vital information.
- Committed to excellent service and customer satisfaction.

▸ Work History

- 1985-Pres. **Owner/Manager**, DJB Enterprises, Honortown, MI.
- 1992-1994 **Computer Systems Specialist/MIS Manager**, Fontaine Engineering, Hester, MI.
- 1987-1992 **Senior Technical Specialist**, Compworld Computer Center, Detroit, MI.
- 1986-1987 **Technical Services Manager**, Honortown Computer Center, Honortown, MI.
- 1984-1986 **Field Technician**, INAKOMP, Inc., Royce Oak, MI.

▸ Technical and Computer Skills

- Thorough knowledge of PC's, Laptops, terminals and mainframes to include IBM, Apple, Macintosh, IBM 34, 36, 38, AS400, D.E.C., and related networks.

Progressive development in:

- Custom design and application of interface cables; controllers; and industrial electronics.
- Design and construction of specialized circuit boards and related equipment.
- Setup and operation of scopes; transistor checkers; capacitor checkers; and a full range of electronic test equipment.
- Repair and setup of printers/plotters, monitors/terminals, operating systems, harddisk and RAID systems, printhead, tapehead, data recovery, optical/laser equipment and CD Roms, office equipment; VCR's, cameras, modems, telephones, microwaves, copiers, and fax machines.
- Computer languages to include: C++, Basic (including visual), Cobol, Fortran, Pascal, RPG.
- Accounting, spreadsheet applications, databases, desktop publishing, and tax preparation.
- Video imaging, barcoding systems, and computer graphics.

26

Combination. *Randy Clair, location unknown*

A powerful resume whose strong page border is matched by substantial information (originally six pages condensed to two pages). Notice the Specialist and Expertise lines.

Proficient in:
- Setup, repair, and maintenance of CAD and mapping programs,
- Power plant and water treatment instrumentation, railroad signals and controllers, satellite receivers and transmitters, robotics, emergency communications systems, and computerized machinery and medical equipment.

▸ Education
- Michigan Institute of Technology, working toward B/S:
  Computer Science. *Planned graduation date - December:*   1997.
- Honortown Community College, A/S: *Data Systems Management*.   1986.

Seminars:
- Mobile Data Terminals (MDT), Motorola.   1995.
- Global Video Teleconferencing,   1994.
  3-D Modeling, Silicone Graphics.
- Robotics and Vision Systems.   1993.
- Motion & Motor Control, Allen-Bradley.   1991.
- Laser Printer Repair, Panasonic.   1991.
- Dot Matrix Repair, Panasonic.   1990.
- Dot Matrix Repair, Star.   1988.
- Computer Systems Repair, CORDATA   1986.
- Fortran Language, Michigan Technological University.   1981.

Certifications:
- Data Processing.   1986.
- Electronics.   1985.
- Industrial Controls.   1982.
- Electricity.   1979.

▸ Accomplishments
- Michigan Council of Teachers of Mathematics, MCTM.
  Placed top 50 in the state of Michigan two consecutive years.
- Vocational Industrial Clubs of America, VICA.
  Achieved third in state (Michigan) for radio and television repair.
- The Electronics Technician Association, ETA.
  Authorized Electronic Repair Technician.

▸ Community Service
- Volunteer speaker (youth education), Honortown Area Career Center. 1995.
- Volunteer firefighter, Honortown, MI.   1991 - Pres.
- Medical First Responder, State licensed.   1992 - 1994.
- American Red Cross Systems Repair.   1987.

▸ Training
- Firefighter I and II.   1994.
- Hazard Material Awareness.   1993.
- Hazard Material Operations.   1992.

Excellent professional references available upon request.

The applicant needed a resume to meet with banking representatives for a venture with another computer business. Almost the whole resume is like a summary of skills. Right-pointing triangle bullets call attention to section headings.

JOHN A. DOE

555 Main Street
Anytown, USA, 00000
(000) 000-0000

COMPUTER OPERATIONS & SYSTEMS PROFESSIONAL

Personable, conscientious, and resourceful individual with seven *plus* years of progressively responsible experience in Computer Operations, leading to current position of **Lead Operator** within a sales/manufacturing firm; excellent supervisory and managerial skills; well-versed in *Total Quality Management;* oversee department activities to assure delivery of reports on a timely and accurate basis; serve as an effective liaison and chief information source to all company departments.

TECHNICAL SUMMARY

- *Software:* MVS/ESA, JES2, DOS/VSE, IDMS, CICS, RESOLVE, PANVALET, TSO, ISPF/PDF, SPF, NET(VTAM), CMF, SARSTC, ODE, BIMWINDOW, TMON, BBMCAS, MVSPAS, TSSO, SUPERCALC 5.0 (pc-based spreadsheet)

- *Hardware:* IBM ES/9000, IBM 3083, IBM 4341, IBM 3203 printers, IBM 3380/3880 (controller) disk drives, MEMOREX 3288/3282 (controller) tape drives, MEMOREX 5450 Tape Cartridge Drives, IBM 3274 terminal controllers, XEROX 4850 Laser Printer.

- *Languages:* JCL, COBOL.

PROFESSIONAL EXPERIENCE

ACME MANUFACTURING, Anytown, USA   *February 1982 - Present*
Reseller of product identification and bar coding systems, and manufacturer of industrial labels.

Lead Operator (1st Shift), ISD Information Services Department *4/89 - Present*

Train and direct operations staff (one 2nd shift and two 1st shift operators) on an IBM ES/9000 mainframe system, utilizing MVS/ESA, JES2, IDMS, CICS, PANVALET, TSO, ISPF/PDF, NET(VTAM), CMF, BIMWINDOW and TMON; generate reports within a timely manner to various departments, including: Order Entry, Production Control, Accounting and Customer Service; ensure an effective overall operation through careful monitoring of hardware, and ordering and maintaining inventory; respond as first-level technical support (software and hardware) to in-house users; provide CICS security to new employees; perform weekly backups for IBM PS/2 PCs; perform daily backups for LAN, plus upload and download procedures between LAN and mainframe.

- Directly involved in conversion from IBM 4341 to IBM 3083 to current IBM ES/9000 mainframe system.
- Co-lead *Total Quality Management Work Team,* involving all company departments; resulted in a 50 percent improvement in computer operations.
- Increased department efficiency through developing a TSO-based online documentation system, and correcting JCL and system-related errors and abends.
- Created JDEs and designed forms, including billing invoices and time sheets, for the Xerox 4850 Laser Printer, eliminating the need for the purchasing of pre-printed forms.
- Promoted after serving as *Computer Operator Trainee (2/82-6/83), Computer Operator, (7/83-7/85)* and *Senior Computer Operator (7/85-3/89).*

EDUCATIONAL BACKGROUND

ANYTOWN COMMUNITY COLLEGE, Anytown, USA
Associate in Applied Science Degree, Computer Information Systems, May 1992

References and Salary History Will Be Furnished Upon Request

27

Combination. *Joellyn Wittenstein, Arlington Heights, Illinois*

A resume for someone who earned a degree while working full-time. Small square bullets set off categories in the Technical Summary. Triangle bullets point to accomplishments.

Scott Bodarmel

0000 Harrison Street - Somewhere, IN 00000
(000) 000-0000

OBJECTIVE

A position in Computer Data Analysis/Service or Entry Level Management where I can utilize my education in Management Information Systems; accounting, decision making and leadership strengths to contribute to the success of your company.

STRENGTHS

◆ Personable, confident, and highly motivated with a strong work ethic.
◆ Self-starter, able to work independently or as a team member.
◆ Quick learner, accurate and able to react effectively to challenges.
◆ Excellent verbal and written communication skills; would utilize research skills to effectively exceed my professional goals for the benefit of the company; to contribute in an informed manner to challenges facing the department.
◆ Demonstrate high performance standards: attention to detail, deadlines, and quality of work.

EDUCATION

Somewhere University, Somewhere, Indiana: 0000-0000 (GPA 3/4.0)
Associate of Science Degree: Business Administration - Management Information Systems.
Relevant coursework: Business Computers (LOTUS 1-2-3, Word Perfect, dBASE, COBOL, DOS, PASCAL), Accounting, Calculus, Business Legal Environment, Consumer Science, Statistics.

EXPERIENCE

Biermann & Sons, Somewhere, Indiana: 0000-0000.
Warehouse Worker. Efficiently and quickly processed orders and loaded shipments. Operated Fork lift.
◆ Exceeded average piece count of 90, to 160.
◆ Recommended processing in-town orders separately - resulted in an increase of efficiency.
◆ Set a standard for excellence; trusted by management to train new workers, lead by example.

Rule Insurance, Thisplace, Illinois: 0000-0000.
Shipping Clerk. Processed company documents to develop client insurance packets. Attended meetings regarding company procedural changes and quality control. Oversaw all functions of mail processing. Operated UPS machine, figured weight and location for accurate postage.

Wal-Mart Company, Somewhere, Indiana: 0000-0000.
Shipping/Receiving Clerk. Responsible for receiving merchandise and checking for accuracy, determining status of shipment (items missing, damaged goods, etc.).
◆ Made quick accurate assessments of shipments - routing to sales floor or to holding areas in the warehouse. Kept mental log of where items were stored for quick access when needed in the sales store.

28

Combination. *Colleen S. Jaracz, Vincennes, Indiana*

Large diamond bullets point to transferable skills and achievements for this individual who is ready to move from warehouse work to computer data analysis or entry-level management.

DOROTHY A. GRACHECK

2332 Ellyn Street
Bloomingdale, IL 60108   708/555-5191

OBJECTIVE: *NETWORK / COMPUTER SERVICES:*
A position utilizing a strong aptitude for learning new computer systems.

PROFILE:
- Comprehensive skills in the programming, configuration, and troubleshooting of IBM and Apple systems, as well as plotters, modems and all types of printers and peripherals.

- Familiar with Token Ring, Ethernet, Local Talk, IPX, and E-mail systems; handle customer service and problem solving in a professional manner.

- Perform system analysis, software installations and debugging; experience with DOS 6.1, OS2, Windows, Excel, Lotus, WordPerfect and MS Word on a full range of IBM clones.

EMPLOYMENT: Electrorent Corporation, WoodDale, IL
Lead Technician   3/94-Present
Effectively train and supervise eight technicians in the testing, programming, repair, and configuration of computer and peripheral systems listed above.
Communicate daily with clients from business and private accounts to determine and meet their needs for new systems or repairs.
Repair and maintain peripherals including all types of plotters, printers and modems.
Perform cleaning of hard drives and install/remove memory and components; load software to customer specs.
* Rated outstanding in all categories, including customer service, on last review.
* Recognized by management for the ability to quickly learn new systems.

Computer Technician   3/93-3/94
Responsible for repairing a wide range of laptop and desktop computers and related equipment.

Geen Industries, Addison, IL   3/91-3/93
Office Manager / Administrative Assistant
Performed all office support for seven midwest representatives.

Mr. David's Carpet, Carol Stream, IL   6/90-3/91
Office Administration / Customer Service

Tube Sales Company, Carol Stream, IL   8/87-6/90
General Office

EDUCATION: College of DuPage, Glen Ellyn, IL   Present
Seeking to attend courses in Novell and Computer Science.

Willowbrook High School, Bloomingdale, IL   Graduated 1986

29

Combination. *Steven A. Provenzano, Schaumburg, Illinois*

Once an administrative assistant, this computer technician with a knack for learning new computer systems looks for a position in network services after taking Novell courses.

Jennifer Marie Lastname

55 Apple Hill Drive • River, NY 55555 • (000) 555-5555

PROFESSIONAL PROFILE

Results-oriented professional with extensive experience in MIS, operations, programming and TQM. Ability to coordinate and manage multiple projects. Proven supervisory and training abilities. Hardware: AS/400, IBM 3090, IBM System 38, PC's, Token Ring Network. Software: CMS, CICS, IDMS, MAPICS, MAPICS DB, ASI, COPS, IIN/Advantis, WordPerfect, Windows, Novell NetWare/LAN, Paradox, Excel.

EXPERIENCE

RIVERVIEW TECHNICAL COMPANY, River, New York
MIS Coordinator/TQL Coordinator, 1992 to XXXX
- Provided information management support for all plant users. Assisted users in defining and developing Information Systems Support Requests, and developing communications/data transfer capabilities.
- Presented PC training programs including operating systems, communications, data back up and applications. Administered PC networks.
- Cataloged and managed location, configuration, cabling, and maintenance of all computer devices. Implemented configuration to support future business activities.
- Coordinated Plant's Total Quality Leadership (continuous improvement process) program, involving problem selection/approval, creation and training of teams, monitoring team performance, measuring results and communicating status. Staff member, Plant Management Team.

Programmer Associate, 1991 to 1992
- Monitored and controlled computer processing, including output queues, printing and output distribution. Ran various jobs in accordance with schedule of operations.
- Made modifications to existing programs, created new programs to enhance productivity.

Computer Operator, 1988 to 1991
- Operated AS/400 computer system. Provided system support and back up.

RIVER SPRINGS INSURANCE, River, New York
Data Entry Operator, March 1988 to November 1988
- Responsible for the input and output of data for car and home insurance policies.

HANDY DANDY COMPANY, River, New York
Data Entry Clerk, June 1986 to March 1988
- Interpreted legal documents and input data in system for use in court proceedings for automated litigation firm. Handled microfilming and quality control.

PRIOR EMPLOYMENT:
  Manager/Assistant Manager - Small Company, 1982-1986
  Cashier - River Boutique, River Square, 1981-1982
  Crafts/Sports Director/Park Floater - Town of Riverview, Summers 1980 & 1981
  Assistant Supervisor - Toddler Summer Program, 1978-1979

EDUCATION

A.A.S. Data Processing, 1989 - River Community College, River, New York
A.A.S. Business Administration, 1986 - River Community College, River, New York
Training Certificates - TQL Training; PC Maintenance Repair Update; 8-D Training; Facilitator Training; EDI Course; Leadership & Supervisory Skills for Women; Powerful Communication Skills for Women; Novell Networking Technologies; NetWare 3.11 Advanced System Manager; System Administration for NetWare 3.11; Systems Integration Project; Paradox; WordPerfect Windows; Excel 4.0; Windows 3.1; Novell LAN End User; Intro to DOS/Hard Disk Management; Managing Change.

30

Combination. *Betty Geller, Elmira, New York*

The writer considers this resume "very targeted" with its specific information in the Profile and wealth of focused Experience. The series of training certificates is a strong conclusion.

NATHAN G. LEVINSON
455 Armory Street
Philadelphia, PA 00000
(000) 000-0000

QUALIFICATIONS:
- Calibrate, program, and provide support for computer-controlled test equipment
- Technical trainer and as-needed crew supervisor for test and assembly personnel
- Experienced in self-managed, goal-oriented team environments
- Experience in setting up and configuring PC systems including peripherals from multiple vendors
- Adept at managing multiple simultaneous projects/work responsibility areas
- Knowledge of ISO 9002 certification process
- Coordinated industrial project in foreign cultural milieu

EXPERIENCE:
New Ideas Technology Corp., Philadelphia, PA   1993–present
Engineering Technician: Provide technical and on-call support for three cleanrooms;
    repair/refurbish eleven disk drive product lines for five manufacturers (Maxtor.
    Micropolis, Seagate, Connor, DEC). Spec and purchase equipment parts for engineering
    and production.
- Managed transfer of entire cleanroom test and repair facilities from Pacific Rim and domestic locations: studied existing site operations (including software, hardware, procedures, etc.) in order to replicate them at Springboard, coordinated workstation layout, acquired tool capacity and spare parts, trained employees at new location, etc.
- Create and revise documentation for ISO 9002 certification

Computers R Us Equipment Corp., Trenton, NJ   1979–93
Engineering Technician, 1987–93: Supported DEC servowriters in a Class 100 cleanroom.
    Debugged at system, board, and component levels. Performed mechanical and electrical
    analysis and alignment/calibration of a laser positioning system. Upgraded and debugged
    pneumatic controls. Performed resonance and Bode plot measurements.
- Identified and solved root cause of a persistent servowriter resonance problem

Manufacturing Technician, 1979–87: Performed failure analysis and debugging of disk drives.
    Analyzed product data; recommended solutions. Evaluated parametric test software.
    Wrote diagnostic programs for production equipment.

EDUCATION:
Information Systems, Informative University, Philadelphia, PA   1988–present

A.S. in Computer Electronics Technology   1983
Penn's Landing Community College, Philadelphia, PA

COMPUTER SKILLS:
Operating Systems: VAX VMS, MS-DOS (with and without Windows)

Languages: DCL, Pascal, BASIC

Applications: PowerPoint, Harvard Graphics, Corel Draw, AmiPro, WordPerfect, Microsoft
    Word, Lotus 1-2-3, specialized diagnostic tools.

REFERENCES:
Available upon request.

31

Chronological. *Shel Horowitz, Northampton, Massachusetts*

Boldfacing down the left margin enables you to see quickly the section headings and key topics.
Bullets of the same intensity point to important qualifications and accomplishments.

Ricardo Santianna

28 Kirkland Street • Cambridge, MA 02139 • (617) 555–5555

Qualifications

Specialized training in the basics of computer operation, assembly, installation, diagnostics, and networking. Excellent technical aptitude, willingness to learn, and hands-on ability. Skilled problem-solver, adept at operating, troubleshooting, and repairing electronic and mechanical equipment. Basic understanding of DOS and Windows operating systems and MS Word software. Highly motivated team player, with strong work ethic.

Relevant Achievements

- Built fully functioning pc from scratch, including installation of hard drive, floppy drive, motherboard, IOE cables, jib jumpers, CD-rom, ethernet adapter, sound card, and modem; partitioned hard drive.
- Received U.S. Army technical training in communications systems and radar repair; performed equipment inspections and routine maintenance.
- Repaired and maintained smooth operation of automated grocery store scanning equipment and cash registers under high pressure during periods of high volume.
- Analyzed inventory data to track demand for promotional items.
- Exceeded monthly productivity quota as warehouse shipper/receiver.

Education

Certificate	**Computer Career Institute, Clark University**, Worcester, MA		xxxx
U.S. Army	**Fort Devens**, MA		May–July xxxx
U.S. Army	**Technical Training School**, MA		December xxxx–May xxxx

Work History

Front End Manager - Star Market, Somerville, MA   xxxx—present
- Promoted to manage increasingly larger stores with more responsibility.
- Troubleshoot scanning equipment and cash registers to ensure smooth operations.
- Monitor hours and submit payroll paperwork.
- Supervise and schedule 34 employees.
- Entrusted with bank deposits of $25,000/day in cash receipts.

Assistant Night Auditor - Charles Hotel, Cambridge, MA   xxxx—xxxx
Provided general customer assistance and transportation services.

Warehouse Shipping/Receiving Manager - Caldor's, Framingham, MA   xxxx—xxxx
Managed 10 employees; unloaded and stocked inventory, filled customer orders, and operated forklift.

Machinery Operation - Parker Bros., Salem, MA   xxxx—xxxx
Operated plastic molding machinery, processed and packaged final product for delivery.

Military Service

U.S. Army, Corporal, Fort Devens, MA   xxxx—xxxx

32

Combination. *Betty Geller, Elmira, New York*

The opening Qualifications paragraph serves as an Areas of Expertise section, a Summary of Skills, and a Profile all in one section for this ex-military person looking for computer work.

Nathaniel A. Martin

8899 Blustery Drive, #10 ▪ Orchard, Illinois 60000 ▪ (555) 555-8765

PROFILE	Competent **Network Support Professional** with 16 years experience in computer systems and network support. Manage design, installation, testing, and support of systems/networks and applications in multi-user corporate environment.

Strengths include:

- Fluency in all LAN topologies, along with Macintosh, DOS, Windows, and Win95 operating systems.
- Netware and NT server administration; CNA/CNE certification studies in progress.
- E-mail systems maintenance and support; 3270 and 5250 mainframe communications.
- Excellent communication skills; able to establish and maintain effective relationships with vendors and subcontractors.

PROFESSIONAL EXPERIENCE	**Computer Services Technician** MASTERPIECE, INC., St. Louis, Missouri	1993-Present

Assist Computer Services Manager (and fill in during his absence) with hardware, software, and network installation and support of 200-400 user system. Backup servers and e-mail/post office. Ship, receive, and relocate computer hardware systems and software. Instruct and support BCS users on hardware and software applications. Install and upgrade software. Maintain support contracts and coordinate with software vendors.

Service Manager   1989-1993
BIGG COMPUTER STORE, St. Louis, Missouri

Supervised 3 technicians in installation and maintenance of networks and computer systems (PC and Macintosh) to various client sites including Anheuser-Busch corporate. Managed service department, ordered parts, controlled inventory, and scheduled repairs. Earned certification as IBM, Compaq, Epson, Hewlett Packard, and NEC Authorized Repair Technician.

Customer Service Engineer   1979-1989
ABC CORPORATION, St. Louis, Missouri

Tested, repaired, and maintained central processing units and peripherals on NCR equipment. Provided third party maintenance on mainframes, data communication lines, and preventative maintenance on computer electrical and mechanical equipment.

SPECIAL TRAINING	**CNA / CNE** Certification study	in progress
	NT Server Administration Certification study	in progress
	NCR Technical Training	1979-1989
	Graduate, CONTROL DATA INSTITUTE Completed 750 hours hands-on training in computer repair technology.	1980

REFERENCES	References and training credentials furnished upon request.

33

Combination. *Carla Culp Coury, Glen Carbon, Illinois*

An outstanding variant of a resume like that of Pat Kendall (see Resume 15 in *Gallery of Best Resumes*). Applying for his supervisor's job, this person wanted to be competitive.

ROGER J. SEMPKINS

23 Venus Drive
O'Fallon, IL 62269
(618) 555-9851

HIGHLIGHTS OF QUALIFICATIONS

- Six years experience and proven ability to analyze, design and implement unique computer solutions based on company needs.
- Excellent technical and supervisory skills involving installation, maintenance and troubleshooting.
- Proficient knowledge of numerous software applications and programming languages: Xbase, C, COBOL, Assembly, FORTRAN, BASIC, and RPG.

PROFESSIONAL EXPERIENCE

Computer Systems Manager   *1991-Present*
BELLEVILLE AREA COLLEGE, Belleville, IL
- Supervise 10-person staff on host-terminal network for specialized transportation system.
- Developed database applications; gained dramatic increases in productivity and efficiency.
- Automated manual reporting procedures to improve tracking and documentation capabilities.
- Created inventory control system equipped to centralize diverse supply methods.
- Coordinate with several state and local agencies to ensure compliance with Americans with Disabilities Act.

Computer Consultant   *1986-Present*
KENNETH JOHNSON REALTY, INC., Belleville, IL
- Oversee installation and maintenance of software, providing on-call support when necessary.
- Designed new property management application to company specifications.

EDUCATION

BELLEVILLE AREA COLLEGE, Belleville, IL
- A.A.S. Computer Information Systems
- A.S., Computer Science
- Vice President's List; 4.0/4.0 GPA

REFERENCES AVAILABLE UPON REQUEST

34

Combination. *John A. Suarez, location unknown*

This resume with a page border highlights management and consulting experience before mentioning dual associate degrees. The 4.0/4.0 GPA is a strong resume ending.

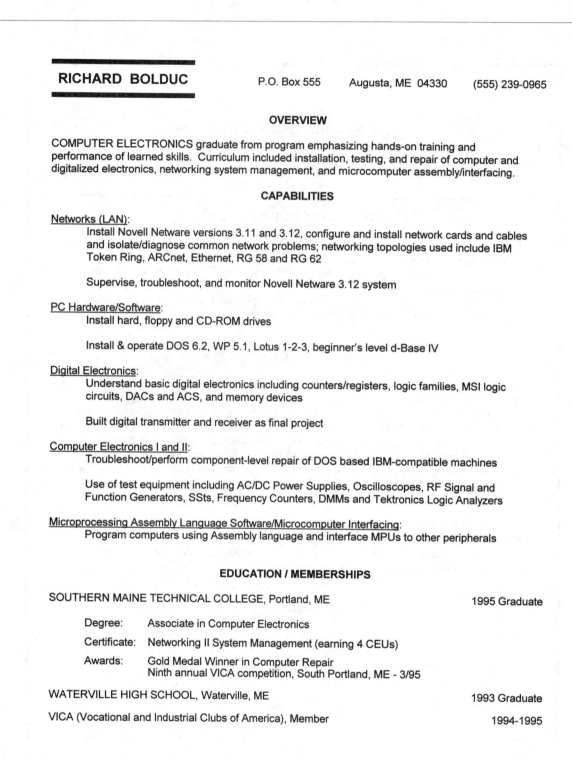

RICHARD BOLDUC

P.O. Box 555   Augusta, ME 04330   (555) 239-0965

OVERVIEW

COMPUTER ELECTRONICS graduate from program emphasizing hands-on training and performance of learned skills. Curriculum included installation, testing, and repair of computer and digitalized electronics, networking system management, and microcomputer assembly/interfacing.

CAPABILITIES

Networks (LAN):
 Install Novell Netware versions 3.11 and 3.12, configure and install network cards and cables and isolate/diagnose common network problems; networking topologies used include IBM Token Ring, ARCnet, Ethernet, RG 58 and RG 62

 Supervise, troubleshoot, and monitor Novell Netware 3.12 system

PC Hardware/Software:
 Install hard, floppy and CD-ROM drives

 Install & operate DOS 6.2, WP 5.1, Lotus 1-2-3, beginner's level d-Base IV

Digital Electronics:
 Understand basic digital electronics including counters/registers, logic families, MSI logic circuits, DACs and ACS, and memory devices

 Built digital transmitter and receiver as final project

Computer Electronics I and II:
 Troubleshoot/perform component-level repair of DOS based IBM-compatible machines

 Use of test equipment including AC/DC Power Supplies, Oscilloscopes, RF Signal and Function Generators, SSts, Frequency Counters, DMMs and Tektronics Logic Analyzers

Microprocessing Assembly Language Software/Microcomputer Interfacing:
 Program computers using Assembly language and interface MPUs to other peripherals

EDUCATION / MEMBERSHIPS

SOUTHERN MAINE TECHNICAL COLLEGE, Portland, ME   1995 Graduate

 Degree: Associate in Computer Electronics
 Certificate: Networking II System Management (earning 4 CEUs)
 Awards: Gold Medal Winner in Computer Repair
    Ninth annual VICA competition, South Portland, ME - 3/95

WATERVILLE HIGH SCHOOL, Waterville, ME   1993 Graduate

VICA (Vocational and Industrial Clubs of America), Member   1994-1995

35

Functional. *Elizabeth (Lisa) M. Carey, Waterville, Maine*

Two short bold lines enclosing the name draw attention to it. Adequate white space and indented information in the Capabilities section make this resume easy to read.

Customer Service

Resumes at a Glance

RESUME NO.	LAST OR CURRENT OCCUPATION	GOAL	PAGE
36.	Customer Service Representative	Customer Service Representative	75
37.	Collections/Visa Coordinator	Not specified	76
38.	Cashier	Customer service position	77
39.	Manager of Customer Care	Not specified	78
40.	Customer Service Manager	Services management/ Hardware management/ Product management	80
41.	Team Leader/Asst. Manager	Not Specified	82
42.	Site Manager	Not specified	84
43.	New Car Salesman	Not specified	86

CARYN C. ESSAR

6602 Marcus Lane, Newman, NJ 00000   **(555) 555-5555**

OBJECTIVE

Position as a Customer Service Representative

SUMMARY OF QUALIFICATIONS

- 6 years of customer service experience; strong phone skills.
- Superior listening and probing abilities.
- Extremely articulate; clear, pleasant speaking voice.
- Professional and personable in relating with clients and coworkers.
- Ability to remain calm, patient, and productive in fast-paced environment.
- Effective in working with other departments to resolve problems.

SKILLS AND ACCOMPLISHMENTS

CUSTOMER SERVICE REPRESENTATIVE (1994 - Present)
Chilton-Elms Insurance Corporation, Newman, NJ

<u>**Client Relations and Problem Solving**</u>

- Processed dental enrollments and changes for hundreds of corporate accounts with 50-3000 employees.
- Responded to over 100 phone calls daily (on the employer hotline) from benefits administrators, regarding enrollment, eligibility, and termination.
- Received numerous requests from benefits administrators at client companies to personally handle their accounts.
- Consulted with underwriters, group representatives, and other hotline personnel to obtain additional information and resolve problems.
- Earned a "Bravo" letter of recognition for performance and helpfulness.
- Scored in 90-100% range for productivity and accuracy on quality reviews.

<u>**Product Knowledge**</u>

- Studied and learned details of dental insurance enrollment, eligibility, and termination.
- Selected by supervisor to manage more complex accounts due to product knowledge, professionalism, and problem-solving abilities.

CUSTOMER SERVICE REPRESENTATIVE (1990 - 1994)
Barrington Clothing, Newman, NJ

<u>**Initiative**</u>

- Promoted from sales associate to service representative within a few months.
- Took control of problem situations swiftly and competently.

<u>**Communication**</u>

- Developed the ability to relate effectively and professionally with customers when processing returns/exchanges, providing information, and handling complaints.
- Selected as Employee of the Month in June 1994.

EDUCATION

A.A., Liberal Arts, Arnell Community College, Arnell, NJ (in progress)

36

Combination. *Rhoda Kopy, Toms River, New Jersey*

Note that the Work Experience section is labeled SKILLS AND ACCOMPLISHMENTS. With this heading, the reader is primed to look for them rather than duties for each position held.

Krysten S. Hollister
33994 South Shore Drive
Sand Lake, MI 00000
Day Telephone: 222-555-0000 - Evening Telephone: 000-222-5555

Profile
Creative individual with strong organizational, communication, and business skills.

Summary of Qualifications

- Over 10 years experience in credit union member services.
- Demonstrated problem-resolution abilities.
- Results-oriented; goal-directed with a sharp eye for detail.
- Proven performance record in full-circle collection procedures.
- Team player; ability to work with individuals on all levels.
- Committed to excellent service and member satisfaction.

Professional Experience

MEMBER SERVICES   *COMMUNICATION*   *PUBLIC RELATIONS*

"Combining knowledge and experience to accomplish the task."

SAND LAKE CREDIT UNION, (S.L.C.U.), Sand Lake, MI
Job Title: Collection Department/Visa Coordinator: 1988 to Present.
Job Title: Customer Service Representative: 1984 to 1988.
- ▸ Responsible for the collection of monies due on all delinquent and charged off loan accounts.
- ▸ Oversee and manage S.L.C.U. visa credit card program.
- ▸ Serve as liaison between S.L.C.U. and District Court; interact with attorneys on all legal matters involving but not limited to: bankruptcies, garnishments, tax levies. Represent S.L.C.U. in small claims disputes.

Other primary duties:
- In charge of S.L.C.U. redemption and repossession procedures: assist members with refinancing alternatives and solutions; document, track, recover merchandise on defaulted loans; prepare merchandise for resale.
- Function as department administrator and report quarterly to S.L.C.U. Board of Directors; provide detail on charge-offs, skip tracings, and collection investigations and outcomes.
- Verify individual credit reports through Trans Union and TRW credit bureaus.
- Interact with radio and newspaper advertising staff for marketing and promotion of S.L.C.U. member services.
- Balance all collection department and visa department general ledgers; maintain records on bankruptcies and payments.

SAND LAKE OPTOMETRY P.C., Sand Lake, MI
Job Title: Doctor's Assistant/Contact Lens Specialist: 1982 to 1984.
Job Title: Office Manager/Receptionist/Bookkeeper: 1977 to 1979.
- ▸ Responsibilities included training patients in proper eye care. Managed and maintained accounting activities, clerical, administrative work and patient services; served as customer service representative.

Other primary duties:
- As Lens Specialist: prepped patients; assisted with eye examinations; blood pressure tests; glaucoma, visual fields, color-blindness checks; and lensometer readings.
- Involved in insurance, Medicaid; ordered, stocked, maintained inventories.
- Involved in collection of past due accounts, end-of-day cashout and closeout procedures, and inner-office assignments as needed.

Education and Seminars
A/A Degree, 1988, Sand Lake Community College, G.P.A. 3.75
Seminars in: Dun & Bradstreet: Collection Techniques; National Business Institute: Collecting Judgments in Michigan.
Michigan Credit Union League, Star Independent Study: Certifications in: Member Relations; Member Services; Consumer Lending.
Classes in WordPerfect 5.1

Hobbies/Activities
Enjoy interior decorating, co-ed volleyball, softball, tennis.

37

Combination. *Randy Clair, location unknown*

The client wanted information on one page. The result was this layout, which caught the eye of the interviewer, plus a Bank Loan Officer position for a salary increase of 10 percent.

SUZANNE S. WEISMAN
9822 Larkwood Court, Apartment 1-B
Zeeland, MI 22222
222-000-5555

Objective
A challenging position in Customer Service where my ability to interact with a broad customer base will promote an opportunity for personal and professional development.

Summary of Qualifications
- 8 years experience in customer service with a major retailer.
- Proven abilities as full-time Cashier; sincerely enjoy helping people.
- Excellent reputation with customers as a competent and knowledgeable professional.
- Expertise in anticipating and responding to customer needs.
- Enjoy my work and consistently greet customers with a smile.
- Excellent attendance; punctual; timely; reliable; realize the importance of my job and being at my work station as scheduled.
- Honest and productive; like to stay busy.

Relevant Skills and Experience
1987 - Present
J-Mart, Inc., Kentwood, MI

 CASHIER. Diverse responsibilities within this large, busy, multi-department organization. Take pride in providing excellent customer service. Hands-on experience in numerous departments providing a variety of services and needs:

• *Courtesy Desk*	• *Layaway*	• *Gas Station*	• *Bakery*	• *Pricing*
• *Café*	• *Video Center*	• *Lotto*	• *Tobacco*	• *Merchandise Returns*
• *Money Orders*	• *UPS*	• *Bagging*	• *Phones*	• *Aisle Assistance*

- ▸ Responsible for beginning shift banks as high as $4,000 and organizing end-of-shift monies and receipts for turn-in.
- ▸ Thorough knowledge of store system. Train and assist coworkers when asked; fill-in when needed.
- ▸ Excellent ability in memorizing number patterns: 10-digit computerized codes and PLU's.
- ▸ Fast and accurate keyboard and cash register skills.

Education
⇒ Davenport College, Holland, MI. 2 years. 1990 - 1992. Studies: <u>Travel and Tourism</u> and <u>Business Management</u>. Working toward double A/A Degree.
⇒ Kalamazoo Valley Community College, Kalamazoo, MI. 1 year. 1988. Studies: <u>Intro to Computers</u>.

Volunteer/Community Involvement
▪ Girl Scouts Of America, Galesburg, MI, Fall Co-District Chairperson. 1991 - 1995. Oversee monies and validate cookie orders.

References available on request.

38

Combination. *Randy Clair, location unknown*

The individual is working toward a double A.A. degree. Horizontal lines showcase bulleted areas of service. The outcome: an interview and an entry-level package with higher pay.

IRENE CENTORINO
409 Bay Road
Milton, Massachusetts
(617) 698-1043

PROFESSIONAL SUMMARY:

Dynamic, self-directed executive with 15 years in the communications industry. Successful in developing market strategies and new business opportunities; training, managing, and directing over 300 employees; establishing and overseeing start-up operations; and reengineering/streamlining operational programs systems and processes. Creative and entrepreneurial; skillful in combining financial leadership with sound business operating and management practices to position service companies for long-term growth and profitability. Qualifications include:

- New Business Development
- Customer Relations Management
- Facilities Planning
- Multi-site Management
- Budgetary Planning and Control
- Motivational Training & Development
- Reengineering Analysis

- MIS Technologies
- Financial Analysis and Planning
- Compensation and Benefit Systems
- Marketing Strategy and Analysis
- Executive Presentations/Negotiations
- Public Speaking and Training
- Competitive Strategies

PROFESSIONAL HIGHLIGHTS:

- Redefined hiring/customer service practices, while streamlining process and procedure flows, **to successfully maintain Western Region's "Highest Customer Satisfaction" rate for three consecutive years.**
- Attained Top Performing Region in customer attrition through the implementation of innovative customer service/marketing techniques.
- Conducted employee development and education programs for 800 regional employees.
- Developed and presented customized Tele-sales training program to over 500 employees of large publishing company. **Successfully increased volumes per facility by 50%.**
- Streamlined/consolidated customer care activities, **reducing operating costs by 200% and marketing acquisition costs by 300%.**
- Launched a series of innovative marketing and customer service techniques **resulting in improved customer satisfaction, increased revenue per subscriber, and 200% reduction in customer service costs.**
- Successfully facilitated the transition of employees during company merger, **resulting in a 98% retention rate.**
- Analyzed and developed process flow mapping to maximize internal resources for large paper manufacturer.
- Customized a Customer Service Quality Services training program for Southwestern Bell Mobile Systems.
- Conceptualized and implemented "Wheel of Fortune" program to crosstrain customer service staff in each department to improve service impact to the customer. **Successfully reduced call transfers from 63% to 4%.**
- Set up and directed 7 new customer care offices. Hired and trained staff; developed marketing plan for all facilities.
- **Secured 60% of new communications market and increased market share by 49% within one year of market operational control.**
- Created and implemented an aggressive training program to decentralize new customer service requirements to individual service centers. **Successfully redirected 40% of new customer activity to regional service centers.**
- Conceptualized and developed a tele-sales training program for Apple Computer, focusing on incremental selling to inbound callers.

39

Combination. *Cheryl Ann Harland, The Woodlands, Texas*

The next step for this person, who received a two-year degree from a four-year university, is a senior-level management position without having a bachelor's or a graduate degree.

IRENE CENTORINO   **PAGE TWO**

PROFESSIONAL   **ACE MOBILNET**, Boston, Massachusetts   1994 - Present
EXPERIENCE: <u>Manager of Customer Care</u>
Direct management and support staff of 265 in customer service operations, servicing over 150,000 calls per month, with $10 million budgetary responsibility.

DORSEY & ASSOCIATES, West Roxbury, Massachusetts   1992 - 1994
<u>Consultant Training and Development</u>
Provided consultative training and development expertise, and customized programs for telecommunications, manufacturing, and publishing companies.

SYSTEM COMMUNICATIONS, INC., Arizona/Nevada/California   1986 - 1992

SYSTEM CELLULAR COMMUNICATIONS, INC., California and Nevada
<u>Director of Customer Development</u>   1988 - 1992
Directed 300 employees in the management of 16 customer care locations servicing over 285,000 customers.

<u>Manager of Customer Care</u>   1987 - 1988
Managed and implemented all customer care and marketing strategies for Las Vegas region. Established vendor distribution network; developed pricing strategies; created product positioning.

SYSTEM CABLEVISION OF TUCSON, INC.
<u>Controller</u>   1986 - 1987
Directed Accounting and MIS departments in the preparation of monthly financial forecasts, cash flow analysis, and budgetary planning and control.

<u>Prior</u>
<u>Assistant Controller</u>, Smith Cablevision of California, Inc.   1984 - 1986
<u>Accounting Manager</u>, Big Valley Cablevision   1980 - 1984

EDUCATION: Oklahoma State University
Oklahoma City, Oklahoma
A.S, Accounting 1980

SPECIALIZED   **Legendary Service Certified Trainer**
TRAINING: Bluebeard Training and Development, Inc.
Professional Development
Merkin and Associates

After an impressive first page, filled with a Professional Summary and Professional Highlights, this second page shows continual employment since the year of the degree. Underlining makes the various job positions easy to see.

ROBERT R. WILSON

9 West Mountain Avenue · #324
Boilingbrook, Illinois 00000
(708) 555-5555

CAREER OBJECTIVE:

EXPERIENCED professional seeks a position with advancement opportunities that will utilize acquired skills and experience to contribute to the success of a progressive organization. Areas of concentration include:

SERVICES MANAGEMENT ◆ HARDWARE MANAGEMENT ◆ PRODUCT MANAGEMENT

PROFILE SUMMARY:

An accomplished manager with solid skills in retaining and expanding client base and increasing revenue. Strong interpersonal skills are evident in the ability to interface with others at all levels. Excels at developing and motivating staff, creating a synergistic team unit. Exposure to financial management has developed a keen eye for profitability and cost reduction. Adept in computerized environments.

· *THOROUGH UNDERSTANDING OF CLIENT SERVICES WITHIN FAST PACED ENVIRONMENTS.*
· *RECOGNIZED AS A CONSISTENTLY STRONG PROFESSIONAL WITH THE SKILLS AND TALENTS NECESSARY TO RESOLVE DIFFICULTIES WHILE MAINTAINING POSITIVE RELATIONS.*

PROFESSIONAL EXPERIENCE:

<u>**A.S. CORP.**</u> · Boilingbrook, Illinois   *1972 - Present*

CUSTOMER SERVICE MANAGER · 1995 - Present

· Directs all customer service functions for a manufacturer of high performance storage and retrieval products.
· Trains, develops and manages a staff of 19 Customer Service engineers.
· Coordinates coverage for clientele consisting of 80 Fortune 500 companies.
· Interfaces with all levels of management and acts as a liaison between company staff and client personnel.
· Utilizes PC's and MAC's for e-mail, general correspondence and presentations.

Achievements:

◆ *Manages the largest of 15 departments in the eastern region, due to superior leadership and managerial skills.*
◆ *Developed a synergistic team of customer service engineers to peak levels of performance and productivity.*
◆ *Consistently met or surpassed organizational objectives.*
◆ *Eliminated problems associated with on-line system schedules by developing and implementing procedure changes.*
◆ *Improved response to customers' service requests; established and maintained rapport with clientele.*
◆ *Recipient of numerous awards for outstanding customer satisfaction.*

(CONTINUED...)

40

Combination. *Alesia Benedict, Rochelle Park, New Jersey*

Another strong resume to help a two-year degree graduate compete successfully against applicants with four-year or higher degrees. Note again the use of type (see Resume 25).

ROBERT R. WILSON · (708) 555-5555 · Page Two

PROFESSIONAL EXPERIENCE continued...

<u><u>A.S. CORP.</u></u> continued   *1972 - Present*

REGION PRODUCT MANAGER · 1993 - 1995

· Administered strategic customer service and retention strategies to protect service base from competition and prevent service revenue erosion.
· Traveled to sites to conduct comprehensive presentations at customer locations and to internal company personnel.
· Developed proposals and contracts to increase revenue and expand client base.

Achievements:

♦ *Developed the 1995 Customer Services Operating Plan ($56.8 million budget) which was implemented throughout the region.*
♦ *Developed a response for professional services for a major metropolitan city and was awarded prime Vendor Status for the contract.*
♦ *Maintained a retention ratio of 100% during tenure as manager.*

CUSTOMER SERVICE MANAGER · 1987 - 1993

· Accountable for troubleshooting and resolving customer relations concerns.
· Fostered superior relations with customers.
· Promoted to Region Product Manager in recognition of outstanding leadership skills.

DISTRICT SUPPORT MANAGER · 1982 - 1987

· Supervised 6 technical specialists and coordinated customer support.
· Interfaced with worldwide technical support and engineering personnel in Company's headquarters.

TECHNICAL SPECIALIST · 1979 - 1982

· Assisted customer service engineers with complex technical problems.

SENIOR FIELD ENGINEER/ASSOCIATE FIELD ENGINEER · 1972 - 1979

EDUCATIONAL BACKGROUND:

New York City Community College · Brooklyn, New York
A.A.S. in Electronics

Regularly attends company sponsored management and marketing training courses sponsored by the American Management Association.

COMPUTER PROFICIENCY:

IBM PC's · Macintosh PC's · Windows · Excel · Word · Power Point

Page borders, tiny bullets for duties, and diamond bullets and italic for achievements help to tie together the two pages. Work for the same company since 1972 also unifies the resume. Double-underlining makes the company name stand out on both pages.

Adrian Masters

5555 So. Jackie St.
Unit #4444
Arlington, OR 55222

Phone:
(555) 555-1147

Alternate Phone:
(555) 555-8416

Professional Profile

- ✒ Customer service specialist with a global vision toward excellence, support, and service
- ✒ Accomplished trainer and presenter, including creation of materials and manuals
- ✒ Over six years experience in personnel training, motivation, and management
- ✒ Enthusiastic and reliable with high work ethic and superb record of accomplishment
- ✒ Well traveled, with four years experience in Chinese culture and business customs
- ✒ Speak and understand basic conversational Chinese and studied Latin for five years
- ✒ Computer background includes PC word processing and custom designed applications

Employment History

Blue Cross Blue Shield of the National Capital Area, Washington, DC   1987-Present
- ✒ *Team Leader/Assistant Manager* (1991-Present)
  - ○ **Team Trainer/Consultant** to a subsidary company in Arlington, Oregon, overseeing intensive 14-week customer service training classes (since 12/94)
  - ○ Managed and coordinated activities of seven customer service representatives, each handling up to 70 phone and written inquiries and complaints daily
  - ○ Team has maintained 99% accuracy record and consistently met deadlines
  - ○ Presented annual national specialized training course for the BC/BS Director's Office
- ✒ *Customer Service Representative - Federal Division* (1989-1991)
  - ○ Assistant to team leader, handling complex customer inquiries and research
- ✒ *Correspondent - Federal Customer Service Division* (1987-1989)
  - ○ Researched, resolved, and wrote personalized responses for up to 300 inquiries monthly

The Limited Corporation, Landover, Maryland   1985-1987
- ✒ *Retail Manager—Lane Bryant and The Lerner Woman*
  - ○ Managed all the operations of two retail clothing outlets in the Washington area, employing 28 sales associates, assistants, and laborers

Design and Production, Inc., Alexandria, Virginia   1983-1985
  Company designs and fabricates museum exhibits for clients such as Disney World, The Smithsonian, Presidential Libraries, and the Ellis Island Museum in New York
- ✒ *Assistant to the President, Sales, & Purchasing*
  - ○ Assisted with the preparation of proposals to multimillion dollar clients
  - ○ Assisted sales account executives and acted as liaison between clients and sales executives

Education

- ✒ Associate Degree, Liberal Arts, Suffolk County Community College, Selden, Long Island
- ✒ Business Administration Graduate, Katherine Gibbs Business School, Huntington, Long Island

41

Combination. *Barbie Dallmann, Charleston, West Virginia*

This individual wanted to work in an international customer service market, so the writer chose paper with a world map. Note the balanced format for the contact information.

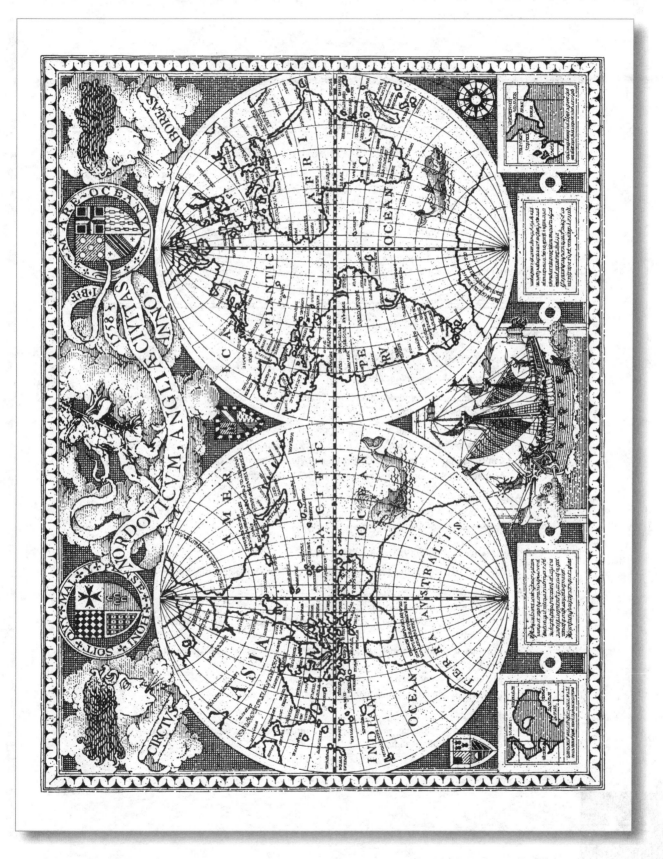

This is the preprinted back of the resume sheet and is a full-page enlargement of the Sixteenth Century world map at the top of the first page. The map's Latin fits the person's study of Latin.

MARIO CRUZ

(407) 578-1826
mcruz@hotmail.com

110 Alafaya Woods Court
Winter Park, Florida 32789

OPERATIONS MANAGER

Results-driven operations manager with a proven track record of success in developing, restructuring and reorganizing operations to produce maximum efficiency and profitability. Hands-on manager and team builder with excellent communication and leadership skills. Qualifications include:

- Budget Administration
- Cost Reductions / Profit Improvements
- Workforce Development / Management
- Strategic Planning / Scheduling
- Work Order Processing
- Customer Service / Relations

- Fleet / Maintenance Management
- Contractual Monitoring / Compliance
- Facility Maintenance / Management
- Labor Efficiency Planning
- Safety Enforcement / Management
- City / County Communications

PROFESSIONAL EXPERIENCE:

ENVIRONMENTAL WASTE MANAGEMENT, Orlando, Florida   April 1996 to May 1999

Site Manager – Recycle Plant (1999)

Selected to improve overall operations and facility maintenance for the Orlando site which included two small off-site locations.

- Directed a staff of 3 supervisors and approximately 57 employees.
- Oversaw operating budget and cost containment strategies.
- Contacted multiple recyclers for price quotes and selected company with best rates.
- Monitored operations to insure compliance with all contracts.

Achievements

- Led a series of maintenance improvements to meet county official's expectations and re-establish favorable relations.

Site Manager – Hauling Division (1996 to 1999)

Promoted to manage all phases of operations for the Port Orange hauling division.

- Lead a team of 25 employees including one supervisor.
- Accountable for a monthly budget of $300,000.
- Directed all phases of operations including staffing, routing, fleet maintenance, purchasing and cost control.
- Responded to all commercial and residential customer service issues and insured excellent customer relations.
- Monitored and enforced all safety programs.
- Handled all communications with city and county officials.

Achievements

- Restructured operating procedures to eliminate on-going county fines saving the company thousands of dollars annually.

42

Combination. *Beverly Harvey, Pierson, Florida*

A resume that displays increasing responsibility over more and more employees. (To get a sense of an individual's career path, read a resume from the end to the beginning.)

MARIO CRUZ

PROFESSIONAL EXPERIENCE: (Continued):

BFI formerly IWS, Orlando, Florida   1981 to 1996

Promoted through a series of increasingly responsible management positions including Supervisor, Operations Manager and Supervising Troubleshooter.

Operations Supervisor

Selected to troubleshoot and turnaround operations for several locations including Orlando, Lakeland, Lake County, DeLand, and Daytona Beach which also included Deltona and Port Orange.

- Oversaw labor budgets, hiring, fleets, route orders, mapping and customer service.
- Consistently led profitable operations and eliminated fines.

<u>Achievements</u>

- Turned around the Lakeland site which was losing $5,000 per month. Slashed labor budget, raised rates and led operational improvements generating $3,000 in profits monthly.
- Led a massive reorganization of the Deltona operations which was in total disarray. Restructured the workforce, recruited quality employees, reorganized the routing, added a truck, and improved general operations. Reduced workforce hours from 17-hour days to 9-hour days. Slashed county fines.
- Reorganized Orlando's commercial routes and driver problems and slashed fines.

EARLIER CAREER included positions as a heavy equipment mechanic and operator.

EDUCATION:

Seminole Community College, Sanford, Florida
Business Management Courses

College of Technical Mechanics, Bayonne, New Jersey
Technical Degree (Machinery)

LANGUAGES:

Fluent Spanish

The opening section within horizontal lines indicates the person's qualifications and areas of expertise. In the Professional Experience section bullets point to duties and achievements. The achievements are put under an Achievements subheading for each position held.

Mr X

1200 Way Drive, Jacksonville, Florida, 11111, Apartment #150, (904) 444-3333

Skill Profile

Service: Handling customer complaint; good listening skills; customer relations; patient in dealing with difficult people; good telephone skills; willing to help and relate to others.
Office: Word Processing; record keeping; filing; composing correspondence.
Computer Software: WordPerfect 5.1; Power Point; Lotus 123; DBase; Word for Windows.
Interpersonal: Ability to get along well with others; excellent teamwork ability; diplomatic; dependable.

Education

Graduate: Fernandina Beach High School, 1991
Kansas State University, Manhattan, Kansas - One Quarter

Employment Highlights

Buddy Hutchinson Toyota, Jacksonville, Florida, 7/94-Present
        New Car Salesman: Interact, assist and provide product knowledge to customers; product
        and price negotiation; demonstration of vehicles; closing sales.

United States Army, Fort Riley, Kansas, Home of the First Infantry Division, 5/93-4/94
        Administrative Secretary: Responsible for financial papers, medical records, personnel files
        which included orders for promotions, awards and disciplinary actions, generated memos,
        performed typing, filing and bookkeeping; shared responsibilities for upkeep of 700 files;
        prepared monthly training schedules, organized immunization clinics; organized and
        administered physical fitness test.

Ritz Carlton, Amelia Island, Florida, 7/91-9/92
        Roomservice Waiter/Telephone Sales Agent: Responsible for taking and delivering orders
        to guests; handling daily reports, complaints from customers and guest menus; enlightened
        guest about sights and attractions on the island and surrounding areas.

Community Service

Special Olympics Volunteer, Amelia Island Care Center
        Amelia Island, Florida, Sponsor from 1987 to 1971

References

Available Upon Request

43

Combination. *Rose Montgomery, Charlotte, North Carolina*

No lines, bullets, or boldfacing appear in this scannable resume. Without highlighting, the resume features keywords, skills, and abilities. Nouns are more important than verbs.

Design

Resumes at a Glance

RESUME NO.	LAST OR CURRENT OCCUPATION	GOAL	PAGE
44.	Head Floral Designer	Not specified	89
45.	Buyer	Not specified	90
46.	Graphic Artist/Illustrator/ Art Director	Not specified	91
47.	Technical Illustrator	Not specified	92
48.	Offset Stripper/Supervisor	Technical Services Representative	93
49.	Director of Store Design	Position in store design/ interior design	94
50.	Graphics Artist	Not specified	96
51.	Graphics Artist	Not specified	97
52.	Graphic Designer/Artist	Not specified	98

Rebecca Jean Robinson

9876 North Leland Avenue ❧ Janeway, Illinois 60000 ❧ (555) 555-1234 ❧ (555) 555-5678 *messages*

PROFILE

Award winning **Floral Designer** with 9+ years professional experience and specialization in wedding designs and original creations seeks position with progressive firm offering creative opportunities in innovative and artistic environment.

QUALIFICATIONS

- ❧ Earned **FTD Master Designer** designation; **AIFD certification** in progress.
- ❧ Experienced wedding designer, ranging from very small to elaborate double weddings.
- ❧ Strong horticultural background; knowledgeable in care of cut flowers and green plants.
- ❧ 22-year affiliation with garden clubs and flower shows. Frequently recognized for outstanding design and creativity in silk, fresh, and live plant arrangements.
- ❧ Strong communication and customer service skills. Experienced presenter of floral designing programs, workshops, and demonstrations.

PROFESSIONAL DEVELOPMENT

Floral Designer

AIFD National Symposium, Chicago, Illinois ❧ *AIFD Certification in progress (Phase I)*	1995
"Tradition Is Not a Static Concept" (4 days) ❧ AFS, Oklahoma City, Oklahoma	1995
"The Bouquet" Wedding Class (1 day) ❧ Redbook, St. Louis, Missouri	1994
Personal study with Sandy Wersching at *Surprise!* (8 weeks) ❧ St. Louis, Missouri	1993
FTD Master Designer designation	1993
Coursework toward A.A. Horticulture ❧ Belleville Area College, Belleville, Illinois	2 years

PROFESSIONAL EXPERIENCE

Head Designer — 1992-1995
GEOFFREY LEWIS FINE FLORISTS, Mount Jennings, Illinois

- ❧ Lead designer of 5-designer team for full-service florist. Created specialty pieces for banquets and formal displays at City Gateway Center as well as standard house and hospital designs and funeral work. In charge of all wedding work, from initial consultation with bride through designing flowers and servicing the wedding. Designed and arranged all floor and window displays; consulted in all creative matters. Cared for and cultivated plants in on-site greenhouse.

Designer — 1988-1992
ZENIE'S FLOWERS, Cavesboro, Illinois

- ❧ Created fresh, cut, silk, and live plant arrangements for small full-service floral shop. Assisted with wedding coordination. Designed and arranged floor and window displays.

Designer — 1986-1988
FLOWER POWER, Cavesboro, Illinois

- ❧ Created arrangements for all-occasion supplier; specialized in silk and dried arrangements.

PROFESSIONAL AND COMMUNITY AFFILIATIONS

Illinois Department of Agriculture, Master Gardener	Janeway Garden Club
District V Garden Clubs of Illinois (past president)	Janeway Historic Preservation Board
Mount Jennings Community Appearance Board	

"I am very creative and enjoy learning and applying new design styles and techniques. Clean line designs are my trademark."

44

Combination. *Carla Culp Coury, Glen Carbon, Illinois*

Because degree work was interrupted for family considerations, the writer emphasized continuing education and labeled the section Professional Development. A superior resume.

DENORA K. FEITSAM

234 Thunderbolt Road
Belleville, Illinois 62221
(618) 555-9246

KEY STRENGTHS

Architectural Drafting	Rendering
Accessories Selection	Textiles
Specification Writing	CAD
Construction Documents	Space Planning

SUMMARY OF QUALIFICATIONS

Solid training and hands-on experience including team design and floor plan projects for residential and commercial buildings. Familiar with numerous design documents from proposals and bid invitations to thank-you letters. Additional background in retail business functions: budgeting, customer service, bookkeeping, and sales.

EDUCATION

ASSOCIATE OF APPLIED SCIENCE DEGREE, INTERIOR DESIGN

Catonsville Community College, Catonsville, Maryland, May 1995
- Team design project: the Historic Ellicott City Designer Showhouse
- Treasurer, Interior Design Association
- Student member, International Interior Design Association; contributed to an award-winning design charette

RELATED EXPERIENCE

BUYER

Model Home Interiors, Inc., Jan. 1995-May 1995
- Purchased accessories to complete model home designs.
- Prepared paperwork for proper billing.

INTERIOR DESIGN LIBRARIAN

Catonsville Community College, Feb. 1994-Dec. 1994
- Collected and organized library items from local interior designers.
- Ordered and filed new samples, and discarded outdated products.

FLORAL DESIGNER

Broadmoor Florist, June 1990-May 1991
- Created floral designs using fresh, silk, and dried flowers.

ADDITIONAL EXPERIENCE

Teller, American National Savings Association, Oct. 1992-July 1993
Bookkeeper, PEAK Parent Center, Feb. 1991-Dec. 1991

REFERENCES AND PORTFOLIO AVAILABLE UPON REQUEST

45

Combination. *John A. Suarez, location unknown*

The original version of this sans serif resume was on "decorator" paper, making a visual statement that matched the person's career field. Boldfacing accentuates the positions.

Joel R. Smith

555 Main Street
Elmira, NY 55555-0000
(000) 000-0000

Profile

Graphic Artist/Illustrator/Art Director with experience in all facets of commercial design and graphic communication needs.

Experience

SMITH DESIGN STUDIOS - Elmira, NY   1987 - Present
Owner/Art Director
Provide a wide array of commercial design services including:
- ◆ **Graphic Design:**
  Promotional material, packaging, logos, corporate identity.
- ◆ **Illustration:**
  Cartoons, architectural renderings, general illustration using media including pen/ink, air brush, oils, and enamels.
- ◆ **Signs/Lettering:**
  All types of indoor and outdoor signage; plexiglass, aluminum, wood, wall murals, banners, trucks, vans, boats and RV's.
- ◆ **3-Dimensional Display Design and Construction:**
  P.O.P., displays, floor displays (trade shows), scale models and mock-ups.
- ◆ **Cell Animation, Cell Coloring and Animatics:**
  Client: Hanover Pizza Company.
- ◆ **Set and Prop Design:**
  Clients: Howard Communications, Wedge Toy Co., Video Stores (children's video game show).

Retained on freelance basis by numerous commercial clients, including:
- **International Refrigeration**, Harris Point, NY
- **John Green Video**, Howard Beach, NY *(contact: James Howard)*
- **Ann Maire Printing/Sherman Graphics**, Elizabethtown, NY
- **Betty Grey Studios**, Elm Creek, NY *(contact: Betty Attenboro)*
- **Graphics of Hancock**, East Hancock, NY
- **John Doe Illustration & Design**, Harreytown, NY

HAMILTON SCREENPRINTING - Hamilton, NY   1987 - 1988
Art Work Subcontractor

HARRY BENEDICT COMPANY - Germantown, NJ   1985 - 1987
In-House Artist
In charge of hand lettering, layout, and design of signage. Oversaw production of camera ready art for silk-screen printing department. Presently retained as sub-contractor.

ARTISTIC STUDIOS - Germantown, NJ   1983 - 1985
Head Artist
In charge of design, hand lettering, illustration. Hands on experience in all types of signage and 3-D display design and construction.

Education

Elmira Community College - Elmira, NY
School of Arts and Letters
A.A.S. in Commercial Art (1984)

Currently pursuing independent studies in **Desktop Publishing** and **Illustration**.

46

Chronological. *Betty Geller, Elmira, New York*

The writer emphasized current projects and clients for this self-employed Graphic Artist. The name and side headings in a Brush Script font contrast nicely with the angular page border.

George M. Butler

1023 Seymour • Eastpointe, Michigan 48021 • (810) 555-6493

PROFILE

Technical Illustrator with solid experience in all areas of automotive design illustration. Superior concept illustration skills with emphasis on speed, accuracy, and clean line quality. Will meet client needs, through clear communication, with artwork that is clean and accurate. Prefer challenging work.

- Excellent comprehension of layouts, details, and 3D computer wireframe.
- Good perception of schematic diagrams.
- Keen sketching ability.
- Good final art capabilities in all media (ink, plastic lead, and graphite).
- Computer literate in IBM Personal Designer 3D Illustration & Surfacing.

EXPERIENCE

CREATIVE DESIGN ENGINEERING, Madison Heights, MI	1994 - Present
MASCOTECH TRAINING & VISUAL SERVICES, Warren, MI	1989 - 1994

- Illustrated '97 W-car (MS-2000), on site at GM Engineering Staff.
- Illustrated '96 GM ST Electrical for Truck & Bus Group.
- Illustrated for W Car platform on-site at GM Tech Center.
  - Electrical
  - Engine dress
  - Body, sheet metal
  - Fuel line routing
  - Suspension
  - Interiors
- Illustrated U-Van '95 prototype
  - Electrical; Suspension
  - Rear & Front ride level control
- Created geometric dimensioning & tolerance illustrations for D Car platform.
- Experience with GM SPO group, Truck & Bus.
- Created sketches from mock-up on site at GM Tech Center, Ford Motor Weight Assessment Program, and various shop mock-ups.
- Freelance work has included:
  - GM SPO
  - Ford Motor Company final art
  - Corporate logo for international company

EDUCATION

Ferris State University, Big Rapids, MI
Associate's Degree in Technical Ilustration, May 1989

Alpena Community College, Alpena, MI: **Basic Electronics**, 1982 - 1985

PORTFOLIO PRESENTED UPON REQUEST

47

Combination. *Kathleen McConnell, location unknown*

Strong bullets unite visually the Profile and the Experience section. Hyphens serve as bullets for a second level of bulleted items. Section headings stand out with hanging indentation.

Phinneas T. Martens, 3986 116th Avenue, Lawrence, MI 22222, 000-555-2255

Career Objective

Position as Technical Services Representative with major film company.

Background Summary

- 12 years experience as offset stripper. Hands-on supervisor with computerized scanning and camera skills. Familiar with the complete process of print production from sales through camera, press, delivery.
- Acquired an overall understanding of small newspaper publishing by working in each production area: understand processes related to 4-color scanning; film processors; plate processors; image setters; raster image setters; chemical mixing units.
- Committed to high quality production. Resourceful; skilled in analyzing and solving problems. Thrive on opportunity to apply technical knowledge and analytical skills in projects involving people at all levels.
- Proven abilities in web press, sheet fed press, stitch and trim layout. Working knowledge of a wide variety of camera art and multi-image production.

Professional Experience

1983 - Present.
Distefano Services, Inc., Bradley, MI.
OFFSET STRIPPER/SUPERVISOR. Diverse responsibilities with this S.W. Michigan web printer. Involved in full-circle department management. Supervised 9 production employees on 3 shifts.
- In charge of scheduling and production within the Camera/Stripping Department.
- Coordinated production activities to meet deadlines; managed last-minute production decisions.
- Trained employees in offset camera work; laying out stripping flats; making printing plates; spot color breaks; and assembling 4-color process film.
- Purchased department materials and supplies. Conferred with vendors and performed cost-efficiency studies.

1982 - 1983.
Horizon Graphics, Bloomingdale, MI.
PRODUCTION ASSISTANT. Learned 4-color stripping. Performed pre-press work for web and sheet fed presses.
- Gained invaluable offset camera experience and developed technical skills that later qualified me for the position at Distefano Services.

Technical Skills

- Experienced on IBM P.C. and software: MacIntosh, PhotoShop 3.0, Fotolook, Illustrator 5.0, Quark 3.2

Seminars/Training

- Padgett/Thompson, Employee Performance Evaluations, 1994.
- SkillPath, Inc., Managing Negativity In The Workplace, 1994.
- Fred Pryor Seminars, Coaching Skills For Managers And Supervisors, 1994.
- Dun & Bradstreet, Business Education Services, Managing Multiple Tasks, 1994.
- Dale Carnegie, Human Relations Training. Elected: Highest Award For Achievement, 1985.
- Kodak Half-Tone Classes, 2 days, 1984.

Education

- Colliard Technical Institute, Ann Arbor, MI. Graduate. Studies of special interest: Mathematical Science I, Print Shop Graphics, Advertising Art & Design.

References

- Professional and personal attached.

48

Combination. *Randy Clair, location unknown*

Horizontal lines separate the sections and make them easy to identify. Narrow left and right margins and a small font size make the resume seem like one for an executive.

PETER E. BRAUNSTERN
20020 Andrews Avenue • Washington, DC 00000 • **(202) 555-5555**

CAREER OBJECTIVE

EXPERIENCED PROFESSIONAL in STORE DESIGN/INTERIOR DESIGN seeks a position with growth opportunities that will utilize a proven track record of obtaining company goals.

AREAS of SKILLS AND STRENGTHS

IMAGINATIVE THINKING	**BUDGETING**	**PURCHASING**
INTERPERSONAL SKILLS	**TIME MANAGEMENT**	**LEADERSHIP SKILLS**

PROFESSIONAL EMPLOYMENT

M.S.O. • Washington, D.C.
DIRECTOR OF STORE DESIGN   **1990 - PRESENT**

- Serves as a Showroom Display Director and buyer for upholstery casegoods and accessories.
- Accountable for showroom floor layout.
- Maintains stock inventory on merchandise in showroom.
- Interfaces with sales force to address purchasing samples for floor.
- Aids sales representatives in closing sales.
- Maintains fabric books.

Highlights:

- **Increased sales volume by 20% through showroom merchandising.**
- **Significantly impacted weekly revenue and generated an additional $20,000 per week by controlling warehouse stock and moving merchandise to showroom floor.**
- **Effectively controlled budgets and spending.**
- **Coordinated all aspects of relocation to a new 40,000 square foot showroom.**
- **Implemented new computer systems to organize warehouse inventory and financial accounting.**

CASTRO CONVERTIBLES • New York, New York
DIRECTOR OF STORE DESIGN   **1984 - 1990**

- Controlled and coordinated all visual merchandising and space planning for 12 showrooms.
- Served as the Buyer for all casegoods and accessories.
- Supervised and developed a professional staff of 5 assistants.
- Interfaced with top management concerning store merchandising, sales and merchandising and inventory control.
- Accountable for daily store operations for a retail furniture store including purchasing, renovating model rooms and front window displays.

Highlights:

- **Created stage set for national Castro Convertible television commercials.**
- **Completely directed the renovation of 4 showrooms from concept to full implementation of merchandise into stores.**
- **Produced special sale closeouts which generated weekly sales increases of 25% for 4 consecutive months.**
- **Conducted training seminars for sales staff, addressing customer service and satisfaction in the home furnishings market.**

49

Combination. *Alesia Benedict, Rochelle Park, New Jersey*

Another aggressive resume by this writer to help a two-year degree graduate be competitive against other applicants with a four-year or higher degree. Note the use of

PETER E. BRAUNSTERN   **(202) 555-5555**   - Page Two -

PROFESSIONAL EMPLOYMENT continued... ———————————

MACYS • New York, New York
VISUAL DISPLAY MANAGER   **1983- 1984**

- Oversaw home furnishing display throughout the store.
- Specialty merchandising included tabletop, china, stemware and cookware.
- Accountable for creative planning, setting up, maintaining and changing visual displays.

CASTRO CONVERTIBLES• Totowa, New Jersey
SENIOR INTERIOR DESIGNER   **1980 - 1983**

- Addressed interior design for clientele, furniture sales and in-store design.
- Travelled to residential clients and performed needs analysis, estimating and creative consultation.
- Produced highest sales volume over a 3 month period.
- Obtained highest sales to one client for 1987 ($64,000).

EDUCATION

A.A.S. in Interior Design • New York School of Interior Design

ADDITIONAL EXPERIENCE

Served as an Instructor of Interior Design for an adult education class.

small caps in the Areas of Skills and Strengths section. Diamond bullets call attention to highlights for the last position held and the current position. Page borders unify the resume. Partial horizontal lines point to several of the section headings to make them readily seen.

Donna Ann Coleman   80 VINEYARD ST., APT. 36A, SYRACUSE, NY 10000 ✳ (315) 555-0000

Graphics Artist
dedicated to the principles of good design, with a vision toward innovation

Gerber Scientific System, including scanners, plotters, vinyl lettering and Graphix 4B plotters;
vinyl peeling & masking for glass, metal, wood, plexi, foamboard, Sintra and banner material

computerized vinyl lettering	press plates—Web & Omni	PMTs and halftones
race car decals & airbrushing	rubylith plates for silk screen	PMS color mixing
banners & small signs	layout, design & thumbnails	Aldus PageMaker
window & in-store lettering	design work for special promos	PC & Macintosh
lettering for billboards	camera (shoot, strip, develop)	Lotus 1-2-3, Basic & DOS
planning & scheduling	supervisory, inventory, ordering	newsletter layout

Awards & Memberships
placed 1st & 2nd at Onondaga Community College Art Show
Certificates of Achievement 1990 to 1993—Fountaine Art Show
Popular Museum Scholastic Art Award 3 yr. in a row (h.s.)
Jr. Achievement for Architecture Member (h.s.)
N.Y. Secretary for American Industrial Arts Student Association

Work History
Graphics Artist
Fountaine, Incorporated
Anytown, NY
5/87 to present

Sales Clerk
Petman Pets
Anytown, NY
9/90 to present (p.t.)

Admis. & Customer Relations
New York State Fair
Anytown, NY
8 to 9/92 & 8 to 9/90 (p.t.)

Graphics Signmaker
Cashier/Service Desk
Weinman's
Syracuse, NY
5/83 to 10/87 (p.t.)

Education
A.A.S.—Graphics Arts, 1987
Minor in Photography
County Community College
Syracuse, NY

Regents Diploma, 1985
Anytown High School
Syracuse, NY

worked since age 16 ... detail-oriented ... challenged by variety & diverseness ... competent under pressure
... enjoy seeing projects from start to finish ... adept at maintaining multiple priorities

50

Combination. *Beverley Drake, Rochester, Minnesota*

The first of two resumes with almost the same information for the same person by the same writer. With two sets of three columns, this resume is more symmetrical than the next.

80 VINEYARD ST., APT. 36A, SYRACUSE, NY 10000 ✳ (315) 555-0000

computerized vinyl lettering ✳ decals and airbrushing on race cars ✳ banners and small signs ✳ window and in-store lettering ✳ billboard lettering ✳ planning and scheduling ✳ rubylith plates for silk screen and for Web and Omni press ✳ layout, design, thumbnails ✳ design work for special promos ✳ camera work (shoot, strip, develop), PMTs and halftones ✳ vinyl peeling and masking for glass, metal, wood, plexi, foamboard, Sintra and banner material ✳ newsletter layout ✳ supervisory, inventory and ordering

Donna Ann Coleman

Gerber Scientific System, including scanners, plotters, vinyl lettering, Graphix 4B plotters

IBM & Macintosh Computers, Aldus PageMaker, Lotus 1-2-3, Basic & DOS

AWARDS and MEMBERSHIPS

1st and 2nd Prize at Ourcounty Community College Art Show
Certificates of Achievement 1990 to 1993—Fountaine Art Show
Popular Museum Scholastic Art Award 3 yr. in a row (h.s.)
Jr. Achievement for Architecture Member (h.s.)
N.Y. Secretary, American Industrial Arts Student Assoc.

WORK HISTORY

Graphics Artist
Fountaine, Incorporated,
   Printing Svcs. Dept.
Anytown, NY
5/87 to present

Sales Clerk
Petman Pets
Anytown, NY
9/90 to present (p.t.)

Admissions & Customer Relations
New York State Fair
Anytown, NY
8 to 9/92, 8 to 9/90 (p.t.)

Graphics Signmaker
Cashier/Service Desk
Weinman's
Syracuse, NY
5/83 to 10/87 (p.t.)

EDUCATION

A.A.S. Degree–Graphics Arts, 1987
Minor in Photography
County Community College
Syracuse, NY

Regents Diploma, 1985
Anytown High School
Syracuse, NY

worked since age 16 ... detail-oriented ... challenged by variety and diverseness ... competent under pressure ... enjoy seeing projects from start to finish ... adept at maintaining multiple priorities.

51

Combination. *Beverley Drake, Rochester, Minnesota*

The second of the pair of resumes. Not evident in either version is the special paper on which each resume was originally printed. Text on the left is balanced by the oversize caps.

KELLY ALBERTSON *Graphic Designer*

7 Mt. Olive Way
Budd Lake, New Jersey 07867
(201) 457-9856

Background includes practical experience and education, which have provided excellent working knowledge of these key areas:

Magazine layout and production	**Commercial illustration**
Computer assisted page and layout	**T.V. graphics**
Computer assisted illustration	**Graphic design**
Advertisement layout and production	**Typography**

Highly skilled and creative artist with a proven talent for generating striking ideas and layouts. Demonstrated ability to consistently produce high quality work under deadline. Able to work well with a wide variety of technical and support staff. Proficient in Adobe Illustrator and Photoshop, QuarkXpress, Ofoto, and Applescan.

EXPERIENCE

All American Crafts/MSC Publishing, Sparta, New Jersey   1994 - Present
Graphic Designer/Artist

- Responsible for design and layout of various magazines, including *Craftworks, Paintworks, Traditional Quilter, Fashion Knitting, Crochet Fantasy*, and *Woodworks*.

- Designed effective and visually pleasing multi-house ads, as well as ads for specific magazines.

Sir Speedy Printing, Rockaway, New Jersey   1991
Assistant

- Responsible for layouts and mechanicals of advertisements. Set up presses for printing.

ADDITIONAL DESIGN EXPERIENCE

- Business cards   • Logos   • T-shirts   • Photo books

EDUCATION

A.A. Degree in Applied Science   County College of Morris
(Recipient of the New Jersey Cooperative Education Student of the Year Award in Graphic Design)

PORTFOLIO AND PROFESSIONAL REFERENCES UPON REQUEST

52

Combination. *Shari Favela, location unknown*

This person had some work experience, but here educational courses were more important. Both her education and her experience are shown to offset her limited hands-on experience.

Education and Training

Resumes at a Glance

RESUME NO.	LAST OR CURRENT OCCUPATION	GOAL	PAGE
53.	Substitute Teacher	Teacher's Aide	101
54.	Director of National Sales/Training & Management Development	Not specified	102
55.	Teacher's Assistant	Position in care and education of young children	104

HOPE I. CANAIDE
2 Kindergarten Lane
Readiness, NH

OBJECTIVE

A teacher's aide position in the school system for the
opportunity to utilize and build on previous experience
in education and demonstrate a caring for young people with
special needs.

SUMMARY OF EXPERIENCE

<u>Substitute Teacher</u> for the Greater Academic Learning
Collaborative working with special students on elementary,
junior high, and secondary levels (1993-).

<u>Leader, Co-Leader</u> for Girl Scout Troop 14 coordinating
workshops and activities, including merit badge advancement
programs, arts and crafts and costume making, plus special
weekend outings at Camps Whinneehaha and Minniehaha (1987-).

<u>Room Mother</u> for Grades 2 and 5 at Don Sparetherod Memorial
School, Readiness, NH (1990-)

RELATED ACTIVITIES

Volunteer, Readiness Recreation T-Ball Program.
Assistant at Progressive School, Readiness
Member Readiness Parent-Teacher Association.

EDUCATION

Graduate Area Regional Cooperative High School, Readiness,
NH - Business Course
Enrolled in Early Childhood Education Certification Program,
Field Day, NH

TRAINING

Essentials of Leadership - Sweetbriar Girl Scout Council
Children as People - Bye For Now Mommy Child Care Center

OTHER WORK EXPERIENCE

9/90-9/91 First Money Bank, Readiness, NH - Bank Teller

8/88-9/90 Hinge On Success Door Company, Readiness, NH - Office
Assistant

53

Combination. *Stephen H. Mazurka, Exeter, New Hampshire*

Not every job seeker wants a resume desktop published and printed in high resolution. This
resume looking typewritten is a good match for this teacher's aide as she looks for work.

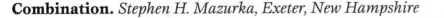

GEORGE M. ELLIS

61 King Drive, Windermere, Florida 34700
(407) 876-8571

SENIOR SALES, OPERATIONS & MANAGEMENT EXECUTIVE

Interval Ownership Resort Industry

High-performance executive delivering phenomenal growth in the interval ownership industry for over twelve years. Consistently successful in driving increased revenues within highly competitive markets. Dynamic leadership and training style, motivating sales and management teams to peak performance. Strong closer. Qualifications include:

- Operations / Efficiencies Management
- Leasing Management
- Acquisition / Procurement
- Team Building / Development

- Sales Training / Management
- Sales Team Development / Leadership
- Competitive Positioning
- Strategic Planning / Development

Delivered strong and sustainable revenue and profit gains
positioning Vistana as the #1 on-site sales resort.

PROFESSIONAL EXPERIENCE:

VISTANA RESORTS, Orlando, Florida   1987 to Present
A Division of Peck & Peck Investment Inc., Orlando, Florida

The Vistana Family of Resorts is the largest timeshare resort in the world with over 1,000 villas.

Promoted through a series of increasingly responsible sales and management positions based on contributions to Vistana's progressive financial growth.

Director of National Sales / Training & Management Development *(1997 to Present)*

Senior sales, leasing and operations management executive leading the corporation through tremendous growth, from one location generating $35 million in annual revenues to four locations with revenues surpassing $300 million.

- Requested by CEO to develop and institute a comprehensive training program to develop expert closers and sales managers to compliment the existing sales training program.
- Member of a three-man acquisition and procurement team leading the corporation's aggressive expansion initiatives worldwide.
- Establish infrastructures, processes and management efficiencies for new acquisitions and resolve operational issues for established properties to repeatedly drive record revenues.

General Manager / Director of Leasing *(1995 to 1997)*

Promoted to General Manager of Vistana Resort Villas' operations and directed a staff of 75.

- Assumed management of leasing operations and doubled year-to-date production from 5% to 10% within 60 days. Expanded leasing management responsibilities to include all of Vistana's resorts.

54

Combination. *Beverly Harvey, Pierson, Florida*

After a career in tradesman positions in the construction industry, this individual switched to sales, and his career path then climbed impressively: from Sales Rep to Sales Manager to

GEORGE M. ELLIS   Page   2

- Designed an incentive program for non-buyers improving conversion rate from 35% to 43% on a consistent bases.
- Recognized for development and leadership of the #1 Producing Leasing Department, 1996.
- Won recognition for development and leadership of the #1 Producing Sales Line, 1995.

Sales Manager *(1987 to 1995)*

Senior Sales Manager overseeing all sales, support and training operations. Led resort through explosive growth and consistent record-breaking revenue gains closing over $30 million in sales within 7½ years.

- Won Rookie of the Year, 1987.
- Won Sales Manager of the Month, 2/89, 3/90, 4/90, 7/90, 12/90, 5/91, 2/92, and 3/93.
- Awarded Sales Manager of the Year in 1990 for delivering record breaking annual revenues of over $4.25 million.

Sales Representative *(1987)*
- Began in interval ownership industry as sales representative and within first month earned Closer of the Month.
- Promoted to Sales Manager within nine months.

Earlier Career included tradesman positions in construction industry.

LICENSURE:

Florida Real Estate License

MEMBERSHIPS:

ARDA, Certified Member
United Way, Pewter Member

General Manager to Director of National Sales. Bold italic makes the various sales positions easy to spot. Horizontal lines enclose a profile (not named as such) near the top of the first page. Bullets here point to multiple areas of expertise.

REBECCA T. MATHEWS

5000 Beach Street • Cape May, New Jersey 00000 • (000) 000-0000

OBJECTIVE: An opportunity to contribute to the care and education of young children.

EDUCATION:

Trenton State College, Trenton, New Jersey - B.A. Degree in progress
Majors: Elementary Education / English Literature

Brookdale Community College, Lincroft, New Jersey - A.A. Degree, 1994
Major: Liberal Arts / Dean's List Student

EXPERIENCE:

GREEN GIANT NURSERY SCHOOL, Chatham, New Jersey   1995-Present
Teacher's Assistant

- ▸ Assist in all preschool classes from two years through five years old.
- ▸ Plan arts & crafts projects to complement weekly educational theme.
- ▸ Supervise children in playground. Interact with parents delivering and picking up children. Communicate special requests and information to staff.
- ▸ Lead storytelling sessions. Follow up with thoughtful questions to make sure children understand concepts correctly.

WHITMAN SQUARE CLEANERS, Camden, New Jersey   1990-1994
Assistant Manager

- ▸ Supervised staff in all daily operations of high-volume dry cleaner.
- ▸ Interfaced extensively with customers, troubleshooting problems and generating solutions.

NEWARK TEEN CENTER, Newark, New Jersey   1987-1990
Group Staff Leader

- ▸ Planned and conducted group sessions for adolescents recovering from addictive disorders. Followed up with one-on-one conferences.
- ▸ Participated in clinical conferences to determine treatment goals. Worked with group staff and families to implement.
- ▸ Scheduled staff over a seven-day work week. Trained new staff members.
- ▸ Advanced through the ranks from Trainee to Senior Staff. Achieved the highest-level group staff position.

SUPPLEMENTAL EXPERIENCE:

Worked as a Nanny for private clients, taking care of preschool and elementary age children.

References available upon request.

55

Chronological. *Vivian Belen, Fair Lawn, New Jersey*

A teacher who earned an associate degree before receiving a bachelor's degree. Note the different levels of indentation to distinguish the workplaces, positions, and duties.

Engineering and Technology

Resumes at a Glance

RESUME NO.	LAST OR CURRENT OCCUPATION	GOAL	PAGE
56.	Field Service Engineer	Not specified	107
57.	Master Journeyman Automotive Technician	Automotive Technician	108
58.	Shop Foreman	Not specified	110
59.	Mechanic	Not specified	112
60.	Technician	Position in airframe or power plant maintenance	113
61.	Overhauler of aircraft components	Aircraft Mechanic	114
62.	Team Manager/Installer	Position in aviation	116
63.	Department Manager	Aviation or Industrial Maintenance Technician	118
64.	Quality Assurance Supervisor	Railcar Consultant	119
65.	Custodian (interim position)	Not specified	120
66.	Production Operator	Electronics Technician	122
67.	Supervisor	Communications Technician with fiber optics	124
68.	Mechanical Technician	Not specified	125
69.	Technical and supervisory positions (USAF)	Electronics Technician	126
70.	Electronics Technician	Position in repair of electronic/ electromechanical equipment	127
71.	Development Production Support Supervisor	Not specified	128
72.	Carpenter	Not specified	129
73.	MRO/Buyer	Not specified	130
74.	Technician Team Leader	Technician in the industrial field	131

RESUME NO.	LAST OR CURRENT OCCUPATION	GOAL	PAGE
75.	Maintenance Mechanic	Power Plant Technician/ Foreman	132
76.	Library Page	Theatrical Electrician	133
77.	Production Supervisor	Not specified	134
78.	Industrial Engineer	Not specified	135
79.	Industrial Engineer	Not specified	136
80.	Project Engineer	Project Engineer in tool & die industry	137
81.	3-D Product and Tooling Designer	Position in design engineering	138
82.	Design Engineer	Not specified	139
83.	Vice President Sales, document conversion software	Not specified	140
84.	Senior Lab Technician	Position in quality engineering	142
85.	Commercial Roofing Co. Laborer	Not specified	143
86.	Unigraphics Senior Layout Detailer	Position in product design/ detail	144
87.	Position in engineering dept.	Position in mechanical, architectural, and production drafting	145
88.	Underwater Construction Project Manager	Position in instrumentation technology	146
89.	Laborer	Position in commercial diving industry	148
90.	Not specified	Position in construction estimating, sales, or project coordination	150
91.	Production Worker	Production Specialist	151
92.	Substitute Engineer	Position in surveying/material testing	152

ROBERT E. FORD

72727 Gateside, Suite #305
Royal Oak, Michigan 48009
800 555.1234

QUALIFICATIONS

- ‣ Problem solving professional with over 14 years experience
- ‣ Excellent communicator and liaison between customer and management
- ‣ Specialist in assembly line field
- ‣ Supervisory/management experience

EMPLOYMENT HISTORY

INGER RANDSOLL – Automated Production Systems Division   Farmington Hills, MI
Manufacturer of assembly lines for major companies including: Ford, Chrysler, General Motors, Caterpillar and Navistar.
FIELD SERVICE ENGINEER — 1985 to Present
- ‣ Supervise the installation and build of projects
- ‣ Communicate customer details and issues to management
- ‣ Instruct customer on procedure and up-keep of system
- ‣ Accomplished field installations, set-up and calibration of nut runner systems
- ‣ Trouble shoot and resolve issues on all electrical, electronic and mechanical functions of the system

FEDERAL ELECTRIC COMMUNICATIONS   Madison Heights, MI
Manufacturer of assembly lines for automotive assembly plants
FIELD ELECTRONIC TECHNICIAN — 1984 to 1985
- ‣ Managed in-house panel wiring and printed circuit board changes to reflect engineering modifications
- ‣ Handled trouble shooting in plants and bench analysis of faulty circuit boards

ABLE MEDICAL INSTRUMENT COMPANY   West Bloomfield, MI
Medical instrument manufacturer
BENCH TECHNICIAN — 1982 to 1984
- ‣ Responsible for servicing and trouble shooting Holter Recording Units, ICR Scanners and Treadmills

AUDIO WORLD   Farmington Hills, MI
FIELD TECHNICIAN — 1981 to 1983
- ‣ Responsible for installing Intercom Systems and Alarm Systems for commercial, residential and government applications

EDUCATION AND CERTIFICATION

OAKLAND COMMUNITY COLLEGE — Auburn Hills, MI
ASSOCIATE OF SCIENCE DEGREE IN ELECTRICAL TRADES TECHNOLOGY & INDUSTRIAL ELECTRONICS

NATIONAL INSTITUTE OF TECHNOLOGY
CERTIFIED IN ELECTRONIC ENGINEERING TECHNOLOGY

SOUTHWEST OAKLAND VOCATIONAL CENTER
CERTIFIED IN INDUSTRIAL ELECTRONICS

DOW CORNING for Ingersoll Rand — **QUALITY CONTROL** Courses

ALLEN BRADLEY — PLC Seminar

56

Combination. *Lorie Lebert, Novi, Michigan*

Notice a pattern of indentation like that in the preceding resume. Note also the brief italic description of several of the companies mentioned in the Employment History section.

DAVID M. JOHN

111 E. South
Candlewood, OK 000000
(000) 000-0000

JOB TARGET ◇ AUTOMOTIVE TECHNICIAN

QUALIFICATIONS & STRENGTHS

◇ MDS
◇ DRB III
◇ Diversified Automotive Knowledge

◇ Diagnostic Abilities
◇ Technical Electrical Training
◇ Strong Work Ethics

CERTIFICATION

Engine Repair
Automatic Trans/Transaxle
Manual Drive Train & Axles
Suspension & Steering
Brakes
Electrical Systems
Heating & Air Conditioning
Engine Performance
Refrigerant Recovery & Recycling

PROFESSIONAL EXPERIENCE

GALLERY AUTOMOTIVE   USA
MASTER JOURNEYMAN AUTOMOTIVE TECHNICIAN   1978 - Present
   ◇ Proven ability to successfully perform diagnostic analysis, verification, and
      complete repair of automotive technology including:

      Driveability   *Suspensions*
      Electrical   *Air Conditioning 134R*
      Anti-Lock Brakes   *Air Bag Systems*
      Transmissions   *Complete Car Maintenance*

   ◇ CSI Conscious
      Contribute to promoting dealership's standards of performance
   ◇ Provide professional customer service regarding automotive repairs, including
      taking road tests with customers for the purpose of duplicating troubleshooting
   ◇ Selected as 1st technician for new products development and training

JOURNEYMAN AUTOMOTIVE TECHNICIAN   1978 - Present
AUTOMOTIVE TECHNICIAN   1976 - 1977

EXCELLENT AUTOMOTIVE   USA
JOURNEYMAN   1973 - 1976

EDUCATION

Community College, Community, OK
   Emphasis on Automotive Transmission & English Classes
Private Pilot's License, Planemasters of Dupage
Community High School, Community, OK, Graduate

REFERENCES AVAILABLE UPON REQUEST

57

Combination. *Betty Callahan, location unknown*

Journeyman training and certifications are an alternative to a two-year degree. All
sections display skills—even the Education section in the reference to the pilot's license.

DAVID M. JOHN_____

SPECIALIZED TRAINING

TOTAL TRAINING HOURS - 1981 - 1995

NEW CAR OVERVIEW

GROUP	SUBJECT	TOTAL HOURS
L.H.	OVERVIEW	24
NEON	OVERVIEW	16
CIRRUS	OVERVIEW	16
MINI VAN	OVERVIEW	24

GROUP	SUBJECT	TOTAL HOURS
5	BRAKES	8
9	ENGINE REPAIR	40
8	ELECTRICAL	24
14	FUEL & EMISSIONS	32
18	DRIVABILITY	24
21	AUTO TRANSMISSION	60
21	MITSUBISHI TRANSMISSION	16
23	BODY	16
24	AIR CONDITIONING	8
26	MAINTENANCE	8

GROUP	SUBJECT	TOTAL HOURS
G.M.	SPECIALIZED ELECTRONIC TRAINING	64

An impressive table that indicates the total number of hours assigned to each group and subject. Blank line spacing within the table makes evident the different group clusters.

WAYNE P. TECHNICIAN

55 U.S. Route One ◆ Saco. Maine ◆ 04072
(207) 555-5055

OBJECTIVE

Seeking a challenging position where my acquired skills and educational background will be utilized toward continued growth and advancement.

SUMMARY OF QUALIFICATIONS

- Master Automobile Technician, ASE certified 1995.
- ASE Refrigerant Recovery & Recycling certified 1994.
- Accustomed to working in a fast-paced environment; ability to work well under pressure.
- Exceptional organizational skills; highly motivated and results oriented.
- Equipped with over $35,000 worth of self-purchased tools.
- Excellent communication skills; effective working both independently and as a cooperative team member.

EDUCATION

Automotive Repair Technician
Gloucester Vocational School - Gloucester, Massachusetts.
Degree Date: 1985

SPECIALIZED TRAINING

Subaru Company Training
Turbo • Fuel Injection • Manual Transmission Overhaul • Automatic Transmission • Carburetion and Emission.

Mitsubishi Company Training
Battery • Starter & Alternator • Diagnostic and Repair • Chassis Electrical • Electrical Fundamental • Electrical Diagnostic & Repair.

Mazda Company Training
Manual Transmission • Automatic Transmission • Diagnostic & Repair • Air Conditioning & Heating Diagnostic & Repair • Fuel & Emission Systems.

WORK EXPERIENCE

Shop Foreman • 1992 to xxxx
Maine Mazda - Biddeford, Maine
- Shop Foreman for the #1 Rated Mazda Dealer in the United States for CSI Service Satisfaction for the last three consecutive quarters.
- Directly responsible for supervision of six automotive technicians; assigning job duties, and assisting technicians in repairs as needed; provided ongoing support and training to other technicians in transmission work and brakes; and provided innovative ways to perform service in the most cost effective manner reducing time spent on repairs and thereby increasing dealership profits on flat rate warranty service.
- Trained personnel in effective upselling service techniques which effectively increased upsell service work performed by 30%.
- Performed diagnostics and utilized analytical skills to determine most cost effective method of repair; performed transmission repairs, overhauls and engine renewals on automatic and manual transmissions; familiar with all types of braking systems, including hydraulic assisted, air, power and anti-lock systems.
- Accustomed to performing all aspects of preliminary service work, i.e. tune-ups, brakes, etc.

58

Combination. *Patricia Martel, Saco, Maine*

Diamond and conventional bullets are used variously in this two-page resume for a well-trained technician—as separators horizontally and eye-catching markers vertically in lists.

WAYNE P. TECHNICIAN
55 U.S. Route One ◆ Saco, Maine ◆ 04072
(207) 555-5055

WORK EXPERIENCE (cont.)

Automotive Technician • 1990 to 1992
Galway Mitsubishi - Cape Elizabeth, Maine.
- All aspects of diagnostics and repairs for a Mitsubishi dealership.

Heavy Equipment Mechanic • 1988 to 1990
R.M. Truck Maintenance - Scarborough, Maine
- Provided diagnostics and repair services on tractor trailers and construction vehicles including backhoes, bulldozers, loaders and excavators.
- Rebuilt hydraulic pistons, cylinders and pumps.
- Performed complete engine overhauls.

Heavy Equipment Mechanic • 1987 to 1990
Gillis & Sons - West Buxton, Maine
- Provided diagnostic and repair services to maintain heavy equipment in excellent working order. Successfully rebuilt a previously dismantled 1972 Ford backhoe and returned same to excellent working condition.
- Acquired extensive knowledge of maintenance and repairs to heavy duty equipment including performing adjustments to arms, buckets, bucket pistons, and hydraulic piston replacement.
- Operated construction equipment assisting at construction site; drove a C70 dump truck to deliver sand or crushed rock, and operated a bulldozer and backhoe on an as-needed basis.

Automotive Technician • 1986 to 1987
Coastal Subaru - Old Orchard Beach, Maine
- All aspects of diagnostics and repairs for a Subaru dealership.

Automotive Technician • 1985 to 1986
Gauthier Motors - Saco, Maine
- All aspects of diagnostics and repairs for a Subaru dealership.

Automotive Technician Apprenticeship • 1980 to 1985
Conley Pontiac - Biddeford, Maine
- Vocational work/study program attending Biddeford Vocational School providing for one week of educational instruction and one week of on the job training on a rotating week by week basis.
- Obtained an in-depth familiarity in all aspects of diagnostic and repair services.
- Utilized excellent customer service skills; responsible for answering the phone and responding to customers requests; assisted in locating requested vehicle parts, and performing pick-ups and deliveries; and provided inventory control services.

The last entry on this page explains the five-year, work/study, Automotive Technician Apprenticeship. Beyond that is other training for certain automobiles and heavy equipment. Boldfacing makes this training and job titles easily seen.

Michael Babcock

1227 Millersport Rd. • Manchester, NY 00000
(555) 555-5555

SUMMARY OF QUALIFICATIONS

Vehicle Maintenance & Repair

- Responsible for the maintenance of a fleet of paving and road building equipment.
- Handle all aspects of heavy truck and highway equipment repairs.
- Extensive experience in general welding repairs and fabrication.
- Also experienced in general repairs to passenger vehicles, engine tune-ups, repairing agricultural equipment, diesel engine repairs, body work, and paint refinishing.
- Trained in use of computer-controlled emission systems and on-board diagnostics for automotive applications.

General Construction

- Able to operate a variety of construction vehicles and equipment
- Responsible for upkeep of service records and service calls to the job site, filing daily vehicle inspection reports and keeping them in compliance with Department of Transportation (DOT) regulations, and keeping maintenance and repair records of on-highway vehicles over 10,000 lbs. as required by the DOT.
- Stock parts department and appropriate supplies and equipment for road building jobs.
- Maintain and repair mixing and screening plants, and hot mix asphalt plants.

EDUCATION	SUNY Agricultural and Technical College at Alfred, NY **Associate in Occupational Science Degree** Specialization: Heavy Equipment, Truck and Diesel Specialist	1983
	BOCES, Belmont, NY Graduate of 2-year Auto Mechanics program	1981
ADDITIONAL TRAINING	Caterpillar, diesel engine training (Models 3116, 3176, and 3406) Week-long seminar at Ag Tech, Wellsville, NY	1992
	Ford Motor Company, trouble-shooting and diagnostic training — 6.9 diesel truck engine and 2 liter light duty diesel engine	1984
EXPERIENCE	A.L. Blades, Belmont, NY **Mechanic**	4/84 to Present
	Lamacchia Ford and Mercury, Inc., Hornell, NY **Mechanic**	10/83 to 4/84
	Lamac Pontiac, Inc., Hornell, NY **Mechanic**	9/83 to 10/83
CERTIFICATES	• NIASE Certified Master Truck Technician • Certified Group 1 NYSDMV Inspector	

References available upon request.

59

Combination. *Catherine Seebald, Wellsville, New York*

A layout change midway through the resume distinguishes the Summary of Qualifications from the sections that follow it. Starting with Education, the heads are in a left column.

John James Doe

000 West End Avenue
Anderson, NY 55555
(000) 555-5555

**CAREER
OBJECTIVE:** Entry level position in **Airframe** and/or **Powerplant Maintenance.**

EDUCATION: EMBRY RIDDLE AERONAUTICAL UNIVERSITY, Daytona Beach, Florida
Associate of Science in Aviation Maintenance Technology
Date of Graduation: May 1993

LICENSES: FAA Airframe and Powerplant Mechanic's License, May 1993

**TECHNICAL
SKILLS:**
- Constructed a wood and fabric winglet and a sheet metal winglet.
- Tested environmentals, de-ice, fire, and fuel systems.
- Inspected disc brakes, tires, and wheels.
- Trained on Boeing 747-400 computer-based program.
- Trained on use of dye penetrant, eddy current, and magnetic particle non-destructive inspection methods.
- Inspected and tested hydraulic actuators.
- Troubleshot mock electrical boards.
- Overhauled MA-4SPA magnetos.
- Troubleshot Lycoming O-320 series reciprocating engines.
- Overhauled Lycoming O-320 E2D reciprocating engine.
- Overhauled cylinders on Continental TSIO-520 reciprocating engine.
- Overhauled and test ran Lycoming T53 turboshaft engine.
- Ran up General Electric J85 turbojet engine.

**WORK
EXPERIENCE:** ANDERSON TELEPHONE COMPANY, Anderson, New York
June - September 1992 / April - September XXXX
Technician
- Duties included installing buried telephone cables.
- Located and repaired broken cables.

**COMPUTER
SKILLS:**
- WordPerfect 5.1
- Lotus 1-2-3
- Windows

REFERENCES: Available Upon Request

60

Combination. *Betty Geller, Elmira, New York*

This 1993 graduate was relatively short on experience, so the writer chose to target the individual's education, licenses, and technical skills but play down his work experience.

John DeFlyer

5005 Beechcraft Court, Apartment 5 ✈ Jennersville, Iowa 55555   (555) 555-0000

OBJECTIVE

Employment as an **Aircraft Mechanic**.

PROFILE

A quality team member and leader, who sets and accomplishes personal and unit goals; a good listener, able to interpret and follow through. Responsible and efficient with an excellent work ethic.

EXPERIENCE

Clark County Airport. *Aircraft Special Transfers, Inc.* Sellersburg, Iowa: 1995-present
Overhaul aircraft components including propellers, governors, magnetos, and field-systems components. Responsible for paperwork, AD research, and service bulletins.

O'Nions Airport. Viceroy, Iowa: 1993-1995
Hands-on experience dealing directly with type-certificated aircraft; aircraft systems and structural parts, including propellers, electrical systems, fuel systems, hydraulic systems, vacuum and static system, plus relevant log book entrees, AD research, and paperwork.

IBEW Local 369. **Electrician's Assistant**. Louisville, Kentucky: 1992-1993

United States Marine Corp. **Corporal (E-4)**: 1988-1992 (Participated in Desert Shield and Storm and Southwest Asia Cease-Fire Campaign)
Four years hands-on experience as an **Aviation Structural Mechanic and Tool Room NCO**.
- ✈ Repaired sheet metal, fiberglass structural parts, and fiberglass rotor blades of helicopters according to design specifications.
- ✈ Made honeycomb repairs to aircraft, and examined parts to determine fabrication procedures and machine and tool requirements.
- ✈ Responsible for inventory and upkeep of all squadron tools; attended meetings, and trained appropriate personnel.

61

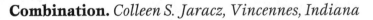

Combination. *Colleen S. Jaracz, Vincennes, Indiana*

Plenty of white space and larger headings spread this resume over two full pages. It includes military experience to highlight advanced technical skills. An easy-to-comprehend layout.

John DeFlyer

(Page 2)

(555) 555-0000

United States Marine Corp. (Continued)

↛ Completed numerous technically oriented courses emphasizing Line Maintenance Safety and Tool Control.

Assistant NCOIC of an operational sea-based aircraft facility.
↛ Assisted in supervising activities of night crew personnel engaged in operational maintenance of sea based aircraft; responsible for their health and welfare.
↛ Continually assigned to positions requiring the highest degree of personal responsibility normally held by individuals of higher grade with outstanding results (both in the United States and Southwest Asia).
↛ Responsible for maintenance related training and supervision of personnel.

EDUCATION

Viceroy University. Viceroy, Iowa: 1993-Present
AS Degree in **Aviation Maintenance Technology** with airframe and powerplant certification. (GPA 3.8)
Related Coursework: General Aviation maintenance; inspection and rigging; power plant installation and trouble shooting; turbine overhaul; sheet metal, materials, and processes; hydraulics and welding; basic electricity; instrument systems; nonmetallic structures; and general studies.
↛ **Resident Assistant** while attending V.U., responsible for welfare of students residing in Manning Hall.

TECHNICAL TRAINING

(*United States Marine Corps.*)

Aviation Structural Mechanic and Metal Smith (1989)
NALCOMIS and Terminal Operations (1990)
Fiberglass Rotor Blade Repair (1989)
Corrosion Control (1989)

REFERENCES

Available upon request.

Airplane bullets unify the two pages. The writer prefers to use bullets before only *special* information or strong points. Putting bullets before generic information reduces their impact. Ample white space is achieved through extra blank lines between main sections.

William G. Guder

P. O. Box 000 ◆ Oakview, Indiana 00000 ◆ (555) 555-0000

PROFILE

- Reliable troubleshooter; a quality team player with proven leadership abilities. Recognize proper steps to achieve efficient solutions, even under pressure situations.
- Excellent <u>manual dexterity</u>, with the knowledge and consistent 'attention to detail' to effectively apply it.
- Out-going, calm, dependable, and straight-forward. Perceptive with sound interpersonal and oral communication skills.

SPECIAL SKILLS

OSHA instructed forktruck operator.
Fire-fighting and life saving training.
Hazardous waste containment and clean-up training.

FAA certified A&P Technician.
Certified Scuba Diver.

EDUCATION

Vincennes University. Vincennes, Indiana: 1995 (Graduated, **Summa Cum Laude**: GPA 3.8)
AS Degree in **Aviation Maintenance Technology**. Mechanic Certification with Airframe and Powerplant Ratings. Financed 100% of educational costs.

> **Related Coursework:** General Aviation maintenance including: inspection/rigging; power plant installation/trouble shooting; sheet metal, materials, and processes; hydraulics/welding; basic electricity; instrument systems; nonmetallic structures; and general studies including computer awareness class.

TECHNICAL EXPERIENCE

Vincennes University-O'Neal Airport. Vincennes, Indiana: 1993-present
Certified Repair Station Facility. Professionally completed all assigned tasks, actively pursued additional work and educational experiences. Helped fellow students as needed and assisted professors. <u>Proficiencies Include:</u> Paperwork, including relevant log book entrees, and AD research; aircraft systems and structural parts (propellers, electrical systems, fuel systems, hydraulic systems, vacuum and static system); and Federal Air Regulations.

- Excellent hands-on technical experience. Deal directly with all phases of aircraft repair - structural, powerplant, and systems.

62

Combination. *Colleen S. Jaracz, Vincennes, Indiana*

Another resume by the same writer. Similar strengths are evident: ample white space, larger headings, two full pages, and an easy-to-grasp layout. A difference is *centered* headings.

William G. Guder (Page 2)
(555) 555-0000

Vincennes University-O'Neal Airport   (Continued)

◆ Currently pursuing pilots license, treasurer of Vincennes Flying Blazers, and active PAMA member.

EMPLOYMENT HISTORY

Team Manager / Installer. *WAA, Inc*. Indianapolis, Indiana: 1992-Present
Install restaurant furniture and fixtures throughout the U.S. Survey and verify measurements paying careful attention to blueprints - capably meet unexpected challenges utilizing drawing skills as necessary; thorough knowledge of tools. Absolute on-site authority; take necessary steps to find practical solutions, insuring client satisfaction and good PR. Coordinate with on-site tradesmen. Total supervisory responsibility for crews of three to six employees. Utilize excellent inter-personal skills with clients; able to motivate and encourage team members who are often away from home for extended periods of time.
◆ Advanced quickly, seven months to management position.
◆ Excellent time management skills.

Machine Repairman. *Garret Engine Division*. Phoenix, Arizona: 1990-1992
Machine maintenance, perform light mechanical repair on CNC (Computer Numerically Controlled) machines. Assisted with upkeep and major repairs.
◆ Conceptualized and developed new filter system for CNC coolants resulting in substantial savings to company.

Mechanic. *American Auto*. Chandler, Arizona: 1988-1990
Rebuild front-end structures. Repair late model cars for resale. Stock parts and operate forktruck.

Foreman. *Dwyer Painting*. Scottsdale, Arizona: 1984-1988
Painted custom homes and commercial properties; remodel work. Supervised three, ten-men crews. Experienced with oil, latex, epoxy, lacquer, stain, and acrylic enamels - air and airless application.

ABOUT ME

A lifetime family interest in flight, and the machines that make flight possible, have led me to study many aspects of aviation maintenance and management. Although successfully employed in a lucrative position with great potential for advancement, my enthusiasm for aircraft has challenged me to follow my desire - to seek professional employment in the field of Aviation.

Another difference in this resume is the concluding About Me section. Its purpose is to explain why the individual wants to follow these interests in a new career direction. The prose paragraph offers pleasant relief from bulleted lists commonly found in resumes.

AMY JONES

444 Bold Blvd. • Janesville, OK 00000 • (000) 000-0000

OBJECTIVE: Aviation or Industrial Maintenance Technician.

EDUCATION:

JONES SCHOOL OF AERONAUTICS, Jones, Arkansas
Certificate of Aviation Maintenance Technician, 1990
- Equivalent to 92 college credit hours (lack only 9 hours for Associate's Degree).
- G.P.A.: 3.66/4.00. Honor Roll student.

MAJOR VOCATIONAL-TECHNICAL SCHOOL, Janesville, Oklahoma
- Attended classes in paint and body work over an 18 month period, 1982 - 1983.

EXPERIENCE:

ROGERS SUPERCENTER, Janesville, Oklahoma　　　　　　　**2/94 - Present**
Department Manager
- Promoted from **Set-up Helper** to **Cashier Trainee** to **Clerk** to **Department Manager** within 18 months.
- Supervise the stocking of inventory, handle paperwork, and check sales.
- Contribute to consistent average weekly department sales increases of 5%.

TRISTATE AIRCRAFTS, Houston, Texas　　　　　　　　　　**6/91 - 6/93**
Airframe and Powerplant (A & P) Mechanic
- Position included duties both as corporate mechanic and as airliner refurbisher.
- Inspected and performed technical repairs of aircraft systems including electrical, hydraulic, pressurization, heating and cooling, powerplants, and airframes.
- Heavy maintenance on Beechcraft, Cessna, Leer, Piper, Saberliner, and Mitsubishi aircraft.

JAY'S CAFETERIA, Jonesburo, Arkansas　　　　　　　　　**3/85 - 5/91**
Supervisor / Maintenance Engineer
- Supervised 8 - 10 kitchen staff employees and all aspects of food preparation.
- Maintained restaurant's electrical equipment, plumbing, heating, and cooling systems.

MILITARY EXPERIENCE:

OKLAHOMA NATIONAL GUARD, Janesville, Oklahoma　　　　**2/84 - Present**
Motor Pool Sergeant / Mortar Crewman
- Supervise the maintenance of Army vehicles and their dispatch, documentation, and licensing.
- Operate a Mortar Ballistic Computer which ensures accurate trajectories.
- Engineer experience includes demolition, surveying, and bridge and road construction.
- Awarded Secret Security Clearance.

CERTIFICATION:
- Airframe & Powerplant (A & P) Mechanic's License

63

Chronological. *Laura C. Karlak, Bartlesville, Oklahoma*

This individual wanted to reenter the aviation maintenance field after working in retail. The Education section shows how to indicate that a degree is a certain number of hours away.

William Van Hoose

123 Stoney Way ▪ St. Louis, Missouri 60000 ▪ (555) 555-4000

RAILCAR CONSULTANT

Quality Control ▪ Wreck Estimation ▪ Aluminum Freight Cars
AAR Billing/Auditing ▪ AWS Certified Welding Inspector

20-year career in quality control management for freight railcar business with leading railcar manufacturer and rebuilder. Special expertise in aluminum wrecks with extensive training from leading aluminum railcar manufacturer. Strong project management, communication, supervisory, and negotiations experience.

PROFESSIONAL EXPERIENCE

LAMBERT RAILCAR COMPANY, St. Louis, Missouri
(a wholly owned subsidiary of Smythe-Westin, Inc.)

Quality Assurance / Estimation   1988-1995
Supervised quality assurance for government contractor to build, maintain, and repair railroad freight cars. Assured compliance with AAR and FRA rules and standards. Wrote estimates based on AAR billing/auditing system. Solely responsible for estimating aluminum wrecks.
- Wrote $1.5 - 2.5 million annually in train wreck estimates.
- Achieved superior TTX company audit 6 consecutive years, outperforming other company shops.

Manager, Quality Control *(position eliminated in company reorganization in 1988)*   1986-1988
Managed quality control of 11-man division responsible for in-bound and in-process railcar inspection. Personally inspected outbound trains for perfect 20-year safety record.
- Earned new car builder certification as a result of outstanding performance.
- Worked extensively with aluminum railcar estimation and repair.

Quality Assurance / Estimation   1978-1986
Supervised inbound inspection and wreck estimation. Assumed responsibility for aluminum estimates.

Welder / Carman   1970-1975
Built and repaired freight cars. Worked with design engineers, blue prints, and welding equipment.

KEEVAN RAILWAY, Madison, Illinois
(a wholly owned subsidiary of Smythe-Westin, Inc.)

Quality Assurance Inspector   1975-1978
Supervised inbound inspection and wreck estimation. Assisted chief inspector, filled in during absences.

TRAINING & CERTIFICATIONS

Commitment to Excellent/TQM, SMYTHE-WESTIN, St. Louis, Missouri	1994
Series of Leadership and Supervisory courses, AAIM, St. Louis, Missouri	1988
AWS Certified Welding Inspector	1985
Testing & Inspection of Welds, Certified Welding Inspector Training	1985
BELLEVILLE AREA COLLEGE, Belleville, Illinois	
Certificate, Combination Welder, GYPSUM COUNTY TRADE SCHOOL, Gypsum, Kansas	1970
Certificate, HVAV, COLLINS INSTITUTE OF TECHNOLOGY, St. Louis, Missouri	1975

64

Combination. *Carla Culp Coury, Glen Carbon, Illinois*

This 50-year-old wanted to do railroad consulting. Because he lacked a management degree, the writer used the term TRAINING & CERTIFICATIONS instead of EDUCATION.

GO GETTER
123 X Street, #000 • Anywhere, America 00000 • (000) 000–0000

SUMMARY OF QUALIFICATIONS

Electronics/
Industrial
Electricity

- Experience repairing and operating A/V equipment, VCRs, fans, answering machines and vacuums, toasters, microwaves on an independent basis, for Lindsey Hopkins Technical Education Center
- Skilled in wiring branch circuits, electrical load hook–ups, wiring motor control circuits, installing and checking motors, troubleshooting motors/motor control problems
- Knowledge of hooking–up and program equipment control circuits through programmable controllers and industrial computers
- Familiar with industrial electricity as it relates to electronics, air conditioning, industrial systems maintenance, building maintenance, computer repair...
- Industrial Electricity and Electronics formal training

Customer
Service

- Excellent people and public relations skills
- Natural ability to explain complex items in layman's terms
- Skilled in handling customer complaints: Attend to problems before they become major issues and reduce complicated situations to their basic components for resolution
- Work well with others at all levels: counseled boys ages 10–15 on three shifts, 24–hours each day; tutored vocational and assisting handicapped students; provided superior service to customers requiring cellular installation

Management

- Instrumental in the start–up of Maritime Communications
- As Supervisor for Cel–Tec Communications, supervised a staff of six
- Motivate others to perform at their best and to like what they do
- Encourage productivity and cross–training
- Communicate in a positive way and entice staff to be productive
- Effective instructor with excellent command of both English and Spanish; conversational sign language

EDUCATION

Lindsey Hopkins Technical Education Center, Miami, FL
Industrial Electricity and Electronics (two–year certificate), 1992

The High School of Art & Design, New York, NY
Majored in Commercial Art, 1972

SPECIAL SKILLS

- Extensive mechanical knowledge includes working with: lathe; acetylene torch; all wrenches, saws and planes; voltmeter; computerized machinery
- Experienced in arc welding and soldering
- Repaired sewing machines and a wide variety of small appliances
- Certified SCUBA diver
- Competent illustrator with knowledge of colors and their effect on people

65

Combination. *Beverley Kagan, North Miami Beach, Florida*

This Electronics Installer and Repairer was willing to be a part-time Custodian in order to get a full-time position in the field of electronics. The first page targets that field.

GO GETTER   Page 2

EMPLOYMENT HISTORY

INSTANT ZAP TECHNICAL EDUCATION CENTER, Anywhere, AK   1992 – present
  Custodian (interim position in order to become full–time), 1995–present
  In addition to routine custodial functions, repair A/V equipment, prepare tape recorders for English labs.
  Teacher's Aide, Self–Assisted Instructional Learning (SAIL) Lab (part–time), 1992–95
  Tutored and prepared vocational students to meet TABE tests.
  Volunteer
  Assisted wheelchair–bound and hearing impaired students getting to and in the classroom, and to execute classroom assignments.

SPLICERS GALORE, Anywhere AK   1991 – 1992
  Machine Operator for national manufacturer of electronic connectors.

NAVIGATION COMMUNICATIONS, Anywhere, AK   1990 – 1991
  Cellular Installer/Electronics Repair
  Strategically installed cell phones, cellular pay phones and fax machines on cruise and commercial ships. Position required 50% travel throughout the U.S.

CEL COMMUNICATIONS, Anywhere, AK   1988 – 1990
  Service Manager, 1989–90
  Installed cellular phones in autos, trucks and limousines. Interviewed and trained new hires; scheduled appointments; advised how product should be installed. Supervised a staff of six.
  Installer, 1988–89

LIMOUSINES UNLIMITED, Anywhere, AK   1987 – 1988
  Chauffeur/Bodyguard

HALFWAY HOUSE, New York, NY   1983 – 1987
  Counselor in house for 250+/– teenage delinquents

U.S. MERCHANT MARINE   1977 – 1979
  Civilian Engineer's Apprentice (Wiper) – assisted in all Engine Room mechanical repairs.

LANGUAGES

Fluent in Spanish and English. Conversational signing.

References available upon request

He returned to school after being in the workforce since 1983. No explanation is given for the gap between 1979 and 1983. Dates right-aligned at the right margin make it easy to see continual employment since 1983. Positions are in boldface to help them stand out.

JEFF J. KORMACK
84312 EAST UTE CIRCLE
PHOENIX, ARIZONA 85044

CONFIDENTIAL RÉSUMÉ
WORK: 602/524-1940
HOME: 602/587-3993

OBJECTIVE

To use proven abilities as an ELECTRONIC TECHNICIAN to advance within the MOTOROLA family, using skills in wafer production and applying knowledge of corporate objectives.

OVERVIEW OF QUALIFICATIONS

Combines education, certification, and more than 15 years hands-on experience in positions requiring strong technical skills, sound judgment, and initiative. Areas of ability include:

Electronic Technology   **Chemical Processing**
Quality Checks   **Testing & Evaluation**
Spec Compliance   **Troubleshooting & Repair**
Clean-Room Protocol   **Documentation & Reports**

- Analytical, intelligent, and logical. Able to recognize and resolve operational malfunctions.
- Hard-working and exceptionally dependable. Takes pride in quality work performed in a timely, professional manner.
- Communicates effectively with both technical and non-technical personnel, establishing a strong team relationship.
- Energetic, enthusiastic and cooperative. Eager to meet new challenges, increase capabilities and contribute to overall productivity.

EDUCATION
Current

Mesa Community College   Mesa, Arizona
AA Degree Candidate*: December 1995   GPA: 3.2
Chemical Engineering
* To be applied toward **BS Degree** in **Chemical Engineering** from ASU
Courses Taken To Date:
Chemistry; Physics; Calculus; Engineering Programming

March 1991

I T T Technical Institute   Phoenix, Arizona
Associate of Specialized Technology Degree   GPA: 3.9
Electronics & Computer Engineering

ADDITIONAL TRAINING

U. S. Air Force - SACCS Courses/Certifications include:
Electronic Computer & Switching System Certification
Advanced Mainframe & Sub-system Repair Certification
Test Equipment/Advanced Modem Maintenance Certification

Bucks County Technical School   Fairless Hills, Pennsylvania
Certification of Completion
Computer Maintenance; Instrumentation; Basic Electronics

EXPERIENCE
5/95 - Present

Motorola COM-1   Phoenix, Arizona
PRODUCTION OPERATOR
Works in clean-room environment in the Diffusion & Implant area. Rapidly developed knowledge of all diffusion and implant area operations as well as overall corporate policies and procedures.

- Changes wafer chemical structure using:
  Oxide, Nitride, TEOS and **Poly-Dep Furnaces.**
- Adept with all metrology tools used for processing and checking wafer quality and conformance to stringent standards and specifications.

Continued > > >

66

Combination. *Brooke Andrews, Chandler, Arizona*

This resume has some nice touches: the phrase for confidentiality in the upper-right corner of the first page, lines that separate main sections, the use of all uppercase for key words in

JEFF J. KORMACK   PAGE 2   WORK: 602/524-1940

Motorola Experience Continued:

- Software experience includes MAUI, Promis and Data-Log.
- Received **positive performance reviews; excellent on-time/absence record.**
- Working toward BS Degree in Chemical Engineering. Participates in continuing education programs to up-grade skills and remain current with new developments in modern technology.

1986 - 1995 & 1985 - 1986

Sears, Roebuck & Company   Pennsylvania & Arizona
ELECTRONIC & ELECTRO-MECHANICAL TECHNICIAN
Excellent performance in Pennsylvania, resulted in re-hire upon relocation to Arizona and advancement to Field Service Technician. Following graduation from I T T in 1991, promoted to Electronics Shop.

- Served as troubleshooter and repair technician providing in-shop and field service for audio/video equipment including VCR, FAX and copiers as well as appliances of all types.
- In previous position trained new technicians in proper procedure and company policy.
- Recipient of "Courtesy Award" for outstanding customer relations, and positive performance reviews for quality workmanship.

1981 - 1985

United States Air Force   * Honorable Discharge
COMPUTER &   * Top Secret Clearance
ELECTRONIC SWITCHING SYSTEM SPECIALIST
Advanced from Technician to Specialist, offering training to other military personnel as needed, in analysis, testing, maintenance, and repair of communication systems.

- Performed operational and diagnostic checks, troubleshooting to component level, and ensured compliance with stringent military standards.
- Prepared detailed documentation and ordered supplies.
- Equipment included ITT, Hewlet-Packard, Techtronics and others.

REFERENCES   References and additional information available upon request.

the Objective, boldfacing for important information throughout the resume, and the "Continued > > >" note in the lower-right corner of the first page. For convenience, the work phone number is put also in the header on page two.

Mr. McBain, Jr.
P.O. Box 9999
Yulee, Florida 22222
(904) 111-1111

OBJECTIVE

Seeking a position as a Communications Technician with fiber optics specialty.

EDUCATION

Graduate, Andrew Jackson High School, 1989
Florida Community College, Jacksonville, Florida
  Attended 1 year
Fiber Optic Fusion Splice Certificate from Siecor, August 94
  Presently studying for Registered
  Communications Distribution Designer

SKILLS AND ABILITIES

10 Base T wiring and configuration; token ring configuration; relocate, prewire and test local area networks; install and program Norstar DR5 Key service; experience with amplifiers, taps, splitters and connectors; can install and terminate cable television (CATV), unshielded and shielded twisted pair cable, 110 and 66 patch panel.

EMPLOYMENT HIGHLIGHTS

Telesystems Atlanta, Inc., Lawrenceville, Georgia, 7/94-present
  Supervisor - supervising a crew of five; checking for accuracy and effeciency on the job; installing voice and data lines.

Bradley Communications, Jacksonville, Florida, 5/91-5/94
  Telephone Technician - Installed and maintained telephones and voice data lines; installed and terminated fiber optics 62.5; supervised a crew of five; scheduled employees; checked employees work for accuracy and efficiency; evaluated employees and filled out job assessment reports.

Brunswick Ramona Lanes, Jacksonville, Florida, 6/89-5/91
  Mechanic - Prepared and conditioned lanes for bowling; cleaned and performed file maintenance on pinsetter machines.

INTEREST

Professional Bowlers Tour

VOLUNTEER WORK

Nassau County Sheriffs Reserve for four years

References Available Upon Request

67

Combination. *Rose Montgomery, Charlotte, North Carolina*

This resume was composed with a specific objective in mind: to show skills and previous experience that qualified the applicant for the position. Previous positions are in boldface.

WALTER M. HAMLEN
2510 Rowan Avenue
Wilmington, North Carolina 28401
(910) 123-4567

EDUCATION

CAPE FEAR COMMUNITY COLLEGE, Wilmington, NC
AAS - Electronics Engineering Technology   Expected 1996

EXPERIENCE

Programmable Logic Controllers (PLC's)
Digital Electronics I and II
Electronic System Design and Construction
Troubleshooting digital circuitry
Robotics/Computer Aided Manufacturing
Fabrication techniques - soldering and desoldering

Computer Experience:
Electronics Work Bench (EWB) Windows 3.1

Equipment Used:
Oscilloscopes   Logic Probes
Digital Volt Meter   Bread Boarding

TRAINING

Sun Electric Company - Transistorized Ignition Systems
Allen Institute - Carburetor and Computer Control and Fuel Injection
USAF Electronics School - Auto Pilot and Compass Systems

CERTIFICATION

ASE Certified - Special training in electrical and electronic computer controls on
automobiles and trucks.

EMPLOYMENT HISTORY

Mechanical Technician
Carolina Cab, Wilmington, NC   1994 to Present
Jones Corporation, Wilmington, NC   1993
Jake's Garage, Inc., Wilmington, NC   1992 to 1993
Pete's Auto Service, Wilmington, NC   1991 to 1992
Frey's Garage, Whiteville, NC   1977 to 1991

MILITARY SERVICE

United States Air Force - Honorably Discharged

References Are Available Upon Request

68

Combination. *Sandy Adcox Saburn, Wilmington, North Carolina*

A way to show a degree in progress. The Experience section is like a skills section. The purpose
of the first four sections is to show the transition to a career in electronics.

RONALD J. CLARK

0000 North West Avenue
Anywhere, USA
(000) 000-0000

OBJECTIVE

Career opportunity as ELECTRONICS TECHNICIAN where my degree in Industrial Technology and 12-year career in the troubleshooting, repair, calibration, and quality control of telecommunications equipment will be of benefit.

EDUCATION

DENTON CITY COLLEGE, Anywhere, USA   5/95
A.S., Industrial Technology. Representative Coursework: Programmable Controls; Logic-Line Diagrams; AC Manual Contactors and Motor Starters; AC/DC Contactors and Magnetic Motor Starters; Single-Phase, Poly-Phase and DC Motor Types; Power Distribution Systems; AC/DC Fundamentals; Solid-State Devices; Microprocessors

UNITED STATES AIR FORCE
Air Assault School; Model 40 School (advanced telecommunications); Mode 5 School (digital electronics logic circuitry); Basic Non-Commissioned Officer Course (administrative management)

PROFESSIONAL EXPERIENCE

Promoted through increasingly responsible technical and supervisory positions   1979-1992
during tenure with the United States Air Force:

Test, Measurement & Diagnostic Equipment Coordinator (2/90-6/92), Riyahd, Saudi Arabia

Managed maintenance division which performed intermediate maintenance on radio telecommunications systems and associated equipment valued in excess of $350,000. Supervised total staff of 15. Provided technical and procedural assistance to electronics technicians. Performed administrative duties including scheduling shop operations and report writing.

> ‣ Comments from performance evaluation: "exceptionally competent"; "his advice is sought by others"; "totally devoted to success of the [team]".

Telecommunications Repair Technician/Repel Master (2/88-2/90), Freezenberg, Alaska

Performed test, troubleshooting, fault isolation and repairs of communication assemblages. Supervised and coordinated with motor pool concerning PMCS and maintenance of vehicles and generators. Additionally supervised the rigging of helicopters and safety of soldiers during repel exercises.

> ‣ Comments from performance evaluation: "technical skills and ability to perform under pressure has greatly improved the operational readiness of ... systems"; "earned the respect of all supported customers"; "outstanding in all areas".

Assistant Non-Commissioned Officer In Charge (11/80-2/88), Fightingforces, Germany

Assisted in management of telecommunications maintenance section servicing over $500,000 in equipment for the European Command Headquarters. Reviewed maintenance scheduling and oversaw duty assignments for staff of 21. Additional duties included site training, crime prevention, safety, publications, and physical security. Promoted as Supervisor, Shop Foreman, and Assistant NCOIC over more experienced personnel.

> ‣ Comments from performance evaluation: "readily and competently accepts responsibilities and duties performed by [superiors]"; "an outstanding NCO"; "streamlined his operations to reach peak efficiency"; "a tremendous asset to this unit."

AWARDS

Three Army Achievement Medals for technical repair support (managed repair shop which was rated #1 among 45 throughout Europe) and Certificate of Achievement Citation.

References Upon Request

69

Chronological. *Susan Britton Whitcomb, Fresno, California*

This individual had the benefit of military experience before getting an A.S. degree. Note that a transition from military to civilian life may happen not quickly but over several years.

JUSTIN R. SINGLETON

101 North Campbell, Phoenix, AZ 85219   (602) 555-3200

OBJECTIVE: Troubleshooting and repair of electronic and electromechanical equipment.

SUMMARY:

- Ten years of experience building and repairing microcomputers.
- Proficient in all types of electronic and electromechanical repair.
- Sole responsibility for all manufacturing and repair aspects of business.
- Excellent customer relations skills.
- Supervisory experience.

EXPERIENCE:

Electronics Technician
COMPCO
Phoenix, Arizona   January, 1985 - Present

(Manufactures, markets and repairs IBM compatible computers.)

- Have sole responsibility for all manufacturing and repair aspects of the business.
- Build and test "IBM Clone" systems and peripherals, including upgrades.
- Repair computers, including IBM, Apple, Mac, Epson, and Packard Bell.
- Build and custom-build phase conversion equipment.
- Service sophisticated studio and portable photography flash equipment.
- Repair alarm systems and phone systems.
- Handle customer relations, including customer service and support for all of the above functions.
- Solid knowledge of DOS and Windows.
- Supervise two part-time employees.

EDUCATION:

DeVry Institute of Technology   1982 - 1984
Phoenix, Arizona

Mesa High School   Graduated in 1982
Mesa, Arizona

70

Combination. *Deborah L. Schuster, Newport, Michigan*

Notice a lot of white space in this easy-to-read format. The tall, condensed font (Aurora Opti Condensed)—shown in small caps—complements the circuit board logo.

Kevin James

444 Cray Street
Jersey City, NJ 22222
(201) 555-5555

SUMMARY

Detail-oriented **Electrical Engineering** professional, with considerable expertise in Development Production Support, Manufacturing Technology, Test Engineering, Quality Control and Assurance. Proven record of accomplishment and growth, with solid leadership, organizational and time-management abilities.

EXPERIENCE

Production Support:
- Supervision of ECO development update and failure analysis.
- Extensive knowledge of Statistical Process Control (SPC) and Total Quality Improvement System (TQIS).
- Prescreening RMA of field returns and inventoriable product and making disposition based on findings.
- Supervision of customer service and production support; researching of problems and troubleshooting.

Manufacturing Test Engineering:
- Collection and generation of monthly DOAs and field failure statistics; implementation and maintenance of hotroom yield statistics; collection and maintenance of failure data in Final Test RTV material.
- ECO expeditor and documentation distribution.
- Writing of test specifications, ATP's, STP's and various other technical reports. Working knowledge of Mil-1-45208, Mil-STD-45662 and Mil-Q-9858.
- Testing of various electronic components, including circuit boards, tuned circuits, capacitors, generators, analog and digital circuits, among others.

Quality Control & Assurance:
- Areas of responsibility and expertise encompass metrology; inspection planning; training; nonconformation; system delegation; material reviews; moving and tagging; and impounding information.

HISTORY

Datability, Carlstadt, NJ   **3/89 - Present**
Development Production Support Supervisor (12/92 - Present)
Chief Inspector (2/91 - 6/92)
QA Lab Technician, Quality Control (3/89 - 2/91)

Superior Manufacturing & Instrument Corp., Long Island City, NY   **1/83 - 3/89**
QA Lab Technician

JFD Electronics Components, Corp., Oceanside, NY   **7/79 - 1/83**
Electronic Lab Technician

EDUCATION

New York Technical College; A.A.S. Degree, *Electrical Engineering,* 1980

SKILLS

- DOS; WordPerfect; Ethernet; Systems Management

71

Combination. *Judith Friedler, New York, New York*

Boldfacing highlights key words throughout this resume. If your eye follows the boldfacing from top to bottom (including the bullets), you can grasp the key information quickly.

MICHAEL MARSHALL
333 Baxter Place, Ringwood, NJ 77777
(222) 999-9999 / mm1111@aol.com

A position requiring strong mechanical and technical skills.

Profile	**Highly qualified construction professional** experienced in all aspect of building trades, covering residential and commercial work…. Proven ability to work independently as well as a supportive team member…. Considered an effective communicator, who interfaces well with clients and other trades professionals.
Highlights	• Achieved excellent safety record for industry standards. • Acted as a subcontractor on jobs, estimating material/labor costs. • Ensured high work standards through close attention to detail and technical specifications.
Expertise	Framing — Sheetrocking — Finished Trim — Door Hanging — Siding Interior/Exterior Finishing Blueprint Reading — Plumbing — Electrical — Masonry — Roofing

—— CAREER EXPERIENCE ——

XXXX-Date   **Carpenter**, Best Construction, Ringwood, NJ
- Utilize all construction trades, including plumbing and electrical, on a wide range of residential and commercial projects for this general contractor.
- Follow work order specifications from blueprints. Order materials, keeping waste to a minimum.
- Interface extensively with clients and subcontractors. Established excellent rapport with both groups.

XXXX-XXXX   **Carpenter**, Home Construction, Fair Lawn, NJ
- Part of a two-person team, working on residential remodeling jobs for this general contractor.
- Worked up estimates when asked to serve as a subcontractor for same company.

XXXX-XXXX   **Carpenter**, Advantage Construction, Fair Lawn, NJ
- Started career in construction for this general contractor and adjusted quickly to demands of the industry. Gained excellent experience and developed strong work ethic.

—— EDUCATION ——
Advanced Technical Institute, Philadelphia, PA
Associate in Specialized Technology, 1991

References available on request.

72

Combination. *Vivian Belen, Fair Lawn, New Jersey*

A strong resume for a person with strong skills. The objective in boldface, italic, and underlining sets the tone for the resume. Lines enclose the most important information.

Don Saltman

0000 Elbert Drive
Somewhere, IN 47591

(812) 888-0000
e-mail: @somewhere.net

profile
- Highly experienced professional. Thirty + years in the metal working industry.
- Excellent work ethic; trusted and respected. Enjoy challenges and handle stress well.
- Troubleshooter, listen and determine best way to proceed – conservative and willing to compromise. Conversant – able to communicate ideas effectively.
- Skilled supervisor. Utilize motivation/mediation skills effectively.
- Computer (CNC Programming, Excel, Symix, Windows, Internet).
- Read blueprints accurately – advanced technical skills – knowledgeable of precision instruments and machines including milling machines, grinders, lathes, and precision measuring instruments.

experience
MRO/Buyer. *BRG Industries* (Brite Resource Group ➡ Formerly Somewhere Manufacturing ➡ formerly Bristol Squib)
Purchase production operations, maintenance, and repair materials (including parts and supplies). Contact suppliers, negotiate purchase agreements, pursue supplier contracts, handle purchase orders and schedule deliveries. Supervise tool crib and attendants. Attend meetings and troubleshoot/mediate when appropriate. Handle payables. Assist with production planning and goal setting.
- Supervise ten member production management team (Team Management Style). Supervise tool room attendants. Delegate work load appropriately to optimize efficiency.
- Research best product purchases including cost/effectiveness of product. Organize tasking to accommodate efficient use of materials for optimal production. Insure efficient handling of inventory.

Tool Room Supervisor: 0000-0000
Supervised sixteen tool and die makers in the maintenance and repair of dies, tooling, and other equipment. Scheduled working hours for all shifts and maintained records of tooling repairs and maintenance.

Machinist/Toolmaker. *Cantel Tool, Inc*. Somewhere, IL: 0000-0000

Tooling Supervisor. *Ready Manufacturing Company*. Somewhere, IL: 0000-0000

Shop Foreman. *Custom Tool Inc*. Somewhere, IL: 0000-0000

education
University of Arkansas at Monticello. 1964-1965

interests
Private Pilot and member of the Mid Aero Club. Somewhere, IL: 0000 to present

73

Combination. *Colleen S. Jaracz, Vincennes, Indiana*

All lowercase letters in the section headings make the resume different. A slightly larger first bullet draws the eye to the first item of the profile section—the section that must be seen.

Mary E. Canter

323 West 47th Street
Elmira, NY 00000
(000) 000-0000

Objective
A challenging position as a technical in the industrial field.

Experience

1987 to XXXX
ELMIRA TECHNICAL, P.C. - *Elmira, NY*
Technician Team Leader
Performed multiple procedures requiring constant upgrading of technical skills and detailed knowledge of state-of-the-art equipment. Supervised scheduling, training, and job assignments for 8 team members. Administered appointment booking, oversaw patient flow and patient/physician case assignments.
Highlights of accomplishments:
- Initiated cost containment program which resulted in 25% reduction in office supply and pharmaceutical expenditures.
- Led Patient Flow Efficiency Team which significantly reduced patient waiting time, resulting in improved patient relations and an increase in quality of technicians' work.
- Designed and conducted customized in-house OSHA and CLIA Compliance Workshops for all staff members.
- Developed "Patient Instruction Sheets" to explain patient responsibilities for both pre-procedural preparation and post-procedural follow-up care.

1980 to 1987
JAMES GIFTWARE - *Johnson Hill, MI*
Manager/Buyer
Responsible for complete management of 2 stores including hiring and supervision of 12 employees, seasonal help, and outside janitorial services. Handled inventory control, register cash outs, bank deposits, and radio-newspaper promotions.
Highlights of accomplishments:
- Installed "Wedding Room" resulting in greatly increased sales of wedding-related merchandise and increased customer traffic.
- Installed glass-etching machine resulting in increased sales of engraveable glass and metal items.
- Initiated extremely profitable balloon delivery service.

1978 to 1980
BAUSCH & LOMB (Research and Development) - *Marietta, NY*
Chemistry Technician
Responsible for direct testing and logging of test results, data analysis, quality control documentation, and troubleshooting during development of Ectachem Blood Analyzer. Trained sales representatives in use of machine and customer education.
- Earned bonus award for development of new test procedure.

Education
Elmira Community College - *Elmira, NY*
Associate in Applied Science Degree (1978)

Continuing Education:
- JET Communications Seminar
- JET Management Course
- OSHA Training Course
- OSHA Hazardous Chemical Seminar
- OSHA/CLIA Compliance Seminar
- Supervisory Skills Course
- Career Track - Power Communication Skills for Women
- JET Transformation Workshops (Management Skills)
- Intermediate Computer Course (Bausch & Lomb)

Credentials
- Ophthalmic Assistant - JCAHPO-OMA
- CPR (certified until 1998)
- Emergency Medical Technician Training

74

Chronological. *Betty Geller, Elmira, New York*

The resume fits on one page without smaller type for the person's name or less white space on the left. Smaller top and bottom margins and tighter line spacing did the trick.

DANIEL RICKS
76 Marionette Drive
New Baden, Illinois 62265
(618) 555-2623

POWER PLANT TECHNICIAN/FOREMAN

- Extensive hands-on experience supervising the operation and maintenance of mobile and stationary power plant equipment ranging from 3kw to 1000kw. Strong knowledge of:

Boilers	HVAC systems
Diesel/Gasoline Engines	Turbines
Generators	Pumps
Condensers	Compressors
Waste Heat Recovery	Heavy Maintenance Vehicles
Process Controls	Electrical Distribution Systems

- Skilled at performing building maintenance involving carpentry, plumbing, electrical repair, and masonry.

- Effective at planning work projects, coordinating with other tradesman, and overseeing completion with attention to deadlines, detail and overall quality.

- A reliable and safety-conscious worker; missed fewer than five days of work in the last 20 years. Supervised and trained personnel on safe work practices.

WORK HISTORY

Prairie Farms, Granite City, Illinois   1994-Present
  MAINTENANCE MECHANIC

United States Air Force   1974-1994
  POWER PLANT FOREMAN
  POWER PRODUCTION SHOP SUPERVISOR
  ELECTRICAL POWER PRODUCTION TECHNICIAN
  POWER PLANT OPERATOR

EDUCATION/SPECIALIZED TRAINING

- A.S. Degree coursework, Power Plant Technology, Belleville Area College
- EPA Hazardous Waste Training: Hazardous Waste Removal and Clean-up, Asbestos Removal, and Protective Equipment Usage
- Additional Military Training: Electrical Power Production Courses, Solid State Circuits, Battery Bank Maintenance

REFERENCES AVAILABLE UPON REQUEST

75

Combination. *John A. Suarez, location unknown*

A resume for a blue-collar worker who didn't quite finish his degree work but received supplemental education by specialized training, including military training.

ALISON PETERS

43 Danvers Street
Dobbs Ferry, NY   10522
(914) 693-8888

OBJECTIVE	A position as a Theatrical Electrician which will utilize my technical training and benefit from my experience with lighting, sound systems and back-stage electrical equipment.
PROFILE	• Organized, goal oriented individual with demonstrated ability to independently carry projects through to successful conclusion. • Punctual; possess strong time management skills and excellent sense of style. • Demonstrated ability to work well with others. • A quick learner; proven capacity to rapidly master information and technical skills.
SPECIAL SKILLS	• Knowledge and experience in all phases of residential circuitry. • Ability to wire circuits from fuse or breaker box to varied switches, outlets and fixtures. • Able to work with conduit and other types of cable. • Ability to install and maintain electrical equipment. • Possess expertise in stage lighting operations and maintenance. • Exposure to snaking wires through walls.
SPECIALIZED TRAINING	**SOUTHERN WESTCHESTER TECHNICAL CENTER,** Valhalla, NY **Majoring in:** <u>Trade Electricity</u> Graduation: June 1996 • Mastered two year curriculum in just over one year.
EXPERIENCE September 1993 - Present	**DOBBS FERRY PUBLIC LIBRARY,** Dobbs Ferry, NY **Page** • Assist patrons with wide variety of needs. • Accurately shelve returned books to the proper location. • Shelf Reading • Discharge books. **HUDSON RIVER MUSEUM,** Dobbs Ferry, NY **Administrative Assistant: Public Relations Department**

EDUCATION	**DOBBS FERRY HIGH SCHOOL,** Dobbs Ferry, NY Graduation: June 1996
	• Member: Stage Crew
	   Lend technical expertise to wide variety of concerts and stage productions.
	   Set-up, operate and ***maintain lighting, projection, and audio equipment.***
	• Extensive participation in both ***set design*** and ***consturction.***

PROFESSIONAL AFFILIATIONS	**V.I.C.A.** (*Vocational Industrial Clubs of America*) the major leadership organization for career minded students.
REFERENCES	Available upon request.

76

Combination. *Mark D. Berkowitz, Yorktown Heights, New York*

The individual's name is integrated with the page border—an interesting touch. Targeting of skills important to the job objective offsets experience in another field and a future degree.

Daniel D. Smithson

1880 McIntyre Drive
Flint, MI 48507

810-555-9231
or 810-555-8244

QUALIFICATIONS SUMMARY

➡ Associate degree in business supplemented by 15+ years' experience in manufacturing environments
➡ Proven ability to build rapport and camaraderie with hourly employees
➡ QS9000 trained and certified

AREAS OF EXPERTISE

➡ Production floor operations
➡ Production scheduling

➡ ISO9002 and QS9000
➡ Quality control

➡ Employee supervision
➡ Shipping and receiving

EMPLOYMENT HISTORY

GM TRUCK & BUS ASSEMBLY • Saginaw, MI   **Production Supervisor**   xxxx-Present
Contract position through Aerotek
- Manage activities of 35+ employees on Repair Deck and Special Paint Line.
- Lead area preparations for ISO certification including employee training, development of documentation, and interaction with auditor during certification inspections.
- Interact with union representatives; maintain understanding of grievance procedures, negotiate with involved parties to resolve grievances at lowest level whenever possible.
- Ensure adherence to components of local and national contracts.
- Utilize inhouse computer system for timekeeping and related documentation.

Accomplishments:
- Recognized by ISO9002 inspector for having thoroughly prepared area for inspection.
- Ended trend of short-tenure supervisors by earning respect and building rapport with employees in area which had seen 8 supervisors in 8 years.

VEMCO DISTRIBUTING • Flint, MI   **Dock Supervisor**   xxxx-xxxx
- Oversaw shipping and receiving of production parts to GM Truck & Bus Assembly.
- Ensured inbound loads were unloaded in timely manner; logged incoming traffic.

ALL-PRO MANUFACTURING • BURTON, MI   **Die Setter**   1995-1997
- Set progressive dies into automatic presses processing tonnage of 100-500 tons.
- Monitored robotic equipment including Allen-Bradley probe system.
- Ensured equipment operated under normal parameters; troubleshooted problems.
- Facilitated die change-overs; obtained first piece approval.
- Contributed to preparations for QS9000 certification inspections.

PLASTIC PRODUCTS INC. • Pontiac, MI   **Production Supervisor**   1990-1995
- Coordinated all aspects of production floor operations including quality control, production scheduling, and employee management.
- Oversaw proto-typing of all new tools.
- Involved in QS9000 certification process.

MASON MANUFACTURING • Mason, MI   **Line Leader**   1984-1990

EDUCATION

MICHIGAN TECH COLLEGE • Houghton, MI   **Production Management** courses   1982-1984
MOTT COMMUNITY COLLEGE • Flint, MI   **Associate of Business** (Dean's List)   1981

— REFERENCES AVAILABLE ON REQUEST —

77

Combination. *Janet L. Beckstrom, Flint, Michigan*

Bold lines and bold, all-uppercase section headings make it easy to see at a glance the design of this resume. Unusual bullets make key skills and qualifications stand out.

Michael D. Evans

2000 Bellingham Drive
Toledo, OH 43610

Residence: (419) 000-0000
Office: (313) 000-0000

Profile

Industrial Engineer

Sixteen years diversified engineering experience, with expertise in Industrial Engineering, as well as a working knowledge of Civil, Electrical, and Mechanical Engineering. Proven ability to enhance productivity and cut costs through workplace design, planning, and goal-setting.

Computer Expertise: CAD/CAM (Teach employee refresher classes), MAXIMO.

Experience

A MAJOR NATIONAL COMPANY ▪ Midtown, Michigan   1985 to Present

Industrial Engineer III (1990 - Present)
Industrial Engineer II (1988 - 1990)
Industrial Engineer (1987 - 1988)
Manufacturing Engineer (1985 - 1987)

Develop and maintain long-range plans for facility requirements at 16 factories. Develop systems to analyze production costs. Measure and record production factors as they relate to people and methods of operation. Identify production problems and recommend solutions to upper management. Redesign work environment to improve efficiency and cut costs. Coordinate new equipment installations and maintenance. Forecast future plant needs, and set goals for improving productivity.

Selected Accomplishments:

- Spearheaded the modernization of raw lumber processing operation at all of our major assembly plants. *Result:* A savings of $1.3 million corporate-wide.
- Coordinated installation of computer-controlled fabric cutting machines at 13 of our facilities. *Result:* A labor savings of $133,000 and an increase in quality.
- Conducted feasibility study for in-house mattress-making. *Result:* A savings of $500,000 at one facility; $205,000 at another facility.

GREYSON CORPORATION ▪ Milan, MI   1980 - 1985
Industrial Engineer

Education

UNIVERSITY OF TOLEDO ▪ Toledo, OH
Associate Degree in Industrial Engineering   1981

78

Combination. *Deborah L. Schuster, Newport, Michigan*

An impressive makeover. A Profile (Who I am) replaces an Objective (What I want to become). The rest of the resume "proves" the statements made in the Profile.

Michael D. Evans

2000 Bellingham Dr., Toledo, OH 43610
(419) 000-0000

Profile

Industrial Engineer

Sixteen years diversified engineering experience, with expertise in Industrial Engineering, as well as a working knowledge of Civil, Electrical, and Mechanical Engineering. Proven ability to enhance productivity and cut costs through workplace design, planning, and goal-setting.

Computer Expertise: CAD/CAM (Teach employee refresher classes), MAXIMO.

Experience

A MAJOR NATIONAL COMPANY ▪ Midtown, Michigan   1985 to Present

Industrial Engineer III (1990 - Present)
Industrial Engineer II (1988 - 1990)
Industrial Engineer (1987 - 1988)
Manufacturing Engineer (1985 - 1987)

Develop and maintain long-range plans for facility requirements at 16 factories. Develop systems to analyze production costs. Measure and record production factors as they relate to people and methods of operation. Identify production problems and recommend solutions to upper management. Redesign work environment to improve efficiency and cut costs. Coordinate new equipment installations and maintenance. Forecast future plant needs, and set goals for improving productivity.

Selected Accomplishments:

- Spearheaded the modernization of raw lumber processing operation at all of our major assembly plants. ***Result:*** A savings of $1.3 million corporate-wide.
- Coordinated installation of computer-controlled fabric cutting machines at 13 of our facilities. ***Result:*** A labor savings of $133,000 and an increase in quality.
- Conducted feasibility study for in-house mattress-making. ***Result:*** A savings of $500,000 at one facility; $205,000 at another facility.

GREYSON CORPORATION ▪ Milan, MI   1980 - 1985
Industrial Engineer

Education

UNIVERSITY OF TOLEDO ▪ Toledo, OH
Associate Degree in Industrial Engineering   1981

Combination. *Deborah L. Schuster, Newport, Michigan*

The same as Resume 78 but with the name enlarged and a logo added. Note that responsibilities are put in paragraph form, but accomplishments are listed with bullets.

RESUME

Troy H. Michaels

897 Stone, Trenton, MI 48183
Home: (313) 555-0000   Office: (810) 555-0000

Objective

Project Engineer in the Tool & Die Industry

Qualifications

Project Engineer (Tool & Die)
Journeyman Tool & Die Maker
Associate of Applied Science Degree

Experience

Project Engineer	July, 1994 - Present
Sampson Machine Tool & Die Company	Warren, Michigan

Estimate job cost, purchase materials, estimate and incorporate engineering changes, and track chosen die lines from design to final buyoff. Work with General Motors, Ford, and Budd engineers to ensure critical delivery dates are met. Arrange for and oversee outsourcing of machine work.

Diemaker, Journeyman/Apprentice	June, 1990 - July, 1994
T-Craft Incorporated	Fraser, Michigan

Duties included die processing, building of wheel cover dies, as well as progressive dies, machining, die tryout, and CNC Wire EDM.

Labor-Shipping/Receiving	June - September, 1987 - 1990
Monsanto Chemical Company	Trenton, Michigan

Education

Associate of Applied Science Degree, 1994
& Applied Technical Tool & Die Program, 1992
Macomb Community College, Warren, Michigan

CNC Wire EDM Operations and Programming
Leblond Makino Machine Tool Company, Mason, Ohio

Future Plans: Bachelor's Degree in Business

80

Combination. *Deborah L. Schuster, Newport, Michigan*

This resume was going to be faxed, so the writer customized a "By Design" template that would look good in black and white and withstand poor fax resolution.

EDWARD G. MASTERSON
456 River Lane
Trenton, MI 48183
(313) 555-0000

CAREER GOALS

Seeking growth opportunity in Design Engineering field.

EDUCATION

Computer Aided Design/Mechanical Design
(Associate Degree, Schoolcraft College, Dec. 1992)

Overall grade average: above 3.9 (on a 4.0 scale)
Member: Phi Theta Kappa fraternity

EXPERIENCE

2/93-Present;	AutoAlliance	Flat Rock, MI.

3-D Product and tooling design on PDGS software, using both the Prime Lundy and Unix systems. Set up an wrote manual for Plant Layout system using AutoCAD version 12. In order to improve efficiency, performed system administration duties on the Prime, DOS, and UNIX based systems.

1/91-12/92;	Attended Schoolcraft College.	Livonia, MI.

Utilized creative abilities by working as a musician.

3/83-1/91:	Renewal Piano & Furniture Restorers	Detroit, MI.

Owned company and supervised eight employees. Applied fine furniture finishes, refurbished and rebuilt antiques and piano. We built a reputation for producing quality work, while maintaining efficiency and profitability.

1981-1983;	Dearborn Piano and Organ Company.	Dearborn, MI.

Problem solving was my primary function while working as a Piano Tuner and Technician at Dearborn Piano and Organ Company.

1975-1981;	Traveled extensively as a Professional Musician.	

Completed apprenticeships in Piano Tuning, Piano Rebuilding, Furniture Finishing and Antique Restoration.

PERSONAL DATA

Strong commitment to continued education and improvement in all aspects of my life. Fueled by past successes, I strongly believe that the achievement of all of my goals is within my reach.

81

Chronological (Before). *Provided by Deborah L. Schuster, Newport, Michigan*

An over-50 person who recently changed careers from owner of a piano and furniture restoration business to design engineer. The writer reworked the original to fictionalize it.

Edward G. Masterson

456 River Lane, Trenton, MI 48183
(313) 555-0000

Profile

Design Engineer

Product designer with extensive experience in 3-D (PDGS). System administrator for Unix-based operating system. Extensive training in PDGS – have mastered most advanced techniques of the system. Fast learner....eager to learn new skills and new systems.

Excellent management, leadership, and supervisory skills, with the ability to train and motivate staff. Good troubleshooter, with a record of increasing efficiency and saving costs. Work well with people from all backgrounds; can serve as team leader or team member.

Experience

Design Engineer   February, 1993 - Present
AUTOALLIANCE   Flat Rock, Michigan

Design catalytic converters, springs, and stabilizer bars in 3-D, using PDGS software and Prime Lundy / Unix systems. Surfacing: Provide surfaces for toolroom and for prototype lab. Implement training for technical personnel. Supervise AutoCAD plant layout personnel. Redesign work elements to improve efficiency and cut costs. In order to improve efficiency, perform system administration duties on the Prime, DOS, and Unix-based systems. Earlier experience also included tooling design.

➢ Set up and wrote a training manual for Plant Layout System using AutoCAD version 12. Result: Within six weeks, the new system increased efficiency by 600%. It also enabled employees with little computer training to access and edit plant layout files.
➢ By troubleshooting data collection system, increased efficiency and greatly reduced the number of outside service calls, saving money as well as time.

Owner   March, 1983 - January, 1991
RENEWAL PIANO & FURNITURE RESTORERS   Detroit, Michigan

Education

Associate Degree, Computer Aided Design/Mechanical Design   1992
SCHOOLCRAFT COLLEGE   Livonia, Michigan

Studies toward Bachelor's Degree in Mechanical Engineering   (Ongoing)
LAWRENCE TECHNOLOGICAL UNIVERSITY   Southfield, Michigan

82

Combination (After). *Deborah L. Schuster, Newport, Michigan*

In this makeover the font for the name and headings is Grail New Condensed, and the lines were made with Word's Draw feature. The bullets are part of standard Word "Wingdings."

JAMES F. METZER

623 Woodland Boulevard, Daytona Beach, Florida 32100

Office: (904) 257-5826   Home: (904) 252-8214   Cell: (904) 202-5874   Email: metzer@bellsouth.net

SENIOR SALES EXECUTIVE / REGIONAL MANAGER

Advanced Technology Industry

Consistent Success in Start-up, Turnaround and High Growth Corporations

Top-producing management executive experienced in building and directing strong sales organizations. Expert qualifications in identifying and capturing market opportunity to accelerate expansion, penetrate new markets, and drive sustained revenue, market and earnings growth. Outstanding record of achievement in introducing technologically sophisticated products to government and commercial markets and managing account relationships.

PROFESSIONAL EXPERIENCE:

FIRSTBCS, INC., Orlando, Florida   1995 to Present

Vice President Sales – *Technology: Document Conversion Software*

Member of a 3-man team challenged to conceptualize, form and launch a marketing company specializing in the sale of document conversion software and conversion services to the federal and commercial markets. Held key responsibility for sales, marketing, new business development and account management.

- Established all organizational infrastructures and delivered sales of $1 million within first year and $9 million by 1999.
- Lobbied Congressman for allocation of funding and placed over 1500 systems within the DoD.

HITEK, INC., Washington, D.C.   1991 to 1995

Vice President Sales – *Technology: Document Conversion Software*

Recruited by VP Commercial Sales in San Diego to completely turnaround and restructure the sales operation. Upon accomplishment of turnaround mission, accepted offer to move to Washington, D.C and concentrate on improving federal government sales.

- Led aggressive reorganization of commercial sales operation and delivered revenues of $2.1 million, up from $467K.
- Closed over $4.2 million in DoD contracts in 1994.

CARDON TECHNOLOGY, Orlando, Florida   1989 to 1991

Regional Sales Manager – *Technology: Artificial Intelligence Software*

Led high growth initiatives through penetration into the Southeast market for this Boston-based software company. Developed a technologically-advanced artificial intelligence software prototype for presentations to commercial prospects.

- Closed major contracts with Siemens, Martin Marietta, and Lockheed and delivered over $4 million in revenues in less than 18 months.
- Achieved 288% of quota in 1990 and ranked second in sales in the company.
- Personally closed a $4 million order with Siemens.

83

Combination. *Beverly Harvey, Pierson, Florida*

Designated as a combination resume because of the opening profile, which calls attention to the individual's experience, qualifications, and record, this resume in all other respects is a

JAMES F. METZER

PROFESSIONAL EXPERIENCE (Continued):

CADMATRIX, INC., Orlando, Florida   1984 to 1989

Regional Sales Manager – *Technology: Electronic Design Software*

Recruited by VP of Sales to launch and manage the sales initiatives and operations for this start-up company and drive rapid growth throughout the Southeast region. Developed sales territories and established offices in Birmingham, Washington and Orlando, and developed a team of 11 representatives.

- Led startup operations and delivered sales of $50 million within five years.
- Drove growth revenues at a 40% rate while the industry average was only 12%.
- Personally achieved sales of $975,000 within first year and closed the first million dollar order in the second year.

M & E SYSTEMS, Orlando, Florida   1982 to 1984

Regional Sales Manager – *Technology: Mechanical and Electronic CAD Products*

Recruited by VP of Sales to turnaround declining business trend. Held full autonomy for all sales operations throughout the Orlando and Atlanta market and a sales team of six.

- Restructured the entire sales operation and developed Fortune 500 clients including Martin Marietta, Lockheed and NASA.

ELECTRO TECHNOLOGY, Orlando, Florida   1980 to 1982

Eastern Region Sales Manager – Computer Mapping Software

Established the Eastern region sales office for this Austin-based start-up company and hired a team of two representatives.

- Increased market share and generated revenues of $1.1 million in 1981 (115% of quota) and $1.8 million in 1982 (125% of quota).

AUTOMATION, INC., Orlando, Florida   1971 to 1980

Eastern Region OEM Sales Manager – Graphic Workstations

Began as a Sales Representative and was promoted through a series of increasingly responsible sales and management positions including District Manager and Eastern Region OEM Sales Manager. Independently led penetration into the Southeast market and built sales operations to support six offices and a team 14 sales representatives.

- Built OEM business from $12 million to over $37 million through major account development with major corporations.

EDUCATION:

University of Alabama, Huntsville, Alabama

---

chronological resume. Lines enclosing the profile make it visible as the lead area of interest. Bold and italic for the job positions make them stand out. Bullets point to noteworthy accomplishments. Note that each is quantified in dollars, numbers, or percentages.

John W. Engineer

5555 East Main Street
Elmira, NY 55555-3333
(555) 555-0000

Objective: A challenging position in Quality Engineering.

Experience: ELMIRA SYSTEMS COMPANY - *Elmira, NY*   1983-Present
Senior Lab Technician
Responsible for inspection of production line, engineering spec review, lab analysis including destructive testing, and all other facets of quality assurance. Interface with customers and vendors to design product and draw up specifications to meet customer criteria. Assure adherence to Federal regulations for military/government customers. Handle disposition of defective product. Provide extensive training to floor and engineering personnel in Quality Assurance procedures.

Notable Accomplishments:
- Saved company $80,000 by finding ways to use alternate parts to make scrap product functional.
- Devised improved automated product time-dating system, resulting in savings of approximately 1,000 man hours per year.
- Received recognition from U.S. Department of the Navy for locating alternate source of cabling, avoiding a four month delay in project completion.

ELMIRA ELECTRIC CORP. - *Elmira, NY*   1979-1983
Quality Control
Worked on production line preparing and testing tubes. Responsible for quality assurance.
Administrative Assistant
Responsible for mail distribution and complete charge of stores, including supervision of storeroom personnel.
Security
Provided plant security and fire protection.

Education: Elmira Community College - *Elmira, NY*
A.A.S., Engineering Technology - 1982

Multiple company-sponsored seminars/workshops including:

- Statistical Process Control
- Chemical Safety
- Leadership Training
- Group Problem-Solving
- Government Security and Regulations
- Written Communication Skills
- Basic Computer Skills

Interests: **Group Leader,** Elmira Systems Athletic Team
League Softball
League Bowling

References Available on Request

84

Chronological. *Betty Geller, Elmira, New York*

A design that is easy to comprehend at a glance. Boldfacing provides a path for reading down the page. Duties are in a paragraph, but accomplishments are listed and bulleted.

Brian D. Thomas

1435 Broadway Street, Vincennes, Indiana 47591   (812) 882-0294

PROFILE
- A fast learner and enthusiastic hard worker.
- Display excellent manual dexterity and hand-eye coordination.
- Dependable, able to persevere when presented with challenges.

EDUCATION
Vincennes University. Vincennes, Indiana: Associate in Construction Technology Degree: May 1995 (GPA 3.2)
Relevant Coursework: Architectural Drafting, Business, Retail Sales, Residential House Construction (including hands-on training), Framing, Carpentry, Concrete and Masonry, Mechanical Systems, Electrical Wiring.
- Received Bierhaus Full Tuition Scholarship.

Lincoln High School. Vincennes, Indiana: 1989-1993
Highlight: Performed in marching, concert, pep, and jazz bands (alto and baritone saxophone - percussion).

EXPERIENCE
Ralph R. Reeder & Sons, Inc. Indianapolis, Indiana: 1995-Present
Commercial roofing company laborer.

Bridges Construction Company. Mooresville, Indiana: 1994
Repaired water cooling towers at G. E. Plastics, Mt. Vernon, Indiana.
Gutted towers, removing and replacing damaged and/or rotting wood.
Repaired top decking.
- Developed more efficient method of clipping grids for more efficient and faster installation.
- Performed capably as a valuable team member.
- Attended *G. E. Safety Seminar* and gained working knowledge of tower structure and applications.

Melon Acres. Vincennes, Indiana: Laborer, 1991; Laborer/**Supervisor**, 1994
Supervised 20+ farm laborers. Motivated and communicated effectively with Spanish speaking labor. Operated farm equipment. Organized field work and shop pallets to efficiently process fruit from field to markets.
Assisted customers and market representatives.
- Gave careful attention to detail, insured that only quality produce was marketed.
- Developed excellent rapport with employer, team members, and laborers.

Kentucky Fried Chicken. Vincennes, Indiana: 1993-1994
Papa Johns Pizza. Vincennes, Indiana: 1992

COMMUNITY AFFILIATIONS
Boy Scouts of America. Vincennes, Indiana. **Patrol, Senior Patrol Leader, and Assistant Scout Master**. Assigned work rotations, supervised up to forty youth, and performed administrative duties. Mentored young scouts.
Junior Civitan Member.

Combination. *Colleen S. Jaracz, Vincennes, Indiana*

On one page with special bullets. The format changes near the bottom of the page: the last heading does not wrap, and text extends to both margins like the information at the top.

143

Richard Klein

129 Bussfield Road • Flint, MI 48501 • (810) 555-1234

EMPLOYMENT OBJECTIVE

Seeking a Product Design/Detail position utilizing extensive Unigraphics experience.

HIGHLIGHTS OF QUALIFICATIONS

- Highly skilled in Unigraphics detailing and modeling; over 1600 hours V12 solid modeling experience including electrical, instrument panel, and chassis components.
- Comprehensive knowledge of Cadillac Luxury Car Division (CLCD) data creation and data management standards.
- Trained in Unigraphics V10 (no hands-on experience due to lack of implementation by work group).
- Eight years experience as a Machinist, including six years experience as a Computerized Numerical Control (CNC) Machinist. Duties included programming, setup, and operation of various 3- and 4-axis horizontal and vertical machining centers, and training of other production operators.
- Accomplished in the use of Statistical Process Control (SPC) for quality control of manufacturing processes.
- Experienced in the use of Auto-Trol software under the AEGIS environment to digitize blueprints into 3-D wireframes for graphic illustration.
- Excellent written and verbal communication skills.

ACCOMPLISHMENTS

- Developed and implemented new standards of Diametric Geometric Dimensioning & Tolerancing (GDT) details for work group.
- Serve as unofficial leader and trainer of three other detailers.
- Member of Phi Theta Kappa (International Academic Honors Society); named to Delta College Dean's List (cumulative grade point average: **4.0**).

EDUCATION and TRAINING

Delta College • University Center, MI
Associate of Applied Science in Drafting and Design Technology   1995
Drafting Certificate of Achievement   1993
  Highlights of coursework: Advanced Dimensioning & Tolerancing, Descriptive Geometry, Geometric Dimensioning & Tolerancing. Served as Drafting Peer Tutor for 10 drafting classes.

General Motors Corporation • Flint, MI
Advanced Solid Modeling (six-week training seminar)   1993

Mott Community College • Flint, MI
Unigraphics Basic Drafting class   1993

EMPLOYMENT HISTORY

Unigraphics Senior Layout I	Quality Engineering • Flint, MI	xxxx-Present
Working on 2003 Cadillac Deville Instrument Panel Diametric details		
Computer Graphics Illustrator	Tech Products • Burton, MI	1995-xxxx
CNC Machinist	Galaxy Engineering • Lake Orion, MI	1994
CNC Machinist	Jackson Precision Machining • Jackson, MI	1988-1990 & 1993
Auto-Trol Graphic Illustrator	Masters Design • Port Huron, MI	1991-1992
Auto-Trol Graphic Illustrator	Express Graphics • Pontiac, MI	1990-1991
CNC Machinist	Simpson Machine Products • Auburn Hills, MI	1986-1988
Prototype Machinist	Gerrard Manufacturing • Northville, MI	1984-1986

86

Combination. *Janet L. Beckstrom, Flint, Michigan*

Headings in boxes extending to the left and right margins are the distinctive features of this resume. The boxes function like horizontal lines in separating the resume sections visually.

Lennart A. Cadman

113 South Fitzgerald • Grant, Michigan 48333 • (616) 955-5555

FOCUS: Mechanical, architectural, and production drafting, with emphasis in layout design. Proficient with Auto CAD and other software.

STUDIES: **Associates Degree in Drafting**
Muskegon Community College, Muskegon, Michigan   1991
Related coursework: Fundamentals of Industrial Drafting, Elements of Machine Drafting, Geometry of Drafting, Die Design, Jig & Fixture Design, Production, CAD, Advanced Computer Aided Design, Technical Math, NC/CNC Maching, Welding, Cast Metals

HISTORY: *CAD Consulting and Experience*

Gerber Products Company, Fremont, Michigan   1991 - present
Engineering Department
- ✔ Design and layout of food processing equipment and detail drawing of baby care products
- ✔ Work closely with engineers from conception to final production drawing resolving design details and problems
- ✔ Utilize computer-aided design (CAD) system to generate computer artwork for use in review and analyzing
- ✔ Make presentations to management to illustrate changes and updates for equipment and products
- ✔ Responsible for domestic and international plant layout designs and drawings for processing and packaging equipment for final presentation to USDA

Herman Miller, Inc., Zeeland, Michigan   1991 - 1992
- ✔ **CAD Technician** responsible for asbuilt architectural and HVAC drawings for manufacturing and environmental engineering departments

Muskegon Community College, Muskegon, Michigan   1990 - 1991
- ✔ **CAD Lab Assistant** responsible for assisting drafting instructors and students with Auto-CAD

Other Experience

Anderson Residential Construction, Montague, Michigan   1985 - 1988
- ✔ **Carpenter** involved in the construction of new homes and remodeling

Palco Lining, Stanton, California   1981 - 1985
- ✔ **Field Supervisor** responsible for hiring and training of labor and excavation of construction site

87

Chronological. *Pat Nieboer, Fremont, Michigan*

A font that calls to mind printed characters in drafting gives this resume a unique appearance. Novel headings (Focus, Studies, History) make the resume seem less formal.

DARREN S. HODGES
1066 Brown Boulevard
Wilmington, North Carolina 28403
(910) 123-4567

OBJECTIVE

A position where I can utilize my skills in Instrumentation Technology and strong experience in the construction industry.

SUMMARY

- Educational foundation in Instrumentation Technology including industrial electronic applications.
- Skilled in project management, supervising employees and budgeting.
- Team player—well developed interpersonal skills contribute to team success.
- Thorough knowledge of scheduling using Critical Path Analysis (CPM).
- Seek opportunities to learn new information and skills.

EDUCATION

Cape Fear Community College, Wilmington, NC
A.A.S. - Instrumentation Technology   May 1995

Divers Institute of Technology, Seattle, WA
Commercial Diving School   1986

SKILLS

Process and Control	Basic Electricity
Microprocessors	Computer Integrated Manufacturing
Digital Electronics	Physics Light and Sound
Physics Heat and Fluids	Programming C++
Electronics	Interfacing to Microcontrollers and
Programming PLC G.E.	Stepper Motors
Fanuc Series 90-30, Lm6	Industrial Motor Controls

- Designed and built a Heating and Cooling Loop for ISA Trade Show.
- Designed process plant, labeled and explained operation.
- Designed stop light with emergency system using GE Fanuc 90-30 PLC.

EXPERIENCE

Professional Diving and Construction, Wilmington, NC
Underwater Construction   1993 - Present
- Project management for commercial and governmental projects.

Coastal Engineering, Wilmington, NC
Project Inspector   1992 - 1993
- Acted as liaison between owner and contractor.
- Solved problems that occurred on all projects and made sure all projects were built to plans and specifications.
- Oversaw pay requests for approval, charge orders, and transmittals.

88

Combination. *Sandy Adcox Saburn, Wilmington, North Carolina*

A nontraditional student returning to college for a degree to broaden his career path. His impressive work history was related to his quest, so the writer made the resume two pages.

DARREN S. HODGES   Page 2

EXPERIENCE (CONTINUED)

Duncan Projects, Raleigh, NC
Site Superintendent   1991 - 1992
Assistant Superintendent
- Responsible for commercial renovations and additions.
- Scheduled activities using CPM to make sure no conflicts occurred.

Dynamic Developers, Raleigh, NC
Superintendent   1991

Johnson Construction, Cary and Durham, NC
Superintendent   1988 - 1990

Marine Constructors, Raleigh, NC
Assistant Superintendent   1987 - 1988

Creative Building, Wilmington, NC
Carpenter/Foreman/Assistant Superintendent   1982 - 1986

MILITARY EXPERIENCE

United States Navy, Norfolk, VA
Honorable Discharge

SCHOOL & COMMUNITY ACTIVITIES

Instrumentation Society of America - Current Member; Vice President of Student Chapter
Student Government Association - Vice President
Winter Park Optimist T-Ball Coach
Cape Fear Youth Soccer Association Coach
Wrightsville Beach Underwater Clean Up Society

SPECIAL TRAINING

CPR & First-Aid Qualified
Advanced SCUBA Diver
Rescue Diver

REFERENCES

Letters of reference and reference lists available upon request

With white space throughout, this two-page layout can be read more quickly than a one-page resume crammed with facts in tiny print—a point sometimes disregarded by supporters of one-page resumes.

WILL CASE

1234 - Totem Avenue SE ♦ Mytown, USA 99999 ♦ 555/555-5555

OBJECTIVE

A position in the commercial diving industry as a diver/tender where knowledge of construction, a high mechanical aptitude, and an unyielding commitment to safety can effectively contribute to the successful and profitable operation of an offshore or inland diving project.

EDUCATION

♦ DIVERS INSTITUTE, 1994-95
  Graduating June 2, 1995 with:

  ◊ Certificate of Training   ◊ Certificate-Hazardous Materials
  ◊ Certificate-Nondestructive Testing   ◊ Certificate-Advanced Scuba (#11194)
  ◊ Rigger Certification

QUALIFICATIONS

Five years of construction experience enhanced through specialized training in commercial diving. Highly reliable self-starter, disciplined, cooperative, and a supportive team member. Particularly skilled in problem-solving. Demonstrated ability to adapt to new equipment and technology. Trained in medical aspects of diving, with a clear understanding of how to handle decompression and treatment of disorders when decompression is not required. Trained in:

♦ *Breathing Apparatus:*   ♦ *Construction Techniques:*
  ◊ Desco Hard Hat ◊ KMB   ◊ Concrete (slabs, footing, retaining walls)
  ◊ Super Lite   ◊ Mark V   ◊ Foundation placement, repairs of pre-existing bases
  ◊ Swindel   ◊ Jap Hat   ◊ Utilities (sewer, gas, water, electric)
  ◊ Miller   ◊ Aquadine   ◊ Heavy equipment (bobcats, backhoes, trackhoes, etc.)
  ◊ Jack Brown Mask   ◊ Scaffolding and shoring systems

EXPERIENCE

PAT'S CONSTRUCTION, Anytown   *Laborer*   1993 to 1994

♦ Managed demolition and rebuild of Seymour's Restaurant and AJ's Supermarket:
  ◊ Took out second floor to make large room, shoring up roof
  ◊ Did all tile work and flooring, installed refrigeration system and cabinets
  ◊ Installed emergency lighting system
♦ Built an environmentally clean car wash from pre-caste concrete
♦ Assisted in laying 5 foundations: apartment complex, new home, and 3 underneath existing homes
♦ Roofed 10 houses and commercial buildings

XYZ CONSTRUCTION, Anytown   *Owner*   1992 to 1993
♦ Remodeled 19th century home, including new kitchen
♦ Built 2,400-square foot home with 16-feet by 30-feet truss system for roof

OTHER EXPERIENCE

UNIVERSITY UNOCAL, Mytown	*Mechanic, Cashier*	1995 to Present
STATE NATIONAL GUARD, Mytown	*Military Police E3*	1988 to 1994
BOSCOE BUILDING SUPPLY, Mytown	*Yard Worker*	1991 to 1992
HAMMER & NAILS SUPPLY, Mytown	*Yard Manager*	1990 to 1991

89

Combination. *Carole S. Barns, Woodinville, Washington*

Some fields consider experience and certain certifications as an alternative to a two-year degree. This commercial diver's interests were underwater construction and safety.

WILL CASE   Addendum to Résumé

1234-Totem Avenue SE ♦ Mytown, USA 99999 ♦ 555/555-5555

DIVING SPECIALTIES

- ♦ Diving Medicine Training
  - ◊ Able to judge severity of symptoms
  - ◊ Evaluate a stricken diver's response to therapy
  - ◊ Diagnosis and treatment of diving disorders when decompression is not required
  - ◊ Diagnosis of arterial gas embolism and other pulmonary overinflation syndrome and decompression sickness
  - ◊ Thermal stress
  - ◊ Near drowning
  - ◊ Operational hazards (blowup, otitis externa, underwater trauma, chemical injury, injuries caused by marine life
  - ◊ Medications and diving
  - ◊ Recompression therapy

- ♦ Nondestructive Testing Training
  - ◊ Origin and nature of defects
  - ◊ Characteristics of metal
  - ◊ Manufacturing of steel
  - ◊ Base metal product forms and finishing
  - ◊ Types and evaluations of defects
  - ◊ Magnetic particle testing methods
  - ◊ Ultrasonic testing methods

CONSTRUCTION EQUIPMENT AND TOOLS

- ♦ Heavy equipment
  - ◊ Bobcats and all accessories which attach
  - ◊ Backhoes
  - ◊ Excavators (trackhoes)
  - ◊ Trucks: 5 ton, 2 1/2 ton, boom
  - ◊ Forklifts
  - ◊ Cherry pickers
  - ◊ Manlifts

- ♦ Smaller Tools
  - ◊ Jackhammers
  - ◊ Large air drills
  - ◊ Gas-powered cut-off saws
  - ◊ Concrete floor saws
  - ◊ Hydraulic tools
  - ◊ Jumping jacks
  - ◊ Viber plates
  - ◊ Chain saws
  - ◊ Beam saws
  - ◊ Power trowel (under supervision)
  - ◊ Hilti gun
  - ◊ Arc and acetylene welders
  - ◊ Concrete vibrators
  - ◊ Large post hole diggers
  - ◊ Pressure washers
  - ◊ Sand blasters

TECHNICAL EQUIPMENT

- ◊ Laser leveling systems
- ◊ Builder's level
- ◊ Transits
- ◊ Scaffolding and shoring systems

This second page is an Addendum that was not attached to the resume but which the individual gave to interviewers. Such a page, matching the resume's style, is a strong addition. Similar bullets help to unify the two pages visually.

JERRY D. MORRELL ⸻⸻⸻⸻⸻⸻⸻⸻

235 W. Thayer Ave. ▪ Bismarck, ND 58501
(701) 255-3141

OBJECTIVE: Seeking a position in Construction Estimating, Sales, and/or Project Coordination.

SKILLS & ABILITIES:

Management
- Supervised and managed the building of a retail lumber yard.
- Ordered all lumber, hardware, and miscellaneous materials.
- Maintained inventory levels adequate to achieve sales goals.
- Hired, trained, and supervised all personnel.

Scheduling
- Set up production schedules based on customer needs and fabrication plant work loads.
- Coordinated shipment of finished product with customer's needs always in mind.
- Coordinated work crews from job to job.

Sales
- Generated over a quarter of a million dollars in annual sales from new retail lumber yard after only three (3) years of operation.
- Prepared labor and material bids from structural engineer drawings.
- Bid projects to general contractors throughout western North Dakota, eastern Montana, and parts of South Dakota.
- Consultations with homeowners resulted in successful sales record.

EDUCATION: BISMARCK STATE COLLEGE, Bismarck, ND
40 hour course in *Autocad* (Computer-aided drafting).

NORTH DAKOTA STATE SCHOOL OF SCIENCE, Wahpeton, ND
Associate Degree—Architectural Drafting and Estimating
Courses included drafting, estimating, math, blueprint reading, and public speaking.
Named to Who's Who in American Jr. Colleges.

MILITARY: **United States Air Force**
Aircraft Support—located parts not readily available from base supply.

American Legion Post 40
15 year member—serving two years as commander, also held various other offices and served on many committees.

HOBBIES: Enjoy outdoor activities including boating, hunting, and fishing. Also enjoy carpentry and woodworking.

REFERENCES: Available upon request.

90

Functional. *Claudia Stephenson, location unknown*

For an older worker, a resume with no Work Experience section or Work History! For many years he worked in a variety of jobs, levels, and locations, so the writer focused on his skills.

Marianne Valdez

Objective

Production specialist position that will benefit from my quality workmanship and reliable performance. Willing to work daytime or evening shifts.

Highlights of Qualifications

- Nearly 4 years experience as a production worker and supervisor.
- Detail-oriented, patient and meticulous. Possess excellent hand/eye coordination and manual dexterity.
- Learn new procedures quickly. Follow written and verbal directions well; do not hesitate to ask for clarifications.
- Enjoy fast-paced environment where quality and efficiency are valued. Team player who can be relied upon to deliver excellent work on time.

Work History

Production Worker
Pentronics, Murray, Utah, 1996-1997

- Assembled circuit boards installing capacitors, transformers, and resistors.
- Prepared small parts for circuit boards on a resistor cutter and a transformer spacer.

Bindery Worker
Consolidated Printing, West Valley City, Utah, 1996

- Packaged booklets, video and audio cassettes in plastic binders. Boxed materials for shipment. Operated shrink wrap machine.
- Collated and punch pressed documents, applied bindings.
- Performed quality control inspection of products before shipment to customers.
- Selected required materials from inventory. Restocked products and supplies.

Production Supervisor
Pen National, West Valley City, Utah, 1994

- Assembled computer cables. Crimped cables, wrapped wires, stripped and tinned wires, soldered cables together.
- Maintained production logs. Trained new workers.

Production Worker (various assignments)
Intermountain Temporaries, Salt Lake City, Utah, 1988-1990

- Assembled molding and inspected balloons for heart procedures. Removed burs from IV needles. Wrapped and inspected IV tubes. Packaged surgical scrub brushes.
- Cleaned homes and hotels. Washed and detailed cars for airport. Packaged airline meals.
- Assembled exercise equipment.
- Manufactured furniture, gluing parts and cutting sponge on a wire cutter machine.
- Packaged nuts, bolts, screws, springs, books, cards in bags and boxes.

Education and Training

People Helping People, Salt Lake City, Utah, 1999
Solder class, Pen National, West Valley City, Utah, 1994
G.E.D., University of Utah, Salt Lake City, Utah, 1992
General Studies, Bingham High School, Riverton, Utah

Address

555 East 5500 South #55 • Salt Lake City, UT 84115 • (801) 555-5555

91

Combination. *Lynn P. Andenoro, Salt Lake City, Utah*

A resume that can be made as a one-row, three-column table with horizontal and vertical lines deleted. Section headings in the left column are easily seen. Positions are in boldface.

Raymond E. Perry

5555 Dumore Road   Deer Lodge, MT 59722   (406) 555-5555

CAREER OBJECTIVE

Surveying/Material Testing position.

EDUCATION

DIVISION OF TECHNOLOGY, MONTANA TECH OF THE U of M, Butte, MT
A.A.S. - CIVIL ENGINEERING TECHNOLOGY, May 1995

MONTANA COLLEGE OF MINERAL SCIENCE AND TECHNOLOGY, Butte, MT
ACCOUNTING/COMPUTER CURRICULUM

TECHNICAL COURSEWORK

- Plane Surveying I, II
- Materials Testing
- Strengths of Materials
- Civil Engineering Drafting

- AutoCAD I, II
- Materials Science
- Engineering Physics
- Statics

SPECIAL PROJECTS

Montana State Department of Transportation Internship - performed soils testing.

Grant Kohrs Ranch - surveyed and mapped buildings, fences, etc.

SKILLS AND ABILITIES

MACHINERY
- Skilled in operation of backhoes, front-end loaders, 2-ton trucks, catapillers, log skidders, jackhammers, and dump trucks.
- Proficient in operating swathers, balers, combines and tractors.
- Practiced in using chainsaws, post drivers, and post hole augers.
- Perform ranching duties including fencing, cultivating, weed spraying, irrigating using necessary equipment.
- Experienced in welding and mechanical maintenance/repair.

COMMUNICATION
- Extensive experience teaching/advising young people from various academic, economic and cultural backgrounds.
- Able to relate to all age groups due to easy-going personality.
- Good listener -- functions well in team and individual project settings.

WORK HISTORY

1/93 - Present   EMORY PUBLIC SCHOOLS, DISTRICT #10, Emory, MT
                    SUBSTITUTE ENGINEER

3/78 - Present   BAR 555 RANCH, Deer Lodge, MT
                    OWNER/OPERATOR

1/92 - 6/94   EMORY PUBLIC SCHOOLS, DISTRICT #10, Emory, MT
                    SUBSTITUTE TEACHER

COMMUNITY ACTIVITIES

- Past Exalted Ruler, Youth Activities Chairman, B.P.O.E., Deer Lodge Elks Lodge.
- Past Advisory Council Chairman, Deer Lodge Chapter of Future Farmers of America.

92

Combination. *Kathlene Y. McNamee, Butte, Montana*

This writer uses a "hook" to organize a resume. The hook for this resume was stating the individual's machinery skills and highlighting his crossover skills to his new career path.

Environment

Resumes at a Glance

RESUME NO.	LAST OR CURRENT OCCUPATION	GOAL	PAGE
93.	Golf Course Superintendent	Not specified	155
94.	Field Guide	Not specified	156
95.	Environmental Technician	Position in hazardous/ solid waste management	157
96.	General Manager, country club	General Manager, country club	158
97.	Golf Course Intern	Golf Course Superintendent	160
98.	Senior Environmental Coordinator	Not specified	162

Lyle V. Snodgrass

9500 Hickory Road
Homestead, Maryland 22226
(505) 555-9392

Qualifications . . .

➤ Degree in Golf Course Technology with ten years of course maintenance experience
➤ Responsible environmentalist and certified commercial pesticide applicator
➤ Highly skilled and knowledgeable in overseeding, irrigation, construction, and grow-in
➤ Superior public relations skills and a propensity for effective personnel management
➤ Well-established working relationships with national equipment and supplies vendors
➤ Creative problem solver with a reputation as a proficient, authoritative decision maker
➤ Strong believer in designing maintenance programs that continually improve course quality

Education . . .

➤ Associate Degree in Agriculture with a major in Golf Course Technology, 1988
Horry-Georgetown Technical College, Conway, South Carolina, GPA 3.66/4.0
➤ Golf Course Superintendents Association Continuing Education:
  • Water Quality, Dallas, Texas, 1994
  • Options and Their Applications in Pest Management, Dallas, Texas, 1994
  • Disease Identification and Control, Birmingham, Alabama, 1989

Professional Experience . . .

➤ **Superintendent**   1992 to Present
Towering Oaks Country Club, Homestead, Maryland
  • Hire and manage the activities of six full-time and eight seasonal employees
  • Renovated the greenside irrigation system, installing all new heads and valving
  • Rebuilt one greens complex and two tee complexes
  • Refurbished the bunkers and installed proper drainage
➤ **Assistant Superintendent**   1990 to 1992
Haig Point Club, Daufuskie Island, South Carolina
  • Supervised fifteen permanent and three seasonal employees
  • Scheduled maintenance for and oversaw operation of computerized irrigation system
  • Supervised applications of pesticides and fertilizers; managed overseeding program
➤ **Chemical Applicator**   1989 to 1990
Augusta National Golf Club, Augusta, Georgia
  • Crew leader during the 1990 Masters tournament
  • Applied chemicals, constructed tees and greens, and controlled supply inventories
➤ **Assistant Superintendent**   1988 to 1989
St. Ives Country Club, Duluth, Georgia
  • Participated in initial course construction, from dirt through grassing
  • Managed construction crew of thirty, including non-English speaking workers
➤ **Internships**   1986 to 1988
Gator Hole Golf Course, North Myrtle Beach, South Carolina
Waterway Hills Golf Course, Myrtle Beach, South Carolina

Professional Affiliations . . .

➤ Class A Member, Golf Course Superintendents Association of America
➤ Member, West Virginia Golf Course Superintendents Association

93

Combination. *Barbie Dallmann, Charleston, West Virginia*

Graphics, Wingding and conventional bullets, boldfacing, and ellipses (. . .) after headings are
features of this resume for a Golf Pro trying to double his salary at a private club.

Kelley A. Brandon

116 East Smithfield Drive ● Millerton, Pennsylvania 00000 ● 717-000-0000

Professional Objective

To foster an appreciation of **nature** in children
in order to nurture **environmentally conscious** individuals.

Profile

- Lifelong interest in and study of birds, plants and animals enhanced by educationally-focused studies and experience at nature centers.
- Ability to conceptualize, develop and implement age-appropriate activities designed to encourage hands-on participation and to stimulate curiosity.
- Thoroughly enjoy interacting with the very young child through geriatric population in a manner that is conducive to creating a learning environment through open dialogue.

Education

SUNY Delhi, Delhi, New York
A.S. - Liberal Arts; Concentration: **Sciences**, May 1992
  *   Honor Forum; GPA: 3.5/4.0
  -     Science Courses: Biology, Chemistry, Geology & Astronomy
  -     Additional Studies: **Field Guide Training Course**
  -     Attended: NYS Outdoor Education Assoc. Conference which focused on collaboration of schools and nature centers to develop and present environmental programs.

Elmira Free Academy, Elmira, New York
Regents Diploma, June 1981
  *   Selected to provide support to elementary age students with emotional problems.

Experience

Valley View Nature Center, Endicott, New York
Field Guide, April 1991 to 1993
  -     Conducted tailored nature walks/hikes to meet comprehension level of students.
  -     Incorporated themes, role playing and a variety of era games to encourage interaction and to provide a learning experience on nature's impact on daily living.
  *   Recipient of the Eleanor Mercy Inroy Award.
Honors Project - Independent Research, 1992
  -     Developed a proposal for the Binghamon Area School District which would comply with NYS Regents Science Curriculum Guidelines. Proposal encompassed the development and instruction of hands-on activity-based projects at the Nature Center which would complement classroom studies.
  *   Proposal was enthusiastically received by Joseph Brown, Founder/Director of the Nature Center & Professor of Biology at SUNY Delhi, as well as School District administrators. Funding is currently being sought through grants.
Volunteer, 1992 to present
  -     Develop and conduct nature tours/hands-on activities to pre-schoolers.

Spencer Crest Nature Center, Corning, New York
Volunteer, 1990 to present
  -     Provide a stimulating educational experience for home-schooled students,
  -     Assisted with Winter Bird Program.

Mustico's, 1991 to present; *Spruce Inn,* 1993; *Pizza Hut,* 1984 to 1987, Binghamton, New York
Customer Service/Management
  -     Experienced in training and supervision of a staff of up to 25.
  -     Well versed in customer relations working with diverse populations.

94

Combination. *Lynda C. Grier, Elmira Heights, New York*

A resume for an individual returning to work to pursue her interest in nature and environmental issues. Volunteer work was part of her preparation for her work field.

HENRY W. SMITH, CHMM

| 541 Ventura Street | Madison, Wisconsin 53666 | (608) 562-1234 |

OBJECTIVE

To properly manage hazardous and solid waste to comply with local, state, and federal environmental regulations at the corporate level.

EDUCATION

COMMUNITY TECHNICAL COLLEGE, Janesville, WI

Associate Degree in Applied Science, Hazardous Material Technician, 1993
  Hazardous Materials Technician Training, 1993
  Hazardous Waste Site Worker Safety, 1993
  Hazardous Material Training Program, 1993
  Hazardous Waste Site/General Supervisor Program, 1993

CERTIFICATIONS AND MEMBERSHIPS

Certified Hazardous Material Manager, CHMM, #1234
Superfund Site Worker Training for OSHA 29 CFR 1910.120
Certified State of Wisconsin Wastewater Treatment Plant Operator #12345
Certified Site Assessor, 1994
Certified Remover/Cleaner, 1994
Federation of Environmental Technologists (FET) - Member

WORK EXPERIENCE

VIRGINIA CORPORATION, Madison, WI   1993-Present
Corporate Manufacturing Services/Environmental Compliance and Chemicals Management Department
Environmental Technician, CHMM
Responsible for compliance with local, state, and federal environmental regulations. Develop compliance documents: SPCC Plans, Contingency Plans, Spill Reporting Forms, and Waste Analysis Plans. Establish satellite inspection procedures for all facilities. Maintain compliance records and prepare manifests, sampling plans, reports, and other hazardous waste documents including site specific waste handling procedures. Completed PCB capacitor removal project. Implemented UST tank management program for thirty-three tanks. Trained employees on DOT, OSHA, and NR 600 requirements. Inspected facilities to correct deficiencies in waste handling areas. Conduct environmental audits at vendor facilities. Assisted in Title V air permits, stack testing, and training requirements.

ENVIRONMENT PLUS CONSULTING, Racine, WI   1992-1993
Environmental Technician
Installation of remedial systems at LUST sites throughout Wisconsin.

COMMUNITY TECHNICAL COLLEGE, Madison, WI   1992
Hazardous Material Equipment Technician (Part-time)
Assisted with OSHA Training 1910.120.

WASTE HANDLERS INC., Kenosha, WI   1983-1991
Project Coordinator
Negotiated with municipalities, private industry, and landowners to coordinate liquid agricultural waste disposal projects throughout the Midwest. Worked with DNR to secure site approvals and as a liaison between private industry and municipalities. Performed sludge analysis and calculated application rate, then coordinated application work teams. Worked with US Geological surveys for soil and soils testing. Assisted with Emergency Response training programs and worked with all safety equipment. Interpreted Material Safety Data Sheets, then distributed them to customers and employees. Completed state reports and disposal records.

REFERENCES AVAILABLE UPON REQUEST

95

Combination. *Marie Keenen Mansheim, location unknown*

A Certifications and Memberships section functions as a Skills section, making the line thin here between a chronological resume and a combination resume. Note the capital letters.

Robert L. Norwood

3220 Mountain Ridge Road   Montgomery, Alabama 36100   ☎ [334] 555 -1575 Residence

"In club management, he has no peers."
– Two star general and club board chairman

"Bob Norwood is the finest club manager I have known in over 27 years."
– Executive and board member

"Brilliant organizer."
– Senior decision maker

OBJECTIVE: To give members of The Four Hills Country Club unsurpassed service and outstanding value.

PROFILE: ❖ Seasoned manager in all aspects of club operations ❖ Expert in delivering great service and great value ❖ Master at building and leading teams of employees to *want* to be the best.

SELECTED EXAMPLES OF SUCCESS:

SEASONED MANAGER WHO GETS RESULTS: Selected to manage a club that might not have met its next payroll. Literally lived in the club for the first week. Turned fragmented staff into well-trained team. Put reputation on the line with members.

Payoffs: **Cut $19,000 a month** in personnel costs without reducing staff. Designed and executed programs that attracted *and kept* membership. One indicator of success: **food revenue up** nearly **50% in four months**.

DELIVERING GREAT SERVICE AND GREAT VALUE: Not satisfied with the high membership he inherited when hired as new manager. "Sparkplug" behind an all new program of benefits for families: gave them more services at great savings. Children's serving line — built to their height — a big success.

Payoffs: **Membership up 18%** in eighteen months. Cash flow considerably improved.

LEADING EMPLOYEES TO BE THEIR BEST: Transformed the cleaning staff from "time-clock punchers" to pros. Gave them new uniforms, new lockers — and total responsibility for making our club shine.

Payoffs: **Sick leave dropped by 60%** across the board. **Turnover went** from nearly 100% a year **to zero**. All our staff couldn't wait to get to work. Members prouder than ever to show visitors their club.

96

Combination. *Donald Orlando, Montgomery, Alabama*

Three testimonials capture attention and sell the individual before any part of the rest of the resume is read. After the testimonials, the reader is primed to side with all of the glowing

Robert L. Norwood, General Manager   [334] 555-1575 Residence

WORK HISTORY:

❖ *General Manager*, Awahnee Country Club, Clartin, Alabama
  1996 – Present

  Hired to guide $2 million restoration and expansion for this full-service, 600-member club. Facilities include dining room, grill, snack bar, swimming pool, tennis courts, 18-hole golf course, and driving range.

More than 25 years of increasing responsibility in club management with the United States Air Force, including these most recent positions:

❖ *Club Manager,* Sharpton Officers' Club, Sharpton Air Force Base, Texas, January 1994 – 1996

  Chosen over 33 other experienced applicants, including others with years more experience, to manage this 3,000-member club. Facility entertained very senior decision makers from Federal and state governments, business and community leaders, and high ranking representatives of some 32 foreign governments. Supervised staff of 83.

❖ *Club Manager* later promoted to *General Manager,* Club Complex, Royal Air Force Compton, Compton, England, June 1991 – January 1994

  Selected from 25 well-qualified applicants to run this complex of three clubs. Served nearly 2,200 members and their families. Provided nearly 20% return on sales despite currency fluctuations that eroded buying power. Responsible for 200 full and part time employees.

❖ *Director,* International Club Complex, Brunssum, The Netherlands, June 1983 – December 1989

  Reported directly to boards and committees representing 16 foreign nations. Turned around restaurant losses of $50,000 a year to generate profits of $200,000 annually. Oversaw $100,000 in improvements in a single year: all completed on time, all paid for before renovations completed. Led staff of 200.

CERTIFICATIONS:

❖ In top two percent of managers who held credentials as a Certified Military Club Executive, International Military Club Executive Association, 1978.

❖ Formerly Air Force's chief instructor preparing club managers to handle food and beverage operations, manage finances, conduct marketing and accommodate special functions.

MEMBERSHIP:

❖ Club Managers Association of America

EDUCATION:

❖ Associate of Arts, **Restaurant Management,** Community College of the Air Force, Maxwell Air Force Base, Alabama, June 1978

Page two

information that follows. Achievements are presented as examples of success and as payoffs to the employer. Unusual bullets point to managerial positions. Stellar achievements and top certifications close the deal. At the end, who cares about only an associate's degree?

Paul R. Schultz

Current Address: 1260 Oak Ridge, Apartment 306, East Lansing, Michigan 48823
Current Phone: (517) 332-5180
Home Address: 4187 Broomhead Road, Williamsburg, Michigan 49690
Home Phone: (616) 267-9304

OBJECTIVE AND GOAL

Golf Course Superintendent Position.
My professional goal is to manage the grounds of a U.S. Open Tournament.

PROFILE

- Knowledgeable of turf types, diseases, and insects.
- Skilled in soil management and artistic spacial landscape design. Utilize research skills to incorporate best-suited trees, shrubs, and flowers to achieve maximum aesthetic value.
- Self-motivated, with quality leadership potential.
- Excellent work ethic, flexible, eager to learn, easy going.
- Patient and calm, hard working, fascinated with the profession. Able to accept and efficiently solve challenges as they occur.
- Enjoy physical aspects of Turfgrass Management.
- Computer experience in program set-up, data entry, irrigation design programs (to determine water usage and evaporation quotas), WordPerfect, QuatroPro.

EDUCATION (Personally financed 100% of education)

Michigan State University. East Lansing, Michigan: 1993-1995
Turfgrass Management, graduating in March 1995
Relevant Coursework: Technical Mathematics, Fertilizer and Pesticide Application Technology, Agricultural Chemistry, Engine and Equipment Maintenance, Communication and Business Management

EXPERIENCE

The Farm Golf Club. Rocky Face, Georgia: 1994
Intern.
Duties: Mowed and fertilized fairways, greens, tees and landscaped areas. Repaired and maintained irrigation heads. Completed tee construction projects, including resodding. Maintained course set-up and grounds, placed pins on greens, and moved tee markers. Performed bunker renovations, replacing liners as needed for proper weed control. Sprigged Bermuda Grass throughout course rough.

- Initiated power washing program to clear course of mud accumulating from tornado.
- Suggested improvements on sod removal procedure by promoting machine use in appropriate areas instead of hand labor, resulting in time saved and increased efficiency.

97

Combination. *Colleen S. Jaracz, Vincennes, Indiana*

Distinctive pencil bullets on this page highlight the individual's knowledge, skills, traits, work ethic, interests, and computer experience—matters that set him apart from the crowd.

Paul R. Schultz

EXPERIENCE (Continued)

Twin Beach Country Club. West Bloomfield, Michigan: 1988-1993
Grounds Foreman. 1990-1992
<u>Supervised club grounds and golf course during management transition</u>.
Duties: Screened, hired, trained, scheduled and supervised four full-time and two part-time grounds employees. Evaluated employees monthly. Met with board, reporting ground conditions, work scheduled and work in progress. Justified budget recommendations. Managed inventory, maintained equipment, ordered materials and supplies. Performed mechanical duties on all types of equipment (lawn mowers, trucks, etc.), including irrigation system.

- Established work procedure routines insuring frequent job rotation of employees to relieve boredom, rewarded employees through praise and incentives.

- Hands on management style, willing to work with employees as needed to complete assignments right the first time, gaining their respect and striving to make each task as interesting as possible.

- Quickly assessed streaked hydraulic leak on fairway, initiated broom, soap and water procedure before hydraulic fluids ruined turf, saving cost and substantial resodding time.

- Initiated efficient mowing patterns to save time and improve course appearance by insuring a smooth and accurate cut. Suggested purchase of mowing equipment to implement increased efficiency and cost effectiveness.

- Developed irrigation procedures and suggested alternate ways of fixing leaks and handling break downs.

- Repaired blower during leaf pick-up season by jury-rigging motor from used blower parts.

Crew Leader. 1988-1990

PROFESSIONAL SEMINARS

Construction and Trades Seminary, Pontiac, Michigan: 1989
Landscape Design Certificate. Oakland Technical Center, Walled Lake, Michigan: 1988-1989
Jacobson Mechanic Training Program, Racine, Wisconsin: 1992

AWARD AND PROFESSIONAL AFFILIATIONS

Oakland Technical Center. **Academic Landscaping Award: 1989**

Michigan Turfgrass Foundation
Member of GCSAA

Bullets on this page highlight the individual's achievements and management style. These bullets show how the individual has saved his employer money and enhanced his employer's reputation. Boldfacing makes the job positions stand out in a visual sweep of the resume.

Thomas Haslinger

R.D. #2, Box 189A
Travis, LA 00000
(555) 555-5555

SUMMARY OF EXPERIENCE

Thirty years of pipeline experience including project manager, superintendent, technical analysis, monitoring of construction compliance and broad-scope environmental field work. These projects have ranged from small gathering systems and cross-country pipelines to unique systems, such as anhydrous ammonia, urea and brine. Involved in over 35 projects in 20 states, lasting from one month to over a year, which have been located in a variety of settings, ranging from rural agricultural areas to densely populated areas and industrial sites. Also conversant in D.O.T. safety and API 1104 and ASME codes.

QUALIFICATIONS

Environmental Consulting

- Assure compliance with Environmental Protection Regulations.
- Coordination of all construction and environmental activities with the appropriate federal, state and local regulatory agencies.
- Preparation of all required status and compliance reports.
- Provide complete environmental training for all on-site personnel.
- Daily on-site observation of construction activities to adhere to environmental commitments as defined by the contract documents, specifications, drawings, federal, state and local permits, applicable laws and regulations, environmental plans, and good environmental practices.
- Worked with Corps of Engineers on projects in Pennsylvania, Maryland and Florida.
- Liaison to natural resources and regulatory agencies on numerous projects.
- Participated in Environmental Impact studies and a Historic Preservation study.
- Established routes for new pipelines, permitting, preparing soil and erosion plans, coordinating construction activities with regulatory agencies.
- While working in environmentally-sensitive areas, have had my crews featured in articles and on cover photos for different trade publications (*Pipeline Digest* and *Pipeline Industry*).

Pipeline Inspection

- As Chief Inspector, have been responsible for:
  — Gas well hookups and construction of mainline, natural gas, jet fuel, urea, and anhydrous ammonia pipelines, as well as necessary injection and receiving stations
  — Hydrotesting and commissioning of urea systems
  — Requalification of jet fuel pipelines, and relocation and change-outs of anhydrous ammonia pipeline
  — Installation of metering facilities
  — Compliance of subcontractors with the various codes and procedures, materials control, cost control, and project management
  — Inspection of coating process for internal coating of jet fuel pipelines.

Pipeline Construction

- Have experience in and in-depth knowledge of all areas of pipeline construction including installation of pipelines and meter stations, construction of well locations and roadways, as well as clean-up and restoration after construction.

98

Combination. *Catherine Seebald, Wellsville, New York*

Three pages are used for this Environmental Consultant/Pipeline Inspector with 30 years of experience. Qualifications are grouped according to three categories for easier reading.

Thomas Haslinger

PROFESSIONAL EXPERIENCE

1994–Present   **Senior Environmental Coordinator** — Spreads 8 and 9 (Third Party)
FLORIDA GAS TRANSMISSION, Phase III Expansion Project

1990–1993   **Chief Environmental Compliance Inspector** (Third Party)
CONSOLIDATED NATURAL GAS TRANSMISSION

JOYCE WESTERN CORPORATION
1985–1990   **Superintendent**
     Also responsible for all environmental issues related to the Joyce-owned companies.
     Crew Superintendent — 1982
     Construction of 10 miles, 12" natural gas pipeline for National Fuel Gas at Cooks Forest, PA.
     Cleanup Foreman/Construction — 1979, 1980
     Construction of 26 miles, 30" pipeline for Consolidated Natural Gas Transmission.

1985   **Chief Inspector**
ATOKA PIPELINE, McAlester, OK
     Gas well hookups and construction of 50 miles of 12" mainline.

1984   **Chief Inspector**
CARSWELL PIPELINE COMPANY, Abilene, TX
     Construction of 80 miles of 6" jet fuel pipeline.

     Chief Inspector
PRIDE REFINING, Abilene, TX
     Requalification of 25 miles of 6" jet fuel pipelines, installed metering facilities. Prepared 50 miles of 6" pipeline for internal coating. Inspected the coating process.

1983   **Welding Inspector**
TAMPA ELECTRIC COMPANY, Tampa, FL
     Responsible for assurance of codes and procedures promptly instituted throughout construction of a fossil fuel power plant.

TAMPA BAY PIPELINE, Tampa, FL (Third Party)
1979, 1982   **Chief Inspector**
     • Relocation and change-outs of 6" anhydrous ammonia pipeline.
     • Construction of 22 miles of 4" lateral pipeline and 2 receiving stations.
     Foreman — 1974–1977
     Construction of pipelines for natural gas, oil and other petroleum products.
     Roustabout — 1970–1973

1981, 1982   **Chief Inspector**
TAMPA PIPELINE TRANSPORT COMPANY, Tampa, FL
     Building 13 miles of 4" anhydrous ammonia pipeline, including injection and receiving stations.

Professional Experience spans two pages but covers only the last half of the individual's career. Years of employment are centered within a left column. Boldfacing the job positions makes them easy to spot at a glance. Once a job is done, the inspector must find a new job.

Thomas Haslinger

PROFESSIONAL EXPERIENCE (continued)

1981	**Chief Inspector**

SYSTEM SERVICES & INDUSTRIAL CORP., Garden City, GA
14 miles of 6" anhydrous ammonia pipeline, including injection and receiving stations.

1980   **Chief Inspector**
INTERNATIONAL MINERAL & CHEMICAL CORP., Bainbridge, GA
Construction of 15 miles of 8" urea pipeline, including injection and receiving stations, hydrotesting and commissioning.

Chief Inspector
AIRCRAFT SERVICES, Tampa Airport, Tampa, FL
Relocation of 6" jet fuel line for construction of new hangers, and construction of a new 8" fuel pipeline and refueling system.

1979   **Chief Inspector**, (Third Party)
CHRISTINA RESOURCES, Riverside, FL
Construction of 18 miles of anhydrous ammonia line.

Chief Inspector
ST. LOUIS PIPELINE COMPANY, St. Louis, MO
Lowering and updating 65 miles of 6" jet fuel pipeline.

EDUCATION   **A.A.S. in Construction Engineering Technology** — 1968
State University of New York, Alfred, NY

ADDITIONAL TRAINING   Erosion and Sediment Control and Stormwater Management Course — 1995
SYRACUSE UNIVERSITY, Syracuse, NY

Compliance Training:
- Hazardous Waste Operations and Emergency Response (HAZWOPER)
- Federal Energy Regulatory Commission training
- Environmental auditing and natural resources damage assessment

Continuing studies of Agronomy and Soils Science — 1981
STATE UNIVERSITY OF NEW YORK, Alfred, NY

Completed Industrial Radiology School — 1970
Radiation Safety Schools (annually) — 1971–1974
Consolidated X-Ray, Woodbridge, NJ

Have also attended many workshops, courses, seminars, and conferences sponsored by numerous states and state agencies.

CERTIFICATES   Level III Radiography Certification, March 1983

Job hopping is therefore not a problem with this work record: frequent job changing goes with the position. The constant is the role of Chief Inspector. A recent university course and a note about state training events show that the person updates his education.

Health Care

Resumes at a Glance

RESUME NO.	LAST OR CURRENT OCCUPATION	GOAL	PAGE
99.	Materials Manager	Practical Nurse	167
100.	Training Coordinator	Not specified	168
101.	Charge Nurse	Staff nursing position	170
102.	Staff Nurse: Same Day Surgery	Nurse in emergency room or immediate care center	172
103.	Nurse Technician/Mental Health Assistant	Registered Nurse	173
104.	Certified Hospice Nurse/Case Manager	Not specified	174
105.	Nursing Supervisor/RN	Not specified	175
106.	Not specified	Registered Nurse	176
107.	Registered Nurse	Registered Nurse	177
108.	Registered Nurse	Registered Nurse	178
109.	Psychiatric Nurse Supervisor	Nursing position	180
110.	Nursing Services Manager/Staff Nurse	Not specified	182
111.	Nurse Coordinator, Radiology	Not specified	183
112.	Home Health Care Registered Nurse	Not specified	184
113.	Respiratory Technician	Respiratory Therapist	185
114.	Secretary	Registered Nurse	186
115.	ER Registration Clerk	Not specified	187
116.	Licensed Vocational Nurse	Position in nurse training	188
117.	Registered Nurse	Not specified	189
118.	Rehab Equipment Specialist	Not specified	190
119.	Staff Nurse	Emergency Room Nurse	192
120.	Occupational Therapist Aide	Occupational Therapist Assistant	193
121.	Occupational Therapist Aide	Pediatric COTA position	194
122.	Shift Leader/Cashier/Cashier Trainer	Physical Therapist Assistant	195

RESUME NO.	LAST OR CURRENT OCCUPATION	GOAL	PAGE
123.	Not specified	Physical Therapy Assistant	196
124.	Home Health Aide	Registered Nurse	197
125.	Case Manager/Community Health Nurse	Not specified	198
126.	Account Specialist—Health Resources	Not specified	200
127.	Medical Assistant/Laboratory Technician	Medical Assistant/Laboratory Technician	201
128.	Certified Medical Transcriptionist and Accredited Records Technician	Not specified	202
129.	Senior Health Care Consultant	Not specified	204
130.	Certified Nursing Assistant	Not specified	205
131.	Psychic	Not specified	206

ELIZABETH M. BARKLEY
104 Maple St.
Montgomery, AL 00000
(000) 000-0000

PROFILE: *Licensed Practical Nurse desirous of securing a nursing position in fulfillment of a lifelong dream. Stable and promotable with over seventeen years with the same organization.*

EDUCATION:

Tri-County Technical College, Montgomery, AL
Practical Nursing   1995

Tri-County Technical College, Montgomery, AL
A.S. Business Education   1989

Honors:

Distinguished Practical Nurse Graduate
Magnolia Leadership Graduate
Board of Visitors - Tri-County Tec
Montgomery County Highest Academic Achievement Award
USAA Academic Collegiate All-American
Phi Theta Kappa Honor Society
Collegiate National Dean's List
President's List
Dean's List

**WORK
EXPERIENCE:**

Synthetic Technologies, Montgomery, AL   1988 - XXXX
Materials Manager
Supervised materials management department including purchasing, traffic, materials control, production planning and distribution. Developed objectives, policies and programs covering the administration and operation of materials management.

Davidson Cable Corp., Montgomery, AL   1970 - 1988
Distribution Center Manager (1986 - 1988)
Directed all aspects of distribution center for manufacturing facility with $95 million sales. Supervised 8 managers and 40 hourly associates.

Manager of Materials and Services (1982 - 1986)
Managed purchasing, customer services, shipping/receiving, primary warehouse and plant services departments. Supervised 5 management employees and 8 hourly employees.

Warehouse Manager (1979 - 1982)
Assumed responsibility for shipping finished goods and maintaining $2.5 million in inventory.

Purchasing Agent (1974 - 1979)
Negotiated competitive prices and delivery of raw materials, supplies, small tools, office and janitorial supplies. Performed physical inventories and periodic cycle counts.

Buyer (1970 - 1974)
Procured raw materials by means of bills of materials. Expedited delivery of raw materials, manufacturing, janitorial and maintenance supplies.

99

Combination. *Gwen P. Noffz, Greenwood, South Carolina*

The original resume was on decorative "stethoscope" paper (from Beckett-Highland Publishing). The Profile explains her career change after many years in management.

Sherry Harmon

"... has a real skill in understanding behavior and motive of those she works with. Promotes open conversation. Able to confront & praise easily. Works well with all people.
... is easy to get along with, truthful, and straight forward."

PROFESSIONAL EXPERIENCE

Training Coordinator. *Preventive Home Health Care*. Somewhere, IN: 0000-0000

Began employment as Certified Home Health Aide → Filing Clerk → Staffing Coordinator → Office Manager → Medical Records Manager → present.

Ensure effective branch office operations. Coordinate efforts and provide education, training, and support for staffing coordinators and medical records secretaries at five branches. Excellent troubleshooter - enjoy finding solutions to challenges. Thorough knowledge of all staffing positions, fill in on a temporary basis as needed. Research and stay up-to-date on Medicare/caid regulations. Attend general staff meetings, corporate office meetings, and quarterly CQI meetings with Training Coordinator and Administrators. Assure proper documentation and quality assurance of charts meeting JCAHO and State Survey standards and proper entry of referral source files. Assign compatible staff person to clients and mediate difficulties arising from assignments. Write, audit and revise training manuals. Computer - HAMS, WordPerfect, RMS, First Choice.

▌ Develop and present educational/training seminars stressing problem-solving solutions to challenges. Find speakers and facilitate logistics. Develop paperwork, conduct research, coordinate activities, and administer tests. Assisted in Genasus Project.

▌ Effective listener/communicator/mediator - ask proper questions to facilitate efficient, cost effective, and often creative results-oriented solutions. Lead and instruct by example - encourage motivational leadership qualities and personal standards of high ethical work product in others.

▌ Developed efficient filing systems, color-coding for pay-source identification, and a *Financial Information Reference Guide*.

Rural Route #0, Box 00, Somewhere, IN 00000   **(812) 000-0000**

100

Combination. *Colleen S. Jaracz, Vincennes, Indiana*

Ample white space makes this resume easy to read and spreads it across two full pages. A different font for the name helps it stand out. The opening testimonial wins the reader over

Sherry Harmon (Page 2)

"Excellent teacher!" "Sherry is a willing and able employee. Able to deal with people with a wisdom and insight beyond her years. Always treats others with respect and dignity."

**PROFESSIONAL
EXPERIENCE** (Continued)

Developmental Assistant → Residential Manager. MRC. Somewhere, IN: 0000-0000

Certified Nurses Aid. *Nursing Home*. Somewhere, IN: 0000-0000

**EDUCATION/
AWARDS**

Recognition & Appreciation Award. Preventive Home Health Care: 0000
HAMS 3.5 Update Training Certificate: 0000
Q.E.D. Saliva Alcohol Test Training Course: 0000
ICD-9-CM Coding Clinic for Home Health Care Certificate: 0000
Washington High School, 1985

**PROFILE/
SKILLS**

▌ Energetic manager with excellent planning and organizational skills. Thrives in active professional environment. Thoughtful, accomplished facilitator; able to coordinate multiple/complex projects. Detail oriented and determined, proven ability to identify, analyze, and solve problems.

▌ Highly reliable self starter - jump in and do what must be done. Excellent team member, usually advanced into leadership role, calm influence/flexible.

▌ Straight forward, truthful, and direct - but tactful and self controlled. Skilled at maintaining a balanced, objective yet compassionate viewpoint during problem mediation and resolution while successfully upholding the company's objectives.

▌ Motivate personnel to increase efficiency, quality of service, and productivity resulting in progressive staff development.

Rural Route #0, Box 00, Somewhere, IN 00000 | **(812) 000-0000**

to the side of the applicant even before the rest of the resume is read. Thick-thin bullets echo the lines in the headers and footers—a creative touch. A Profile/Skills section is unusual at the end but makes the resume strong throughout.

Cathleen Luttrell

555 North Fifth Street, Rolla, Missouri 00000 ◆ (555) 555-0000

OBJECTIVE

Staff nursing position providing the opportunity to expand professional skills, while allowing myself to apply my education and experience to administer maximum health benefits for patients receiving my care.

PROFILE

◆ Registered nurse administering all aspects of health promotion and maintenance by assessing, planning, implementing, and evaluating patient care, including: illness care, restoration, rehabilitation, health counseling, and education. Participate with other health care providers in promoting health and well-being of each patient, utilizing the safe performance of nursing skills requiring cognitive, psycho-motor, and affective capabilities. Accepts responsibility as provider of care, manager of care, and member within the discipline of nursing.

◆ Interact well with patients utilizing excellent therapeutic communication skills. Understanding, give individualized attention to each patient gaining their trust by listening; sensing their needs, and seeking to truly understand their concerns and desires.

◆ Mature, organized, and dependable, maintain good rapport with physicians and staff. Eager and energetic, believe strongly in setting positive goals and following them through successfully.

EXPERIENCE

Charge Nurse. *Cresent Convalescent Center*, Hilldale Corporation. Rolla, Missouri: 1994-Present

Provide quality care to residents in the Skilled Care wing. Efficiently perform diversified nursing duties including observing complications and symptoms requiring attention or drug modification; maintaining professionally accurate and complete documentation (Medicare/caid) utilizing excellent written and verbal communication skills; and supervise Personal Care Assistants. Interact well with residents and maintain good rapport with physicians and staff. Handle medical emergencies and pressures intelligently and quickly.

101

Combination. *Colleen S. Jaracz, Vincennes, Indiana*

This resume by the same writer also has lots of white space and is easy to read. It should not "intimidate a harried human resources person with a pile of resumes on the desk."

Cathleen Luttrel

VOLUNTEER EXPERIENCE

American Red Cross Blood Mobile Drive.

Obtained vital signs and managed information questionnaires while maintaining strict client confidentiality.

EDUCATION

Rolla University Associate Degree in Nursing. Rolla, Missouri: 1994

Rolla University Certificate of Graduation, Surgical Technology. Rolla, Missouri: 1991

LICENSE AND CERTIFICATION

State of Missouri Health Professions Bureau Registered Nurse: 1994 **License # 00000000, Expiration Date 10/31/95**

Certificate of Surgical Technology: 1991

HONORS AND ACHIEVEMENTS

Rolla University Dean's List: 1991, 1992, 1994
Rolla University Student Nurse Organization: 1994
Stella Richart Delta Theta Tau Scholarship: 1993
Rolla University Alumni Scholarship: 1992
Barbara Deoer Nontraditional Student Scholarship: 1991
Rolla University:
    Bronze Service Pin, 1991
    Gold Service Pin, 1990
    Leadership Cord, 1990
Rolla University Student Senate: 1989-1991
Rolla University Student Alumni Representative: 1989-1990

REFERENCES **Available upon request.**

Like the preceding resume, this resume uses as part of the header on page 2 the dual horizontal lines that appear on page 1 below the name of the individual. Effective diamond bullets link visually the contact information with the Profile.

KAREN LEWIS
234 Sand Street
Carol Stream, IL 60188
708/555-7596

OBJECTIVE:	A Nursing position in an Emergency Room or Immediate Care Center.

PROFILE:
- Comprehensive skills in immediate patient care and advanced cardiac life support, including experience as unit preceptor.

- Skilled in pre/post operative care, as well as urology, gyny, ortho, ENT, and pediatrics.

EMPLOYMENT:

Community Memorial General Hospital, Schaumburg, IL
Staff Nurse: Same Day Surgery 1992-Present
Perform all aspects of pre and post-operative care for up to 17 patients.
Supervise one assistant and all functions of assessment, documentation, discharge, and readiness.
Work extensively with patients, families, physicians and fellow nurses with professional, yet personal communication skills to determine and meet specific patient needs.

Emergency Room Nurse 1980-1992
Certified Mobile Intensive Care Nurse, responsible for all unit and charge duties at this Level 2 Trauma Center.
Trained and supervised students and paramedics.
Involved in emergency room care and a wide range of procedures.

Central DuPage Hospital, Winfield, IL
Emergency Room In-House Registry 1985-1987
Urgent Care In-House Registry 1991-1992

Northwestern Memorial Hospital, Berwyn, IL
Staff Nurse: General Surgery, and Emergency Room 1976-1980

Loyola University Medical Center, Maywood, IL 1973-1974
Staff Nurse / General Surgery Unit

CERTIFICATION: **Basic Cardiac Life Support (CPR), Advanced Cardiac Life Support (ACLS), Trauma Nurse Specialist (TNS).**
Advanced Cardiac Life Support Recertification, 10/94.
State of Illinois License #041-151737

EDUCATION:

Triton College, River Grove, IL
A.S. Degree: Science/Nursing Graduated 1973

Illinois State University, Normal, IL
General Education courses 1971

Riverside-Brookfield High School, Riverside, IL 1970

102

Combination. *Steven Provenzano, Schaumburg, Illinois*

A clean design with bullets only for skills mentioned in the Profile. Places of work and instruction are underlined; positions, certifications, and the degree are in boldface.

W. JAMES SMITH
123 Mason Avenue
Anytown, Tennessee 00000
(000) 000-0000

OBJECTIVE:

To gain valuable experience as a **Registered Nurse** in the medical-surgical unit of a major hospital with rapid progression to other departments, such as Emergency, CCU, and ICU.

SUMMARY OF QUALIFICATIONS:

- Will obtain A.D. in Nursing from Central State University in May 1995
- One year of psychiatric experience at University Medical Center/Jackson Hospital in Anytown, Tennessee, with some experience in medical-surgical and physical rehabilitation
- Have gained experience in CCU, ICU, ER, and OR during nursing rotation
- Maintain excellent relationships with patients, family, staff, and administration
- Ability to decisively handle trauma situations and deal effectively with difficult patients
- Motivated and dedicated to providing professional, quality patient care

EDUCATION:

A.D. Nursing ■ May 1995
Central State University ■ Capital City, Tennessee

Scheduled to take Tennessee Nursing Board exam for R.N. license in June 1995

HEALTH CARE EXPERIENCE:

Nurse Technician/Mental Health Assistant ■ January 1994 - Present
Jackson Hospital ■ Anytown, Tennessee

- Provide patient care, counseling, and support
- Have assisted with "Code Blue" and "Code Yellow" situations and performed CPR
- Remove sutures and wound dressings, give injections, draw blood, insert urinary catheters, and administer other treatment as required
- Provide assistance to medical-surgical unit and physical rehabilitation unit

Home Health Care Sitter ■ February 1990 - December 1993
Acme Estates Home Health Care ■ Anytown, Tennessee

- Provided at-home care to patients, developing excellent technical skills and personable bedside manner

References and Additional Information Available Upon Request

103

Combination. *Carolyn S. Braden, Hendersonville, Tennessee*

This person wanted to stress his training and experience and to indicate his desire to move rapidly to different areas of hospital nursing. Original on eye-catching stethoscope paper.

Rana A. Michaels

453 SE 122nd Street ▪ Washburn, California 55555
555-555-5555

CERTIFIED HOSPICE NURSE

More than eight years in hospice and staff nursing positions plus 11 years as nursing technician. Excellent communication and interpersonal skills to establish and maintain emotional support for patients, caregivers, and family members. Enjoy serving others. Calm, dependable, friendly, and adaptable.

- Hospice case management
- Pain management and symptom relief
- Liaison between physicians, caregivers, and outside agencies

- Patient needs assessment
- Oncology nursing
- Dietary monitoring
- Caregiver and nursing staff instruction

RELEVANT PROFESSIONAL EXPERIENCE

PROVIDENCE HEALTH & HOSPICE, Elphrata, California   Part time -- 1995 to July 1999

Certified Hospice Nurse/Case Manager
Provided palliative home care support and pain management for terminally ill patients and their families through regular visitation to assess environment and ensure physician's orders implemented. Supervised home health aides. Coordinated pastoral, social worker, and physician care for hospice patients in hospitals and nursing homes.

GENERAL HEALTH SYSTEMS, Dakota, California   Part and full time -- 1993 to 1995
Older Adult Services & Adult Day Care   Concurrent

Primary Nurse
Developed and implemented primary nursing plan for 110 clients. Assessed eligibility for adult day care. Coordinated interdisciplinary teams of social workers, recreational, occupational and physical therapists. Liaison between physicians, hospitals, and nursing agencies to facilitate smooth transition to Older Adult Services.

Monitored medications and dietary regimens. Instructed caregivers and nursing staff members. Supervised three staffpersons.

RAINBOW HOSPICE, Peterson, California   Full Time -- 1993 to 1994

Weekend On-call Hospice Nurse
Home visits to terminally ill patients providing emotional support and supportive care instruction to patients, their families and caregivers. Used aggressive pain management techniques.

ZION MEDICAL CENTER, Peterson, California   1991 to 1993
Clinical Coordinator for Home Solutions, Discharge Planning, Charge Nurse, Staff Oncology Nurse

EDUCATION

Associate of Science, Nursing. Peterson Community College, Peterson, California, 1991

Ongoing education and training in home care, hospice administration, case management, communications, treatment systems, and personal improvement

104

Combination. *Janette M. Campbell, Washougal, Washington*

Profile information and bulleted areas of expertise are put where they are most likely to be seen by a reader. Education without a four-year degree is put last in the least-read location.

Charlotte M. Dapplewood

000 Chicago Ave.
Chicago, IL 00000
(000) 000-0000

Qualifications & Strengths	Strong Communication Skills Supervisory Abilities Positive Rapport with Clients Detailed Documentation Client Care Management TBI Injury
Education	**APPLE VALLEY COMMUNITY COLLEGE** Apple Valley, IL *Associate Degree of Nursing, May 1991* *Practical Nurse Certification, May 1990*
Employment	**APPLE VALLEY NURSING HOME**, Apple Valley, IL May 1991 - Present ***Nursing Supervisor/RN*** Supervise the residential care of up to 247 middle-age through elderly clients. Develop, coordinate, and implement client care management. Prepare and educate client for successful discharge from facility. Monitor, assess, and communicate client progress to attending physician on a periodic basis. Participate and collaborate in care planning meetings with departmental advisors, client, and family members. Traumatic Brain Injury Unit. Train, delegate responsibilities, and evaluate performance of 31 CNAs at variable times. **ELDERLY CARE CENTER** Blossom Village, IL, May 1989 - May 1991 ***LPN*** Provided direct client care and maintained personal hygiene and safety of up to 12 diverse client caseloads. Supervised, delegated responsibilities, and monitored performance of up to 7 CNAs. Oversaw all phases of client care management. **MONOPOLY STORES** Apple Valley, IL, August 1985 - May 1989 ***Supervisor/Customer Service Representative*** Responsible for the daily business operations including scheduling, training, and monitoring performance of service employees, cashiers, and baggers. Balanced and documented cash drawers on a nightly basis. Established positive relationships with customers to ensure satisfaction and encourage repetitive business.
References	Available Upon Request

105

Combination. *Betty Callahan, location unknown*

If you use WordPerfect or Microsoft Word, you can create the body of this resume (that is, everything below the information at the top) as a table and erase all but one vertical line.

Laura McVicar
600 Elmwood Ave.
Smalltown, OH 49000
(419) 000-0000

OBJECTIVE: To work as a Registered Nurse in a
                  setting requiring a more personalized
                  approach to health maintenance, patient
                  care, and follow up.

EDUCATION: SMITH HIGH SCHOOL, Hilltown, Ohio 49000
                       Graduated 1968
                  LUCAS COUNTY COMMUNITY COLLEGE at
                       campuses located in both
                       Perrysburg and Toledo and clinical
                       expierience in various Toledo
                       hospitals. 1980-1983. G.P.A. of
                       3.6

WORK EXPERIENCE: CHILDREN'S HOSPITAL OF OHIO 3214 Toledo
                       Road, Toledo Ohio 48000 555-0000
                       Hired 2-13-84 as an R.N. $9.56 per
                       hr. Current employment.
                  United Parcel Service 95035 Sylvania
                       Blvd., Toledo 48000 Driver.
                       10-79/12-79
                  Big Chain Supermarket 4082 Anderson Rd.
                       Perrysburg, Ohio 49000 Cashier.
                       6-73/5-79
                  Sears, Roebuck and Co. Sales 8-72/6-73
                       Oregon General Hospital, 4550 Main
                       Street, Oregon, Ohio 49000
                       6-68/5-70

PERSONAL: I am married, age 34, in excellent
                  health, dependable in my habits, and
                  thorough in my duties. My maiden name
                  was Smith. My work records and most of
                  my college instructors know me by Teal.
                  I bowl, sew, and follow my husband's
                  softball team, but I especially enjoy
                  my gardening and competing annually in
                  the home canning and baking divisions
                  of the Ohio State Fair, and contribu-
                  ting to the next edition of the "Blue
                  Ribbon Recipes" Cookbook. I also
                  attend Smalltown Baptist Temple.

106

Chronological (Before). *Provided by Deborah L. Schuster, Newport, Michigan*

An out-of-date resume that has been fictionalized and simulated by the writer. It contains
inappropriate information (salary, hobbies, and religion) and non-health-care positions.

Laura McVicar, RN
600 Elmwood Avenue
Smalltown, OH 49000
(419) 000-0000

Objective:	A Registered Nurse seeking a position in a setting that requires a more personal, one-on-one relationship with my patients.
Strengths:	■ Ability to interact with children with severe physical, emotional, and psychological problems.
	■ Ability to establish rapport and communicate well with both patients and their families.
	■ Teaching and training – both other employees, patients, and their families.

Experience: CHILDREN'S HOSPITAL OF OHIO, Toledo, Ohio
Registered Nurse, Same Day Surgery, 2/84 - Present

■ Administer care to patients ranging from the highest acuity level to the well child.
■ Teach and prepare patients and their families for a surgical experience.
■ Closely monitor vital signs immediately after surgery.
■ Train families to administer the home care that will be required after surgery.

Accomplishments:

■ Created a comic book to teach children about the hospital experience and help them know what to expect.
■ Wrote a Parent Information Handout to inform parents about the procedure for same day surgery.
■ Workshop Leader for Positive Action Committee – Revamped Unit Clerk Expectations, resulting in a hospital-wide increase in the clerks' productivity.
■ Awards: Hospitality Award, Image of Nursing Award.

Professional Associations: American Nurses Association
Ohio Nurses Association
Nursing Council Forum

Education/ License: **Associate of Nursing Degree,** 1983
LUCAS COUNTY COMMUNITY COLLEGE, Toledo, Ohio

State of Ohio Nursing License, 1984

107

Combination (After). *Deborah L. Schuster, Newport, Michigan*

The Strengths section lists skills for the goal of pediatric home health care. By getting rid of old information, the writer had space for the Experience section and accomplishments.

JUDY HELPER, R.N.

55555 North 55th Avenue
Anyplace, USA 55555
(555) 555-5555

OBJECTIVE: To obtain a rewarding position where registered nursing experience, education and dedication will be of value.

HIGHLIGHTS OF QUALIFICATIONS

- Current Licensed Registered Nurse in the State of Arizona.
- Fifteen (15) years of registered nursing experience in various settings.
- Broad knowledge of newborn care/obstetrics, adult and home health programs.
- Proven ability to coordinate the efforts of others effectively, and foster an atmosphere of teamwork.
- Genuine concern for and sensitivity to patients.
- Excellent communication skills with aptitude to interact effectively with diverse individuals, such as administration, peers, physicians, patients and families.
- Maintain patience and enthusiasm to educate patients and families.
- Manage time and administrative duties efficiently and effectively.
- Highly reliable self starter; can be counted on to prioritise assignments with little or no supervision.
- Demonstrated ability to adapt to frequently changing environments and situations; remain focused under stress and emergency situations.

SUMMARY OF PROFESSIONAL EXPERIENCE

- Solid experience and knowledge in pediatrics, obstetrics/gynecology, home healthcare, general practice, urgent care, ENT, orthopedic care, nursing home care, and public health.
- Act as charge nurse; oversee all nursing functions/activities, supervise up to 4 number of personnel
- Evaluate patient status by identifying needs, problems, and progress of patients.
- Maintain detailed, accurate records on each patient.
- Suggest nursing care for patients as appropriate.
- Inform physicians of pertinent patient care information.
- Coordinate nursing services with other patient care services.
- Administer medications, IVs, etc.
- Keep abreast of all hospital policies and changes being made; train staff.
- Keep staff informed and ensure policies are being adhered to.

PROFESSIONAL EMPLOYMENT HISTORY

Cigna Healthplans, Anyplace, USA, & Anywhere, USA   1993 to 1995
Position: Registered Nurse - Home Health Discharge Planner
- Coordinate admissions and assessment of post-partum, newborn, and ante-partum patients.
- Conduct patient education sessions relating to post-partum, newborn, ante-partum and routine care.
- Provide instruction on the care of diabetic patients (i.e., proper diet, insulin administration, blood sugar testing, etc.)
- Oversee home health care practices, coordinate necessary referrals between physicians, patients and clinics, and monitor overall case management.

Pacific Hospital of Anywhere, Anyplace, USA   1992 to 1993
Position: Registered Nurse - NSY, Obstetrics & Post-Partum Dept.
- **Level I:** Coordinated admissions and assessment of newborn infants.
- **Level II:** Provided care, assistance and transfers of newborns.

Humana Hospital, Anyplace, USA   1982 to 1992
Position: Registered Nurse - NSY
- **Level I:** Responsible for admissions and assessment of newborn infants, as well as critical care of newborns.
- Administered IVs, set up oxygen apparatus, and administered oxygen and medications.
- Provided post-partum care, assisted in labor & delivery, and provided patient education.
- **Level II:** Performed a wide variety of administrative functions relating to the newborn nursery.
- Trained new personnel, and ensured that medical and record keeping procedures were properly followed.

108

Combination. *Bernard Stopfer, location unknown*

Strong qualifications show that the individual is highly qualified for taking on a responsible position. The Summary eliminates possible redundancy in the Employment History.

JUDY HELPER, R.N. - Page Two

Cottonwood Community Hospital, Anyplace, USA   1981 to 1982
Position: Registered Nurse – Adolescent/Pediatric Medical/Surgical Unit
• Served in the Pediatric Intensive Care Unit (Level II)

Hurley Medical Center, Anyplace, USA   1980 to 1981
Registered Nurse – Pediatric Medical/Surgical Unit
• **Levels I & II**: Served as charge nurse in the Pediatric Unit with responsibilities for patients aged 0-5 years.
• **Level III**: Served as registered nurse in the Pediatric Intensive care Unit.

LICENSES

State of Anyplace, Registered Nursing License, # 085000

EDUCATION

Associate of Science Degree in Nursing, 1980 - Anyplace Community College, Anywhere, USA
G.P.A. 3.6/4.0

REFERENCES PROVIDED UPON REQUEST

The Professional Employment History is a record of increasing responsibility and greater interaction with people. The increase within positions is shown by the distinction of levels of activity. Education—the earliest experience—is put last.

Caring S. Nurse, R.N.
1000 Ohio Avenue
Athens, Ohio 45701
(614) 592-0000

CAREER OBJECTIVE	To obtain a position which will utilize my broad range of nursing experience to the unique needs of individuals. To promote and implement the standards of nursing practice as established by the profession.

EDUCATION

OHIO UNIVERSITY, Athens, Ohio - Spring 1997
Candidate for BSN Degree

HOCKING COLLEGE, Nelsonville, Ohio - 1985
Associates Degree in Nursing, Licensed Practical Nurse

Continuing Education
Psychiatric Update (1988) ... Diabetes Review (1989) ... Skin Cancer Review (1992) ... Depression Update (1993) ... Medication Update (1993) ... Nurses, The Undiscovered Gold (1993) ... Facilitator Skills Instruction (1994)

CERTIFICATIONS

Current CPR and Standard First Aid Certification
Certification in Psychiatric Nursing - Received October 1993
Certified CPR Instructor - Received December 1994

WORK EXPERIENCE

Psychiatric Nurse Supervisor   3/94-present
NORTHWEST PSYCHIATRIC HOSPITAL, Anytown, Ohio
Responsible for ensuring optimal clinical performance and adherance to nursing standards. Provide clinical direction. Assess training needs and recommend training programs for staff. Conduct staff meetings. Serve as member of various committees. Implement scheduling for staff.

Registered Psychiatric Nurse I   2/88-3/94
NORTHWEST PSYCHIATRIC HOSPITAL, Anytown, Ohio
Expertise in psychiatric and mental health nursing practice and understand theories concerning personality development and the behavior patterns involved in the treatment of mental illness. Clinically supervise nursing staff; make assignments. Assist with admissions and implement comprehensive nursing assessments and care plans. Follow through with treatment modalities/nursing interventions.

Registered Home Health Nurse   9/86-12/88
BOBCAT HOME HEALTH, Anytown, Ohio
Administered holistic care on individual clients, integrating family, environmental and community resources to promote optimal level of client well being. Framework of practice in care management included use of Nursing Process, including teaching/ monitoring all levels of care, identifying clinical problems and using research knowledge and advocating for the client's right to self-determination.

109

Chronological. *Melissa L. Kasler, Athens, Ohio*

The resume of a person with a two-year degree in nursing who is working on a four-year degree. Her experience, dating back to her two-year degree, becomes more supervisory.

Caring S. Nurse
Page 2

WORK   **Medical/Surgical Registered Nurse**   9/87-2/88
EXPERIENCE O'ROYAL MEMORIAL HOSPITAL, Anytown, Ohio
(cont'd)   Provided care for individuals who had a known or predicted physiological
alteration. Followed through with Nursing Process, teaching implemented.
Provided primary, acute and long-term nursing care influenced on health
status, and the related social and behavioral problems arising from individual
patients.

            Community Health Registered Nurse   9/85-12/88
LODI TOWNSHIP FAMILY PRACTICE, Anytown, Ohio
        Synthesized nursing practice and public health practice and apply the
synthesis to promoting and preserving the health of populations.
Implemented general and comprehensive nursing.

References Available Upon Request

Horizontal lines enclosing the Career Objective call attention to it. Boldfacing helps key
Education information and positions stand out. All-uppercase letters make the educational
institutions and the workplaces easily seen. The overall design is readily grasped.

Scott M. Roberts

9 High Street
Eastland, Maine 00000
(207) 555-5555

Profile

Health care professional with five years of nursing and health care experience. Solid knowledge of comprehensive nursing care procedures and excellent direct patient care skills. Successful in managing time, prioritizing tasks, and organizing projects. Creative problem solver. Effective staff and patient relations skills. A.S. degree in Nursing from the University of Maine.

Professional Experience

Seaside Manor, Eastland, Maine   **1994 - Present**
Nursing Services Manager / Staff Nurse

- Oversee the delivery of quality patient care in a 250-bed residential nursing facility. Supervise and manage nursing staff of six, including, registered nurses, licensed practical nurses, and certified nurses' aides.

- Provide problem-focused charting on each patient; approve all admissions and discharges; and ensure accurate medication delivery and recording.

- Perform patient assessments, develop care plans, coordinate with other disciplines including, physical therapy, occupational therapy, dietary, activities, and consult with psychologists and psychiatrists on special cases.

Resthaven Pines, Ocean Beach, Maine   **1992 - 1993**
Medication and Treatment Nurse

- Provided nursing assessment, care, and treatment for geriatric patients in residential nursing facility. Discussed care, conditions, and concerns with patients and family members. Passed appropriate medication, as ordered by physicians, for 45 patients.

Downeast Care Center, Riverside, Maine   **1989 - 1992**
Activities Coordinator

- Coordinated activities in a 150-bed nursing care facility. Set up structured recreational programs. Documented levels and amount of participation. Attended team meetings and conferences.

Education & Professional Development

University of Maine, Riverside, Maine   **1994**
A.S. Applied Science in Nursing

Professional Development:
- Basic Peripheral I.V. Therapy
- Pain Management
- IBM Computer Training
- Nursing Process Workshop

Community Involvement

Elder Care: A Symposium, Planning Committee
Downeast Agency on Elder Service, Board of Directors
American Lung Association of Maine - Bike Trek Across Maine, Winner's Circle Participant

110

Combination. *Joan M. Roberts, Bangor, Maine*

A well-designed resume with text indented so that the headings can be read at a glance. Horizontal lines interrupted by the headings help separate the major sections of the resume.

CANDY BAR
RN, CPAN

9387 Sandway Lane
Indianapolis, IN 46222
(317) 912-0365

SUMMARY OF QUALIFICATIONS:

- Twenty-two years of extensive experience in nursing management.
- Program development for MRI and other areas of Radiology.
- Acquired expertise in Post-Anesthesia Nursing and Acute Pain Care.
- Maintain high personal standards of professionalism, keeping current on treatments and medical literature.
- Skilled in teaching/training roles; preceptor and mentor to fellow nurses; orientation resource to resident physicians.
- Extended knowledge in cardiac and respiratory monitoring and therapy.

TRAINING & EDUCATION:

Certified Post-Anesthesia Nurse, 1990-Current. In-depth studies of pharmaceuticals and procedures.
ACLS Certification, current.
Associate of Applied Science, Nursing, Purdue University; 1972.

EXPERIENCE:

<u>A BIG HOSPITAL,</u> Indianapolis, Indiana   1983-Present

NURSE COORDINATOR, RADIOLOGY, 1994-Present: Responsible for management of patients and nursing care given in MRI, IVR, cat scan, and radiology oncology.
- Direct QI for radiology; provide inservice education for all members of Radiology Department and specialty personnel.
- Serve on numerous committees.
- Administer conscious sedation to Radiology patients in preparation for procedures.

ROTATING CHARGE NURSE, Post-Anesthesia Care Unit, 1988-1994: Provided nursing care to post-operative patients. Assisted Pain Clinic Patients with anesthetic nerve block treatments.
- Quality Improvement Coordinator; member, Standards of Care Committee.
- Provide orientation and instruction to residents and nurses.
- Instituted new paperwork procedures which resulted in improved efficiency.

HEAD NURSE, 31-bed Medical Unit, 1985-1987: Managed staff of 20: Cardiac, renal, diabetic, oncology/chemotherapy, isolation, detoxification, pre/post cardiac catherization, pre/post angioplasty.
- Rotated as relief weekend coordinator for hospital.
- Served on Continuing Education, Clinical Nursing Practice, and Quality Assurance Committees.

EVENING CHARGE NURSE, 24-bed Critical Care Unit, 1983-1985: MICU/CCU, telemetry and step down care.

<u>BIGGER HOSPITAL,</u> Indianapolis, Indiana   1972-1981
SHIFT MANAGER, Emergency Room, 1975-1981.
R.N., Medical/Surgical, Nursing Research, Oncology Units, 1972-1975.

AFFILIATIONS:

- American Radiological Nurses Association
- American Society of Post-Anesthesia Nursing; attend seminars and national conventions.
- Indiana Society of Post-Anesthesia Nursing: Immediate Past President; 1994-1995 President, 1993-1994; Vice President, 1992-1993.

111

Combination. *Carole E. Pefley, Indianapolis, Indiana*

The original was printed on special paper. The person was pleased with its impact and is still working at "a big hospital." Square bullets complement the "box" in the upper-left corner.

SAMANTHA N. COLLEY, RN
4025 Burke
Pasadena, TX 77504
(000) 000-0000

EDUCATION

University of Texas   School of Nursing - Associate Degree
Continuing seminar education to maintain license

PREVIOUS CERTIFICATIONS

American Heart Association CPR Instructor - 1982 - 1984
Certified Emergency Nurse - 8/89 - 9/93
Advanced Cardiac Life Support Certified Nurse - 11/89
Curaflex Intravenous Certified Nurse - 10/91

CURRENT CERTIFICATION

Basic Life Support Certified - 10/93 - 10/95

EMPLOYMENT HISTORY

9/91 - present   Omair Home Health, Pasadena, TX
Home Health Care RN · General Health Care Maintenance · Assess and Evaluate Patients
to Attending Physicians · Evaluate and Change Procedures for Wound Patients · IV Therapy
· Manage and Supervise Cases including LVN and Support Staff · Develop Staff Treatment
and Nursing Care Plan · Schedule Patients According to Insurance and Medicare
Requirements · Market Services to Physicians.

1/91 - 9/91   Brazoria County Hospital District, Houston, TX
Emergency Room Nurse · L & D.

5/84 - 5/90   Southwest Medical Center, Corpus Christi, TX
Emergency Room Nurse · Patient Triage · Assessment · Medication Administration · IV
Therapy · Patient Treatment and Care · Charge Duties · Education · Truma and Acute Care
Delivery.

Labor and Delivery RN · Assessment of Pregnant and Laboring Patients · Patient Treatment
and Care in Active Labor · Fetal Monitoring · Delivery of Infant Vaginally and by C-Section
· Recovery Room Care · Education.

ENT Care RN · Pediatric Care · Patient Treatment and Care · Charge Duties.

Private Duty RN for Dr. John Doe · General Physician in office Patient Care.

REFERENCES AVAILABLE UPON REQUEST

112

Chronological. *Nell Turk, Houston, Texas*

When text is fully justified (having flush left and right margins), a horizontal line near the top of
the resume helps establish a sense of margin width. Bullets separate text in paragraphs.

Maria Eléna Navarro, CRTT
127 Pine Street, Unit D
Morris Plains, NJ 55555

(000) 000-0000

OBJECTIVE | ***Respiratory therapist*** *in a hospital where previous experience in clinical settings such as ICU, CCU, and NICU would be put to use and valued.*

EDUCATION | *County College of Morris, Randolph, NJ*
Completed AMA approved certificate program in Respiratory Therapy, 1992

William Paterson College, Wayne, NJ
Associates in Applied Science, Allied Health, 1988

TECHNICAL SKILLS | ***Equipment:*** *MA-1, Puritan-Bennett 7200, and Bear series ventilator initiation and management, including transport, set up and maintenance.*

Treatment Modalities: *Under the direction of a physician, perform gas, aerosol and humidity therapies; intermittant positive pressure breathing (IPPB); chest physiotherapy; cardiopulmonary rehabilitation.*

Techniques: *Endotrachael intubation/extubation; administration of medical gases, drugs, treatments and tests as prescribed by an authorized physician; drawing and interpretation of arterial blood gases; airway management; bedside spirometry for checking pulmonary functioning and recording patient progress; quality control checks for optimal equipment performance of respiratory equipment.*

Patient Interaction: *Implementation of patient care plans and follow-up treatment on patients of all ages, newborn through geriatric; instruction of patients on use of liquid oxygen, concentrators, c-paps, bipaps and apnea monitors as well as use, care and troubleshooting of their ventilators; direct responsibility for the management of respiratory compromised patients; assistance to crisis team in the administration of basic life support in code situations.*

WORK EXPERIENCE | *3/95 to Present* — ***Respiratory Technician*** *HomeCare Agency, Rockaway, NJ*

2/93 to 3/95 and currently on per diem basis — ***Respiratory Therapist*** *Memorial Hospital, Morristown, NJ*

1/92 to 2/93 — ***Respiratory Technician*** *Wayne General Hospital, Wayne, NJ*

10/90 to 12/91 — ***Telemetry Technician*** *Cardiologics, Inc., Glenridge, NJ*

8/87 to 10/90 — ***Telemetry Technician/Nurses Assistant*** *Beth Israel Hospital, Passaic, NJ*

LANGUAGES | *Bilingual fluency in English and Spanish*

113

Combination. *Melanie A. Noonan, West Paterson, New Jersey.*

A resume in which the headings in the left column are separated from the information in the right column by a vertical line. Make this resume as a table and erase all lines but one.

ELLEN J. MADERES

111 Kane Court
Mendota, IL 00000

Phone / Message
(555) 555-5555

OBJECTIVE

⇒ Seeking a position as a **Registered Nurse**.

OVERVIEW

⇒ Highly motivated new graduate with a compassionate nature and dedicated approach toward patient care.
⇒ Organized and efficient in work habits.
⇒ Effective skills in patient assessment and report writing, including computer charting.

EDUCATION

A.A.S. in Nursing, May 1995
Mendota State College, Mendota, IL
Graduated with **Honors**; Phi Theta Kappa member

⇒ Gained hands-on experience and knowledge in nursing procedures while completing a rotating, two-year internship at these health care facilities:

Madison County Hospital	Ventilator & Cardiology Units
DeKalb Hospital	Orthopedics & Medical-Surgical Units
St. Martin Hospital	OB/GYN & Pediatrics Units
Oakwood Medical Center	Respiratory & Sub-Acute Units
Hope Center	Psychiatric Facility

EXPERIENCE

Secretary, 1980 - 1992
Lion Elementary School, Mendota, IL

⇒ Served as liaison to parents. Routed phone calls, drafted and typed correspondence, and administered first aid. Maintained accurate student records; performed light bookkeeping.

⇒ Remained calm and focused on the task at hand during high-pressure and emergency situations.

Instructor / Member - Fund Raising Committee, 1983 - 1995
Madison Community Foundation, Mendota, IL

⇒ Planned and taught adult and youth craft classes. Made presentations before large and small groups to elicit support for foundation-sponsored programs. Actively involved in planning and organizing fund raising events.

114

Combination. *Jennie R. Dowden, location unknown*

The size of the type is increased to make the resume fill one page. With text being equal, a full page is more impressive than a partial page. Special bullets make the page seem special.

Glenda Benson
455 Melody Lane • Lemont, IL 60581
(708) xxx-xxxx

EDUCATION:

1995   College of DuPage, Glen Ellyn, IL
A.A.S. degree in Nursing
Honor Student Award, 1990-94
*Clinical rotations at Good Samaritan, Edward and Cook County(peds)
hospitals. Observational experience in Home Health setting. Final
quarter included 3 shifts per week.*

1987   Business and Professional Institute, College of DuPage, Glen Ellyn, IL
Computer software courses in word processing, spreadsheet and
graphics programs.

EXPERIENCE:

1993-Present   Community Hospital, Any Suburb, IL
ER Registration Clerk(7/94-Present)
Interview patients to obtain admitting information. Process insurance
information. Initiate billing for ER charges. Extensive use of computer
for data entry.

Patient Care Tech (11/93-7/94)
Central Resource Team. Floated to Medical Oncology, General Surgery
and Pediatrics Units.

1991-1993   Day Surgery Center, Bensenville, IL
Purchasing Coordinator
Developed and maintained systems for purchasing all medical supplies
and equipment. Prepared monthly budget, updated pricing structure.
Negotiated purchases with vendors.

1990-1991   Delta Medical Technologies, Jamestown, IL
Administrative Assistant to President
Responsibilities included customer service, A/P, A/R, purchasing and
inventory control of medical products using computer system.

1982-1989   M-B Sales, Woodridge, IL
Senior Project Manager
Total project management for McDonald's Happy Meal Program.

References Available On Request

115

Chronological. *Julie R. Marshall, location unknown*

Clinical rotations are mentioned in the Education section because the individual applied to
hospitals where rotations occurred. Nursing-related positions are in boldface and underlined.

Ann Nicole Ellison
706 South Thomas Drive
Anaheim, CA 92804
(714) 555-9982

Licensed Vocational Nurse, seeking to utilize professional experience and knowledge in an educational environment. Offering excellent nursing skills, guidance, and leadership to nurses in training.

Education and Training

1993	**Medical Advancement Center,** Culver City, CA
	Intravenous Therapy
1990-1991	**Golden West College,** Huntington Beach, CA
	Nursing
1988-1990	**North Orange County ROP.** Anaheim, CA
	Certified Nurses Assistant, Long Term Care, Acute
	Care, and Vocational Nursing
1981-1983	**California State University,** Fullerton, CA
	Child Development (senior standing)
1979-1981	**Fullerton College,** Fullerton, CA
	Associate of Arts Degree in Liberal Studies

Work History

1989-Present	**Licensed Assistant, North Orange County ROP**, Anaheim, CA
	Ancillary staff working with Certified Nursing Assistant Instructor. Supervise students in a clinical setting. Evaluate performance and progress in direct patient care. Clerical support.
1992-Present	**Licensed Vocational Nurse, Care-At-Home,** Newport Beach, CA
	In \home care. Ventilator dependent quadriplegic, tracheostomy, foley catheter, blood glucose monitor, medications. Spina bifida patient, wound, ADLs, ventilator PRN.
1992-1995	**Licensed Vocational Nurse, Homelife/Staff Builders,** Lake Forest, CA
	In home, assessment, medications, wound, tracheostomy, ADLs.
1992-1993	**Licensed Vocational Nurse, Nursefinders,** Orange, CA
	Sub-acute facilities, resident treatment and medication, direct care.
1988-1991	**Certified Nursing Assistant, Walter R. Schmid**
	Home health care, companionship, prepare meals, ADLs, hygiene, ambulation, nutrition.
1987-1988	**Personal Care Attendant, Saint Joseph Hospital,** Orange, CA
	In home, bed baths, ambulating, personal care, ADLs.
References	Furnished upon request

116

Combination. *Sharon Payne, location unknown*

A strong resume with a lot of boldfacing that complements the intense black in the graphic. The dates are left-aligned at the left margin. The profile in italic indicates a goal and skills.

Natalie M. Hanover, RN

123 Main Street, Anytown, MI 48000 • (313) 555-0000

Strengths:
- Supervision
- Professional Role Model/Mentor
- Recognizing Needs of Patient & Family
- Experienced with Infants, Children, Adults, and Geriatric Patients
- Discharge Planning and Teaching
- Team Member
- Morale Booster
- Good Communicator and Facilitator

Experience:

MAJOR MEDICAL CENTER OF MICHIGAN   Detroit, Michigan
Registered Nurse, NICU, Relief Charge Nurse   April, 1985 - Present

Care for high risk neonates requiring oxygen and assisted ventilation, for premature infants weighing less than 1000 gms, for patients requiring extracorpeal membrane oxygenation, and for infants with various congenital anomalies, as well as those with respiratory, gastrointestinal, cardiac, neurological, and surgical diagnoses. Assumed charge nurse role. Managed 38-bed unit with 14 vents and 14 staff.

Selected Accomplishments:

- Wrote and presented inservices on "Caffeine Citrate" for NICU, and on "Drawing Blood From Peripheral Arterial Line."
- Wrote a pamphlet, "Quiet! Shunting Baby," to help parents understand pulmonary vasoconstriction.
- Preceptor for Wayne State Nurse Extern Program.
- Chairperson and developer of "Lovin' Spoonfuls"– a cookbook fund-raiser that raised over $8,000 for the unit. Proceeds were used to purchase a computer for educational purposes.
- Hospitality award, 1988.
- Committees: Primary Nurse Committee, Developmental Care Committee

Prior Experience, 1976 - 1985:
Held positions as a staff nurse and a charge nurse in a 28-bed short stay toddler medical unit, a staff nurse and a charge nurse in an adult medical/surgical unit, and a medical assistant.

Education:

Associate Degree in Science   1981
HENRY FORD COMMUNITY COLLEGE   Dearborn, MI

Other Professional Training:
   BCLS Certified
   Course in critical care
   Yearly conferences on a variety of topics.

Combination. *Deborah L. Schuster, Newport, Michigan*

A graphic like that in Resume 116 but smaller (one of the By Design package symbols). The writer puts responsibilities in paragraphs but lists strengths and achievements with bullets.

Nellie Mercy, C.O.T.A.

0000 N. 000 E.
Anytown, Indiana 00000
(000) 000-0000

Expertise: Rehab Specialist

Strengths:

- Rehab equipment sales
- Excellent organizational skills
- Exceptional memory
- Effect good judgment decisions
- Thorough assessment of patient needs

- Strong clinical background
- Attention to detail
- Experienced communicator
- Genuine patient advocate
- Skilled leader

Experience:

Only Care Services, Inc., Indianapolis, Indiana   **5/88-Present**

REHAB EQUIPMENT SPECIALIST:

Leader in developing Rehab Division for Onlycare Services, Inc. Opened Indianapolis Division (1990) and expanded to $1.2 million Indiana territory (1995). Manage customer service representative, and create new business with hospitals and medical facilities.

Team with physicians and therapists to ascertain proper rehab medical equipment. Evaluate and measure customers for wheelchairs and seating. Design custom seating orthotics; oversee fabrication. Deliver equipment to clients and ensure proper fitting. Write letters of medical necessity to secure funding, and communicate with case managers to clarify equipment need. Generate billing and assist with inventory control.

- Conduct wheelchair clinics in several facilities throughout Indiana.
- Frequent guest lecturer at University of Indianapolis.
- Train and educate occupational/physical therapists and insurance case managers.
- Extensive clinical assessment to create solutions for patients' needs.

State Home Health Services, Indianapolis, Indiana   **7/87-7/88**

REHAB SPECIALIST: Marketing of customized wheelchair seating devices. Supervised design technicians and customer service representative; in charge of quality control.

- Assisted in development of a growth-adjustable seating system.
- Expanded territory by 200%.

118

Combination. *Carole E. Pefley, Indianapolis, Indiana*

A well-developed, two-page resume. The Experience information alone occupies almost one page. Square bullets call attention to duties of the current position and past achievements.

Nellie Mercy, C.O.T.A.

-2-

<u>**Rehab Engineering and Repair, Inc.**</u>, **Danville, Indiana**   10/85-7/87

REHAB SPECIALIST: Marketing of customized wheelchair seating devices. In charge of
financial management; made major business decisions to facilitate ongoing growth and
development.

- Increased business by 400%.
- Co-owner, 5/86; sold business to State Home Health Services.

<u>**Union Hospital of Indiana, Inc.**</u>, **Indianapolis, Indiana**   1180/-10/85

CERTIFIED OCCUPATIONAL THERAPY ASSISTANT:
- Developed customized seating program.
- Primary therapist for Muscular Dystrophy Association Clinic; implemented Saturday treatment
  program.

Education

Associate Degree, Occupational Therapy; Indiana University, Indianapolis, Indiana; 1979.

Certifications

- Certified Seating Specialist, University of Tennessee
- LaBac Certification
- Pindot, Jay, Roho, Avanti, Silhouette, and Cozy Craft Seating Certification

Specialized Training

- Customer-Oriented Selling
- Hearst Power and Manual School
- Franklin Time Management Seminar
- Nero Developmental Treatment Conference, Indianapolis, Indiana
- Treatment of Spinal Cord Patients, Rehab Institute of Chicago

Professional Organizations

- National Registry of Rehab Technology Suppliers
- American Occupational Therapy Association
- United Cerebral Palsy Association
- Muscular Dystrophy Association

The one-line Education statement is buttressed by separate sections for Certifications and
Specialized Training. All-uppercase letters are used for positions in the Experience section.
Generous white space before and after section headings helps the resume fill two pages.

Irene Stephens

123 Whiteoak Lane ◆ Radcliff, Kentucky 40100 ◆ (502) 555-1111

Objective

Emergency Room Nurse

Summary of Qualifications

- Over 10 years experience in increasingly responsible positions.
- Reliable, honest, and patient-oriented. Excellent leadership and training skills.
- Outstanding communication and interpersonal skills.
- Intensive patient care and emergency medical experience working in diverse environments.

Highlights of Nursing Experience

Baptist Hospital • Radcliff, KY   Jul 88 - Present
STAFF NURSE
- Prepared and administered prescribed medications. Obtained and prepared samples and specimens for laboratory cultures and analysis. Administered intravenous fluids. Performed traction care. Prepared patients for surgery. Assisted with maintenance of nasogastric tubes. Performed care for patients with asthma, pneumonia, or bronchitis with oxygen therapy, bladder catheterization, colostomy irrigation, and intravenous therapy procedures. Observed patients for signs of problems such as dehydration, mental stress, and life-threatening symptoms.
- Read patient charts and diagnostic reports and made entries in medical records.
- Performed preventive, therapeutic, and emergency nursing care procedures.
- Carried out nursing care plans. Cared for patients of all ages who were seriously, chronically, and acutely ill and those who had common diseases and minor injuries. Ensured maximum patient hygiene and safety.
- Obtained admission data and assisted with patient transfer and discharge. Used medical software to input orders, check medications, look up labs, check patient history, x-rays, physician orders, etc.
- Ordered clinical equipment and supplies.
- Supervised 12 personnel. Oversaw their patient care to ensure care and duties were correctly performed. Delegated duties appropriately. Prepared performance evaluations. Acted as Schedule Coordinator and ensured that all shifts were adequately covered.

Martin Burn Center • Martin, KY   Jun 85 - Jul 88
EMERGENCY ROOM NURSE
- Specialized in the emergency medical treatment of chemical, thermal, and electrical burns. Assisted with medical examinations. Took and recorded temperatures, pulse, respiration, and blood pressure. Applied and removed surgical, wound, and skin dressings. Collected and prepared specimens for analysis. Assisted in dispensary. Performed routine admissions tests. Administered immunizations. Maintained health records and clinical files.

Education & Licenses

- Martin College • Martin, KY • **Associate in Nursing** • 1985
- **Kentucky Board of Nursing** • License No. 1234567

119

Combination. *Connie S. Stephens, location unknown*

A multiline border enclosing everything below the contact information is a distinctive design feature. Another is the use of cross bullets, which are smaller in the Education section.

Susan K. Schumm

327 Parkview Place
Carmel, Indiana 46032

(317) 581-1057

OBJECTIVE
Secure Occupational Therapist Assistant position that would utilize and expand my education and hands-on experience to strengthen a facility's operations, that seeks and rewards results.

EDUCATION

Associate of Applied Science (OTA)   XX/XX-XX/XX

OT College, Chicago, Illinois ♦ ACHIEVED: Academic Honors (XXXX, XXXX); Recipient of *Lakeshore Business and Professional Women's* Scholarship Award (XXXX, XXXX); and President's List of Scholars (Fall XXXX) ♦ LICENSURE: Examination (XX/XX) ♦ MEMBER:*The American Occupational Therapy Association, Inc.* (XX/XX); and COTA Temporary Practicing License (XX/XX).

OTA Fieldwork Level II:

♦ *Education Cooperative,* (an early childhood school setting), Chicago, Illinois (XX/XX) ♦ OT UNIT: Children with: Cerebral Palsy, Autism, Down Syndrome, Developmental Delays, and Hearing Loss ♦ RESPONSIBILITIES: Performed sensory integration techniques; Demonstrated proper body positioning; Planned and implemented individualized fine motor activities to achieve IEP goals; Planned and instructed gross motor group activities; Visited and observed area facilities' therapies in children birth to 8 years old; Attended and summarized home visits; and Charted daily progress notes.

♦ *General Hospital,* Chicago, Illinois (XX/XX-XX/XX) ♦ OT UNIT: Inpatient, Acute Care, Orthopedic, Neurological, ICU, Cardiopulmonary ♦ RESPONSIBILITIES: Evaluated and treated total hip and knee replacements; Handled and knowledge of adaptive equipment; Taught compensatory techniques; Implemented and treated upper extremity functions; Assessed and monitored splints; Assessed and retrained in active daily living activities; and Charted progress and discharge summaries.

Child Development Program   XX/XX-XX/XX

Acme University, Chicago, Illinois ♦ Completed one (1) year in the Liberal Arts and Science Department ♦ ACHIEVED: Dean's List, Spring XXXX.

PROFESSIONAL EXPERIENCE

Occupational Therapist Aide   XX/XX-XX/XX

OT Services, Inc., Chicago, Illinois ♦ CONTRACT SITES: Extended Care Facility ♦ OT UNIT: Neurological and Cardiopulmonary ♦ SUPERVISED RESPONSIBILITIES: Implemented and treated upper extremity functions; Retrained feeding techniques; Trained in paraffin baths and heat packs; Assessed and monitored splints; Taught compensatory breathing and energy conservation; Handled adaptive equipment; and Prepped and transferred patients.

Teacher Assistant (Preschool: Special Needs)   XX/XX-XX/XX

Education Cooperative, Chicago, Illinois ♦ RESPONSIBILITIES: Interacted and nurtured preschoolers in developing functional motor and social skills; and **CPR** certification (annually).

Teacher Assistant (Moderate Mentally Handicapped)   XX/XX-XX/XX

Education Cooperative, Chicago, Illinois ♦ RESPONSIBILITIES: Instructed, interacted, signed communication, and developed social skills to mainstream **MoMH** children into public school setting.

REFERENCES
Furnished upon request.

120

Chronological. *Susan K. Schumm, Carmel, Indiana*

This resume looks professional at first glance. One reason is that type is used consistently and with sophistication. Focus words are in small caps (ACHIEVED, LICENSURE, MEMBER, etc.).

Susan K. Schumm

327 Parkview Place
Carmel, Indiana 46032
(317) 581-1057

OBJECTIVE

Secure a Pediatric COTA position that would utilize my positive patient-therapist rapport and interpersonal skills to strengthen a facility's operations that values and rewards results.

CERTIFICATION

♦ Licensed Certified Occupational Therapist Assistant, State of Indiana, XX/XX.
♦ Credentialed Service Provider to the First Steps Program in the State of Indiana.

PROFESSIONAL EXPERIENCE

COTA   XX/XX-Present

FIRSTCARE/A Rehab Provider, Portage, Indiana ♦ RESPONSIBILITIES: Service Provider to *First Care Pediatric Rehabilitation Center*; Service Provider to the Early Intervention Program of *Opportunity Enterprises*; Service Provider to the *Cerebral Palsy Center of NW Indiana*; Facilitate development in special needs children from birth to 8 years old; Chart daily notes; Score and update quarterly program plans; and Demonstrate and involve parental carry over.

Continuing Education

♦ "How Does Your Engine Run?" The Alert Program for Self-Regulation (16 Hours), XX/XX.
♦ Brain Gym Seminar (48 Hours),XX/XX.
♦ Infant-Toddler Institute (3.2 CEU's), *The University of Wisconsin*, Oshkosh, WI, XX/XX.
♦ Technology for Infants and Toddlers Training (7 Hours), *ATTAIN*, XX/XX.
♦ Promoting Sensory Integration in Young Children (6 Hours), *Indiana Association of Rehabilitation Facilities*, Indianapolis, IN, XX/XX.
♦ Introduction to the NDT Approach in the Pediatric Population (31 Hours), *Edgewater Rehabilitation Associates, Inc.*, Northbrook, IL, XX/XX.
♦ Effective Intervention for Children with Oral-Motor Dysfunction (6 Hours), *Clinician's View*, XX/XX.
♦ Issues in Early Intervention (6 Hours), Louis Rossetti, Ph.D., St. John, IN, XX/XX.
♦ The Sensitive Child (3 Hours), *Wee Care Therapy, Ltd.*, Schererville, IN, XX/XX.
♦ Sensory Integration for COTAs: Intro. to Theory & Treatment (12.5 Hours), *The Tramble Co.*, XX/XX.
♦ Treatment of the Baby (31 Hours), *Boehme Workshops*, Milwaukee, WI, XX/XX.

Occupational Therapist Aide   XX/XX-XX/XX

Restorative Services, Inc., Merrillville, Indiana ♦ CONTRACT SITES: Extended Care Facility ♦ OT UNIT: Neurological and Cardiopulmonary.

EDUCATION

Associate of Applied Science (OTA)   XX/XX-XX/XX

South Suburban College, South Holland, Illinois ♦ ACHIEVED: Academic Honors (XXXX-XXXX); Recipient Lakeshore Business and Professional Women's Scholarship Award (XXXX, XXXX); and President's List of Scholars (Fall XXXX).

OTA Fieldwork Level II

♦ *Illinois School/Speed Cooperative*, (an early childhood school setting), Park Forest, IL (XX/XX-XX/XX) ♦ OT UNIT: Children with: Cerebral Palsy, Autism, Down Syndrome, Developmental Delays, and Hearing Loss ♦ RESPONSIBILITIES: Performed sensory integration techniques; Demonstrated proper body positioning; Planned and implemented individualized fine motor activities to achieve IEP goals; Planned and instructed gross motor group activities; Visited and observed area facilities' therapies in children birth to 8 years old; Attended and summarized home visits; and Charted daily progress notes.
♦ *Porter Memorial Hospital*, Valparaiso, IN (XX/XX-XX/XX) ♦ OT UNIT: Inpatient, Acute Care, Orthopedic, Neurological, ICU, Cardiopulmonary ♦ RESPONSIBILITIES: Evaluated and treated total hip and knee replacements; Handled and knowledge of adaptive equipment; Taught compensatory techniques; Implemented and treated upper extremity functions; Assessed and monitored splints; Assessed and retrained in active daily living activities; and Charted progress and discharge summaries.

Child Development Program   XX/XX-XX/XX

Purdue University Calumet, Hammond, Indiana ♦ ACADEMICS: Completed 1 year in the Liberal Arts and Science Department ♦ ACHIEVED: Dean's List, Spring XXXX.

MEMBERSHIPS

♦ *The American Occupational Therapy Association, Inc.*, XX/XX-Present.

REFERENCES

Furnished upon request.

121

Combination. *Susan K. Schumm, Carmel, Indiana*

A one-page resume chock full of information and neatly laid out with two levels of indentation to make the arrangement clear. Strong diamond bullets are used throughout.

Grace T. Drake

Route 1 Box 555
Small Town, ME 00000

(207) 555-5555

Physical Therapist Assistant

Education and Training:

Associate's degree in Applied Science, Physical Therapist Assistant Program (1995)
Kennebec Valley Technical College, Fairfield, Maine

- Foundational coursework in Anatomy & Physiology, Health Concepts, Kinesiology, Pathology, and Neurology

- Hands-on and observational training in acute care and outpatient settings to achieve patients' short and long term therapy goals

- Observation of initial evaluations and participation in treatment planning, use of various modalities and exercises for shoulder, knee, hip, cervical and back injuries

- Participated in gait training, flexibility and strengthening exercises, instruction in the use of assistive devices (walkers, canes, crutches)

Clinical Rotations: Newport Physical Rehabilitation Center, Newport, Maine
Miles Memorial Hospital, Damariscotta, Maine
St. Mary's Regional Medical Center, Lewiston, Maine

Medical Assistant Program (1984 Graduate)
Kennebec Valley Technical College, Fairfield, Maine

Employment History:

1982 - Present Great Big Grocery Store, Home Town, Maine
Shift Leader, Cashier, Cashier Trainer
Supervise/assist in training 30-40 checkout personnel, provide prompt assistance to customers, and perform all other duties with a professional and courteous attitude.

1979 - 1982 Rockwell's Liquidation Center, Our Town, Maine
Cashier

1981 - 1982 The Best Shirt Company, Waterville, Maine
Shirt Folder

122

Chronological. *Becky J. Davis, Waterville, Maine*

The focus of this resume is primarily on recent Education and Training, including clinical experience, followed by a brief Employment History. The shadow oval is a real eye-catcher.

DAVID STEVENS

235 West Thayer
Bismarck, ND 58501

(701) 255-3141

CAREER OBJECTIVE: Position as a Physical Therapy Assistant.

CERTIFICATION

• Board Exams Completed 10/16/95 - Results Pending

EDUCATION

5/95 UNIVERSITY OF NORTH DAKOTA-WILLISTON - Williston, ND
Associate of Applied Science Degree
Major: **Physical Therapist Assistant**

5/90 NORTH DAKOTA STATE SCHOOL OF SCIENCE - Wahpeton, ND
Associate of Science Degree
Major: **Business Administration**

PROFESSIONAL EXPERIENCE

Clinicals: UNIVERSITY OF NORTH DAKOTA REHAB - Grand Forks, ND
Instructor: Laurie Babcock   4/10/95 - 5/18/95

ANNE CARLSEN SCHOOL FOR CRIPPLED CHILDREN - Jamestown, ND
Instructor: Tom Magstadt   2/6/95 - 3/15/95

REFERENCES AVAILABLE UPON REQUEST

123

Chronological. *Claudia Stephenson, location unknown*

A short resume with little information but visually powerful because of the shadow page border; thick horizontal line; and all-uppercase letters in the name, headings, and last line.

ROXANNE REYSER
85 West First Street
Hinsdale, IL 60521
(XXX)XXX-XXXX

CAREER OBJECTIVE

To obtain a Registered Nurse position with a hospital, long-term care facility, or other healthcare organization.

EDUCATION

College of DuPage, Glen Ellyn, IL
A.A.S. degree in Nursing, 1995
GPA 3.7/4.0, President's List, Graduated with High Honors
Member, Phi Theta Kappa, National Honor Society

Triton College, River Grove, IL
Nurse Assistant Program, Awarded CNA Certificate, 1987
President's Honor List

Unicare Health Facilities, Inc., Fond du Lac, WI
Nurse Assistant Certificate, 1985

EXPERIENCE

Nov. 1989-Present

HOME HEALTH AGENCY, River Forest, IL
Home Health Aide
Employed full-time while in school to fund education.

Apr. 1992-Sept. 1993

HOME HEALTH PLUS, Westchester, IL
Home Health Aide

Apr. 1991-Aug. 1992

DR. KOPP, D.D.S., Elmhurst, IL
Dental Assistant

Feb. 1990-Sept. 1990

WESTLAKE HOSPITAL, Melrose Park, IL
CNA - Critical Care

Prior Experience Summary 1983-1988

Rolling Meadows Nursing Home, Fond du Lac, WI
CNA • Activity Assistant • Dietary Aide

St. Agnes Hospital, Fond du Lac, WI
Home Health Aide

North Shore Terrace Nursing Home, North Chicago, IL
Activity Assistant

Care Center East Nursing Home, Fond du Lac, WI
CNA • Dietary Assistant

REFERENCES

Available on Request

124

Chronological. *Julie R. Marshall, location unknown*

Boldfacing calls attention to superior academic work. Boldfacing and underlining make job positions stand out in the Experience section. Prior Experience is downplayed without bold.

CYNTHIA NURSE, R.N., A.D.N.
123 Healthcare Lane
Medville, MA 12345
(222) 222-2222

PROFILE

Efficient, caring registered nurse with well-rounded experience gained through increasingly responsible positions in community health care and clinical settings. Skills include case management to ensure quality and cost-effective care as well as direct patient care. Regularly update knowledge and skills by taking continuing education units. Currently working toward IV and gerontology certifications.

HIGHLIGHTS OF QUALIFICATIONS

- 9 years of nursing experience.
- Received recognition from current employer for developing SIDS consultation standards to be followed by state visiting nurses.
- Knowledgeable about third party payer requirements and experienced in processing paperwork for all types of insurance coverage.
- Excellent organization and time management skills. Complimented by supervisors for concise paperwork.
- Known for being loyal and a good resource person for other nurses; familiarize self with policies and adhere to them.

PROFESSIONAL EXPERIENCE

1991-present   VISITING NURSE & COMMUNITY CARE OF NORTHERN MA, Mountain, MA
Case Manager / Community Health Nurse

Manage caseload and provide direct home nursing care to an average of 35 patients in the towns of Mountain, Scenic, and History. See an average of 8 to 10 patients a day.

- Establish appropriate care plans for patients and their families: consult with physicians and therapists; refer patients to physical therapy, occupational therapy, speech therapy and counselors. Coordinate services with hospice nurses. Make referrals to DCYS and protective services for the elderly.
- Provide family support services: teach families about diseases, precautions and restrictions; counsel families regarding proper medication use, medication side effects and diet.
- Obtain approval from insurance companies for visits. Process paperwork in compliance with third party payer reporting requirements, including Medicare, Medicaid, HMO's, and private insurance companies. Conference with case management company to manage funding.
- Provide direct patient care: geriatrics, adult health, maternal/infant health; care includes physical and disease process assessments, administering medications, changing dressings. Supervise 20 home health aides. Precept student nurses and new employees. Conduct in-services.
- Conduct blood pressure clinics and cholesterol screening.

Honors: Selected as "Nurse of the Month" in recognition of developing SIDS consultation standards. Chosen out of approximately 300 employees.

- Continued -

125

Combination. *Annamarie Pawlina, location unknown*

All-uppercase side headings within dual horizontal lines are the distinctive design feature of this resume. Note the honors in italic in the Professional Experience and Education sections.

CYNTHIA NURSE, R.N., A.D.N.
(222) 222-2222
Page 2

PROFESSIONAL EXPERIENCE (continued)

1986-1991 HISTORY HOSPITAL, History, MA
        Staff Nurse   (1989-1991)
        Licensed Practical Nurse   (1986-1989)

Performed patient care and taught care to patients and families, including discharge planning on a 40-bed Urology unit. Assisted physicians in bed-side procedures. Conducted in-services.

- As **staff nurse,** also performed evening charge duties and functioned as a resource person for staff, students and orientees.
- Wrote two patient teaching guides: cystoscopy and catheter leg bag use/care.

Honors: Nominated for Jane Peters Award for excellence in nursing, 1990.
Promoted from LPN I to LPN II for excelling in clinical skills, 1988.

EDUCATION

Associate Degree in Nursing, History Community College, History, MA, 1989.
Honors: College Scholar, Dean's List (cum laude).

Practical Nurse Diploma, Taylor Voc / Tech School, History, MA, 1986.

CPR certified (current).

Continuing Education Units
Units completed include: ...urology and prostrate cancer ...gerontology (preparation for certificate) ...wound care... psychiatric patients... HIV and AIDS... SIDS.

ACTIVITIES

LPN Council alternate and Employee Counsel LPN representative.
Volunteer for American Cancer Society, "Great American Smokeout."

Note, too, the parallel verbs (Manage . . . Establish . . . Provide . . . Obtain . . . Provide . . . Conduct) at the bottom of the first page. This is good writing style—especially in resumes. Diamond bullets grab attention for the qualifications in the Highlights section.

SANDRA L. COLLECTOR
52 Standing Bridge Road
Thomas, GA 19207
(555) 555-0000

SUMMARY OF QUALIFICATIONS
➤ Excellent written and oral communication skills. Use and understand medical terminology.
➤ Work well with patients, office personnel and insurance companies.
➤ Superior track record of successful private and Medicare insurance collection and reimbursement.
➤ Familiar with CPT and ICD9 insurance codes.
➤ Computer programs: COMPUSYSTEM, ACES, IDX (Thomas Hospital Corp.); WordPerfect.
➤ Type 50 wpm and able to operate all types of office machines.

EXPERIENCE
Account Specialist - *Health Resources*, 1998-Present.
Thomas Health Corporation, Thomas, GA
➤ Handle insurance collection for 34 physicians in the Endocrinology, Pulmonary, Infectious Disease, Urgent Treatment and General Family practices.
➤ File all primary and secondary private insurance claims. Communicate effectively with patients and insurance companies to resolve problems.
➤ Answer all explanation of benefits questions.
➤ Resolved 2 years of delinquent claims in 3 months.
➤ **Increased collection rate from 34% to 116%.**
➤ Currently handling Workers' Compensation claims for all doctor groups (Specialty, Family, and Urgent Treatment Centers).

Office Assistant (Thomas Clinic) - *PT Aide* (St. John Clinic), 1995-1998.
Thomas Sports Medicine & Rehabilitation, P.A., Thomas/St. John, GA
➤ Transcribed notes for 5 physical therapists
➤ Answered telephones, scheduled patients, entered data into computer.
➤ Verified insurance coverage.
➤ Filed all Medicare charges on ACES computerized program.
➤ Worked account receivables and prepared monthly statements.
➤ Handled patient calls and all office procedures in absence of office manager.
➤ **Maintained a 96.6% collection rate.**
➤ As physical therapy aide, assisted therapists with 30 patients per day.

EDUCATION
Medical Business Certificate. 1997
Local Technical College, Thomas, GA
Medical Terminology, Communication, Legal Issues, Professionalism, Financial Billing, and Clinicals.

Professional Bookkeeping and Accounting, 1999
Basic accounting course.
Professional Career Development Institute, Salem, GA

Excellent references available on request.

126

Combination. *Karen Swann, Clemson, South Carolina*

Distinctive bullets pull the reader's vision down the page to ensure that both the Summary of Qualifications section and the Experience section are read. Achievements are in bold.

MELISSA MEDTEK
555 Carlisle Drive
Banton, NJ 00000
(555) 555-5555

OBJECTIVE

Laboratory Technician / Medical Assistant Position

SUMMARY OF QUALIFICATIONS

- Proficient in all phases of back-office and laboratory work; cross-trained to handle front-desk responsibilities.
- Self-starter; take initiative to insure that job gets done properly and efficiently.
- Determined to excel; willing to take on new challenges and responsibilities.
- Thrive in fast-paced environment; able to handle multiple tasks simultaneously.
- Strong documentation skills with focus on insuring accuracy.
- Establish excellent rapport with patients and staff.
- Experienced on computerized billing/scheduling system.

PERTINENT SKILLS

Laboratory Testing: Venipuncture - Capillary collections - CBC testing - Glucose testing Urine cultures - Non-stress testing - Alpha fetoprotein testing

Clinical Assistance: Norplant implants/removals - Colposcopies - Hysteroscopies - Leeps Endometrial biopsies - Cryos - Breast aspirations - Vital signs

Front Office: Appointment setting - Phone screening - Computerized billing - Physican scheduling - Insurance

EDUCATION

Specialized Clinical Assistant, 1994 • Stanton Technical Institute, Stanton, NJ

CERTIFICATIONS

EKG Technician Certificate • OSHA Regulations Certificate • CPR Certificate

PROFESSIONAL EXPERIENCE

MEDICAL ASSISTANT / LABORATORY TECHNICIAN   May 1994 - Present
Banton Obstetrics and Gynecology Associates, Banton, NJ

Developed expertise in a wide range of front and back office responsibilities for this eight-doctor practice. Initially hired as an entry-level laboratory technician; quickly mastered laboratory responsibilities and was asked to oversee laboratory; also functioned as a medical assistant and receptionist.

- Commended by physicians for being a "fast learner," and exhibiting the ability to accommodate the diverse needs of the medical staff.
- Reorganized laboratory, making it a fully functioning, efficient operation.
- Handled all laboratory responsibilities, including: Operating, maintaining, calibrating, and troubleshooting equipment - Maintaining logs - Ordering supplies
- Methodically screened numerous patient phone calls and determined proper handling.
- Developed excellent rapport with patients by being compassionate, upbeat, and informative.

127

Combination. *Rhoda Kopy, Toms River, New Jersey*

A trim resume whose design is easily comprehended. In the Pertinent Skills section, clustering skills according to three categories in boldface is helpful for the reader.

Gina J. Browne, RHIT, CMT

43 Vintage Road
Bayview, Maine XXXXX
(207) xxx-xxxx

Profile

Certified Medical Transcriptionist and Accredited Records Technician with more than twenty years of experience at Downeast Maine Medical Center. Solid knowledge of multiple dictating and transcription software. Strong relationships with medical, administrative and support staff. Excellent organizational, communication and management skills. Successfully completed 40 continuing education credits every two years. Excellent skills in the following areas:

- Office Management
- Scheduling
- Quality Assurance Programs
- Staff Supervision

- Medical Terminology, Anatomy & Physiology
- MS Word, Excel and MS Outlook
- Telephone Communications
- Training & Staff Development

Professional Experience

DOWNEAST MAINE MEDICAL CENTER, Bayview, Maine, 1967 - 1999
HeIS Coordinator (1999)

Liaison between Associated Transcription and DMMC. Accountable for the resolution of transcription issues within departments. Assessed transcription turnaround times and provided a written report in graph format to department heads on a weekly basis. Ensured that quality standards were being met and maintained. Work with physicians' offices on the retrieval of missing transcripts.

- Established excellent working relationships with department heads following the dissolution and outsourcing of medical transcription services.
- Maintained longstanding professional relationships with physicians regarding transcription issues.

Supervisor / Manager Transcription (1980 –1999)

Managed transcription services for DMMC. Spearheaded effort to ensure that turnaround time of all medical dictation was 24 hours or less. Maintained staffing schedule for seven days a week, 24 hours a day coverage. Managed time cards, evaluations and tracking for all departmental employees' continuing education. Maintained productivity figures and quarterly analysis of transcribed documents. Responsible for interviewing, hiring, disciplining and discharging staff. Maintained service contracts. Also transcribed medical dictation when necessary.

- Developed medical transcription training manual for new employees.
- Developed and instituted a quality assurance program in the medical transcription department.
- Oversaw the installation and employee training for two central dictating systems (Lanier 4800 system and Digital Voice System).
- Spearheaded the installation and development of training materials for two transcription software packages (MedPerfect and Medescribe).
- Established the first AAMT Chapter in the State of Maine and served as the first President.
- Acted as liaison between DMMC and the Bayside Job Corps Center and the Training Institute on the development of a one-year program for Medical Transcription training.
- Set up a separate medical records system in the Emergency Department of DMMC of all emergency department records to ensure speed and efficiency in records retrieval.

Medical Records Clerk / Medical Transcriptionist (1967 – 1979)

Responsible for admissions, discharge, chart assembly, chart deficiency, filing/retrieval of records, correspondence, coding, birth certificates, death certificates and any miscellaneous job that needed to be done. Completed an eighteen month medical record technology program and became an Accredited Records Technician.

128

Combination. *Joan M. Roberts, Bangor, Maine*

Thin lines enclosing the individual's name and under each section head make it easy to grasp the overall arrangement of the resume. In the Professional Experience section duties

UNIVERSITY OF MAINE, Bayview Campus, Bayview, Maine
Instructor of Medical Transcription, 1987 – 1988

Instructed students on use of transcription equipment, transcription of medical dictation, use of reference sources, productivity and quality analysis of transcribed work. Graduated two classes of students.

Education & Professional Development

American Association of Medical Transcription, Modesta, CA
Certified Medical Transcriptionist, 1985.

American Health Information Association, Atlanta, GA
Accredited Records Technician, 1975

Professional Development Programs:
MS Office, Excel and MS Outlook
Stress Management
Supervisor Management
Continuing Education through Maine Health Information Association
Continuing Education through Pine Tree Chapter AAM and the National Office

Professional Affiliations

Maine Health Information Association
American Health Information Association
Pine Tree Chapter – AAMT
American Association for Medical Transcription

and responsibilities are put in paragraphs. Under the first two paragraphs accomplishments are listed and bulleted. Italic is used extensively: in the contact information, section headings, job positions, duty paragraphs, and almost entirely in the Education section.

JANE B. DOE
555 Main Street ◆ Anytown, USA, 00000 ◆ (000) 000-000

REIMBURSEMENT SPECIALIST

To obtain a challenging, growth-oriented opportunity within the health care industry where my background and skills can be best utilized.

CAREER SUMMARY

- Fourteen years of progressive experience in the medical field, including 11+ years in health care reimbursement administration within two major pharmaceutical/health care firms.
- Experienced in all phases of computerized patient accounting procedures, patient control records, payor and accounts receivable analysis, purchasing, inventory control and payroll.
- Effective liaison between insurance companies, managed care organizations, patients and employers to ensure timely processing of claims and collectibles.
- Experienced in researching, preparing and formalizing proposed contracts for managed care organizations and insurance companies.
- Strong oral and written communicator; excellent supervisory and managerial skills.
- Licensed Pharmacy Technician since 1984; trained under licensed pharmacist (Get-Well Hospital) for compounded IV medications.

MAJOR ACCOMPLISHMENTS

ACME PROFESSIONAL SERVICE CENTERS:

- Started as Reimbursement Account Administrator; promoted to Reimbursement Service Manager, Corporate Reimbursement Specialist, and Regional Reimbursement Service Manager.
- Assisted in developing business plan of action to regionalize reimbursement functions, including intake, billing and collections.
- Traveled extensively to interview, hire and train personnel in computer system applications, reimbursement policies and procedures, and intake, billing and collections.
- Served as part of a team effort to write the company reimbursement reference and training manuals.
- Expanded Central reimbursement department from one to twenty-five employees.

EMPLOYMENT HISTORY

AUTOMATED HEALTH CARE, INC.	*November 1994 - Present*
Senior Health Care Consultant	
ACME PROFESSIONAL SERVICE CENTERS	*July 1989 - November 1994*
Reimbursement Service Manager (11/93 - 11/94)	
Corporate Reimbursement Specialist (11/92 - 11/93)	
Reimbursement Service Manager (11/92 - 11/92)	
Reimbursement Account Administrator (7/89 - 11/91)	
XYZ PHARMACEUTICALS/ABC HEALTH CARE	*August 1984 - July 1989*
Home Patient Representative/Reimbursement Coordinator	
GET-WELL HOSPITAL, Anytown, USA	*September 1981 - August 1984*
Admissions Coordinator/Pharmacy Technician	

EDUCATIONAL BACKGROUND

General Studies (1979-198), Anytown University, Anytown, USA

References Will Be Furnished Upon Request

129

Combination. *Joellyn Wittenstein, Arlington Heights, Illinois*

The Employment History displays steady growth in reimbursement services. Underlining makes evident the different workplaces. The Career Summary emphasizes experience.

KATRINA A. MEDIC

57 Seaside Boulevard ♦ Gorham, ME ♦ 05505
(207) 555-5505

OBJECTIVE

Seeking a position where I can utilize my education and experience to the benefit of my employer.

SUMMARY OF QUALIFICATIONS

- Dedicated to helping others; people person, sensitive and responsive to their needs.
- Excellent communication skills, able to establish rapport with patients.
- Self-motivated and dependable, capable of handling a variety of task.
- Fluency in medical terminology ~ knowledgeable in CPR.
- Capable of working independently or as a cooperative "team" member.
- Adaptable to new situations; willingness to learn more.

EDUCATION

Certified Dental Assistant
Dental Career Institute - Portland, Maine
Emphasis on: oral anatomy, medical terminology, chair side assistance, sterilization techniques and radiology (qualification for State x-ray certification)
Degree Date: 1993

Certified Nursing Assistant
Southern Maine Vocational Technical Institute - South Portland, Maine
Degree Date: 1991

Scarborough High School - Scarborough, Maine
Diploma: 1990

EMPLOYMENT HISTORY

Certified Nursing Assistant ♦ 1991 to Present
TLC Center, Portland, Maine
- Responsible for basic direct patient care, responding to patients requests and immediate needs.
- Providing assistance to patients at meal times.
- Maintaining patients personal hygiene.
- Monitoring vital signs and charting results.

Dental Assistant ♦ 1993 to Present
Cumberland Dental Health Center - Scarborough, Maine
- Volunteer position - assisting in dental procedures.
- Providing chair side assistance to Dentist.
- Preparing materials for various treatments.
- Cleaning and sterilizing instruments.
- Extensive communication with patients, greeting clients and establishing rapport.

Scarborough Rescue Student Reserve Member ♦ 1988 to 1990
Scarborough Rescue - Scarborough, Maine
- Two year student apprentice training program between Scarborough High School and the Scarborough Rescue educating students about all aspect of emergency medical care.
- Trained and received certification in CPR.
- Responded to 911 calls, and assessed condition of patients upon arrival.
- Monitored vital signs, charted results, and performed basic emergency medical procedures.

Junior Volunteer ♦ 1986 to 1989
Southern Maine Medical Center - Biddeford, Maine
- Summer employment providing a variety of services including transport of patients between rooms/floors; assisting with the discharge patients; general housekeeping including bed making; delivering flowers to patients; and answering the phones.

REFERENCES

Available upon request

130

Combination. *Patricia Martel, Saco, Maine*

The type was made smaller—but margins were not made narrower—so that a considerable amount of information could be put on one page without reducing white space.

Clair Voyant

1000 Moon Circle
Lafayette, LA 70503
318/111-1111

CAPABILITIES   Spiritual Psychic . . . Clairvoyant . . . Lightworker . . . Way-shower . . . Tarot . . . Regular Deck . . . Channeled Information.

PROFILE
◆ A dedicated professional, providing guidance for living in the New Age, with five years experience in providing professional readings and approximately twenty years in providing readings for family and friends.
◆ Possess the ability and willingness to help and heal others through spiritual means.
◆ Offer unconditional love, support and information to individuals seeking to improve their lives.
◆ Concentrate on keeping clients focused on the now moment and teaching them to trust their intuition as a guide to making appropriate choices now, which ensures a more gratifying future.
◆ Provide insight, support and guidance for alien abductees.

EDUCATION   COLORADO PSYCHIC CENTER, Denver, Colorado   1990 - Present
Currently working with Ima Psychic (my personal reader and metaphysical mother) twice weekly by phone to enhance and refine my natural psychic abilities. Travel to the Center at least once per year for continuing education, guidance and exploring new trends.

UNIVERSITY OF SOUTHWESTERN LOUISIANA/T.H. HARRIS VO-TECH SCHOOL
Practical Nursing Degree

PROFESSIONAL   *Psychic*   1990 - Present
BACKGROUND
◆ Provide private readings for individuals.
◆ Work Psychic Fairs as a reader.
◆ Provide readings at Books, Books and More Books (a nation-wide bookstore chain).
◆ Teach meditation classes and manifestation classes.
◆ Work with crystals and teach others to work with crystals for their own private use.
◆ Co-lead weekend retreats for adults desiring to be more spiritually aware and to expand their consciousness.

Private Duty Nurse for a nursing agency.   1990
Charge Nurse for a nursing home.
◆ Provided compassionate and loving care and support to patients and families.

131

Combination. *Leah K. Goodrich, location unknown*

On the very day the writer learned of my use of this resume, she got a call from "Clair," who asked about interest in her resume for the book. "Clair Voyant" must be clairvoyant!

Hospitality

Resumes at a Glance

RESUME NO.	LAST OR CURRENT OCCUPATION	GOAL	PAGE
132.	Kitchen Staff and Waitperson	Not specified	209
133.	Owner of catering service	Position in restaurant management	210
134.	Asst. Manager of natl. training unit for pizza chain	Position in restaurant management	211
135.	Assistant Manager, Dining and Beverage, Country Club	Not specified	212
136.	Restaurant Manager	Management position	213
137.	Restaurant Manager	Position in customer service and management	214
138.	Operations Supervisor	Not specified	216
139.	Broiler/Prep Cook	Assistant or Sous Chef	217
140.	Hotel General Manager	Management position	218
141.	Restaurant Owner/Manager	Not specified	220
142.	Manager of executive dining room	Not specified	221
143.	Server/Banquet Server/Graveyard Captain	Position in hotel and restaurant service	222
144.	Facilities Chef	Director of Food Service or Executive Chef	224

HAROLD B. LONG

| 123 Mainstreet | City, State 10101 | (555) 444-3210 |

EDUCATION

LAURENCE TECHNOLOGICAL UNIVERSITY — City, State
Pursuing a *Bachelor of Science Degree* in **MECHANICAL ENGINEERING**
SCHOOLCRAFTED COLLEGE — City, State
ASSOCIATE OF SCIENCE DEGREE — 1993
Concentration of Studies in *Mathematics* and *Science*

QUALIFICATIONS

- Excellent communicator; able to inform, relay messages and speak with superiors, colleagues and subordinates
- Conscientious and reliable employee
- Able to follow a project through to completion, using decision-making skills
- Efficient in following orders and directions

EMPLOYMENT HISTORY

O'SHUCKS BAR AND GRILL — City, State
KITCHEN STAFF AND WAITPERSON — 1994 to Present
- Responsibilities include: maintaining a pleasant attitude in working with the public while supporting employer in — taking orders from customers, short-order cooking, assisting in kitchen where needed.

RUBY WEDNESDAY — City, State
KITCHEN STAFF — 1990 to 1994
- Assisted in kitchen and general janitorial in a timely, efficient manner.

QUALITY MAINTENANCE and JANITORIAL — City, State
OWNER/WORKER — 1987 to 1990
- Entrepreneurial effort in starting and running a business. Contracted residential and commercial customers for cutting, mowing, edging and maintaining lawns and subdivision entrances.

ADVERTISING SYSTEMS — City, State
ASSEMBLER/DRIVER — 1985 to 1987
- Light production, assembly-line work and managed the hi-lo; some maintenance and janitorial responsibilities.

THE CITY NEWS — City, State
DELIVERY — 1980 to 1985
- Managed paper route, handled customer inquiries and made sure papers were delivered in a timely manner in excellent condition (wrapped in bad weather, etc.), collected and kept account of payments.

EASTERN T.V. SERVICES — City, State
GENERAL LABOR/DELIVERY — 1980 to 1988
- Picked-up, delivered appliances and ran general errands for owner.

ASSOCIATIONS AND AFFILIATIONS

MODEL ROCKET CLUB — **PRESIDENT AND FOUNDER**
- Engineered, built and tested model rockets using physics principles to investigate flight

CITY ASTRONOMY CLUB — **MEMBER**
- Studied, investigated, enjoyed and participated in all aspects of astronomy

References Available On Request

132

Combination. *Lorie Lebert, Novi, Michigan*

An A.S. degree graduate who is pursuing a B.S. degree. Horizontal lines of fixed length make the resume's sections visible at a glance. Bold small caps highlight positions.

Denise A. Robertson
2323 West 121st Street
Piper, Illinois 00000
(555) 555-5555

objective

❑ A responsible position in Restaurant Management.

summary

❑ Creative and technically proficient; over six years of related experience.
❑ Strong organizational skills; demonstrated talent for special event planning and coordination.
❑ Energetic, positive demeanor, with a verifiable record of motivating staff to meet objectives.

education

CHICAGO STATE UNIVERSITY, Chicago, Illinois
Associate in Applied Science, Food Service Management
Graduation date: December 1995 ❑ GPA: 3.4/4.0

STUDENTS IN FOOD SERVICE MANAGEMENT
Member, Program Committee

❑ Assisted in planning and coordinating educational programs for members, e.g., guest speakers, "job shadowing," and tours.

work history

ROBERTSON CATERING, Piper, Illinois
Owner, 1992 - Date

❑ Manage a part-time business while attending college full-time. Establish and maintain strong communication lines with clients to create memorable affairs; emphasis is on traditional American cuisine for groups of 10 to 75.

BOB'S BURGER WORLD, Piper, Illinois, 1988 - 1992
Assistant Manager, 1990 - 1992

❑ Began as a Clerk; promoted to Crew Leader after six months. As Assistant Manager, opened the restaurant, oversaw cash control procedures, reconciled store bank, and made deposits.

❑ Supervised and coached a crew of up to 10, handling customer relations, maintaining inventory for daily needs, and ensuring fast delivery of orders.

❑ Reduced staff turnover 35% in one year by initiating an award and incentive system for employee excellence.

certifications

❑ Certified Red Cross First Aid and CPR Instructor

133

Combination. *Jennie R. Dowden, location unknown*

A different touch is the use of all-lowercase letters for the side headings. It draws attention to them and makes them seem less formal. Boldfacing helps you spot the positions quickly.

MORRIS A. PETERS

5440 Ridge Circle
Norfolk, Virginia 23550
804 • 663 • 9876

OBJECTIVE

To obtain a position at the management level in a food service establishment.

EXPERIENCE

PIZZA PARLOR, Virginia Beach, VA. **Assistant Manager of National Training Unit**.
Trained groups of 8-12 manager trainees from various cities across the U.S. Course consisted of a 3 week program designed to enable the trainees to open new units. Hired, supervised, scheduled, counseled, and trained employees in the concept of company policy. Responsible for maintaining a clean and well organized facility. Maintained and dispatched up to 33 company vehicles nightly. Tracked and analyzed daily sales, labor control worksheet, weekly sales analysis, payroll, operational analysis, ordering and inventory control, profit and loss statement and POOP sheet. 1985-1987

EASTERN STEER FAMILY STEAK HOUSE, Norfolk, VA. **Assistant Manager**.
Supervised, scheduled, and counseled 40-50 employees. Responsible for ordering, receiving, and maintaining stock inventory. Closed out all registers daily, made cash deposits, prepared Daily Sales Report, TAB sheets, profit and loss statements, and payroll. Personnel management included interviewing, hiring and firing of employees. Made personal contact with customers and promoted the restaurant to neighboring businesses. 1985

CIMMARON HOUSE, Norfolk, VA. **Kitchen Supervisor**.
Supervised and trained 30-40 employees in all aspects of a high volume kitchen including inventory, ordering and receiving of all stock. Opened and closed dining room and bar registers, prepared daily sales report and cash drops. Made daily prep sheet assuring that all phases of kitchen operations included sanitation were accomplished in a proper and timely manner. Filled in production slots as needed. 1984-1985

DENMAN'S, Suffolk, VA. **Kitchen Supervisor**.
Responsible for all aspects of kitchen operations including broiler, grill, hot and cold tables, prep, and sanitation operations. Trained new personnel in the same duties. 1984

HOWARD'S AIRCRAFT COMPANY, Long Beach, CA. **Electronics Engineer**.
Provided technical assistance on board naval ships during extended periods at sea. 1983-1984.

U.S. NAVY.
Supervised 20-75 men in a state of the art electronics shop. Honorably discharged as an E5. 1979-1982.

EDUCATION

Naval Electronics School. Associate Degree. Top 10% of class.

134

Chronological. *Anne G. Kramer, Virginia Beach, Virginia*

The eye-catcher is the set of three lines between the name and the contact information at the top of the page. The other lines help you see the length of each resume section.

JACK MARSHALL JONES

4321 ROSEWOOD — NORTHCITY, MICHIGAN 48321
248.555.5555

CAREER FOCUS

Enthusiastic results-driven professional with experience managing operations, business, and people. Extremely good situation manager, remaining competent and confident in stressful situations. Excellent analytical and organizational skills. Diligent problem-solver and decision-maker.

SUMMARY OF QUALIFICATIONS

- Experience dealing with groups, teams, individuals in unique situations within fast-paced environments.
- Knowledge of international culture through numerous travels and experiences.
- Strong background and understanding of regular and reserve wine, and wine selection.
- Computer efficient with knowledge of MAC and PC environments, including Windows 95, Micros, Aloha Point-Of-Sale (touch screen), WordPerfect, PageMaker, and industry-specific software.

EXPERIENCE

WALNUT BROOK COUNTRY CLUB   Northcity, Michigan
ASSISTANT MANAGER — Dining & Beverage, xxxx-current

- Provide excellent management and service for a privately-owned club with 325 class-A members offering excellence in cuisine as well as golf, tennis, swimming, and social activities.
- Manage the dining room and bar area for the club; arrange all weddings, parties, and special events; organize and schedule personnel.
- Prepare and arrange wine auctions and collections; prepare regular and reserve wine lists; organize and design wine dinners.

GENERATION COMPANIES   Southside, Michigan
MANAGER – *Sorté Restaurant*, xxxx-xx

- Managed the floor operations of new, upscale, customer-focused restaurant. Responsibilities included management of food preparation, sanitary requirements, local and state regulations, money management, and security concerns.
- Administered all product management, computer issues, customer relations, employee communications.
- Also worked under Kenneth Trout at company owned Laurel Restaurant.

UNITED STATES MARINE CORPS
CORPORAL (NCO E-4), xxxx-xx

- Managed several assignments and various job responsibilities including repair/maintenance of weapons. Personally responsible for work center (offensive weapons systems). Oversaw troop operations and unit deployment exercises, including moving materials and personnel overseas (Japan, Korea, Norway, the Mediterranean, and Bosnia).
- Directed unit's clerical and operation needs; ordered supplies, organized work details, conducted regular physical fitness programs, and weekly review sessions. Worked with the public and civilian defense contractors for armament systems.
  Awards: Rifle Sharpshooter, National Defense Service Medal, Sea Service Deployment Ribbon, Good Conduct Medal, Navy Unit Commendation.

WESTSIDE FIRE DEPARTMENT   Westside, Michigan
FIREFIGHTER, xxxx-xx

- Responsible for contending with situation management; applying emergency medical techniques; team cooperation; value of order and discipline. Developed strong skills dealing with chaotic situations.

EDUCATION

EASTSIDE COMMUNITY COLLEGE   Eastside, Michigan
General Studies – maintained 3.9/4.0 GPA

Military Courses: ▸ Naval Aviation Dispersed Technical Publications Librarian ▸ Non-Nuclear Ammunition Inventory Accuracy Course ▸ Aviation Ordinance Ammunition Technician ▸ Hazardous Material/Explosive Drivers Course

135

Combination. *Lorie Lebert, Novi, Michigan*

Another resume in which horizontal lines under section headings help to define the section length visually. Note "Career Focus" as an alternative heading for a Profile.

IRENE STEPHENS
123 Whiteoak Drive
Radcliff, KY 40100
(502) 555-1111

OBJECTIVE

Management Position

EXPERIENCE

Manager, 11/92 - Present
Appleton's Restaurant, 555 Elm Road, Hardin, KY 40100
Supervised employees. Responsible for P&L. Ordered
supplies.

Manager, 8/89 - 11/92
Costello's, 111 Maple Lane, Hardin, KY 40100
Supervised employees. Full P&L responsibility. Used
computer.

Assistant Store Manager, 7/86 - 8/89
Computer Center, 555 Ash Drive, Radcliff, KY 40100
Full range of management responsibilities. Directed sales
floor. Supervised employees.

Cashier (part-time), 1/86 - 5/86
Food Mart, 111 University Drive, Lexington, KY 40200

EDUCATION

Associate degree in Business, 1986
University of KY, Lexington, KY

REFERENCES

Available upon request.

136

Chronological (Before). *Provided by Connie S. Stevens, location unknown*

This do-it-yourself attempt to write a resume has too much white space. Actually, what you see here is the professional writer's fictionalized copy of the client's original resume.

Irene Stephens

123 Whiteoak Drive	Radcliff, Kentucky 40100	(502) 555-1111

Objective

A responsible position that will utilize my expertise in customer service and management

Summary of Qualifications

- Demonstrated ability to provide significant contribution to bottom line results. Noted for streamlining operations and increasing profits.
- A strategic planner who is able to creatively anticipate the needs of the future.
- Skilled in directing, coordinating, and motivating staff to successfully complete business objectives.

Relevant Experience

APPLETON'S RESTAURANT • Hardin, KY   Nov 92 - Present
Manager
- ♦ *Directly responsible for cost reduction and improved efficiency by significantly reducing labor and food costs.* Effectively controlled cost in order to successfully operate within monthly budget. Successfully fulfilled profit and loss projections based upon last year's performance.
- ♦ Facilitated and coordinated marketing and advertising strategy. *Raised delivery sales by 20% due to excellent sales strategy and superior marketing skills.*
- ♦ Hired, trained and developed, supervised, scheduled, promoted, terminated, and evaluated staff. Managed and controlled all payroll functions including maintenance of records and payroll adjustments. Monitored all payroll taxes, filings, journal entries, and accounts payable. Ordered and purchased supplies and monitored inventory.
- ♦ Exhibited excellent customer service, liaison, and follow-through skills.

COSTELLO'S • Hardin, KY   Aug 89 - Nov 92
Manager
- ♦ Full P&L responsibility. Conducted study of operations methods and costs. Pinpointed key cost improvement opportunities. Reorganized, trained, and motivated staff to higher levels of productivity. Significantly improved customer service, product, and store maintenance, expanded delivery area. *Result: Successfully directed profit improvement program which increased net sales and profits by 25% over previous year.*
- ♦ Hired, trained, supervised, scheduled, terminated, and evaluated staff. Maintained records of hours worked for payroll.
- ♦ Successfully utilized skills in diplomacy, tact, and problem-solving to effectively handle irate customers and defuse potentially explosive situations. Provided weekly reports on sales, labor, food costs, and inventory. Utilized Lotus 1-2-3 for payroll and inventory. Further utilized computer programs to track figures which were used as guidelines for making the P&L.

137

Combination (After). *Connie S. Stevens, location unknown*

The writer's rewrite of Resume 136—a self-contained lesson in resume development, design, and desktop publishing. Listing the ways Resume 137 differs from 136 can be instructive.

Irene Stephens Page 2

COMPUTER CENTER • Radcliff, KY   Jul 86 - Aug 89
Assistant Store Manager
- ◆ Developed and instituted the "Department Manager" system. *Took the nominally profitable department, expanded it, revamped the operating procedures, and increased sales by 50% in less than one year.*
- ◆ Oversaw full range of management responsibilities. Purchased and ordered for all departments. Met with sales representatives and fostered accounts with new vendors to better serve the store's needs.
- ◆ Coordinated special promotions and events. Prepared sales reports. Directed sales floor activities. Delegated responsibilities, monitored work done, and gave final approval upon completion. Hired, trained, and supervised employees. Utilized skills in diplomacy and tact to handle irate customer situations.

Education

University of Kentucky • Lexington, KY
Associate in Business Administration • 1986

Computer Skills

IBM-Compatible Computer • MacIntosh Computer
DOS • Windows • Lotus 1-2-3 • WordPerfect

Professional Memberships

Martin County Chamber of Commerce
Martin County Small Business Association

If you were an employer who thought Resumes 136 and 137 were from two different individuals, which person would you want to hire—the one described in 136, or the one in 137? The resume begins and ends with center-justification. Experience is doubly indented.

BRUCE BAILY

1000 North Street
Blandvile, IL 00000
(000) 000-0000

QUALIFICATIONS & STRENGTHS

◇ Time Management & Organizational Skills   ◇ Team Player & Problem-Solver
◇ Supervisory & Leadership Abilities   ◇ Self-Motivated
◇ Multi-Level Management   ◇ Training of Support Staff
◇ Strong Work Ethics   ◇ Computer Proficient

PROFESSIONAL EXPERIENCE

SUPERVISOR OF OPERATIONS
ANY COMPANY, Plano, VT, 1994 - Present
◇ Manage overall business operations for territory covering 150 mile radius, 17 branch locations, and 375 support staff
◇ Hold team meetings with support staff on a periodic basis
◇ Provide hands-on training with emphasis focused on generating increased sales and revenues

ASSISTANT MANAGER
FAMILY STYLE RESTAURANT, Family, NY, 1993 - 1994
◇ Performed extensive responsibilities including hiring, training, and scheduling of support staff
◇ Monitored business operations in coordination with company goals and objectives
◇ Provided excellent customer service relations

RESTAURANT OPERATIONS
NUMBER ONE IN TOWN, Anytown, MI, 1992 - 1993
◇ Primary responsibility included ordering of perishable food products
◇ Determined menu selections through thorough testing procedures
◇ Supervised 25 support staff in daily functions

ASSOCIATE MANAGER
TOP CLASS RESTAURANT, Top Class, NB, 1989 - 1992
◇ Provided exclusive service to patrons
◇ Generated additional revenue through establishing positive rapport with patrons
◇ Consulted on menu selection and accompanying wines

EDUCATION

<u>ASSOCIATES DEGREE in RESTAURANT MANAGEMENT</u>
National Restaurant College

Exclusive Meal Selection Seminar
Institute for Better Eating

Supervisory & Leadership Management
Professional Sales Management Training

REFERENCES - *Available Upon Request*

138

Combination. *Betty Callahan, location unknown*

The bullets are small, hollow diamonds that "lighten up" this resume whose type appears uniformly dark. An optical illusion is that each hollow bullet is light gray, not white.

François J. Boudreau

88 Harbor Place
Rock Cove, ME 00000

(207) 555-5555

Objective:

Assistant or Sous Chef

Summary of Qualifications:

- ✦ Associate's Degree in Culinary Arts with training in American and International Cuisines
- ✦ Restaurant experience has included broiler, grill, sauté, fryer, expo, breakfast and salads
- ✦ Able to handle a multitude of tasks at once, meeting deadlines under pressure
- ✦ Demonstrates ability to respond with speed and accuracy in a highly productive setting
- ✦ Works cooperatively and harmoniously with coworkers and supervisors
- ✦ Dedicated to quality in service and product

Experience:

Broiler/Prep Cook	Jacques Restaurant, West Cove, Maine (9/94 to Present) 200-seat Four Diamond restaurant featuring an extensive menu of French and American cuisine
Fry Cook	The Lobster Net, Port Hancock, Maine (1992-94) Indoor and outdoor dining, specializing in fresh lobsters and seafood; take-out and banquet service
Fry/Prep Cook	The Weathervane, Rocky Coast, Maine (1991) Traditional New England seafood served in a casual setting

Education:

Associate's Degree in Culinary Arts – Newbury College, Brookline, Massachusetts (1992)
Curriculum and Training included:

- ✧ Soup, Stock and Sauces
- ✧ Breads and Rolls
- ✧ Desserts
- ✧ Classical Bakeshop

- ✧ American Cuisine
- ✧ International Cuisine
- ✧ Yarde Manger
- ✧ Sanitation and Dining Room

139

Combination. *Becky J. Davis, Waterville, Maine.*

The graphic tells you that this resume is about food—the eating or preparation of it—before you have had a chance to read one word. In the Education section are more "gray" bullets!

MICHELLE M. MADISON
P. O. Box 7 ♦ Solomons Bay, Florida 11111
(555) 555-5555

Professional Objective: Management position in the Hotel/Hospitality or Service industries.

Highlights of Qualifications
» Ten years experience in the hospitality industry. Progressed through the ranks to General Manager of hotel and marina.
» Strong sales and customer service representative. Bottom line oriented.
» A team player. Motivates staff to go above and beyond.
» Received Gold Hospitality Award in 1993 and 1994; awarded to less than 3% of Choice Hotels' 3,000 hotels.

Professional Experience

Currently **General Manager** of a 60 room hotel and 187 slip marina. Recognized expertise in the following areas.

CUSTOMER SERVICE AND SALES
- Successfully augmented a variety of market segments including travel and leisure as well as business and government to assure highest occupancy.
  - Supervised sales staff in telemarketing and outside sales.
  - Negotiated corporate and government group rates.
- Developed marketing plans for the hotel and marina.
  - Established marketing focus to schedule advertising and public relations programs.
  - Created advertisements for various media and interacted with media representatives.
- Supervised food and beverage manager with banquet functions and restaurant operations.

MANAGEMENT AND ADMINISTRATION
- Supervised up to 30 hospitality personnel in all aspects of hotel operations for 100 room facility.
  - Was responsible for hiring, scheduling and supervising daily performance.
  - Provided performance evaluations, discipline, counseling and dismissals, as necessary.
  - Taught on-the-job training in all areas of hotel operations.
- Prepared annual budget for facilities. Tracked expenditures within budgeted guidelines.
  - Met or exceeded all revenue goals by at least 10%.
  - Managed accounts payable, receivables and collections and payroll.
  - Provided daily and monthly reports to corporate financial staff.

FACILITIES MANAGEMENT
- Performed quality assurance inspections of rooms, common areas and grounds. Ensured all facilities were safe, clean and well maintained.
- Oversaw decorating renovations.
  - Negotiated best value contracts with decorating companies.
- Managed 187 slip marina at waterfront hotel site.
  - Leased slips for short and long term berthing.
- Designed landscape layout, coordinated ongoing grounds planting. Supervised grounds maintenance staff.

140

Combination. *Janet Hanke, location unknown*

A new layout that secured a job interview. Three different kinds of bullets are used: chevrons (»), conventional filled circular bullets, and hyphens. Compared to the Employment

Madison, Michelle M.   Page 2

Education and Training

Associate of Arts degree in <u>Hotel, Restaurant and Institution Management</u>   1987
Midwestern County College, Edwards, MI

                Choice Hotel Management Training Course
                Holiday Inn Guest Service Management
                American Hotel and Motel Management Association:
                    Front Office Operations
                    Introduction to Hotel and Restaurant Management
                    Supervisory Development
                    Supervisory Housekeeping

Employment History

GENERAL MANAGER	Humphrey Hotels Comfort Inn · Solomons Point, FL	1992 - Present
GENERAL MANAGER	Humphrey Hotels Comfort Inn · Dorcester, TX	1990 - 1992
GENERAL MANAGER	Comfort Inn · Woodlawn, MN	1989 - 1990
ASSISTANT GENERAL MANAGER	Holiday Inn · New Carrolton, MA	1988 - 1989
ACCOUNTING MANAGER **NIGHT MANAGER/CHIEF AUDITOR** **FRONT DESK CLERK**	Holiday Inn · Somersville, OR	1986 - 1988
WAITRESS/BARTENDER/CASHIER	Ramada Inn · Somersville, OR	1985 - 1986
STORE SUPERVISOR	Drug Fair · Highland Lakes, SD	1982 - 1985

References available upon request.

History on page 2, the Professional Experience section on page 1 is a list of achievements grouped by three categories as side headings. The use of all-uppercase letters for the job positions in the Employment History emphasizes the person's managerial roles.

Robert F. Bailes

793 Broadway, Revere, Massachusetts 02151 • (617) 251-0000

Qualifications Summary

- **Business Management:** documented abilities in overseeing production, building a business, performing marketing and sales functions, and assuming total responsibility for business operations.
- **Financial Management:** skilled and experienced in budgeting, accounting, analyzing expenditures and focusing on bottom-line results.
- **Concept Development:** strong skills in envisioning, planning, implementing and streamlining new ideas.

Experience
1997-20XX

Owner / General Manager, FRIENDS RESTAURANT, Marblehead, Massachusetts
Overall management, direction and employee supervision of 40-seat restaurant and active take-out operation.
- Analyzed and reviewed all operations, both initially and on an ongoing basis, to assure efficient and profitable operation of the restaurant.
- Hired, trained, supervised, reviewed and disciplined staff of 20.
- Directed all sales, marketing and advertising efforts.
- Worked cooperatively with town and state agencies.
- Positioned business to respond rapidly to capitalize on restaurant-industry trends.

Accomplishments
- Increased business 42% from 1992 and grew to total sales of $250,000.
- Instrumental in reviving business and restoring to a profitable and thriving status.
- Achieved favorable restaurant review in the *Boston Globe*.
- Negotiated and accomplished profitable sale of the business.

1989-97

General Manager, TOWN & COUNTRY RESTAURANTS, Boston, Massachusetts
Assumed management and training responsibilities for various Town & Country-owned restaurants in Boston and suburbs.
- Managed the opening of four restaurants.
- Trained managers and staff for both back and front operations at locations throughout the Town & Country chain.

1987-89

Kitchen Manager, CHATEAU BANQUETING HALL, Quincy, Massachusetts
Managed all food service operations of high-volume banquet and functions facility.

1985-87

Night Chef, SHERATON BOSTON HOTEL, Boston, Massachusetts
In charge of kitchen servicing hotel dining room and room service for 300 guest rooms; also provided food service for banquets and functions.

1982-84

Owner / General Manager, THE COVE RESTAURANT, Bar Harbor, Maine
Purchased and managed 125-seat fine-dining establishment.
- Key accomplishment was in cost control of labor and food expenses, resulting in a highly profitable operation.
- Purchased restaurant from bankruptcy, restored to solvent operations, and sold for a substantial profit.

Education

FLORIDA INTERNATIONAL UNIVERSITY, Miami, Florida
Course work in International Management and Accounting, 1981-82

BUNKER HILL COMMUNITY COLLEGE, Charlestown, Massachusetts
Associate Degree in Restaurant Management, 1981

141

Combination. *Louise M. Kursmark, Cincinnati, Ohio*

An individual with extensive management experience who wanted to apply his skills in a different field. The challenge was to present his achievement in general business terms.

Barbara Stein

1000 Hudson Street ● New York, NY 11111 ● (212) 555-5555

CAPABILITIES:

- Detail-oriented, with strong analytical, research and problem-solving abilities.
- Enthusiastic and motivated; eager and willing to learn; adapt quickly to new tasks and environments.
- Possess excellent interpersonal and communication (oral and written) skills.
- Enjoy working with people towards a common goal and objective.
- Utilize solid organizational and time-management abilities in coordinating multiple projects at a given time.

ACHIEVEMENTS:

- Within the Hospitality Industry, maintained responsibility for daytime activities at a prominent New York City bar/restaurant.
  - Oversaw purchasing and inventory control of bar goods.
  - Supervised waitstaff and porters.
  - Planned and coordinated theme parties.
  - Placed daily orders and checked in deliveries.

- Assured that the highest quality of service was provided as Manager of the Executive/ Private Dining Room at the Union Bank of Switzerland.
  - Maintained stock and organized bar.
  - Coordinated special requests
  - Directed purchasing of fine, hand-made linens and china.

- Directed $300,000 renovation of 5,000 sq. ft. stone house in upstate New York.
  - Interfaced extensively with contractors and sub-contractors.
  - Obtained necessary local permits for construction.
  - Dealt with vendors, and closely monitored purchasing.
  - Completed project within budgetary and time constraints.

- Participate in various voluntary and fundraising activities, including producing craft goods for fair at the Friends Seminary.

EXPERIENCE:

Union Bank of Switzerland, New York, NY
  Manager, Executive Dining Room, 1979-1980

Morgan's Old New York, New York, NY
  Day Manager / Bartender, 1974-1975

SPECIALIZED TRAINING & EDUCATION:

Stenotype Academy, New York, NY; *Associates Degree: Paralegal Studies, 1994*
University of Paris, Sorbonne; *French Culture & History*
University of Manitoba; *Fine Arts, Sculpture and Pottery*

References Furnished Upon Request

142

Combination. *Judith Friedler, New York, New York*

A resume for a person with a hospitality background but who went back to school for a two-year paralegal degree. Transferable skills are bulleted in the Capabilities section.

Phillip J. Smith

3445 Vista Way, Paradisio, CA 94786 • Telephone: (601) 546-9878

Objective
Hotel and Restaurant Service

Summary
I am seeking steady, long-term employment in a restaurant/leisure/catering business where I can utilize my well developed inter-personal and communication skills to provide superior service and maximize repeat customer business. My goal is to develop my supervisory skills and to receive formal training in restaurant management in order to qualify for future advancement.

Employment History

The Alletella Hotel & Resort   08-22-94- Present
Room Service - Paradisio
    Server
    Banquet Server
    Graveyard Captain
    Assists in training new employees.
    Responsible for Graveyard Room Service.
    Provides an enjoyable dining experience for guests in their rooms.
    Commenced part-time, later promoted to full -time on the basis of performance.

The Coffee Spot   05-17-94 - 08-20-94
Espresso Cart - Paradisio
    Espresso Coffee Maker
    Established top sales record.
    Cleaned and maintained equipment.
    Performed quality control on all drinks sold.

Le Mar Resort   06-27-93 - 04-20-94
The Vista Cafe - Paradisio
    Server
    Averaged 100 guests per day.
    Served up to 800 guests at banquets.
    Served breakfast, brunch, lunch and dinner.
    Received comments on excellent people skills
    General Manager commented on my efficiency.
    Guests expressed appreciation to me for improving their stay.

    Host
    Seated guests.
    Organized breaks for servers.
    Performed supervisory duties.
    Servers expressed appreciation to me for making things run smoothly.

143

Combination. *David Newbold, location unknown*

The Summary is a skills summary that reveals more about the person's career goal. A unique design feature of this resume is the presentation of list items in shortest to longest order.

Phillip J. Smith

Page 2

The Swordfish Grill	12-05-92 - 06-20-93

Cafe & Grill - Paradisio
> <u>Server</u>
> Entertained Guests
> Served wine and drinks
> Served lunch and dinner
> Averaged 90 guests per day
> Worked well with other employees
> Displayed strong product knowledge
> Received many positive guest comments
> Helped guests select things from the menu
> Served up to 110 guests at catered functions
> Advised guests on wines that would compliment meals.

La Cantina Restaurant	09-05-92 - 01-04-93

- Paradisio
> <u>Busser & Host</u>
> Provided support services for servers
> As host, provided excellent first contact for guests

United States Navy	09-01-92 - Present

Active Reserve
> <u>Naval Journalist</u>
> Currently working on producing training films
> Awarded *"Iron Man"* in Naval Physical Readiness Test

United States Navy	09-01-89 - 09-01-92

Aircraft Carrier - *Midway*
> <u>Aviation Ordinance Man</u>
> Responsible for:
> *   Supervision of weapons handling teams
> *   Safe storage and transportation of explosive ordinance.
> *   Cleaning, maintenance and care of weapons/cargo elevators
> *   Calibration of tools & instruments relating to weapons elevators
> Nominated for Weapons Department *Junior Weaponeer*

Education

High School:	**Jonesboro High School**	Jonesboro, CA	Graduated
College:	**Miller College** Mass Communications	Miller, CA	1 Year
	City College, Hotel/Restaurant Management	Paradisio, CA	(In Progress)

The end of the Education section at the bottom of page 2 shows another way (as a minitable without lines) to indicate that work on a degree is in progress. Start and end dates for jobs in the Employment History section are specified with precision to the day.

DENNY DE VITO

555 E. 55th Street, Apt. 55
New York, NY 55555
(Residence) (555) 555-5555

OBJECTIVE

Director of Food Service or Executive Chef Position in a Corporation, Hotel or County Club

SUMMARY OF QUALIFICATIONS

✓ Extensive experience in large scale restaurant and catering operations.
✓ Comprehensive training at the American Restaurant School and Fromage et Pain.
✓ Strong front of the house and back of the house expertise.
✓ Dedication to professionalism and quality, while keeping an eye on costs.
✓ Excellent mastery of classic culinary techniques, with emphasis on French, Italian and American cuisine.
✓ Creative in recipe and menu planning.

PROFESSIONAL TRAINING

American Restaurant School (5/55 - 5/55), New York
Professional Culinary Arts Program

Fromage et Pain (5/55 - 5/55), Paris
Basic Culinary Techniques/Classic French Cuisine

L'Ecole Pomme (5/55 - 5/55), Paris
French Cuisine and Wine

EXPERIENCE

A Well Known Department Store (1955 - Present)　　　　　　　　　New York, NY
Facilities Chef
- In charge of food operations for all restaurants in 26 suburban stores, as well as 4 restaurants and catering facility in flagship New York store.
- Maximize profits through evaluation of food costs and menu prices. Maintain food consistency and prices throughout all facilities.
- Train a total kitchen staff of 725 in New York City and suburban stores.
- Manage all daily and special event catering operations (fashion shows and cosmetic seminars).
- Adhere to federal/state health guidelines. Oversee equipment repair, replacement and maintenance.

ACHIEVEMENTS
- Instrumental in opening new restaurants in New York City and suburban stores.
- Revamped identities/concepts of the above locations including restaurant design and construction, menus, staffing and other aspects of operations.
- Expanded in-house catering department from initial revenue of $500/week to $45,000/week.
- Developed a catering department cited as an "unexpected treat" by the *Daily Chef*.
- Improved gross profit 57% over a period of one year for all suburban units.
- Turned around unprofitable operations in suburban units by improving service, developing point-of-sale displays, enhancing quality control, controlling food costs and creating special promotions.

Pasta Repast (1955 - 1955)　　　　　　　　　　　　　　　　New York, NY
Executive Chef
- In charge of food operations for this 3-star Italian restaurant.

Leonardo Akbar's (1955) (1 month)　　　　　　　　　　　　　New York, NY
Externship (American Restaurant School)
- Developed culinary experience at this Italian/Moroccan restaurant.

References will be furnished on request.

144

Combination. *Etta Barmann, New York, New York*

The first half of this resume is center-justified, and the second half is left-justified. The result is a design that is pleasing in its diversity. Check marks in the Summary are a nice touch.

Human Resources

Resumes at a Glance

RESUME NO.	LAST OR CURRENT OCCUPATION	GOAL	PAGE
145.	Human Resources Manager	Not specified	227
146.	Human Resource Manager	Position in human resources management	230
147.	Human Resource Associate	Not specified	232

PROFESSIONAL

RÉSUMÉ

OF

MARILYN S. BROWN

145

Combination. *Ann Klint, Tyler, Texas*

A resume's title page shown here for its unique page border (or frame). The top and bottom are thicker than the left and right sides. This kind of border appears again on page 2.

MARILYN S. BROWN
0000 Pinetree Lane
Horton, Louisiana 00000
(000) 000-0000

HIGHLIGHTS OF QUALIFICATIONS

- **Certified Employee Benefit Specialist/Medical and Pension Plans** with 20+ years of progressive experience in quality and cost-contained management of employee benefits.
- Highly cognizant of benefit plans; federal, state, disability, and workers' compensation laws and regulations; and payroll/personnel systems and procedures.
- Demonstrated ability to **reduce expenses and complaints** and **increase profit margins, productivity, and efficiency.** Recognized for saving company $269,000.
- Efficient **problem solver** with excellent **decision-making**, **organizational**, and **interpersonal** skills; effectively communicate with people of all socioeconomic levels.
- Astute professional with strong work ethics. Thoughtful **team player. Goal-oriented.**

PROFESSIONAL EXPERIENCE

NETWORK TELEVISION CORPORATION   Horton, Louisiana
Human Resources Manager   1992 – Present

- Interview, hire, train, supervise, and evaluate personnel staff.
- Manage employee benefit plans (ERISA, medical, dental, vision, 401K) for all employees.
- Administer AAP/EEO and workers' compensation claims/disputes.
- **Wrote and implemented safety program** which significantly reduced loss-time injuries.

SOUTHERN TELEPHONE COMPANY – New Orleans, Louisiana   1964 – 1991

Area Manager – Employee Benefits / Personnel (1980–1991)

- Efficiently managed and controlled costs of 40 employee benefit plans for 11,000+ employees and dependents in South Louisiana.
- Trained, developed, directed and coordinated the activities of a staff of 10.
- Interfaced extensively with interdepartmental managers, union, law, and medical professionals, financial institution executives, and federal and state agencies.
- Coordinated disability and workers' compensation matters with Company Medical Director.

Significant Achievements

- Recipient of **VIP Award** (1989); instrumental participant in employee benefit education.
- Recipient of **Key Contributor Monetary Award** (1988).
- Saved company $269,000 through effective management of disability and workers' compensation cases; reduced leave time by two to three weeks per case.
- Successfully resolved 1,500 workers' compensation claims annually; reduced annual workers' compensation premiums by over $200,000.
- Drastically increased efficiency, improved perception of organization, and reduced complaints through effective training and development of employees.
- Significantly increased productivity and efficiency by restructuring benefit group and developing specialty areas; streamlined administrative services; eliminated unnecessary reports.

This is the resume's first page. Larger square bullets appear before the highlights of qualifications; smaller bullets precede duties and achievements in the Professional Experience section. Boldfacing makes keywords stand out.

MARILYN S. BROWN   Page Two

SOUTHERN TELEPHONE COMPANY (Continued)

Staff Specialist – Pension Benefits (1977–1980)

- Administered day-to-day pension benefit issues; interpreted plan provisions for 5,000 retirees.
- Supervised staff of four personnel employees.
- Promptly and proficiently managed death claims to clients' satisfaction.
- Conducted monthly pre-retirement meetings; ensured thorough understanding of entitlements.
- Promoted to Area Manager due to experience and ability to interface effectively with people.

Benefit Analyst (1977–1978)

- Processed Medicare and group insurance claims for 3,500 employees.
- Promoted to Staff Specialist – Pension Benefits due to outstanding performance and knowledge of pension benefits.

Administrative Assistant / Secretary to District Manager (1974–1977)

- Provided secretarial and administrative support to District Manager and staff of 30.
- Transcribed dictation for Medical Director.
- Conducted pre-employment screenings.
- Promoted to Benefit Analyst.

Administrative Assistant (1970–1973)

Senior Confidential Stenographer (1966–1969)

Telephone Operator (1964–1966)

EDUCATION / PROFESSIONAL DEVELOPMENT

LOUISIANA EASTERN COLLEGE - Monroe, Louisiana
Associate Degree in Social Services

TRINITY BUSINESS COLLEGE - New Orleans, Louisiana
Office Management Certification

SOUTHERN TELEPHONE COMPANY

**Hewlett-Packard Automated Office Systems; Financial Communications
Labor Relations; Producing Results With Others; Creating the High Performance Team**

PROFESSIONAL AFFILIATIONS

Member, CERTIFIED EMPLOYEE BENEFIT SOCIETY (CEBS)
Member, SOCIETY FOR HUMAN RESOURCE MANAGEMENT (SHRM)
Member, EAST LOUISIANA PERSONNEL ASSOCIATION
Member, AMERICAN BUSINESS WOMEN'S ASSOCIATION
Past-Member, SOUTHERN PROFESSIONAL WOMEN'S CLUB

Notice that on page 2 the individual's positions go back as far as 1966. No dates, however, are supplied in the Education section. Center-justification at the end matches that on page 1. Boldfacing calls attention to company-related education.

Resume of

JANICE A. HOFFMAN

1954 FM 698	New Haven, Texas 78975	(000) 555-0000

● **PROFESSIONAL OBJECTIVE**

Seeking a challenging Human Resource Management position where my professional experience and education will allow me to make an immediate contribution as an integral part of a progressive company.

● **SUMMARY OF QUALIFICATIONS**

Sixteen years experience in Human Resource Management

Extensive knowledge in current employment / human resource legislation

Coordinate and implement personnel policy, wage, and benefit programs

Special skills in resolving personnel conflicts in accordance with employment legislation

Superior interpersonal and communication skills. Ability to get along well with diverse personalities. Have received numerous commendations for exceptional work

High energy level - good reasoning ability - and a dedicated professional

● **HUMAN RESOURCE MANAGEMENT EXPERIENCE**

SUN VALLEY TEXTILES, INC., New Haven, Texas   March 93 to Present
Human Resource Manager

- Formulate personnel policies for the company
- Direct employment activities, assuring that properly qualified employees are recruited and hired for company positions
- Coordinate and participate in disciplinary and termination proceedings involving employees
- Communicate to employees all changes in personnel policies and counsel with employees on personnel policies and personal problems
- Assure that company employment policies and personnel practices comply with the applicable provisions of federal and state labor laws
- Determine and recommend employee relations practices to establish a positive employer-employee relationship, and promote high level of employee moral
- Develop and implement the company's Affirmative Action Program
- Establish wage structure, pay policies, and performance appraisal programs

146

Combination. *P. J. Margraf, New Braunfels, Texas*

Larger bullets are before the major side headings. These bullets visually tie the two pages together. The eye can sweep across the pages and find major headings quickly.

Resume Continued

JANICE A. HOFFMAN

<u>BATEMEN, INC., West Flores, Texas</u>   October 1989 to February 1993
Employee Relations Specialist

- Investigated EEOC charges of discrimination, developing company's response to charges
- Acted as liaison with the EEOC and Texas Commission for Human Rights
- Responsible for conducting all exit interviews and involuntary terminations for company
- Represented company in employment hearing proceedings, and trained company management on various laws regarding employment practices

<u>PATTON PEPPER, INC., West Flores, Texas</u>   August 1980 to October 1989
Personnel Director

- Administered wage and benefit programs for 900 employees (exempt and non-exempt)
- Developed and implemented company's Affirmative Action Program
- Overseen company's personnel policies and practices, handling grievance procedures
- Interviewed, screened, and referred prospective candidates for employment
- Managed $450,000.00 annual budget, and directed 9 personnel
- Responsible for all personnel, training, safety, and health functions
- Regularly conducted new employee orientation, and met with all employees on benefit and policy changes

● <u>EDUCATION</u>

<u>SOUTHTEXAS UNIVERSITY, ST. PHILLIPS, TEXAS</u> - May 1994.
Associates in Science in Management **(Human Resource Management).** GPA 3.9.
Consistently placed on Dean's List and President's List.
<u>Additional Education:</u> Have attended numerous human resource management seminars to remain current in field. <u>Computer literate:</u> WordPerfect, Paradox, Lotus 123, Freelance, and E-Mail.

● <u>PROFESSIONAL ORGANIZATIONS (Past and Present)</u>

Tri-County Personnel Association. New Haven Chamber of Commerce. Texas Association of Business. American Society of Personnel Administrators.

● <u>COMMUNITY ACTIVITIES</u>

Volunteer mentor at New Havens' Fisher and Kent Elementary Schools, as well, participation in the Habitat for Humanity program.

References Available Upon Request

Another good feature is the extra line spacing between the items listed in the Qualifications and Experience sections. The additional white space is more inviting than single-spacing. Boldfacing directs attention to the person's job positions.

AMY D. MOSSE

444 Old Copper Drive
South Port, Maine 12345

Home: 555 444-3333
Office: 555 666-7777

CAREER HIGHLIGHTS

Created Workers Compensation Protocol

Developed and facilitated in-service presentation for training management

Implemented common review date for all Home Medical Products companies

Administered new system-wide benefit package, and organized annual open enrollment

Initiated and performed on-site visits to be more accessible to satellite locations

EMPLOYMENT SUMMARY

HEALTHY FORT HEALTH SYSTEM

Human Resource Associate *(Diversified Services Group)*

1992 to Present   Bingham Farms, Maine

- ❑ Responsible for the presentation of policies, procedures and benefits to all new-hire employees
- ❑ Member of HRIS (Human Resource Information System) User Group
- ❑ Research data to ensure management is in compliance with policies and procedures and rate adjustments are justified
- ❑ Act as liaison from corporate to all DSG employees
- ❑ Perform on-site visits to satellite locations
- ❑ Update system-wide mainframe for current revisions, new employees, and payroll
- ❑ Process annual salary increase for all DSG employees
- ❑ Quality Improvement Process Committee member

Human Resource Assistant *(Diversified Services Group)*

1992   Bingham Farms, Maine

- ❑ Assisted with compensation, benefit presentations and employment
- ❑ Arranged pre-employment physicals, processed new hire paperwork, conducted new hire orientations
- ❑ Direct involvement with employee relations and relevant issues
- ❑ Processed payroll for various areas of group
- ❑ Maintained current and accurate information on personnel files via computer
- ❑ Demographically tracked benefit and compensation information as well as performance reviews

147

Combination. *Lorie Lebert, Novi, Michigan*

The information at the top of page 1 is arranged in a balanced format with the address on the left side and phone numbers on the right. By far the most distinctive feature is the

EMPLOYMENT SUMMARY *(CONTINUED)*

HEALTHY FORT HEALTH SYSTEM (Continued)
Human Resource Assistant *(Corporate Human Resources – Employment Division)*
1988 to 1991   Dadroya, Maine
- ❑   Assisted with entire employment process; from recruitment through hiring
- ❑   Conducted recruitment events [career fairs, open houses]
- ❑   Assisted in the creation and placement of employment advertisements

Clinic Services Representative
1985 to 1988   Baylor, Maine
- ❑   Maintained patient information on computer
- ❑   Performed new patient registrations, processed hospital admissions and input patient information
- ❑   Generated employee work schedules, kept computerized schedules for physicians, collected payments, maintained medical records

FERN STATE UNIVERSITY
Clerk – 1982 to 1984   Big Bend, Maine
- ❑   Managed verbal and written business communications
- ❑   Adjusted student schedules; handled grade changes and confidential records

EDUCATION

UNIVERSITY OF MAINE   Augusta, Maine
Computer workshops for WordPerfect, Lotus 1-2-3 – 1990

FERN STATE UNIVERSITY   Big Bend, Maine
Associate Degree – School of Business, Office Administration – 1984

References Available On Request

shaded bars in the Career Highlights. Square shadowed bullets look like three-dimensional check boxes that the reader can check while reading down the lists in the Employment Summary. Job positions are highlighted with bold and italic for easy recognition.

Law Enforcement and Criminal Justice

Resumes at a Glance

RESUME NO.	LAST OR CURRENT OCCUPATION	GOAL	PAGE
148.	Emergency Medical Technician	Position in law enforcement	237
149.	Detective Sergeant	Not specified	238
150.	Police Sergeant/Station Commander	Second career in public relations	240
151.	Marine Patrol Officer/Training Officer	Position in law enforcement or medicine	242
152.	Deputy Clerk	Secretary/Administrative support position	243
153.	Police Training Officer	Position in law enforcement	244

LAWRENCE D. ENFORCER

88 Safeway Lane, Crimefree, NJ • Willing to Relocate   **(555) 555-5555**

OBJECTIVE

Position in Law Enforcement

SUMMARY

- Experience in protecting public safety and responding to emergencies.
- Calm, confident and composed in tense situations.
- Academic background in criminal justice.
- Outstanding problem-solving and interpersonal skills.
- Committed to working toward a safe, crime-free environment.

EDUCATION/CERTIFICATION

A.A.S., Criminal Justice, Elton Community College, Elton, NJ, 1994

Emergency Medical Technician - Ambulance (EMT-A)
First Responder/Crash Injury Management (FR-CIM)
CPR - Basic Life Support
CPR - Community

RELATED EXPERIENCE

EMERGENCY MEDICAL TECHNICIAN
Amber Ambulance, Fixum, NJ   1994 - Present
- Evaluated a wide range of emergency situations, administered first aid to sick and injured individuals, and monitored status during transport to health care facilities.
- Worked cooperatively with law enforcement officers and paramedics to control and stabilize critical situations.
- Defused tense situations involving psychiatric cases.
- Oriented new employees; helped to establish a positive work environment.

LOSS PREVENTION OFFICER
L A Nickles, Stopit, NJ   1993 - 1994
- Deterred external theft through constant vigilance, while purporting to shop.
- Personally apprehended over 30 shoplifters and assisted with the apprehension of 40 others.
- Contacted police and provided a full report on each case; thoroughly documented incidents for company records.
- Selected to be part of the internal theft team; set up and monitored cameras to observe employees suspected of theft; documented unusual activity.
- Monitored suspicious credit card activity and notified credit card companies.

SECURITY SUPERVISOR
Funtime Adventure Park, Twister, NJ   1991 - 1993
- Oversaw the safety of 20,000 to 45,000 amusement park guests daily; supervised up to 15 security personnel.
- Promoted to supervisory position within one year of hire.
- Assessed diverse security situations (e.g., related to drugs, drinking, fighting) and implemented appropriate actions, evicting guests when necessary; completed comprehensive incident reports.
- Oriented new security personnel; explained responsibilities, policies and procedures.

148

Combination. *Rhoda Kopy, Toms River, New Jersey*

Hanging indentation makes this four-section resume easy to read. The section headings are evident at a glance, and the lines of information are no more than 4.5 inches wide.

ROBERT V. WEST

1056 RANGE ROAD
CATTLERIDGE, IOWA 00000
(555) 555-5555

HIGHLIGHTS:

- Over 15 years of progressive experience in law enforcement.
- A.S. in Law Enforcement, Graduate of the Iowa Criminal Justice Academy and Continuing Education student with 24 credits in Composition, Social Work and Psychology from the University of Iowa.
- Extensive experience in Public Speaking, Teaching, Interviewing, Investigating, and Report Writing.

PROFESSIONAL ACHIEVEMENTS:

Public Speaking and Teaching:

- Conducting training programs on child abuse dynamics for law enforcement officers and social workers at various law enforcement and social service agencies, including the Criminal Justice Academy, University of Iowa, Community Counseling Services, and Eastern Iowa Medical Center; topics include: "The Role of Law Enforcement as an Initial Responder", "Law Enforcement, Social Service Agencies and Society: Positive Interaction vs. Conflict", and "Child Protection: Myths and Realities".
- Testifying before legislative committees to advocate for the maintenance of services to children and families.
- Conducting presentations for community groups and organizations; facilitating Q & A sessions.
- Facilitating group discussions with Child Protective Services, Battered Women's Projects and other service providers around issues involving interaction with law enforcement.

Communications:

- Performing Public Service Announcements; being interviewed for television programs.
- Assisting in the production of "Innocence For Sale" at WVVJ-TV (1989).
- Writing press releases and detailed investigative reports.
- Formulating and writing policy for the Sheriff's Office on matters pertaining to children.

RELATED EXPERIENCE:

Detective Sergeant; *Smith County Sheriff's Department,* Cattleridge, Iowa (1989 - Present)
- Command the Division of Crimes Against People; supervise law enforcement officers.
- Conduct child abuse investigations; interview children, family members, medical personnel, educators, and social service providers; maintain extensive documentation; testify in court.
- Present seminars and classroom instruction on issues impacting children and families.
- Participate on the planning committee for the annual Child Sexual Abuse Conference.

Investigator; *Somerset County Sheriff's Department,* Davenport, Iowa (1986 - 1989)
- Specialized in crimes against people in addition to performing all other types of criminal investigations.

Security Officer; *Great Western Paper Company,* Westfield, Iowa (1979 - 1986)
- Provided plant security; protected GWP's physical assets; conducted investigations into employee theft, drug usage, and vandalism.
- Prepared cases deemed to be "fair and accurate" by arbitrators.

149

Combination. *Joan M. Roberts, Bangor, Maine*

As in Resume 134, a bar of three horizontal lines is an eye-catcher that draws the reader's attention to the top of the first page and to the name of the individual. The same kind of

ROBERT V. WEST / Page Two

Patrol Officer, *Milltown Police Department,* Milltown, Iowa (1977 - 1979)
- Performed general patrol duties including, writing traffic tickets, checking doors, and responding to emergencies; utilized verbal rather than physical skills to diffuse angry, aggressive, and confrontational people.

OTHER EXPERIENCE:

Licensed Raft Guide; *Falls River Expeditions,* Green Point, Iowa (1990 - Present)
- Safely guide rafts on the Pebble, Kennedy, and Dead Rivers; maintain and repair equipment.
- Knowledgeable of risk and liability management.
- Market rafting company through networking, cold calling, brochure distribution, and innovative promotional techniques.

EDUCATION:

University of Iowa, Cattleridge, Iowa (1986 - Present)
Completing undergraduate courses in English, Social Work and Psychology

Iowa Criminal Justice Academy, Watertown, Iowa (1978)

County College, Smithfield, New Mexico (1976)
A.S. in Law Enforcement

<u>**Professional Development**</u>:

Advanced Interviewing Techniques
Intervention in Child Sexual Abuse
Prosecuting and Defending Child Abuse Cases
Multi-Disciplinary Investigation of Child Abuse

PUBLIC SERVICE INVOLVEMENT:

Pine Hill Abuse Council - *President and Board of Directors (1988 - 1989)*

Child Abuse & Neglect Committee Eastern Iowa Medical Center - *Member since 1989*

REFERENCES AVAILABLE UPON REQUEST

lines forms part of a header on page 2. Notice in the Professional Achievements section the clustering of activities under two main, underlined categories. Boldfacing makes the job positions stand out in the Related Experience section.

15 Anderson Street
Elizabeth, NJ 55555
(000) 000-0000

PAUL DRISCOLL

Goal: **Second career in public relations**, with purpose of increasing enrollment for a higher learning institute using skills developed during 25 years as a law enforcement officer.

Qualified by:
- ☞ Excellent interviewing and evaluation techniques to determine individuals' areas of interest and cultural fit.

- ☞ Ability to develop comprehensive questionnaires with sensitivity to various intelligence levels and social status of intended participants.

- ☞ Strong involvement with delivery of instructional programs for disadvantaged youth and administration of scholarship opportunities.

- ☞ Experience as a public speaker and author of published instructional articles.

Education: **UPSALA COLLEGE**, East Orange, NJ
A.A. in Social Sciences, 20XX

Extensive record of training courses taken throughout police employment to keep up to date on issues of social concern.

Work History: 19XX – 20XX   IRVINGTON POLICE DEPARTMENT

Police Sergeant/Station Commander	6/XX – 12/XX
Shift Commander	11/XX – 6/XX
Detective	8/XX – 11/XX
Patrolman	5/XX – 8/XX

19XX – 19XX   NEW JERSEY DEPT. OF TRANSPORTATION
Traffic Engineer with Traffic Safety Service Department

Highlights of Employment:

... As Certified Police Instructor by New Jersey Police Training Commission, trained rookies in all aspects of police functions. Conducted performance evaluations at prescribed intervals and assessed levels of preparedness for increased responsibility.

... Supervised shifts of four inside and outside officers, making sure that all arrest reports, accidents and investigations were completed accurately.

... Transferred warrants, summonses and bailable offenses into criminal justice system, mindful that all constitutional rights were adhered to, for successful prosecution of criminal cases.

... More

150

Combination. *Melanie A. Noonan, West Paterson, New Jersey*

A resume with a number of interesting touches: the "pointing finger" bullets; the ellipsis (...), used as an embedded marker for each employment highlight; and effective boldfacing.

... Acted as chief hostage negotiator with mentally deranged or drug influenced criminal perpetrators.

... Testified as expert witness at New Jersey Supreme Court trials to identify behavioral patterns of narcotics users.

... In twelve years as Juvenile Officer, worked closely with school systems to develop Drug Awareness Resistance Education (DARE) program. Spoke at student assemblies and arranged for counselors to deal with drug problems in the schools.

... Wrote widely distributed article focused toward parents and teachers, educating them to identify symptoms of drug use and offering alternatives to the criminal justice system in dealing with youth drug problems.

... In charge of setting up new performance evaluation systems at Irvington Police Department using Behavioral Anchored Rating (BAR) scales.

... Received numerous commendations for investigative work leading to criminal convictions.

... Trained various medical personnel and administrators at large intermediate care facility in CPR techniques.

Volunteer Activities:

MEMBER OF ELIZABETH BOARD OF EDUCATION
Chief Negotiator; Chairman of Buildings & Grounds Committee: elected by Board to solicit and review bids for general administrative services. Sat on several policy committees.

CITY OF ELIZABETH ETHICS COMMITTEE
Investigated violations of ethics laws of public officials.

NEW JERSEY POLICE BENEVOLENT ASSOCIATION (PBA)
Scholarship Committee: evaluate criteria for $2000 scholarship award to high school students in Union County; on state level, involved with awards of 30 scholarships annually.

Chief negotiator for all contracts and grievances of PBA Local 109. Liaison between Local 109 and State PBA regarding special legislation. Instrumental in promoting transfer of pension system from eligibility at age 62 to eligibility with 25 years of service.

The boldfacing is effective because it is extra dark in the chosen font. Another difference, which makes the resume more interesting, is the use of less-common side headings (Goal, Qualified by, and Volunteer Activities).

RANDALL J. HOWE
293 Clark Street • Davison, Michigan 48823
810-555-4356

OBJECTIVE   To pursue a career in law enforcement or the medical field.

EDUCATION

GENESYS/FLINT OSTEOPATHIC CAMPUS   *Anticipated completion:*
Paramedic Training   Fall xxxx

GENESYS/ST. JOSEPH CAMPUS
Emergency Medical Technician Course - Licensed EMT   xxxx

UM-FLINT
Criminal Justice coursework   1998

DELTA COLLEGE
Associate of Arts   1997
• *Major:* Criminal Justice
• *Achievement:* Recognized for Outstanding Service to Delta and the Criminal Justice Program

---

TRAINING

• State Training School Instructor (Department of Natural Resources)	1997
• Adult/Infant/Child CPR (American Red Cross)	1994-1996
• Boating & Snowmobile Safety Instructor	1994-1996
• Advanced Self-Defense (Delta College)	1995
• Self-Defense (Delta College)	1995
• Criminal Justice Internship (City of Burton Police Department)	1995
• Advanced Life Saving (American Red Cross)	1994
• Standard First Aid (American Red Cross)	1994
• M.L.E.O.T.C. Pre-employment Written Test (Burton Police Academy)	1994

RELATED ACTIVITIES

• Senator, Student Congress (Delta College)	1997
• Treasurer, L.E.R.N. (Law Enforcement Resource Network)	1996-1997
• Volunteer Tutor (Genesee Adult Literacy Center)	1996-1997
• Member, PPI (Positive Peer Influence)	1994-1996
• Volunteer Lifeguard (L.D.S. Boys' Camp [1-week session])	1992-1994

EXPERIENCE

Oakland County Sheriff Department / Rochester, MI   xxxx-Present
Marine Patrol Officer (summer) and *Training Officer* (winter) — Patrol county lakes to promote safe boating.

Rite Aide Pharmacy / Davison, Michigan   xxxx-Present
Pharmacy Employee — Supervise night employees, operate cash register, provide customer service.

Metropolitan Credit Bureau / Flint, Michigan   1995-1996
Operator/Office Worker— Operated switchboard, processed payments, typed monthly bulletins, filed.

REFERENCES   Furnished upon request

151

Chronological. *Janet L. Beckstrom, Flint, Michigan*

A different kind of resume because of the cascade of right-aligned dates (years). The horizontal lines make it easy to see the separate sections and get the gist of their contents.

Linda L. Rhodes

2188 Gibbs Road
Shade, Ohio 45776
(614) 696-0000 (H) • (614) 592-0000 (W)

QUALIFICATIONS

- Experienced in all facets of office work and capable of handling a great deal of responsibility
- Detail oriented person with strong organizational abilities; very accurate in all areas of work
- Excellent interpersonal skills with ability to deal effectively with people of all backgrounds
- Extremely well organized and efficient; quickly learn procedures and methods

---

OBJECTIVE

Seeking a position in a secretarial or administrative support area utilizing extensive experience in office organization and management.

WORK HISTORY

SHADE COUNTY JUVENILE COURT, Shade, Ohio (1994 to present)
Deputy Clerk
- Utilize excellent interpersonal skills handling fee payments and greeting visitors to the Court
- Demonstrate good organizational skills maintaining smooth flow of operations in fast-paced environment
- Maintain strict levels of confidentiality handling court reporting for Juvenile Court cases

TRADEWINDS RECOVERY SERVICES, Anytown, Ohio (1986 to 1994)
Secretary
- Provided clerical support to counselors including typing all correspondence; familiar with WordPerfect
- Utilized good time management and communication skills maintaining 6-line telephone system
- Maintained positive image of office greeting clients and handling fee payment
- Demonstrated good organizational skills scheduling all assessments for counselors

Client Accounts Clerk; Administrative Services/Fiscal Department
- Acted as liaison between residential programs and fiscal services
- Responsible for follow-up calls and written statements for residential and outpatient services
- Prepared billing mailings and reports to fiscal; responsible for general billing documentation
- Initiated, maintained and updated Medicaid cards for eligible recipients with Department of Human Services
- Also serve as clerical and billing support backup as needed

Intake Case Manager
- Handled referral calls determining the appropriateness of a client for the program
- Prepared all admission materials and handled verification of insurance and Medicaid eligibility
- Responsible for completing all paperwork involved in obtaining Medicaid cards for clients
- Acted as liaison for Billing Services and Insurance and Self-Pay clients
- Interaction with drug and alcohol abuse clients; provided emotional support when needed

OHIO UNIVERSITY, REGISTRAR'S OFFICE, Anytown, Ohio (1964 to 1977)
Clerical Supervisor/Secretary
- Responsible for schedule of all academic classes for Ohio University
- Collected class material from all departments on campus
- All classes offered on campus were charted; required knowledge of all buildings and classroom sizes within
- Responsible for meeting deadlines for printing schedule of classes; proofread material giving final approval
- Supervised three employees; responsible for Registration, Student Records and Dean's Office switchboards

Excellent References Available Upon Request

152

Combination. *Melissa L. Kasler, Athens, Ohio*

The frame enclosing the Qualifications section ensures that it will be seen. Similarly, boldfacing for the various job positions makes it likely that these too will be noticed.

William J. Smith

555 Monroe Park Circle   (000) 000-0000
Cresthaven, New York 55555

OBJECTIVE: Seeking a career position in **Law Enforcement** utilizing educational qualifications and hands-on training.

SKILLS:
- ♦ Solid education in all aspects of criminal justice and law enforcement.
- ♦ Knowledge of investigations and surveillance techniques; proficient in handling all types of complaints.
- ♦ Familiar with concepts of justice, due process, and criminal procedure.
- ♦ Strong organizational, research, analytical and problem solving skills.

EDUCATION: CRESTHAVEN LAW ENFORCEMENT ACADEMY, Cresthaven, New York
Certified Police Officer Program - June 1993

CRESTHAVEN COMMUNITY COLLEGE, Cresthaven, New York
A.A.S., Criminal Justice - June 1992
GPA: 3.5   Graduated with Distinction

CRESTHAVEN HIGH SCHOOL, Cresthaven, New York
Regents Diploma - June 1988

ACADEMIC ACHIEVEMENTS:
Honors/Recognition:
- Cresthaven Community College Dean's List (5 semesters)
- Graduated Top 10% of Class, Cresthaven Law Enforcement Academy
- 2nd Place in Firearms Training, Cresthaven Law Enforcement Academy

Certifications:
- PR-24 Police Baton
- Breathalyzer - New York State Department of Health
- First Responder - St. William's EMS Training Program
- Radar Operator - Bureau of Municipal Police
- Emergency Water Safety - American Red Cross

Relevant Courses:
Criminal Justice, Criminal Procedure Law, Criminal Investigation I&II, Police Operations, Police Training & Tactics, Basic Firearms, Sex Crimes, Interviews/ Interrogations, Identifying & Preserving Evidence, Forensic Science I&II, Criminal Evidence & Procedure, Intermediate & Advanced Firearms, Penal Law, Social Crime Delinquency, Highway Drug Interdiction, Administration/Justice Theory, Police Proficiency, Community Relations Theory, Fire Behavior & Arson Awareness, Police Procedures, Critical Incident Management, Handcuffing, Self Defense, Evasive Vehicle Operation Control.

EXPERIENCE: **Training Officer** - Cresthaven Police Department, Cresthaven, NY   1992-XXXX
Observation, patrol and traffic enforcement. On-the-job training in police operations.

Security Officer - Cresthaven Temporary Services, Cresthaven, NY   1990-1991
Provided security at Cresthaven International Race Track. Checked passes, directed traffic and guarded assigned areas.

REFERENCES: Excellent References Available Upon Request

153

Combination. *Betty Geller, Elmira, New York*

For a relatively recent graduate, a resume that emphasizes technical training and honors. With little experience, the individual relies on relevant courses to indicate acquired skills.

Legal Support

Resumes at a Glance

RESUME NO.	LAST OR CURRENT OCCUPATION	GOAL	PAGE
154.	Typesetter, newspaper	Legal Secretary	247
155.	Assistant to mortgage broker	Paralegal in real estate industry	248
156.	Legal Assistant/Paralegal	Not specified	249
157.	Warehouse Foreman	Paralegal Intern	250

JILL EHLI
235 West Thayer Avenue
Bismarck, ND 58501
(701) 255-3141

SKILLS
- Type 65 wpm
- Speedwriting
- Excellent Speller
- Detail-Oriented
- Receptionist
- Filing
- Office Machines
- Good Communicator

COMPUTER EXPERIENCE

IBM PC models, IBM compatible, and Zenith

SOFTWARE EXPERIENCE

WordPerfect 5.0, 5.1, and 6.0   MicroSoft Word
Key Entry III   Ventura
Word for Windows

EDUCATION

1995
BISMARCK STATE COLLEGE - Bismarck, ND
Associate of Applied Science Degree
Major: **Legal Secretarial** GPA: 3.34

COURSES

Legal Office Procedures   Business English
Legal Terminology   Business Math
Office Filing   Business Communications
Business Law   Psychology
Accounting   Geology/Physics
Legal Machine Transcription   Information Processing
Word Processing Machines   Data Entry

EMPLOYMENT HISTORY

12/94 - Present
The Bismarck Tribune - Bismarck, ND
Responsible for typesetting, answering telephones, filing, and customer assistance.

5/94 - 7/95
10-Spot Lanes - Bismarck, ND
Handled money and cash register, assisted customers.

7/90 - 8/91
Knutson's Cafe - Bismarck, ND
Served as hostess and waitress, greeted and served the public.

154

Combination. *Claudia Stephenson, location unknown*

Column formats for Skills, Software Experience, and Education sections help to provide white space and therefore make this resume more readable at first sight.

MARLENE STEPENDO
2975 Standard Street
Des Plaines, Illinois XXXXX
(XXX) XXX-XXXX

OBJECTIVE

To secure a paralegal position in the real estate industry where I can utilize my paralegal education together with my 11 years of experience as a loan officer/processor.

EXPERIENCE

Raising young child while offering assistance to my husband with his mortgage broker position by pre-qualifying applicants, preparing loan packages, and writing/coordinating advertising.   **May 1990 - Present**

CAPITAL MORTGAGE SERVICES; Elmhurst, Illinois
<u>Co-Owner</u>   **April 1986 - May 1990**
- Pre-qualified applicants.
- Interviewed applicants and requested specified information to complete loan application.
- Processed applications by obtaining titles, credit reports, surveys, and various sources of financial information.
- Reviewed and evaluated information on mortgage loan documents to determine if buyer, property, and loan conditions met lender and government standards.
- Cleared titles of all liens and encumbrances. Assisted individuals in clearing poor credit records.
- Prepared contracts, deeds, RESPAs, notes and mortgages, good faith estimates, and truth in lending disclosures.
- Performed bookkeeping functions and prepared payroll and tax forms.
- Coordinated all marketing and advertising activities, which included direct mail, radio advertising, and cold calling local businesses.
- Knowledge of commercial, F.H.A., V.A., conventional, and home equity financing and refinancing.

HOUSEHOLD MORTGAGE SERVICES; Bloomingdale, Illinois
<u>Loan Officer</u>   **November 1983 - April 1986**
Held same responsibilities as above other than accounting work. Also more heavily involved in assisting individuals with credit problems by contacting creditors and negotiating settlements. Developed many contacts which could help expedite difficult loans.

EDUCATION

Currently pursuing a Bachelor of Science degree in Political Science
Northeastern University; Chicago, Illinois

Certificate in Paralegal Studies, January 1995, G.P.A.: 3.9/4.0
Triton Junior College; River Grove, Illinois

Completed several lending courses throughout career, including a 40 hour course in F.H.A. financing

COMPUTER KNOWLEDGE

Microsoft Word and Windows

AFFILIATIONS

Assist in distributing media packages for political campaigns, 1987 - Present
Election Judge, February 1995 - Present
Mortgage Bankers Association, 1986 - 1990

155

Chronological. *Georgia Veith, Elmhurst, Illinois*

A resume for a recent graduate. The first point, though, in the Education section is that she plans to further her education by pursuing a bachelor's degree as she seeks paralegal work.

MarciaWard

385 Grove Street
Freeport, New York 11111
(516) 555-5555

Profile

Legal Assistant offering substantial experience within both **legal and financial services** settings. Maintain the highest standard of professionalism, performance and integrity at all times. Areas of strengths include:

- Drafting agreements, regulatory filings and Blue-Sky registrations.
- Familiarity with SEC, NYSE, AMEX and NASD regulations and compliance issues.
- Ability to communicate effectively with high-profile and high-net-worth clientele, utilizing discretion at all times.
- Attention to detail, follow-through and time management.
- Proficient in Microsoft Word, Excel and PowerPoint; WordPerfect; Lotus 1-2-3; Lexis-Nexis and Westlaw legal research systems; and Time Slips Deluxe client billing system.

Professional Experience

Law Offices of Thomas J. McCabe, New York, New York   19XX - Present
Legal Assistant / Paralegal

- Provide legal support at corporate and securities practice, which represents parties in securities arbitration and litigation, formation, structuring and governance of broker-dealer organizations.
- Prepare regulatory filings for broker-dealers, Form U-4s, private placements, SRO applications (AMEX, PCX, PHLX, NASD, NYSE), options applications for the CBOE, and Blue-Sky registrations.
- Draft an array of agreements, including Continuing Education for NASD applications, supervisory procedures and operating agreements.
- Draw up documentation for corporate filings, legal opinions, and sole proprietorships.
- Administrative responsibilities encompass payroll input; monthly billings; maintaining appointment calendars; updating administrative lists; computer backup; inventory control and purchasing of office supplies.

Citibank, N.A., New York, New York   1990 - 19XX
Specialist - Commercial Paper Issuance Billing (1994 - 1995)
(Placed by Manpower on long-term assignment)

- Generated daily reports reflecting volume of commercial paper issuances.
- Reconciled in-house Depository Trust Company transactions.
- Maintained relations with commercial paper clients regarding billings and associated problems.

Service Officer - Private Banking Division (1991 - 1993)

- Provided support to two private bankers and assisted in the relationship management of 500 private banking clients. Extensive one-on-one contact with clients.
- Managed client accounts; expedited the transferring of funds; provided mortgage documentation; and initiated investigations as warranted, to resolve account-related problems.

Assistant to Unit Head - Private Banking Division (1990 - 1991)

- Reconciled and paid bills; maintained payroll and personnel records; and updated yearly performance appraisals.
- Managed unit head's calendar, travel arrangements, and organized meetings and special events.

Kimmelman, Sexter, Warmflash & Leitner, New York, New York   1987 - 1990
Head Receptionist

Education

St. John's University, Queens, New York
Major: *Liberal Arts*

156

Combination. *Judith Friedler, New York, New York*

This resume for a legal assistant has characteristics of certain executive resumes: narrower margins, smaller type, and wider lines of text. Blank lines ensure adequate white space.

PETER JAMES BARROON

1234 – 5th Street • Mytown, USA 99999 • 555/555-5555

OBJECTIVE

A position as a paralegal intern in the Consumer Protection Division of the State Attorney General's office where skills in research, communications, organization, and a passion for case law can assist in the protection of the public interest.

PROFILE

A highly motivated student of the law with particularly strong written communication skills, an excellent academic record, and a passion for research. A natural leader who is also comfortable working independently or taking direction as a member of a team. Resourceful, persuasive, and able to effectively communicate ideas to others. Perceptive with the ability to listen, hear, and understand what is wanted and needed. Solid problem analysis/solving skills with the goal of innovative, economical, and efficient solutions. Possess a global outlook with a keen attention to detail. Noted among peers, supervisors, and professors for commitment to quality and desire to excel. Good knowledge of accounting procedures. Obtained Paralegal Certificate, June 1995.

EDUCATION

Associate Technical Arts – Paralegal Studies, 1995
Mytown Community College
G.P.A.: 3.99 in Legal Studies, 3.73 overall

SUMMARY OF QUALIFICATIONS

Legal Knowledge

- Westlaw &Computerized Legal Research
- Business Law: Contracts & Agency/Principal Relationships
- Rules of Civil Procedure
- Bankruptcy & Credit Rights
- Employment & Labor Law (Title VII focus)
- Law Office Management

Organizational Abilities

- Supervised up to 15 blue-collar workers, most of whom were 10 to 20 years older.
- Coordinated freight control, handling, warehousing, and distribution among a variety of internal and external customers for a $151 million marine transport company.
- Worked with 10 Western Alaska and West Coast ports, scheduling pickup and delivery of frozen seafood, groceries, cars, steel buildings, and other miscellaneous materials.
- Reorganized a closed-end warehouse to handle daily storage of up to 50,000 pounds of frozen seafood and 280,000 pounds of groceries.

Research

- Investigated consumer protection laws to successfully challenge car dealer to make repairs as required by law.

EXPERIENCE

CARGO UNLIMITED INC., Mytown   1986 to XXXX

Warehouse Foreman (1990 to XXXX)
Receiver (1988 to 1990)
Warehouseman (1987 to 1988)
Longshoreman (1986 to 1987)

157

Functional. *Carole S. Barns, Woodinville, Washington*

Experience dates are added as a gesture at the end, but the writer's view is that this is a functional resume to identify skills that would be useful in a State Attorney General's office.

Maintenance

Resumes at a Glance

RESUME NO.	LAST OR CURRENT OCCUPATION	GOAL	PAGE
158.	Concrete Truck Driver	Laborer	253
159.	Maintenance Mechanic	Position in maintenance and repair	254
160.	Maintenance Technician	Position using mechanical and technical skills	255
161.	Machine Operator	Position in maintenance and repair	256

Daniel D. Schumm

327 Parkview Place
Carmel, Indiana 46032   (317) 581-1057

OBJECTIVE

Secure entry-level Laborer position with a progressive facility that would utilize my maintenance and electrical experience to strengthen a plant's operations, that seeks and rewards results.

PROFESSIONAL EXPERIENCE

Concrete Truck Driver   XX/XX-Present

Chicago Ready Mix, (Division of DEF, Inc.), Chicago, Illinois

Responsibilities:

Operate and maintain a Class B Commercial Driver's License (CDL); Conscientious clean driving record; Perform facility's maintenance; Provide safety, pride, and productivity; Perform electrical, hydraulic, mechanical, and pneumatic systems troubleshooting for facility/fleet; Perform arc and Mig welding on all types of equipment; Maintain routine upkeep on assigned truck; Operate heavy equipment; Transport and deliver concrete work orders; Coordinate with contractors'/ customers' specifications; Assist in placement and other work-site aspects; Establish customer service to promote and personalize company's image.

Production Leadman   XXXX-XXXX

ABC, Inc., (Commodity Marketing Division), Chicago, Illinois

Responsibilities:

Supervised and maintained a safe workplace; Controlled transfer of feed grains and fertilizers; Experienced in control of three phase motors and conveying systems; Performed electrical and mechanical systems troubleshooting for facility; Appointed Safety Control Auditor; Attended meetings; and Implemented safety standards according to company's policies.

Accomplishments:

♦   State Fumigation License, *Acme University*, Chicago, IL, XXXX.
♦   Federal Grain Inspectors License, *ABC, Inc.*, Chicago, IL, XXXX.
♦   Renewed Fumigation License, *Bi-State Seminar*, Chicago, IL, XXXX.
♦   Promoted from Production to Production Leadman due to job performance, XXXX.
♦   Designed and Installed a Heat Reclaiming Duct System for grain dryers, eliminated production loss and significantly reduced utility costs.

General Laborer   XXXX-XXXX

ABC Corporation, Chicago, Illinois

Responsibilities:

Coordinated, delivered, and worked with commercial and industrial project materials.

EDUCATION

Associate in Applied Science (Electronic Technologies)   XXXX-Present

Technical College, Chicago, Illinois ♦ GRADUATION: Anticipated Fall XXXX ♦ CURRICULUM: A/C, D/C Circuits I and II, Digital Systems I and II, and Solid State I ♦ G.P.A.: 3.40/4.0.

Diploma   XXXX-XXXX

Chicago High School, Chicago, Illinois ♦ VOCATION: Technical Training/Auto Body Repair.

REFERENCES

Furnished upon request.

158

Chronological. *Susan K. Schumm, Carmel, Indiana*

A substantial, well-executed resume that makes a positive impression from beginning to end. Responsibilities are placed in paragraphs, but accomplishments are listed with bullets.

HUVERT F. KETTLE
29873 S. Willow Creek Road
Hollow Creek, MI 55555
000-555-2200

PROFESSIONAL OBJECTIVE
Position in maintenance and repair.

PROFILE
▸ Over 16 years comprehensive experience as a Maintenance Mechanic.
▸ State certified through N.A.P.E.; currently taking classes through N.A.P.E. for:
  · certification in industrial water conditioning and refrigeration, and air conditioning.

HIGHLIGHTS OF QUALIFICATIONS
■ Enthusiastic, self-motivated; excellent attendance record; punctual and reliable; realize the importance of getting to work and being prepared for work on time.
■ Equally effective working alone or as a member of a team; strong skills in organizing work flow, ideas, and materials.
■ Possess good communication and interpersonal skills; excellent understanding of responsibilities: can be counted on to complete projects and assignments with little or no supervision.
■ Utilize a proactive approach to problem solving; exercise a quality-oriented attitude toward work.

■ Employ strategies under preventative maintenance program guidelines; proven ability to identify, analyze, repair problems relating to:

LOW STEAM BOILERS / CHILLERS / WATER SOFTENERS / DE-ALKALIZERS
DE-MINERALIZERS / EMERGENCY POWER GENERATORS / SMALL MOTORS

WORK HISTORY
1979-Present. <u>Maintenance Mechanic.</u>
              Willow Creek Hospital, Willow Creek, MI.
              Serve as second shift mechanic over 400,000 square foot medical facility. Working knowledge of: commercial electrical, plumbing, heating and refrigeration, and fire systems within a modernized, multi-floor complex.

EDUCATION/TRAINING
· Michigan State Association of Power Engineers, Certification - 1995, (4th Class Engineer's License), Kalamazoo, MI.
· Michigan State Association of Power Engineers, Planned Certification - 1995, in: <u>Industrial Water Conditioning and Refrigeration</u> and <u>Air Conditioning</u>, (8 week courses).
· Willow Creek Technical School, 2 years, Graduate: Boiler Operations.

MILITARY
United States Army, SP-4, Honorable Discharge, American/Foreign Duty.

REFERENCES
Available upon request.

159

Combination. *Randy Clair, location unknown*

The writer used a monospaced font on purpose to provide a "typewriter look" that would seem more technical and fit the line of work better than laser printer typefaces.

James Smith

5555 Delivery Road
Elmira, New York 00000

Home: (600) 000-0000
Pager: (800) 000-0000

OBJECTIVE

Seeking a challenging position offering an opportunity to utilize and expand my mechanical and technical skills.

SUMMARY OF SKILLS

- Strong background in mechanical maintenance, building and grounds maintenance.
- Knowledge of building trades: carpentry, masonry, heating, plumbing and electrical.
- Dependable, hardworking, efficient, and highly reliable.
- Detail-oriented with a strong work ethic.

EDUCATION

Elmira Technical College, Elmira, New York
A.A.S. in Construction/Building Trades - June 1992
> *Field of Study:* House Framing I; Exterior Finish and Trim I; Bricklaying, Blocklaying and Finishing; Electrical and Plumbing Introduction; House Framing II and Basic Cabinetmaking; Roof Framing, Roof Finish; Exterior Finish and Trim II; Interior Finish.

Elmira High School, Elmira, New York
General Studies Diploma - June 1992

PROFESSIONAL EXPERIENCE

Elmira Greenhouses Inc., Elmira, New York   1992 - Present
Maintenance Technician
- Responsible for overall building and grounds maintenance, including repair and trouble-shooting of greenhouse equipment.
- Handle small engine repair, maintenance of heating systems (gas and coal boilers);some experience with air conditioning and refrigeration repair.
- Operate and maintain basic equipment, such as forklifts, loaders and dump trucks.
- Train and orient new employees.

Dominick's Family Restaurant, Elmira, New York   1991 - 1992
Dishwasher
- Part-time employment concurrent with high school attendance.

Self-Employed, Elmira, New York   Summer 1990
Lawn Care Specialist
- Responsible for all aspects of landscaping and lawn care maintenance. Maintained excellent customer relations.

- References Available Upon Request -

160

Combination. *Betty Geller, Elmira, New York*

The Objective, Summary of Skills, and Education sections are listed first because this person planned to further his education with a four-year degree in construction management.

◘ SAMUAL A. WILCOX, 3400 Winding Pathway Drive, Allegan MI, 22000, 000-555-5500

Seeking a challenging position in hands-on maintenance and repair where problems and opportunities are matched to my wide range of skills and abilities.

■ **SUMMARY**
• Extensive experience and practical knowledge of high-volume printing operations. Involved in the manual and computerized maintenance of boilers, chillers, air conditioners, and offset printing presses. Proficient in residential home repair. Committed to high quality work in all tasks and projects.

■ **PERSONAL QUALIFICATIONS**
• Enthusiastic, dependable, self-motivated, assume responsibility necessary to get the job done.
• Work cooperatively with a wide range of personalities.
• Excellent skills in organizing work flow, ideas, materials, people.
• Able to start up a project from scratch.

■ **CAPABILITIES**
Demonstrated abilities in carpentry, plumbing, and light electrical. Recent accomplishments include:
Carpentry
• remodeled basement: drywalled, paneled 3 rooms; built dock, deck, small backyard bridge.
Plumbing
• installed residential toilets, sinks, showers, tubs. Replaced and repaired broken plumbing.
Electrical
• wired garage in 220V. Rewired basement in conduit. Installed electrical switches and outlets.

■ **WORK HISTORY**
• 9/56 to 8/94 - Stationary Engineer, L.S. Madison, Chicago, IL. Retired. 38 years machine operation and maintenance experience with this Fortune 500 company; printers of Time, Life, Sports Illustrated, New Yorker magazines. Shift leader over 3 maintenance personnel/2 firemen in 6-building complex.

Responsibilities included the operation and/or maintenance of:
• Heidelberg and roto gravure presses.
• sheet-fed offset/hydraulic printing presses.
• air conditioners, chillers.
• Facsimile machines; film development, full circle, multi-stage "red room" process.
• small engines in boiler room.
• buildings; industrial plumbing, heating.

■ **LICENSES**
• City of Chicago Stationary Engineer's License, National Institute for the Uniform Licensing of Power Engineers, Inc., (Illinois State Association of Power Engineers, Inc.).

■ **SPECIALIZED TRAINING**
• Plumbing, Cleveland Institute of Technology, correspondence course, Certificate, 4 years.
• 200T Hermetic Centrifugal Liquid Chillers, CARRIER, correspondence course in refrigeration and air conditioning, 6 weeks.

■ **EDUCATION**
• LLoyd Technical School, Chicago, IL. Certificate: 2 years.

■ **REFERENCES** Personal and professional available upon request.

161

Combination. *Randy Clair, location unknown*

The person wanted a part-time maintenance position with a hardware store. It was less important to show what he did as a printer and more important to show future skills.

Management

Resumes at a Glance

RESUME NO.	LAST OR CURRENT OCCUPATION	GOAL	PAGE
162.	Bake Shop Trainer	Not specified	259
163.	Store Manager	Not specified	260
164.	Carpenter	Not specified	262
165.	Full-Charge Bookkeeper/Office Manager	Full-Charge Bookkeeper	263
166.	Owner of consulting firm	Not specified	264
167.	Purchasing Manager	Not specified	266
168.	Parts Manager/Operations Control Manager	Position in dealership management, parts and service	267
169.	Gateway Service Supervisor	Transportation Traffic Manager	268
170.	Transportation Supervisor	School Transportation Supervisor	269
171.	Senior Credit Manager	Position in commercial credit management	270
172.	Underwriting Representative	Not specified	272
173.	Credit Manager	Position in credit and collections	273
174.	Collection/Litigation Manager	Position in credit and collections	274
175.	Showroom Manager/Lighting Consultant	Not specified	275
176.	Office Manager	Not specified	276
177.	Vice President of Operations	Not specified	277
178.	Branch Manager	Not specified	278
179.	Corporate Risk Management Specialist	Safety professional	280
180.	Training Store Manager	Not specified	282
181.	Assistant Manager	Client Services Supervisor/ Project Coordinator	283
182.	Supervisor–Quality Control	Not specified	284

RESUME NO.	LAST OR CURRENT OCCUPATION	GOAL	PAGE
183.	Owner and Manager	Not specified	285
184.	Production Manager	Position in inventory or production control	286
185.	Operations Manager	Warehouse position in distribution industry	288
186.	Funeral Director Intern	Funeral Director	289
187.	Project Coordinator	Not specified	290
188.	Owner/Manager of family-owned business	Building Supply Yard Manager	291
189.	Consulting Analyst, bank	Not specified	292
190.	Senior Methods Analyst/Supervisor/ Labor Relations Representative	Not specified	293
191.	Director of Golf Instruction	Position in golf industry	294
192.	Assistant Manager	Not specified	296

GREGORY GALLIANO

989 Market Street
Albuquerque, NM 00000
(000) 000-0000

SUMMARY:
- Four promotions in eleven years with same employer
- Strong office and business management skills, including some computer programming
- Knowledge of customer service, sales and purchasing in a retail environment
- Supervision and training experience

SKILLS:
Office Management: Customer service, scheduling, typing (60+ wpm), filing, in-person and telephone reception.

Computer: *Platforms:* IBM PC and compatible, Apple Macintosh, Wang ordering/inventory database system, computerized point-of-sale scanners, Burroughs mainframe. *Software:* dBASE, Microsoft Word, spreadsheets, *Languages:* Some familiarity with COBOL, BASIC, Pascal, FORTRAN.

EXPERIENCE:
The Food Foray Companies   1984–present
- *Bake Shop Trainer*, 1989–present, for personnel in several stores throughout New Mexico: train part-time staff in all facets of high-volume bakery featuring several dozen products. Ensure compliance with government sanitation and food handling procedures. Order materials. Participate in market research and product development/withdrawal.

- *Assistant Front End Manager*, Albuquerque, NM, 1988–89. Scheduled and supervised cashiers and baggers. Provided on-site troubleshooting and register overrides/voids. Ensured smooth customer flow.

- *Cashier*, 1985–88. Assisted customers and performed daily balances.

- *Bagger*, 1984–85.

Robinson Stores, Albuquerque, NM   1987–89
- *Junior Buyer Trainee*, 1989.

- *Sales Associate*, 1987–89.

EDUCATION:
A.A. in Business, Albuquerque Community College, Albuquerque, NM   1987
Courses in Business Management, Introduction to Accounting, Psychology, Public Speaking, English, Algebra, etc.

Data Processing Certificate, Union Vocational H.S., Albuquerque, NM   1985

REFERENCES:
Available upon request.

162

Combination. *Shel Horowitz, Northampton, Massachusetts*

A focused, easy-to-read resume. Boldfacing helps to point out the overall structure of the resume. Italic is useful for identifying important topics within major sections.

SAM BECKETT
14898 St. Johns Avenue
Commerce, Michigan 48343
248.555.2485
e-mail: sbeckett@bignet.net

PROFILE

Well-qualified leader with a strong history of developing and maintaining excellent work teams, customer relationships, and community recognition. Hands-on management style.

Advocate of team-oriented working environments that demonstrate cohesion and unity in the workplace. Empower others to make qualified decisions and solutions.

EXPERTISE

Management — Proven results in managing with efficiency and attaining high performance from satisfied employees.

Human Resources — Insightful leader, utilizing well-developed skills of determining employee qualifications and requirements.

Training — Respected instructor with quality-conscience priorities and team-focused approach to training, mentoring, and encouraging.

Sales/Marketing — Visionary and personable manager; excellent relationship builder applying 'customer first' attitude and 'quality without exception' initiatives.

Finance — Strong analytical sense; experience setting forecasts, analyzing budgets, and implementing cost-efficient methodologies.

RESULTS

Consistently met and exceeded set goals and objectives, never missed a bonus award.

Trained and encouraged almost 70 people that have now gone on to management positions in the last two years. Trained four Store Managers.

Top 5% of Michigan stores for profitability seven of the last ten consecutive years. Remained in the top 2% of managers that have maintained the lowest percentage of employee/customer safety reports.

Food safety certified.

Positioned at stores with negative results. Invariably built, improved, managed stores to achieve positive growth through implementing excellent operational controls in a perishable product environment.

Developed and wrote a training article on "Effective Hiring Practices" that was incorporated and published in the corporate manual.

Won numerous awards for merchandising.

163

Combination. *Lorie Lebert, Novi, Michigan*

Thick-thin lines enclosing the Profile ensure that it will be seen by the reader. Bold embedded headings in the Expertise section make it easy to grasp the areas of expertise.

EXPERIENCE

FARMER JACK, 1979-current

STORE MANAGER

Scope of responsibilities is extensive and diverse, and encompasses all areas of business including finance, human resources, and management of multimillion dollar operations.

- ▸ Manage multifunctional teams consisting of more than 100 personnel (managers to hourly employees). Empower department managers and supervisors to determine and resolve issues.

- ▸ Oversee all internal/external functions including health and welfare of employees, merchandise and perishable products, landscaping, maintenance.

- ▸ Interact with union officials and union employees to maintain a loyal and dependable working atmosphere.

- ▸ Recruit and train personnel for management positions.

- ▸ Interact with community and actively involved in programs that promote positive corporate awareness in the neighborhoods.

- ▸ Make presentations at annual conferences.

- ▸ Cross-functional team member; cooperate on committee with Zone Manager, CPA, Vice President of Operations to achieve annual forecast and budgets.

Note:

- ▸ Throughout career at Farmer Jack, managed for every department in the store; utilize hands-on knowledge to support current managers.

- ▸ Managed 14 stores in 20 years. Reengineered and supported individual business efforts to successfully improve conditions and strengthen profitability levels.

- ▸ Patronize the managing store; encourage employees to patronize the store as well, to ensure excellence in product quality and customer service.

OTHER INFORMATION

Attended "Models for Management" courses through five levels — an intense team-directed hands-on workshop.

Dale Carnegie "Effective Speaking" course.

Computer competent in Windows applications including Lotus 1-2-3, Ami Pro.

— *Page 2 of Résumé for* —

SAM BECKETT

14898 St. Johns Avenue
Commerce, Michigan 48343

e-mail: sbeckett@bignet.net
248.555.2485

Achievements are presented on the first page as results before the position is mentioned on page 2. Right-pointing bullets direct attention to a selection of key responsibilities. The Note subsection presents three overviews. The last section is for additional training and skills.

John M. Collins

912 Penrose Avenue ▪ Washburn, California 55555
555-555-5555

CARPENTER and WORKING SUPERVISOR
Willing to relocate

SUMMARY OF QUALIFICATIONS

Bidding and drawings
Framing
Finish work: door hanging, base board, casing, crown molding, tiling
Roof and drywall experience

Crew supervision of 1 - 4 people ▪ First Aid training ▪ Hilti-certified for powder actuated tools

Own personal tools including compound miter saw, worm drive Skil saw, 14.4 cordless drill,
Sawzall plus other hand tools

EDUCATION

Washburn Community College, Washburn, California
  Currently working on Associates Degree with an emphasis in business

AAAS in Carpentry. Washburrn Community College, Washburn, California
  Graduated Spring, 1998. Hired for Summer 1997 receiving credits and wages for steel framing offices.
  Other coursework included finish work on one house and participation in the complete construction of
  another house.

Diploma. Washburn High School, Washburn, California, June 1995
  Senior project: constructed drift boat

EXPERIENCE

▪ **KETTING CONSTRUCTION CO.**, Washburn, California   May 1997 to present

  <u>Residential Addition</u> (February 1999 to present). Bid job, prepared and submitted drawings for
  permits. Oversee subcontractors and work crew. Will do framing and finish work personally.

  <u>Log House</u> (June 1998 to November 1998). Log stacking, window and door cut-outs, siding and finish
  work.

  Other jobs involving finish work, framing, concrete, and roofing.

▪ **ACE MANUFACTURING**, Washburn, California   September 1996 to April 1997

  Welding and metal fabrication: sprinkler system parts, slip tanks for wheat trucks, and wheat trailers.
  Installed hydraulic lifts on trucks.

▪ **SILVER STAR CABINETS**, Washburn, California   January to August 1996
  Cabinets and laminates

ACCOMPLISHMENTS

Eagle Scout, Boy Scouts of America
Project: Managed team of volunteers and constructed sand volleyball court. Summer 1994

164

Combination. *Janette M. Campbell, Washougal, Washington*

Education is put early for this craftsman with leadership skills to show that he is pursuing a
second degree to increase his business sense. Square bullets are used throughout.

FRANCES C. BOOKKEEPER
49 Marcie Court
South Tinton, NJ 00000
(555) 555-5555

• Relocating to Boston in August 1995 •

OBJECTIVE: Position as a full-charge bookkeeper

SUMMARY

- 4 years of full-charge bookkeeping experience with supervisory duties.
- A.A. degree in business administration; worked full-time while attending college.
- Record of promotions and increasing responsibilities.
- Self-starter who takes pride in quality work; strong customer service skills.
- Flexible schedule; able to devote the time necessary to complete projects.
- Computer skills: Lotus 1-2-3, Excalibur, CLS (hotel accounting program), WordPerfect; viewed as computer troubleshooter by coworkers.

PROFESSIONAL EXPERIENCE

FULL-CHARGE BOOKKEEPER / OFFICE MANAGER
Rantron Concrete, Ballix, NJ   1993 - Present
Manage all bookkeeping functions for concrete plant with 75 employees, a customer base of over 500 clients, and over $4 million in accounts receivable. Assist with bookkeeping functions for 4 affiliated corporations. Respond promptly to customers' questions. Supervise 5 office workers. Provide office support for general managers and estimators.

Bookkeeping
- Performed full-charge bookkeeping responsibilities, including: Accounts receivable and billing... Accounts payable... Payroll... Collections... Bank reconciliations... Monthly and quarterly reports.
- Played key role in conversion to automated A/P and A/R system: Evaluated and relayed requirements to computer consultant; implemented new system and trained staff in its use.
- Organized and increased collection efforts, resulting in higher volume of payments.
- Prepared reports for Workers' Compensation and Unemployment.

Supervision
- Scheduled and supervised 5 secretaries and file clerks; evaluated staff regularly.
- Delegated office work and insured timely completion.

INCOME AUDITOR
Shoreway Resort, Napton, FL   1991 - 1993
Initially hired as night auditor for this large resort, with golf courses, restaurants and hotels. Promoted to night audit supervisor, then to income auditor. Worked closely with controller. Handled diverse tasks, including reservations and front desk responsibilities. Often worked 7-day work weeks during busy season.

- Oversaw all internal functions of a 7-person accounting department: Reviewed all accounts receivable and payable, payroll and billing reports; generated a daily computerized income report with a detailed breakdown of all areas of operation.
- Supervised and scheduled 4 auditors; reviewed their daily work and reports.
- Posted all cash receipts to general ledger; reconciled bank statements.
- Handled all credit card disputes and charge backs.
- Worked 18-21 hours daily when necessary, handling 2 positions, to meet reopening deadline.

ADDITIONAL WORK EXPERIENCE
Held bank teller positions from 1987 to 1991.

EDUCATION
A.A., Business Administration, 1994 • South Tinton Community College, South Tinton, NJ
Dean's List

165

Combination. *Rhoda Kopy, Toms River, New Jersey*

A well-designed resume. The information before and after Professional Experience is center-justified. That section is left-justified with consistent conventions for italic and bullets.

BEVERLEY DRAKE

950 S. Pinehurst Court
Brookfield Wisconsin 53005

555•343•1371
voice mail: 800•789•4369

- ▸ solid planning, organizational, and time management capabilities
- ▸ high work ethic and attention to detail
- ▸ strong problem resolution skills
- ▸ extensive computer background

OFFICE ADMINISTRATION, INCLUDING HUMAN RESOURCE ISSUES

Extensive experience, including 9 yrs. owning and operating full-service business center. Strong business sense and entrepreneurial spirit of "can do". Committed to team concepts and strong interrelationships among all levels. Advocate of cross training and employee empowerment for increased worker productivity. Skills and strengths include:

- ▸ interviewing, hiring, evaluations
- ▸ policy and procedure writing
- ▸ clerical training and inservices
- ▸ planning, organizing, coordinating
- ▸ decisionmaking and troubleshooting
- ▸ records management
- ▸ marketing, promotion, advertising
- ▸ client / customer service
- ▸ payroll, budgeting, accounting

ACCOMPLISHMENTS AND EXPERIENCE

Administrative

- ▸ directed major functions of business center 9 years, including operations, finance, quality control, marketing
- ▸ serve as mentor on small business and employment issues via Internet
- ▸ knowledgeable regarding OSHA, EEO, unions, Worker's Compensation, disability, unemployment
- ▸ familiar with union contract negotiations, seniority lists, workplace safety, and other labor issues
- ▸ maintain awareness regarding human resource and employment issues through yearly seminars
- ▸ past responsibility for clerical hiring decisions at health facility, university department, and business center
- ▸ achieved increased efficiency of nursing home clerical staff by implementation of cross training program
- ▸ experienced in forms design and writing of job descriptions, reports, press releases, and other materials
- ▸ author of over 20 employment-related articles published in newspapers, business and trade newsletters
- ▸ set up and wrote training and administrative policy manuals for various employers
- ▸ supervised student interns and clerical personnel for various employers, in addition to own business
- ▸ panelist on the topic of resume development at 1995 convention of professional resume writers

Technology Expertise

- ▸ working knowledge of Windows, DOS, WordPerfect, PC Tools, Quicken, 386Max, Check-It, virus programs
- ▸ install software and troubleshoot computer, software, and peripheral problems; maintain hard disk
- ▸ research information and use e-mail via Internet and on-line services
- ▸ conduct private tutoring on PCs of WordPerfect and various business software
- ▸ experienced in computerized typesetting of business, promotional, and marketing documents

EDUCATION

Phi Theta Kappa honors / A.A. degree, Virginia Intermont College, Bristol VA
Seminars—supervisory, human resources, accounting, purchasing, marketing, advertising, and
    promotion, desktop publishing, temporary and permanent placement, publishing, job search
    and career materials, career transitioning, online databases and Internet use

CERTIFICATIONS AND AFFILIATIONS

National Association of Female Executives and Professional Association of Resume Writers — current
Greater Oswego Chamber of Commerce and Small Business Extension Service — past
Credentialed as Certified Professional Resume Writer (CPRW) — current

166

Combination. *Beverley Drake, Rochester, Minnesota*

Compare this resume with Resume 19 by the same resume writer. The first page of each is similar, but the content is different. One design can serve many purposes and interests.

EXPERIENCE HISTORY   **BEVERLEY DRAKE**

DRAKE CONSULTING, Oswego, NY   1994 to present
Owner of consulting firm with 3 main divisions: p.t.
- ► Alternative Professional Temp — quick, short-term office support
- ► CareerVision — resume and job search systems
- ► WordSmart — freelance writing, editorial, desktop publishing, and business services

PRECISELY YOURS BUSINESS SERVICES, INC. and RESUMES U.S.A., Oswego, NY   1985 to 1994
[Ex] Owner/Operator of 2 businesses set up from scratch   9 yrs.

STATE UNIVERSITY OF NEW YORK, College at Oswego, Oswego, NY
Technical Assistant to Director and Associate Director of Campus Life   temp p.t. / 12 wks.

OPERATION OSWEGO COUNTY, Oswego, NY (county's industrial development corp.)
Word Processor   temp p.t. / 5 mos.

METROPOLITAN WATER BOARD, Oswego, NY
Interim Secretary to Plant Manager   temp p.t. / 6 mos.

ITHACA GUN COMPANY, Ithaca, NY
Assistant to Director of Personnel; Executive Secretary to Vice President of Operations   temp / 4 mos.

BABCOCK INDUSTRIES, INC., Ithaca, NY
Executive Secretary to Controller   temp / 8 mos.

PRESBYTERIAN CHURCH, Oswego, NY (renamed Faith United Church)
Office Manager and Secretary to Pastor   p.t. / 2 yrs.

CORNELL UNIVERSITY, Ithaca, NY
Sr. Administrative Secretary to Dir. of Administrative Programming, Computer Services   2 yrs.
Sr. Administrative Secretary to Dean of The Graduate School   6 mo.
Sr. Administrative Secretary to Director of Cornell Plantations   4 mo.

RECONSTRUCTION HOME, Ithaca, NY (Skilled Nursing Facility)
Business Office Supervisor (promoted from Administrative Secretary and Account Clerk)   2 1/2 yrs.

ROBERT KIEFFER, M.D., Ithaca, NY
Office Manager, Medical Office Assistant / Secretary   2 yrs.

The box with the shadowed border is especially a good place to indicate a different focus. The second pages of these two resumes are identical. Note that experience histories can be different depending on what you want to select from the past for a prospective employer.

PETER PAN
76 Fantasyland Place
Spring, Texas 77345
(713) 292-0945

PROFILE:	**PURCHASING MANAGER ♦ MATERIALS CONTROL MANAGER** Fourteen years professional experience in material procurement, inventory control, production scheduling, employee supervision and distribution services for the manufacturing industry. Began career as Electronic Technician calibrating ultrasonic flowmeters utilizing oscilloscope, multimeters, frequency generators/counters and other sophisticated testing equipment. Highly technical and detail oriented; successful in maintaining inventory control costs through the effective negotiation of vendor contracts and the implementation of security control procedures.
PROFESSIONAL EXPERIENCE:	**COLLINS MEASUREMENT**, Houston, Texas 1981 - Present <u>**Purchasing Manager**</u> 1993 - Present *(Manufacturer of Instrumentation for Flow Meter Measurement)* Organize, manage and supervise the purchasing of 6,000 item inventory. Conduct cost analysis on new items; negotiate with vendors in the securing of bids; develop package configurations; and dispose of obsolete inventory.
	<u>**Materials Control Manager**</u 1991 - 1992 Scheduled day-to-day operations of the production department. Generated shop packages for parts allocation. ♦ Restructured million dollar inventory stockroom. ♦ Set up cycle count program and initiated new security control procedures. ♦ Supervised shipping and receiving department handling over $220,000 a month in inventory.
	<u>**Production/Calibration Supervisor**</u> 1985 - 1990 Hired, trained and supervised electronic technicians and final assemblers in the production of ultrasonic flow meters. Formulated new departmental procedures; consulted with engineers on new product development; wrote technical procedures for new instrumentation. ♦ Successfully eliminated production backlog within six months.
	<u>**Electronic Technician**</u> 1981 - 1985 Calibrated ultrasonic flowmeters to customers' specifications utilizing a variety of testing equipment. Acted as troubleshooter for test board maintenance and repair.
EDUCATION:	North Harris Community College Houston, Texas **Associate of Applied Science Degree** **Electronic Technology** 1981 **GPA 3.5**
COMPUTER SKILLS:	♦ Macola ♦ Intelligent Query
CONTINUING EDUCATION:	Supervisory Training Materials Identification Programming Logic

167

Combination. *Cheryl Ann Harland, The Woodlands, Texas*

This person worked for the same company since graduation. His degree had little to do with the new direction his career took within that company. Positions are bold and underlined.

Kenneth Lee
1947 Oklahoma Street
Yorba Linda, CA 92679
(714) 555-7122

Seeking to apply my skills and knowledge to a responsible managerial position in dealership parts or service. Offering award winning leadership and dedication to excellence.

Experience   Twenty-six years experience in dealership management, parts and service. Risk Management experience, interfacing with B.A.R., EPA, EDD, Labor Board, Small Claims Court and Consumer Affairs.

Managerial Skills   Parts Manager, supervising more than twenty-six employees with varying skill levels. Service manager, overseeing thirty-three employees, increasing labor sales 52%. Operations Control Manager, responsible for purchasing, testing, inventory, parts control and supervision of national sales representatives and general operations of manufacturing company.

Budgetary Skills   Developed and implemented budgets, sales forecasting, operational planning, merchandising, advertising and promotions.

Inventory Skills   Supervised inventory control of 7,500 to 16,000 part numbers with values of $220,000 in excess of $590,000. Parts sales increase from 34% to 302% over a one to seven year period, with maximum of over $6,000,000 in sales.

Personnel Skills   Responsible for interviewing, hiring, termination, and training of employees in all areas of dealership operations.

Education   AA Degree in Business Management, Fullerton College, June, 1968
Specialized training by Toyota, Chrysler, Nissan, and Mitsubishi

Personal Qualities   Able to communicate effectively, highly organized, excellent problem solving abilities, positive attitude, high motivation

Employers   Toyota of Anaheim   Yorba Linda Chevrolet
Laguna Beach Toyota   Long Beach Mitsubishi
J.J. Jones Cadillac

References   Available upon request.

168

Functional. *Sharon Payne, location unknown*

Lacking any date except the year of graduation, this resume is skill-oriented. It's good-looking too: The parallel vertical lines distinguish this resume from most others.

JASON BRIDGES
289 Lorhardt
Naperville, Illinois 55555

H: (555) 555-5555

W: (555) 555-5555, x555

PROFILE
- Possess 9 years of experience in freight transportation management which would be valuable in a Transportation Traffic Manager capacity.
- Adept at establishing solid, long-term relationships with airlines through effective communication, interpersonal, and negotiation skills.
- Experience managing and motivating up to 34 personnel; create an effective team-oriented environment.
- High level of enthusiasm and ambition exhibited throughout execution of daily activities.
- Proven aptitude at devising solutions to urgent customer problems.
- Valued as a cost-conscious, efficiency-oriented, profit-minded employee.

EXPERIENCE
MONTROSE AIR EXPRESS; Naperville, Illinois   **JANUARY 1986 - PRESENT**

Gateway Service Supervisor   (December 1992 - Present)
- Successfully negotiate airline contracts and allocations.
- Handle supervision and scheduling for staff consisting of two lead agents, 22 dock personnel, and 10 employees of in-house cartage company.
- Ensure freight is transported on schedule; follow-up on airline failures.
- Quote airline rates to customers in collaboration with sales staff.

Achievements:
- Developed container sizing plan which reduced airline cost by 20%.
- Devised and implemented a strategy focusing on accountability and goal setting which increased efficiency of dock and cartage company personnel by 50%.
- Structured procedural methods for ISO-9002.

Hub Operations Supervisor   (June 1987 - December 1992)
- Performed hiring, training, supervising, and scheduling functions for 20 part-time sorters.
- Reported operational progress to management on a daily basis.

Achievements:
- Played an integral role in the successful transfer of hub operations from Kansas City, Missouri to Schaumburg, Illinois.
- Appointed as hub supervisor trainer.
- Acted as area manager in the absence of area management.

Lead Sorter   (September 1986 - June 1987)

EDUCATION
KTI Technical Institute; Greensleeve, Michigan
Associates degree in **Architectural Engineering**, 1987

Michigan State University - University of Michigan
Certificate, Leadership Development, 1991

Bureau of Dangerous Goods, Ltd.; Blatscuff, Connecticut
Certificate, Handling Dangerous Goods in accordance with international & federal regulations.

Executrain; Rolling Meadows, Illinois
Certificate, Windows 3.0 & Excel 5.0

MILITARY
Michigan National Guard; Ann Arbor, Michigan
Aircraft Armament Systems Specialist (1990 - Present) & Army Team Leader (1984 - 1990)

169

Combination. *Georgia Veith, location unknown*

The individual's two-year degree was not directly related to the career he was pursuing. The Education section was therefore placed after the Profile and Experience sections.

Edward S. Buss

943 East 8th Street ★ Newaygo, Michigan 43333 ★ (616) 699-9999

CAREER OBJECTIVE:

Seeking employment in school transportation supervisor capacity.

QUALIFICATIONS:

Respected and disciplined individual with experience in all aspects of school transportation including driving, maintenance, and scheduling. Safety conscious at all levels. Able to communicate effectively and command respect from student body while maintaining good rapport. Computer literate. Supervisory and management experience.

LICENSURE AND PROFESSIONAL AFFILIATION:

CDL State of Michigan
Michigan Association of Pupil Transportation (MAPT)

RELATED BACKGROUND SUMMARY:

★ Developed and implemented 65 efficient bus routes
★ Experienced in hiring employees, scheduling, training, and payroll for 39 drivers, 4 transportation assistants, 2 mechanics, and one clerical/dispatcher
★ Develop and monitor department budget
★ Submit written and verbal reports to administration, staff, parents, and students
★ Keep up to date on safety and licensing for business and employees
★ Monitor weather and road conditions
★ Implemented safety program for pupils through AAA
★ Participated in Regional and State School Bus Rodeos past seven years
★ Knowledgeable and up to date in state and local laws, rules and regulations and ensure accurate completion of all applicable reports
★ Set up schedule of bus maintenance
★ Worked as teacher's aide and playground supervisor
★ Experienced school bus driver
★ Substitute bus driver for three districts

RELATED WORK HISTORY:

Transportation Supervisor   November 1993 - October 1995
  Cedar Springs Public Schools, Cedar Springs, Michigan

School bus driver/Teacher Aide/Playground Supervisor   1988 - 1992
  Holy Trinity School, Comstock Park, Michigan

EDUCATION:

Associates Degree   July 1992
  Grand Rapids Community College, Grand Rapids, Michigan

BA program in Elementary Education   1992 - 1993
  Western Michigan University, Kalamazoo, Michigan

Certificate in Computer Programming and Operations   1983

170

Combination. *Pat Nieboer, Fremont, Michigan*

What a difference a graphic can make! It can't fix a bad resume, however. The beauty of this resume is that it's strong without the graphic—but stronger with it.

EXPERT N. CREDIT

405 West Check Way, #111
Suburban Township, USA 99999
(555) 999-9999

WORK OBJECTIVE:

Position in **Commercial Credit Management** where my extensive work experience and acquired skills will make a valued contribution to the goals of a company.

HIGHLIGHTS OF QUALIFICATIONS:

Knowledge and Experience: Diverse experience in credit management and credit analysis within divisions/subsidiaries of major companies. Demonstrated record of account coordination and resolution. Highly knowledgeable of procedures, rules, and regulations pertaining to credit, collections, and accounts receivable. Familiar in computer usage.

Analysis, Judgment, Problem-Solving Abilities: Effective in researching area of concern within a timely fashion. Prudent in judgment and efficient in implementing appropriate course of action.

Leadership and Interpersonal Skills: Strive to generate productive and profitable communications with sales and service representatives, customers, and management. Provide guidance and training to employees.

EXPERIENCE:

PRINT INTERNATIONAL, Main Print Division, Small Town, USA
Senior Credit Manager (October 1989 - Present)

Manage accounts receivable portfolio compiling over 5,000 accounts valued at more than $10 million for this major division of a large manufacturing company of printing equipment and supplies. Perform credit evaluations on orders ranging from $1,500 to $200,000 in dollar value. Determine accounts to be placed for collection. Train temporary staff on credit procedures.
◆ Significantly reduced aged accounts with balances over 90 days portfolio through a "take charge, hands-on" approach.
◆ Developed productive working relationships with twelve district sales and service locations, order entry, inside sales, and service dispatch personnel.
◆ Established excellent rapport with distinct customer population comprised of government contacts, in-house printing plants, and small printing companies.

(NOTE: From November 1986 - September 1989, took time off due to home/family responsibilities; from December 1987 - September 1989, worked in part-time position as a **Customer Service Representative** at **Furnishing Experts, in Anytown, USA**.)

DOWN TO BUSINESS COMPANY, Microfilm Products Division, Small Town, USA
Regional Credit Manager (January 1982 - October 1986)

Supervised staff in management of $5 million accounts receivable portfolio. Worked with clients and sales representatives to avoid unnecessary collection agency placement, bad debt, and unnecessary loss of a customer's good will.
◆ Targeted credit evaluation criteria toward goals of maximizing profitable sales, minimizing bad debt write-offs, and optimizing customer relations.
◆ Maximized profitable sales by prudent risk management and creativity with applying special terms or security documents for marginal customers.
◆ Maintained an average DSO of 44 days on terms of Net 30 days.

171

Combination. *Cathleen M. Hunt, Chicago, Illinois*

A quality two-page resume. Like many other resumes in this Gallery, this resume is worth studying to sharpen your use of character enhancements (boldface, italic, underlining).

EXPERT N. CREDIT.....(Page Two)

123 WHOLESALE, INC., Subsidiary of Worldwide Industries, Big Town, USA
Credit Assistant (1978 to November 1981)

Under the supervision of Vice President, Treasurer, and in conjunction with theWorldwide liaison in Other Big Town, USA, conducted investigation and analysis of customer credit and account statuses. Prepared written or verbal communications to customers to render account resolution.

◆ Increased sales on large contract jobs through consideration of secured transactions in qualifying a potential customer.

◆ Travelled with company representatives to help enhance communications between credit department and customers.

◆ Maintained an average DSO of 56 days on terms of 5/30, 3/60, and Net 61.

PAPERS OF AMERICA, INC., Forms Division, Big Town, USA
Manager of Credit, Accounts Receivable/Accounts Payable (1972 - 1978)

Reported to President with responsibility for overseeing credit and collection functions. Generated monthly reports for Budget, Salesman Commissions, Product Analysis, and Collections. Supervised staff consisting of an assistant and part-time employees. Scheduled vendor payments, audited vendor invoices, handled adjustments and inquiries, and processed checks.

◆ Planned and participated in achieving smooth transition of manual ledger system to computerized setup.

◆ Improved relationships with customers and suppliers through attentiveness and timely follow-through.

◆ Maintained an average DSO of 37 days, on terms of 1% 10, Net 30.

PROFESSIONAL MEMBERSHIPS:

Nationwide Credit Management Association
National Association of Credit Management
CMCMA Sponsored Trade Group, Member 19xx - 19xx

TRAINING/EDUCATION:

Seminars:

Zenger-Miller Training in Supervision
American Management Association Training in Managerial Skills

Coursework:

Fellow Award, National Institute of Credit, Lake Success, NY
Coursework included *Financial Statement Analysis*, *Credit Management*, and *Credit Law*.

City Institute of Credit, Small Town, USA

City College, Small Town, USA
Completed coursework in *Business Curriculum*.

In the Experience section, diamond bullets highlight the individual's significant achievements.
The Training/Education section is detailed at the end to show her outstanding credentials.
The horizontal line on page 1 is repeated with a header on page 2.

Carol P. Quinn

3456 Palace Road
New Brunswick, Connecticut 05498
(203) 865-2019

PROFILE

An innate leader / manager with a strong desire for job satisfaction. Thrives on additional responsibilities. Highly self-motivated. Accurate and efficient; a quick learner with good analytical skills. Well-organized; detail-oriented; adaptable. An effective trainer and supervisor. A team player who works well independently. A morale booster with a positive attitude.

Computer literate: WordPerfect, Microsoft Outlook , Lotus, Office Vision. Establishes and maintains strong customer relations. Excellent interpersonal skills at all levels, both in person and on telephone. Professional manner and appearance.

EXPERIENCE

1994-present

MetLife
Griswald, Connecticut
UNDERWRITING REPRESENTATIVE (1997-1999)
- Review current and new business insurance applications for auto, home, boat and personal lines to determine if they are acceptable for MetLife.
- Speak to prospective clients gathering pertinent data.
- Make recommendation to insure or not to insure; pass this information to Underwriter for final decision.
- Handle policy changes.
- Write correspondence to mortgage and finance companies, and additional insureds.
- Work on computer: Microsoft Word and Outlook.
- Interact with insureds, lien holder companies, house inspectors, attorneys and interoffice personnel.
- Review and amend policies when necessary.
- Process / apply money from clients or mortgage companies.
- **Received Producer's License, 1998; took INS 21 Course, 1999.**

TECHNICAL ASSISTANT (1994-1997)
- Acted as Customer Service Representative in Complaint Department.
- Worked on computer: Lotus and Office Vision.
- Responsible for office duties: typing, faxing, email.
- Trained new office personnel in Underwriting Department.
- Coordinated weekly department meetings.

PREVIOUS EXPERIENCE:

1984-1991

MANAGER: Family Scoop, CT: Seasonal ice cream stand.
Supervised, scheduled and trained 6 part-time employees; handled payroll and inventory; bottom-line responsibility for customer service.

172

Combination. *Phyllis Fern, Cranston, Rhode Island*

Horizontal lines enclosing Profile text help to draw the reader's attention to this important part of the resume. Indenting the Previous Experience heading makes it less conspicuous.

JULIE AVANELL
29 Maple Avenue • Apt. 3D • Rye, New York 00000
(914) 555-5555

CAREER OBJECTIVE:

Experienced professional seeks a position with a growing organization that will utilize extensive knowledge of credit and collections.

DEMONSTRATED STRENGTHS:

CREDIT/COLLECTION	PROBLEM SOLVING	COMMUNICATION SKILLS
ANALYTICAL THINKING	TIME MANAGEMENT	SELF MOTIVATED

Consistent ability to win the confidence of others and gain their cooperation

PROFESSIONAL EXPERIENCE:

K & R PRINTING INK   Rye, New York
Credit Manager   *1990 - Present*
- Oversees all credit functions for an ink manufacturer. Revenue exceeds $65 million. Company operates domestically and internationally.
- Manages collections for 4000 customers with accounts receivable balances of $10 million.
- Recruits, trains and manages a professional staff.
- Establishes credit limits for all new customers with unlimited authority.
- Prepared reports using Lotus 1-2-3 for review by upper management.
- Travels to customers and resolves issues to promote superior relations.
- Communicates daily with four regional managers and 22 branch managers.

Accomplishments:
◆ *Served as a catalyst for change and transition, successfully turning around a completely disorganized and poorly functioning department.*
◆ *Significantly reduced past due accounts through diligent research and extensive customer communications.*
◆ *Recognized by the Controller for maintaining superior operations.*
◆ *Member of several Creditor's Committees.*
◆ *Represents Company at court appearances during lawsuits.*

EXECUTIVE AIR FLEET CORP.   Teterboro, New Jersey
Credit Analyst   *1985 - 1990*
- Established and adjusted credit lines based on evaluation of credit worthiness of all clients.
- Actively participated in the collection of accounts receivable.
- Managed the activities departmental staff to peak levels of performance.
- Assessed monthly aging schedules.
- Served as a liaison among credit, collections, sales and marketing departments.
- Initially hired as a Credit and Collection Associate and promoted within one year in recognition of superior achievements.

EDUCATIONAL BACKGROUND:

Bergen Community College • Paramus, New Jersey • A.S. in Business Administration

173

Combination. *Alesia Benedict, Rochelle Park, New Jersey*

A resume in which diamond bullets and italic are used to call attention to important accomplishments. Such a resume as this can help two-year graduates be competitive.

SARITA S. MAYNAARD
2987 Solly Acres Road, Earlsburg, MI 55555, 222-000-0055

SUPERVISION ★ *PROGRAM ADMINISTRATION* ★ *CREDIT MANAGEMENT* ★ *CUSTOMER SERVICES*

Background
Broad base experience serving as: Branch Manager; Office/Department Coordinator; Collection/Credit Supervisor.

Career Focus
Position in credit/collection department utilizing my knowledge and experience in the banking industry.

Professional History
1992-Pres. **Collection/Litigation Manager**, Citizens Commercial Savings Bank, Cedarwood, MI.
1987-1992. **Assistant Manager/Office Supervisor**, Standard Federal Bank, Stanwood, MI.
1971-1986. **Branch Manager/Assistant Manager/Collection Manager**, Comerica Bank, Earlsburg, MI.
1967-1971. **Assistant Credit Manager/Collection Manager**, Earlsburg Credit Union, Earlsburg, MI.

Profile of Experience and Accomplishments
Supervision: managed a staff of 10; in charge of recruiting, hiring, and training new employees in banking operations and procedures; directed weekly staff meetings to maintain cooperative relationships with staff; encouraged ideas for continuous improvement and methods for problem/conflict resolution. Monitored writing of Collection Procedures project to ensure effective follow-through. Promoted an "open door" policy to maintain excellent relations; exercised a proactive management approach.

Program Administration: heavily involved in business development: auto, mortgage approvals, denials, and audits; directed Bank Repossession Program. Assisted in the onset and management of Collection and Litigation Account System. Supervised operation and maintenance of ATM Program. Directed new member application and processing for Consumer and Business Credit Cards Program.

Credit Management: accountable for the dispute and collection of past due account activity: reduction of delinquency-- from 11% to 4%--within 2 years; supervised general accounting responsibilities relating to ledger activity: customer master files; over/short cash reconciliation; trial balance detail; and financial journals and reports. Maintained financials for auditors and banking analysts.

Customer Services: served as community relations representative; conducted banking seminars at local schools to promote branch products: distributed brochures, introduced new services, explained branch policies and procedures. Inspired a customer/client-driven environment exhibiting intuitive problem solving, strong customer service, versatility, and integrity.

Education and Training
Comerica Bank, Cedarwood, MI. Sales and Lending Management; Consumer and Retail Credit.
Numerous in-house financial management seminars.
Graduate: Earlsburg Community College, 1967-1969. Focus: Business and Retail Management

Associations
Earlsburg Credit Managers Association, E.C.M.A.

Community Involvement/Volunteer
United Way, Stanwood, MI. Volunteer.

References
Excellent professional references available upon request.

174

Combination. *Randy Clair, location unknown*

One of the best arranged resumes in this Gallery. The four skill areas within dual lines are discussed in turn in the Profile. The result? Two interviews and a Fortune 500 company job.

MARY JANE COSGROVE
555 Old Church Road • Greenbriar, SC
(111) 555-0055 • 555-0000 - mobile

PROFILE
- ❖ Extremely organized - able to accomplish multiple goals simultaneously.
- ❖ Outgoing personality - enjoy working with people - positive attitude.
- ❖ Excellent written and oral communication skills.
- ❖ Marketing and sales experience - give high quality customer service.
- ❖ Equally comfortable as a leader or team member - very flexible.

EXPERIENCE

Advanced Lighting, Greenbriar, SC
Showroom Manager / Lighting Consultant, 1997-Present.
- ❖ Handle inventory and purchasing from 60+ manufacturers.
- ❖ Supervise and motivate 3 sales personnel.
- ❖ Build relationships with customers and suppliers.
- ❖ Generate $25,000-$30,000 in revenue per month.
- ❖ Consistently meet or exceed company and personal sales goals.
- ❖ Provide quality customer service from on-site measuring to personal delivery of all fixtures.

XYZ of Greenbriar, Greenbriar, SC
Residential contracting firm building 60 homes per year.
Construction Coordinator, 1994-1997
- ❖ Applied for all permits
- ❖ Coordinated deliveries and subcontractor scheduling.
Mortgage Officer, Compton Group, Atlanta, SC
- ❖ Took loan applications and brokered loans.
- ❖ Worked with bank inspectors for draws.

First Federal Savings and Loan, Greenbriar, SC
Mortgage Loan Processor, 1989-1993
- ❖ Processed and closed FHA, VA, SC State Housing, conforming FNMA, and PMI approved loans.
- ❖ Worked directly with 8 bank branch managers.

Central City Bank, Minneapolis, MN
Loan Officer, 1987-1989
- ❖ Top Producer - originated required goal of $10 million/year.

Prior customer service experience:
Florida Power and Light, Miami, FL
Georgia Power Company, Columbus, GA

CIVIC AFFILIATIONS

Greenbriar Area Chamber of Commerce - Chamber Ambassadors, chairman
Leadership Greenbriar Class XII
Home Builders Association

EDUCATION

Executive Secretarial degree, Phillips Business College
University of Georgia, Columbus, GA - basic studies.
On-the-job training: mortgage loan processing, office management, inventory control, relationship building, and scheduling.

175

Combination. *Karen Swann, Clemson, South Carolina*

Distinctive bullets help to set this resume apart from others in a stack of resumes. Paradoxically, the person has distinguished herself as one who works well with others.

ANTOINETTE GOGETTER

1155 Hammond Drive #D-4260, Atlanta, GA 30328 **(770) 000-0000**

EMPLOYMENT OBJECTIVE
To further career growth where dedicated performance is rewarded with an outlook for advancement.

CAREER PROFILE
Professional experience in office administration, client relations, and bookkeeping:
- Dedicated, dependable with a quick learning ability
- Well-organized and adaptable to changing environments
- Self-motivated, works independently or as a part of a team while upholding high quality work standards

EDUCATION
Associate Degree, Liberal Arts
MOREHOUSE COLLEGE, Atlanta, GA

Computer Skills:
- Lotus 1-2-3, MS-Word, dBASE, ACT, Corel Draw, AmiPro, CYMA Accounting

EXPERIENCE

Office Manager
AT WORKS, INC., Atlanta, GA 10/90 - Present
- Supervise administrative functions and implement cost-effective processes.
- Process accounts payable/receivable and assist the accounting department as delegated.
- Perform billing and invoice collections.
- Monitor inventory control and approve purchase of supplies.
- Participate and assist in sales and marketing functions.
- Assist in screening and hiring new staff.
- Interface with vendors and communicate organizational needs.

Reservationist
COMFORT INN MANSION, St. Charles - New Orleans, LA 5/88 - 10/90
- Interfaced with a wide range of customers and responded to various business inquiries.
- Performed guest check-in/check-out functions and carried-out associated work.
- Operated a reservation computer system and updated records while handling large volume.

PRIOR EXPERIENCE
Assistant/Clerk, BLAIRTON MARKET, Apollo, PA 1980 - 1986

176

Combination. *Terek A. Jabali, location unknown*

The individual's name and the section headings are all uppercase and italic. Boldfacing is applied to the name, the phone number, the degree, computer skills, and job positions.

Shannon Forster

(618) 000-0000

E-Mail: sforster@advance.com
P. O. Box 000, Somewhere, IL 00000

PROFILE
➢ Enjoy a challenge, excellent troubleshooting abilities.
➢ Accurate and intelligent researcher.
➢ Flexible, effective in all areas of company operations, learn quickly and prioritizes effectively.
➢ Business and results-oriented manager - Expect much from self and employees (trust individual Manager's integrity to provide best service and loyalty to company). Productive relations with peers, staff and management.
➢ Knowledgeable and efficient - an effective communicator - patient.
➢ Self-confident, effective in group settings.

EDUCATION / SEMINARS
Somewhere University, Somewhere, IN: 1992 Lotus 123
Illinois Eastern Community College. Robinson, IL: Presently working towards Business Management degree.
The Great Game of Business Seminar. St. Louis, MO: 1998
Adonis Conference. Albuquerque, NM: 1998

EXPERIENCE
Vice President of Operations. Micro-Electronics, Inc. Somewhere, IN: 0000-Present
Experience in full range of operations, including strategic business planning, finance/accounting, human resources administration, product sales and customer service, dispatch, shipping and receiving, maintenance contracts, warranties, purchasing, and inventory management. Approve department spending and overtime. Direct supervisory responsibility (screen interview, hire, train and management) for five Department Managers (18 employees).
➢ **Goal:** Improve operations on a day-by-day basis. Sole responsibility for software implementation and streamlining processes for improved efficiency and cost savings. Research and implement software conversions and provide intensive training to company management and employees.
➢ Shut down Product Sales Department and cleaned up accounts resulting in substantial savings to company.
➢ Personally took over Information Leasing Company accounts - cleared errors and insured collections resulting in $2M in a seven month period.
➢ Brought software on-line in three months including management and employee training.
➢ As **Operations Manager** (0000-0000) - selected software package and implemented it within six months.

Part-Time Assistant - Installment Loan Department. National Bank. Somewhere, IN: 0000-0000

File Clerk. Insurance Company. Somewhere, IN: 0000

Part-Time Office Assistant. Chemicals, Inc. Somewhere, IN: 0000

COMMUNITY AFFILIATIONS
Leadership Dade County - Class of '98 / Leadership Dade County - Selection and Recruitment Committee and Alumni Committee.

177

Combination. *Colleen S. Jaracz, Vincennes, Indiana*

Special bullets create interest immediately in the Profile section. Reading the career path backward—that is, from the bottom to the top—displays a big leap to V. P. of Operations.

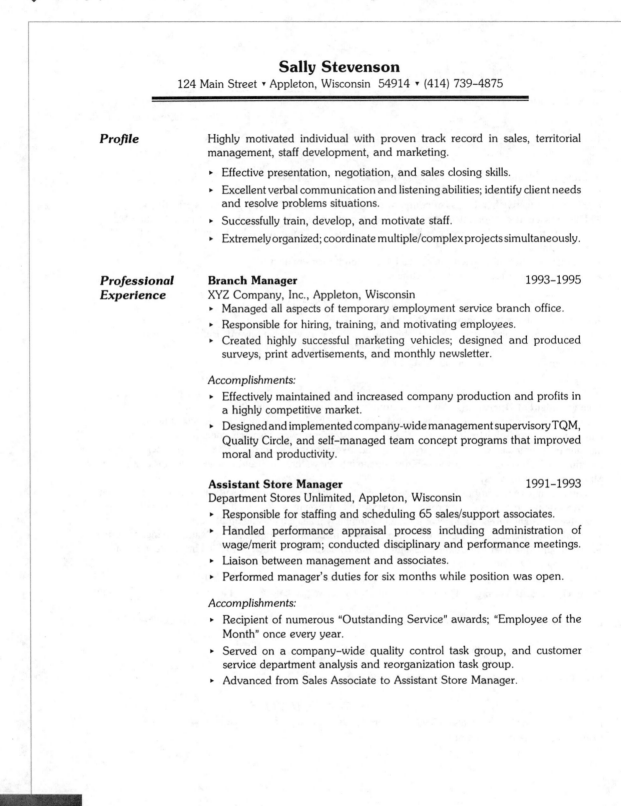

Sally Stevenson
124 Main Street ▾ Appleton, Wisconsin 54914 ▾ (414) 739–4875

Profile | Highly motivated individual with proven track record in sales, territorial management, staff development, and marketing.

- ‣ Effective presentation, negotiation, and sales closing skills.
- ‣ Excellent verbal communication and listening abilities; identify client needs and resolve problems situations.
- ‣ Successfully train, develop, and motivate staff.
- ‣ Extremely organized; coordinate multiple/complex projects simultaneously.

Professional
Experience

Branch Manager   1993–1995
XYZ Company, Inc., Appleton, Wisconsin
- ‣ Managed all aspects of temporary employment service branch office.
- ‣ Responsible for hiring, training, and motivating employees.
- ‣ Created highly successful marketing vehicles; designed and produced surveys, print advertisements, and monthly newsletter.

Accomplishments:
- ‣ Effectively maintained and increased company production and profits in a highly competitive market.
- ‣ Designed and implemented company-wide management supervisory TQM, Quality Circle, and self–managed team concept programs that improved moral and productivity.

Assistant Store Manager   1991–1993
Department Stores Unlimited, Appleton, Wisconsin
- ‣ Responsible for staffing and scheduling 65 sales/support associates.
- ‣ Handled performance appraisal process including administration of wage/merit program; conducted disciplinary and performance meetings.
- ‣ Liaison between management and associates.
- ‣ Performed manager's duties for six months while position was open.

Accomplishments:
- ‣ Recipient of numerous "Outstanding Service" awards; "Employee of the Month" once every year.
- ‣ Served on a company–wide quality control task group, and customer service department analysis and reorganization task group.
- ‣ Advanced from Sales Associate to Assistant Store Manager.

178

Combination. *Kathy Keshemberg, Appleton, Wisconsin*

A well-planned resume showing consistency in the Professional Experience section.
The Profile sets the tone for the resume, telling of the individual's best characteristics.

Sally Stevenson

Professional Experience *(continued)*	**Director of Sales** Institutional Foods, Inc., Oshkosh, Wisconsin	1988–1991

▸ Trained and assisted new sales representatives in prospecting, making presentations, handling objectives, and proper closing techniques.
▸ Facilitated staff planning meetings, promoting goal achievement.
▸ Maintained profitability within product lines.

Accomplishments:

▸ Complete responsibility for development of new division; justification and maintenance of department budget.
▸ Created and implemented a division-wide succession planning program that improved overall organizational efficiency by 15%.

Account Executive   1984–1988
Central Foods, Inc., Appleton, Wisconsin

▸ Responsible for sales calls on new and existing accounts in the hospital and nursing home industry.
▸ Penetrated accounts by increasing product lines and promoting new products as well as value–added services and equipment lease programs.

Accomplishments:

▸ Responsible for territory start–up and management, reversal of non–performing territories, and competitive market analysis.
▸ Successfully persuaded the State of Wisconsin Procurement Office to consider a "Prime Vendor Agreement" versus "Bidding" system for a two-year test, resulting in better cost containment and time management, and reduced storage costs.

Education

Cardinal Stritch College—Milwaukee, Wisconsin
Currently working towards Bachelor of Science–Business Administration
Associate of Arts Degree, 1994

References

Available upon request

Accomplishments are presented at the same location in each position description in the Professional Experience section. This consistency makes it easier to look for information. Education—comparatively the least impressive section—is put near the end of the resume.

═══ ROBERT C. JACOB ═══

942 Sunset Circle
Hampton, Virginia 84217
(555) 555-0000

■ *Professional Objective*

Seeking a position as a safety professional where I can utilize my education and safety experience, and benefit my employer through quality service and dedication.

■ *Summary of Qualifications*

Eight years experience in the safety professional field
Extensive experience working with new O.S.H.A. ergonomic standards
Experience in developing and implementing safety educational programs
Proven results in reducing losses through risk management and accident prevention
Continuous quality improvement and total quality management
Experience in interviewing, educating, and managing safety personnel
Outgoing, hardworking, and goal oriented – excellent attendance record

■ *Education*

Virginia State Technical College, Silvertown, Virginia (90-92)
Associates in Occupational Safety and Health Technology. GPA 3.8.

■ *Certifications*

O.S.H.A. Certified Construction Technician - 91. Certified Blood Borne Pathogen Instructor - 93.
FAA Fire Instructor - 93. Train the Trainer HAZ-MAT - 93. Certified HAZ-COM Instructor - 93.
Department of Transportation, Hazardous Waste Management *(cradle to grave)* - 93. Train the
Trainer Back Prevention Injury - 93.

■ *Professional Safety Work History*

Planned Health Care, Inc., Millington, Virginia   2/95 to Present
Corporate Risk Management Specialist
Responsible for company's loss prevention issues in the states of Virginia, Arkansas, and Kentucky.
Risk management duties include: writing and implementing safety programs and directives for 170
long-term care facilities (involving over 2,000 employees), handling liability claims and settlements,
and consulting with assistant vice-president of tri-state area regarding T.W.C.C., O.S.H.A., and
T.H.C.A. issues. Accomplishments: Reduced claims by 20% throughout by analyzing and revising
new and ongoing company policies. Involved extensively in research concerning losses and
accident prevention in long-term health care facilities.

179

Combination. *P. J. Margraf, New Braunfels, Texas*

By the time the reader has gotten to the Professional Safety Work History, this resume
has made a strong impression through the Summary of Qualifications and Certifications.

Resume Continued

═══ ROBERT C. JACOB ═══

Professional Safety Work History

<u>Ionet Group, Inc., Hampton, Virginia</u>   12/92 to 6/94
Safety Director
Responsible for implementing O.S.H.A. Standards for the airports fixed base operation. Safety director duties included: managing hazardous waste manifests, implementing and training blood borne pathogen's course, first response team, fire training for flight personnel and CPR. Additional duties included: holding regular safety meetings, developing safety contests, managing building and facility environment standards in conjunction with N.F.P.A., and State Fire Marshall's Office, and conducting job hazard analysis. <u>Accomplishments</u>: Completed numerous F.A.A. 1.5 m.m. accident free aircraft restoration projects.

<u>Brite Plastics, Millington, Virginia</u>   10/90 to 11/92
Internship
Implemented 12 new safety programs, consulted with management on workplace productivity in harmony with safety, and performed fire safety inspections.

<u>City of Millington, Virginia Municipal League, Millington, Virginia</u>   7/85 to 10/90
Facilities Maintenance Supervisor
Supervised day to day maintenance operations for 5000 acre city park, including managing and directing 35 personnel. Duties included: directing upkeep and safety improvements on out-door public facilities (public showers, plumbing systems, septic pools, and landscape), job safety analysis, investigating and analyzing accident sites, filing appropriate reports, and follow-up with agencies (TWC, state, and medical authorities). In addition, recommended safety improvements, budgeted manpower, and performed personnel administration. Personnel administration included: scheduling, hazard training, assigning daily work assignments, job coaching, annual personnel reviews, and overseeing daily work assignments. Reported to the City Manager.

■ Professional Organizations

National Fire Protection Administration
Recognized Fellow in American Society of Safety Engineers
American Society Safety Engineers *(former secretary)*, Hampton Chapter
Virginia Chapter, A.S.S.E.
Virginia Health Care Association
National Safety Council

■ Community Activities

Canton Lake Forest Civic Club
Canton Lake Forest Property Owners Association

References Available Upon Request

Each position description reinforces the initial strong impression. The same is true for the Professional Organizations section. Throughout, this resume builds a strong case for the person. Boldfacing highlights job positions; underlining helps the reader see achievements.

CORRINE ANNA SMITH
1500 Main Street
Chatman, Massachusetts
(508) 236-0097

PROFILE:	Professional and articulate manager with seven years experience as a trainer and developer of sales personnel. Outstanding presentation, organizational and leadership qualifications. Consistently successful in the recruitment, training and motivation of sales associates to meet and exceed company goals and objectives.

PROFESSIONAL EXPERIENCE:

TRAINING STORE MANAGER   1992 - Present
Westport Ltd./Westport Woman, Dress Barn Inc., Hyannis, MA
Chosen by regional manager and vice president to train and develop store managers, assistant store managers and district managers, while managing a staff of eight sales associates and troubleshooting for area stores. Responsible for full P&L, recruitment and development, visual merchandising, and new business development.
- Consistently maintained 0% management employee turnover.
- Increased sales 11% over fiscal plan.
- Named #1 store of 765 store chain for sales contest.
- Conducted four grand store openings of different volume levels.
- Completed District Management training program. Currently considered for Area Manager position.

TRAINING STORE MANAGER   1987 - 1992
The Image, Inc., Chatham, MA
Managed four stores of successively increasing volume over a four year period. Appointed district trainer of new management personnel; held regional training seminar for new IBM/POS register system. Maintained $2 million store - highest volume store in region.
- Successfully turned around non-performing store within one year through rigorous recruitment and training efforts and innovative outreach programs. Implemented inventory control procedure lowering shrinkage from 11% to 1.2%.
- Orchestrated the grand opening of six stores.
- Awarded Clothestime Champion twice (1990 + 1992) - first time ever achieved in company's history.
- Perfect Store Presentation Award 1991.
- Completed District Management program.

EDUCATION:

Massachusetts Bay Community College
Boston, Massachusetts
Currently completing Associate's Degree program

PROFESSIONAL TRAINING AND DEVELOPMENT:

Extensive Management Training and Development workshops and seminars at the The Image Inc. and Westport Ltd. Completed District Manager Development program at both companies.

180

Combination. *Cheryl Ann Harland, The Woodlands, Texas*

Good white space in this resume. It can be created by making the body of the resume as a one-row (extended downward), three-column table and then removing the vertical lines.

CHRISTINE JONES

974 North Stanley ▪ Coopersville, Illinois 60000
(555) 555-1234

OBJECTIVE

Client Services Supervisor ▪ Project Coordinator
Experienced manager with 10+ years experience in office management, staff supervision, and project coordination seeks related position in challenging environment. Strong managerial, supervisory, organizational, and customer service skills.

STRENGTHS

- Demonstrated success in planning and completing large, complex projects.
- Adjust well to change; work well under pressure of deadlines or seasonal rushes; quick learner.
- Hands-on manager and skilled supervisor; able to motivate staff for maximum productivity.
- PC knowledge and skills (WordPerfect, Paradox database system).

PROFESSIONAL EXPERIENCE

EASTERN ILLINOIS UNIVERSITY   1985-Present
Coopersville, Illinois

Assistant Manager / Bookstore Textbook Services (1994-Present)

- Supervised staff and operation of Textbook Services division of University Bookstore to distribute more than 48,000 rental textbooks to over 11,000 students per semester. Manage computerized inventory and tracking system of 2000 titles in 200,000 book inventory. Order and replace stock; manage sales and rentals of current and out-of-adoption books.

  - Streamlined entire book distribution and textbook adoption system to reduce warehousing and delays in purchasing.
  - Improved process for collecting student fees and delinquent bills.
  - Initiated and coordinated implementation of system to advertise hours and other information through residence hall cable TV.

Department Supervisor / Bookstore Textbook Services (1992-1994)

- Managed distribution system and setup for semester book rentals and sales. Supervised 8-30 student workers, ordered books, monitored collections, prepared invoices. Acted as department liaison between publishers, faculty, administration, and students.

  - Instrumental in implementing computerized recordkeeping and database system to manage textbook distribution and department records.

Clerk / Administrative Assistant (1985-1992)

- Managed customer service and administrative responsibilities at distribution counter. Tracked purchase orders, invoices, and credit memos.

CITY OF COOPERSVILLE   1981-1984
Coopersville, Illinois

Administrative Assistant

- Provided administrative and office support services for the City Clerk and administrators at City Hall.

EDUCATION

A.S. Business Education ▪ 1981
Greene County Community College, Ashton, Illinois

181

Combination. *Carla Culp Coury, Glen Carbon, Illinois*

A simple, thick, short line is all you need to make a name memorable in a resume. If the rest of the resume is superb (as this one is), the whole resume will be remembered.

ALLISON K. THOMAS
17 Old Carpenter Road • PO Box 72
Breckenridge, SO 99890   (555) 000-5555

PROFILE
- Excellent oral and written communication skills.
- Very organized – able to prioritize and accomplish multiple goals.
- Work well with diverse groups at all levels.
- Computer use: Lotus 1-2-3, Excel, Word, PowerPoint, Word Pro.
- Extremely loyal and dependable.

EXPERIENCE

Seven Worlds, Breckenridge, SO
Supervisor - Quality Control, 1997-Present.
- Coordinate work flow and prioritize tasks.
- Coordinate decisions concerning disposition of received goods with Corporate Office on a daily basis.
- Work with Production, Scheduling, Purchasing and Product Development Departments to ensure an on-time product.
- Maintain inventory and order supplies for QC Department.
- Handle personnel issues for department.
- Maintain department budget.
- Travel frequently to east coast vendor plants.

Supervisor - Receiving Department, 1995-1997.
OPTI Plan Coordinator, 1993-1995.
- Controlled contract and off-shore work flow and maintained production levels.
- Handled all related paper work.

Engineering/Material Utilization Clerk, 1989-1991.
- Performed time studies; calculated time sheets; tracked in-transit goods.

Production Control, 1986-1989.
Production Payroll Clerk / Materials Utilization Clerk, 1983-1986.
Assistant Floor Supervisor, 1981-1983.

Seven Tries Mills, Inc., Breckenridge, SO
Production Administrator, 1991-1993.
- Coordinated deliveries of raw material and finished goods.
- Issued and maintained production schedules and orders.
- Coordinated with Corporate Office to insure proper invoicing/payment.

Pier 1 Imports, Charleston / Breckenridge, SO
Store Manager, 1976-1980.
- Accountable for inventory, sales, customer relations and daily/weekly/monthly reports.

EDUCATION

Communicating with Diplomacy and Tact, American Management Association
Certified Instructor in Zenger Miller's "Working, The Training System."
Management in Today's Workplace, Seven Worlds, Inc.
Various textile courses, Tri County Technical College

Greenville Technical College, Greenville, SC
Business Management curriculum.

182

Combination. *Karen Swann, Clemson, South Carolina*

Notable in this resume is the stack of promotions received during work for the current employer.
Bold and italic highlighting helps to make the various positions stand out visually.

Jane T. Watkins
520 Bournemouth Road
Wilmington, North Carolina 28401
(910) 123-4567

SUMMARY OF QUALIFICATIONS

Excellent management and leadership skills. Able to develop and lead a team of employees who perform to the best of their ability with a very low turnover rate.

Enjoy working with the public and do so successfully. Interact successfully with people from a variety of backgrounds. Strong problem resolution skills.

Experienced in handling all financial matters for a small business including accounts receivable and payable, sales tax and withholding filing and deposits, preparing payroll, managing a budget, and making daily deposits.

Learn new information and tasks quickly and easily.

EXPERIENCE

Sunspot Tanning, Wilmington, NC
Owner and Manager   September 1992 - Present
Manager   June 1992 - September 1992
Achievements:
• Successfully turned around a store that was losing money and unable to cover expenses.
• After less than three years, annual revenue has increased more than 300%.
• Remodeled, expanded and added additional product lines to the business.
Responsibilities:
• Select all advertising and marketing activities. Monitored effectiveness of each source of advertising, and used this information when organizing future campaigns.
• Train all new employees in proper sales techniques and customer service procedures.
• Successful in building a team of employees that has very little turnover.
• Total financial responsibility for the store. Prepare all financial documents, sales tax reports, withholding reports, and make all related deposits and payments.
• Handled all accounts payable and receivable.

Smithson Family, Wilmington, NC
Nanny   1991 - 1992

EDUCATION

Cape Fear Community College, Wilmington, NC
Associate of Science Degree in Business Administration   May 1995

REFERENCES

Provided upon request

183

Combination. *Sandy Adcox Saburn, Wilmington, North Carolina*

A resume that highlights an individual's skills so that she does not remain in retail management. Success in her own business motivated her to complete her degree.

GREG LARSON
5690 Harrison Drive ◆ Knowlton, Illinois 60146
(800) 555-1212

OBJECTIVE   ◆ ◆   Position in inventory or production control   ◆ ◆

PROFILE
- Over 10 years hands-on experience in production and inventory operations.
- Results-driven manager who leads by example. Foster team environment based on respect, fair play and good decision-making.
- Strong analytical skills. Talent for seeing the big picture in problem identification and resolution.
- Detail-oriented, accurate and well organized in project management; able to get the job done.
- C.P.I.M. certification to be completed in 1995.

EXPERIENCE

VACUMASTER ◆ Stanton, Illinois   1990 — Present
Production Manager   (1992 — present)
Supervise production staff in manufacture of vacuum sewage systems to aviation OEM standards. Schedule production, request materials, determine assembly floor procedures and follow OSHA regulations.
- Improved department's morale and overall efficiency by resolving internal conflicts. Evaluated staff placement and made reassignments based on individual traits and skills.
- Greatly improved scheduling, attaining high percentage on-time delivery within industry; only 4% of missed deadlines due to production process.
- Reduced production time of standard unit by 30% (23 to 16 hours) through accurate planning of shop labor.

Inventory Administrator   (1990 — 1992)
- Set up "spare and repair" stock room (independent of production inventory) that allowed more accurate tracking and planning. Identified consumable parts and set minimums. Devised stock numbering modification to differentiate repair and production inventory.
- Managed rotable pool of $2 million inventory with 10-day repair turnaround.
- Directed all aspects of major on-site retrofit program. Coordinated labor force and hardware allocations, including assembly, shipping, scheduling, travel and expense reports.

NELSON UNIFORM ◆ Stanton, Illinois   1988 — 1990
Route Supervisor
Supervised delivery/service operations in tri-state region.
- Determined routes and staffing schedules for six drivers covering 30 routes.
- Conducted sales presentations and negotiated contracts within very competitive market.
- Resolved customer problems and routing emergencies on a daily basis.

CUTTER TOOL COMPANY ◆ Stanton, Illinois   1980 — 1988
Inventory Control/Inside Sales   (1986 — 1988)
- Reduced inventory level by over $1 million through lot size adjustment. Increased inventory turnover from less than once annually to over three turns/year.
- Maintained 92% on-time shipments.
- Generated $1.4 million in sales (average product value of $40) in southeastern U.S. territory.
- Helped implement department's use of monthly sales goals and designated territories.

184

Combination. *Robin Folsom, location unknown*

The Profile, in which the resume first "sells" the reader on the worth of the applicant, has the most bulleted points. For more appeal, the Profile has also more line spacing.

GREG LARSON - 2

CUTTER TOOL COMPANY (cont'd)

Production Control (1983 — 1986)
- Scheduled all manufacturing projects to meet delivery deadlines.
- Identified and corrected operational problems undermining productivity. Standardized floor procedures and established accountability at each step in production process.
- Evaluated outside vendors (bids, facilities, product quality) and coordinated scheduling with work in process.

Machine Operator (1981 — 1983)
Operated O.D. and surface grinders, single and multi-spindle drills, mills and lathes.

Shipping & Receiving (1980 — 1981)

EDUCATION

BARTON BUSINESS COLLEGE ◆ Astor, Illinois   1985
Associate of Applied Science
  Major: Accounting/Business Management

Numerous management seminars through AMA

AFFILIATION

Member, American Production and Inventory Control Society

References Available Upon Request

The position descriptions uniformly have three or four points for each major description. The impression one gets is that each position was an important one because of the person. Bold facing helps the job positions and the degree stand out.

THOMAS A. O'CONNELL
555 Pennsylvania Avenue • Wilmington, New York • 55555
(555) • 555-5555

CAREER OBJECTIVE
A **warehouse position in the distribution industry**, where my
experience and skills will be utilized.

QUALIFICATIONS SUMMARY
- 20 years diversified experience in the wholesale/retail distribution industry.
- Completely versatile in the contractor/retail environment; able to perform any task.
- High energy, self-starter who takes great pride in work.
- Strong interpersonal skills; diplomatic and effective with customer relations.

RELEVANT EXPERIENCE
Rutherford Building Supply, Shelton, NY - 9/95 - xxxx
<u>OPERATIONS MANAGER</u>
Total warehouse operations management responsibility for a leader in wholesale building materials.
- Act as lead person, on and off the dock, to ensure timely and efficient operation of facility.
- Oversee all aspects of receiving, as well as outgoing deliveries, and scheduling of runs.
- Involved in preparing for yearly inventories, cycle counting and daily stock adjustments.
- Set goals and priorities with other team members.
- Ensure safe delivery/protection of company assets, including inventory, fleet, machinery, and personnel.
- Provide next day delivery to broad base of customers, increasing levels of service and resultant sales.

Woodland Lumber, Lakeville, NY - 5/84 - 9/95
<u>OPERATIONS MANAGER</u> - 10/93 - 9/95
Total yard and in-store responsibilities for this leader in the lumber/building supplies business.
- Supervised and delegated work to the Distribution Manager, Dispatcher, and B-Shift Supervisor; oversaw the on-the-job performance of up to 25 employees.
- Responsible for scheduling, internal memos, store relays, retail sales including kitchen department.
- Entrusted with keys for the yard and store as well as the safe combination; opened and closed store on a day to day basis; ran inventories, and conducted safety meetings.

<u>YARD FOREMAN</u> - Monroe, NY - 10/85 - 10/93
Ensured the smooth operation of all aspects of yard operations.
- Responsible for the distribution of goods to 8 store locations
- Oversaw the dispatching of a fleet of 9 vehicles and 6 lifts; all receiving functions; breakdown of pools for shipping including the operation of 2 flatbeds and 2 box trailers.
- Scheduled all personnel for 2 overlapping shifts; conducted monthly yard and safety meetings.

<u>YARD FOREMAN</u> - Middleton, NY - 5/84 - 10/85
Effectively handled the shipping/receiving operations for this high-volume outlet.
- Directed the work force; scheduled employees.
- Responsible for yard layout and resets; running inventory in yard on a semi-annual basis.

EDUCATION/PROFESSIONAL TRAINING
A.A.S. - Electrical Construction & Maintenance - Comstock Community College, Winston, NY
      Cum Laude   President's List
Graduated - Lewiston H.S., Schenectady, NY - College Prep & 2 Year Certificate - Electrical (BOCES)
Completed union (residential 2 year course) as required by local electrical union
Seminar - Role and Importance of the Yard Foreman - Woodbury Lumber - 2 days
Completed Team Odyssey (3 1-week seminars) - provided by Personnel Decisions International
Dupont Seminar - Managing Safety Techniques that Work for Line Supervisors

185

Combination. *Barbara M. Beaulieu, Scotia, New York*

The chronological sections of this resume support the individual's steady work history, duties,
and accomplishments in each position, and his steady progression of responsibility.

Chris Venture

OOO Dogwood Lane, Apartment 9 ◇ Castlewin, IN 00000
(000) 000-0000

OBJECTIVE
A professional Funeral Director career position with an established funeral home where I can utilize my clinical experience and interpersonal relationship/listening skills to benefit your clients.

PERSONAL PROFILE
◇ Accomplished people-oriented team player who is committed to creating a caring, open, and trustful environment to achieve the best possible results for clients.
◇ Personable, out-going, calm, and compassionate; administer excellent personalized care during the grieving period immediately following the death of a loved one.
◇ Demonstrate dedication to provide outstanding clinical results, as well as meeting client's interpersonal needs on a highly compassionate basis.
◇ Motivated by personal sense of achievement by going the extra mile to achieve peace of mind for clients.
◇ Display enthusiasm and willingness to develop continually evolving skills to maximum efficiency.

SKILL SUMMARY
◇ Skilled in embalming procedures and techniques including restorative art techniques.
◇ Adept at representing employer during visitations; first call removals from institutions and private homes; funerals and funeral processions; and post-funeral programs.
◇ Responsible for cleanliness and maintenance of funeral home facilities.

EXPERIENCE
0000-present   **Funeral Director Intern**. *Castlewin Funeral Home*, Castlewin, Indiana

STUDENT EXPERIENCE
0000-0000   *Duesten Fredrick Funeral Home*. Castlewin, Indiana
0000-0000   *Kendall Funeral Home*. Prairieton, Indiana

EDUCATION
Castlewin University. Castlewin, Indiana- 0000 (GPA 3.0/4.0)
   Associate Degree of Science (Funeral Service Education)
   Successfully completed National Boards Examination and registered with the Indiana State License Boards, May 0000.

PROFESSIONAL SEMINARS
National Funeral Director's Convention, Chicago, Illinois- 0000
Zig Ziglar Corporation Seminar "*Achieving Peak Performance*", Indianapolis, Indiana- 0000

186

Combination. *Colleen S. Jaracz, Vincennes, Indiana*

A resume for a Funeral Director Intern seeking to become a Funeral Director. The Personal Profile is an important section because it is a place for the person to display people skills.

DONALD SUMMERS

815 S. Volusia Avenue
Orange City, Florida 32763
(904) 775-0916

PROFILE

Well-qualified Project Manager with over 23 years experience in directing and supervising commercial construction, expansion, and remodeling projects. Qualifications include:

- On-site Project Management
- Budgeting / Cost Controls
- New Construction Coordination
- Troubleshooting
- Crew Supervision
- Deadline Planning / Coordination
- Materials Management

- Subcontractor Supervision
- Blueprint Reading
- Furniture & Fixture Installation
- Building Code Adherence
- Corrective Action Strategies
- Floor Space Assessment
- Liaison

EXPERIENCE

ABC CORPORATION, Troy, Michigan • July 20, 1972 - Present

Project Coordinator – Store Planning Division of Florida

- Direct and supervise all phases of new store construction, expansion, and remodeling for ABC's variety outlet stores throughout Florida with projects ranging up to $2 million.
- Supervise quality control and adherence to specifications set forth by corporate draftsmen and engineers.
- Analyze and assess blueprints and provide recommendations for resolution of any discrepancies.
- Coordinate and supervise multiple layout teams of 7-25 workers.
- Communicate and work directly with local building officials during expansion and remodeling projects to bring buildings up to current construction codes specific to each store's location.
- Consistently run all jobs on time and under budget.
- Supervise and coordinate furniture and fixture installation and setup including all phases of merchandising.
- Advise and report to corporate on project's progress or problems.
- Supervise sub contractors hired for new construction.
- Compile list of unfinished details and follow up on subsequent completion.

EDUCATION

A. S. Degree – Business Administration
St. Petersburg Junior College, St. Petersburg, FL

187

Combination. *Beverly Harvey, Pierson, Florida*

This individual had worked for the same company all his life. Then he was "let go" because of downsizing. This resume helped him get an excellent position at a construction company.

Thomas McGrath

545 Whitney Street ◆ Park Ridge, NJ 55555

Home: (000) 000-0000

Building Supply Yard Manager

Beeper: (000) 000-0000

— SUMMARY OF EXPERTISE —

Building Materials:
- Knowledge of all manufacturers' lines of interior drywall materials and related hardware and supplies used in residential and commercial construction.
- Also familiar with framing lumber, steel, insulation and various exterior systems.

Business Development/ Customer Service:
- Established profitable relationships with numerous contractors by soliciting their business during off-hours when they were most likely to be receptive to sales calls.
- Gained rapport of clients through an honest and personable approach, understanding of their needs, and 24-hour service availability.
- Assured that material deliveries arrived at construction sites on schedule and free of damage.
- Saved contractors' time by having delivered materials distributed properly at different locations of premises where received.

Purchasing:
- Obtained most favorable vendor pricing according to required quantities (by block, contract, commitment, or job).
- Negotiated best deals for high volume purchases.

Inventory Control:
- Bought materials in sufficient supply to cover anticipated sales without carrying excessive inventory.
- Scheduled timing of purchases for best cash flow advantage.
- Turned over stock an average of 2½ to 3 times a month.

Credit:
- Limited risk exposure by checking contractor references prior to business dealings, keeping credit lines on contractors, and requesting job assignments and/or joint checks for their purchases.
- Maintained a diversification of receivables which averted payment problems associated with having a small number of accounts owing large sums.
- Whenever necessary, exercised lien rights in time allocated by law to enable collection of money.

Staff Management:
- Hired and trained a loyal and hard working staff.
- Avoided potential liabilities by stressing to boom truck drivers the importance of precautionary measures in the operation of their vehicles.

— RELATED EXPERIENCE —

1984 - 1993

Owner/Manager of Apex Lumber & Drywall Supply Co. in Tappan, NJ, a building supply yard serving residential and commercial contractors. Generated average annual sales of $2.5 million prior to economic downturn.
- Applied experience obtained since high school to start this business "from scratch." Developed it into a profitable operation within its first year.
- Employed a staff of 10 consisting of boom truck drivers, helpers and a secretary. Equipment included 5 boom trucks.
- Had complete P&L responsibility in addition to purchasing ($150,000 line of credit), invoicing, accounts receivable, and training/supervision of yard workers.

— OTHER EMPLOYMENT —

1993 - Present

Managing family-owned store, Bag-o-Bagels in Cliffside, NJ. Soon to be sold due to father's declining health.

— EDUCATION —

1984

A.A.S. Business Management — Tunxis Community College, Storrs, CT

188

Combination. *Melanie A. Noonan, West Paterson, New Jersey*

Categories in the left column sort out the information in the Summary. Readers not interested in a topic can easily jump to another. Headings are enclosed within dashes.

FRANCES O. POSHMEYER

(555) 123-3456 – Home   *32841 Stablelview Road*
(555) 987-7654 – Work   *Daviston, South Dakota 98765*

SUMMARY OF QUALIFICATIONS AND HIGHLIGHTS
- Consistently meet or exceed performance objectives and goals
- Team player with cooperative, participatory and supportive attitude
- Able to recognize and rectify problems and administer decisions
- Initiated project that eliminated cash loses due to operational dysfunctions
- Effective communicator with customers, clients, vendors and colleagues
- Awarded for outstanding service in support of merger in 1993

EMPLOYMENT
THIRD COUNTY BANK   Daviston, South Dakota
Consulting Analyst   1991 to Present
- Actively participate in special projects; vital part of ATM installation team
- Created training manual and accompanying video for branch ATM training
- Develop, present, document and monitor corporate ATM training
- Provide quality service to internal customers, trainees and co-workers

Customer Information Manager   1987 to 1991
- Recruited, developed, trained and supervised a highly qualified staff (over 60)
- Developed and monitored performance standards for employees within department
- Key member of team which developed and implemented a 24-hour customer information system
- Provided timely and accurate communications to NC branch and interstate personnel
- Continually exceed response goal of 95%

Network Operations Manager   1985 to 1987
- Ensured that Quality Customer Service is a job accountability for all employees
- Prepared departmental budget and monitored expenditures
- Managed communication with branch staff and vendors to ensure timely service of ATMs
- Monitored branch terminals

Teller Supervisor   1983 to 1985
- Delegated responsibilities; recognize weaknesses and implement remedies
- On Task Force which developed a career program for tellers within the bank
- Handled customer issues effectively and efficiently
- Reduced cash loss by improving and monitoring operational functions
- Prepared departmental budget and monitored expenditures

Teller   1975 to 1985
- Maintained a positive, professional manner while instituting service to customers
- Consistently met or exceeded branch sales goals

EDUCATION
EVANS BUSINESS COLLEGE   Wheaton, North Dakota
Associate Degree in Business Administration

CONTINUING EDUCATION
- Manager as Developer
- Principles of Banking
- AT&T Knowledge & Data Communications

- Presentations Skills Workshop
- Management Skills I and II

189

Combination. *Lorie Lebert, Novi, Michigan*

The Employment section displays work for one employer since 1975 and record of growth and promotions. The Summary section tells why the individual has been successful.

Anthony R. Hoya

2418 Fenton Place • Dexter, Michigan 48555 • (734) 555-0933

HIGHLIGHTS OF QUALIFICATIONS

❏ Twenty-plus years' longevity with company in positions of increasing scope and responsibility.
❏ Comprehensive hands-on experience in manufacturing environment including management/supervision, production, employee training and motivation, and issues relating to efficiency and safety.
❏ Proven analytical ability to identify, investigate, assess and solve problems relating to production and performance.
❏ Independent thinker; can be counted on to initiate tasks and follow through to completion with no supervision.
❏ Strong leadership qualities: experienced in motivating employees and leading-by-example.
❏ Polished written and verbal communication skills; able to assess audience and adapt delivery style.
❏ Strive for continual self-improvement: willing to embrace new ideas and methods by building on existing knowledge base to expand personal and professional horizons. Not content to maintain status quo.
❏ Areas of expertise: metal stamping and fabrication.
❏ Fluent in Spanish—speaking, reading and writing.

SUMMARY OF EXPERIENCE

• Conducted investigations to determine causes for decreased production, determined solutions and prepared recommendations for plant management.
• Managed 5 supervisors, 120 production workers and related support personnel; assured consistency of purpose across shifts as well as with other business units.
• Implemented plan developed under PICOS project to reduce manpower and production floor space previously designated to low-demand part production, allowing room for new product development.
• Acted as liaison between production workers, union, plant management and corporation administration.
• Implemented Synchronous Strategies in line with department business plans.
• Ensured safe working environment and compliance with appropriate standards and safety codes.
• Interfaced with union representatives regarding grievances, adherence to agreements, and during other sensitive negotiations.
• Conducted workshops and trained production workers in PICOS theory and implementation; adapted concepts to relate to everyday work place practices and procedures.

EMPLOYMENT HISTORY

GENERAL MOTORS CORPORATION • Ypsilanti, MI   1979-Present
Selectively placed in the following positions to accrue valuable, broad-based experience:

Senior Methods Analyst	**Labor Relations Representative**
PICOS Workshop Facilitator	**Senior Clerk**
General Supervisor - Production	**Supervisor - Mail Handling**
Supervisor - Production	**Personnel Clerk**

EDUCATION

Extensive continuing education through General Motors-sponsored courses,   Ongoing
    GMI Engineering & Management Institute [now Kettering University], and
    Washtenaw Community College (complete list available on request)

Washtenaw Community College • Ypsilanti, MI   1984
Associate Degree in Applied Science - Industrial Supervision & Management

References available on request.

190

Combination. *Janet L. Beckstrom, Flint, Michigan*

The hollow check boxes as bullets offer the reader another way to deal with information in a long section. The reader can check each box to mark progress in reading the section.

RONALD GOLFPRO

5555 North 55th Avenue, #5555
Anyplace, USA 55555
(555) 555-5555

SUMMARY: Experienced Golf Professional offering over 20 years of experience in the golf industry. Highly developed skills in instruction, both individual, groups and clinics....dynamic and harmonic custom club-fitting, club building and repair....golf shop merchandising, inventory and sales....locker and bag storage rooms....and overall operations, both public and private.

HIGHLIGHTS OF QUALIFICATIONS

Teaching
- Possess extensive teaching ability to individuals or groups.
- Explain and demonstrate use of apparatus, equipment, principles, techniques, and methods of regulating movement of body, hands, and feet to achieve proficiency.
- Observe students to detect and correct mistakes; explain and enforce safety rules and regulations.

Management
- Responsible for day-to-day operations of golf course and golf shop.

Club Fitting/Club Repair
- Have worked fitting clubs to customer base.
- Ability to regrip, re-epoxy, reshaft, and rewrap; make lie & loft adjustments; made sets of clubs.

Marketing/Merchandising
- Proven record of success in generating new business for course and pro shop through effective marketing techniques, innovative ideas, promotions and referrals.
- Responsible for a $100,000 inventory; in charge of purchasing, trading, organizing and keeping shop attractive & clean, pricing, and special sales.

SELECTED ACHIEVEMENTS

- Supervised a $60,000 capital improvement to the Glen Lakes Course facility in 1994.
- Annually involved with the National "Hook-A-Kid on Golf Program"; at Glen Lakes, 1991 to Present.
- Designed layout of a 9-hole facility for Good Samaritan Village Retirement Center of Hastings, NB, 1988.
- Designed a 9-hole addition for Southern Hills Country Club of Hastings, Nebraska, which opened the Spring of 1990. A renovation design was also proposed for the original 9-holes, yet to be done.
- Tournament Director and Co-Anchor Narration of the 18th-Hole for the televised Coors 10/11 Midwest Golf Classic.
- Coordinator for such tournaments as the: Nebraska State Cup Matches, State Ladies Match-Play and Stroke-Play Championships, State and District High School Championships, and numerous large corporate tournament outings.
- Helped produce many top-ranking high school players in Nebraska and Arizona.
- Coordinated, directed and facilitated many tournaments, improved and headed marketing and promotions of events; ordering needed inventory and supplies; scoring and supervision of all support staff and personnel.

SYNOPSIS OF PERSONAL ATTRIBUTES

- Strong presentation and demonstration skills; able to make the customers golf experience more enjoyable.
- Manage paperwork efficiently and effectively; achieve maximum time effectiveness.
- Successful in translating, meeting and surpassing organizational objectives and goals.
- Hard working, loyal, dependable, and profit oriented; take pride in doing the best possible job.
- Sharp, innovative, creative, quick learner; proven ability to adapt quickly to new demands.
- Effective communication, and interpersonal skills; able to impart information in a manner easily understood.
- Ability to work effectively with people of diverse backgrounds.
- Work and leadership style that is vigorous, decisive, honest, and straightforward that promotes respect, and trust by the general public, superiors and peers.
- Confident, self-motivated, tenacious, goal oriented, well organized, and perform effectively under pressure.

191

Combination. *Bernard Stopfer, location unknown*

"If you were an employer, would you hire this person?" asked the writer, handing a client this resume with the names changed. "Sure," said the client. "Well, it's *your* resume!" said

RONALD GOLFPRO – Page Two

EMPLOYMENT HISTORY

American Golf Corporation - Glen Lakes Golf Course , Anyplace, USA   1988 to Present
Position: Director of Golf Instruction
- ADAMS "Air Assault" Golf Club Company Custom Club-Fitter.
- Directly involved with development of instructional programs.
- Custom club-fitting, building and repair.

Position: General Manager/Head Professional   1992 to 1995
- Directly involved with all facets of golf course management and operations, corporate policies and procedures, bookkeeping, auditing, budgeting, marketing, memorandums and human resources.

Position: Assistant Professional   1989 to 1992
**   Golf Shop Manager/Teaching Professional**
**   Merchandise Buyer**
- Involved in all facets of golf course management and operations.
- Sales (top salesman repeatedly)
- Buyer for a $100,000 inventory, bookkeeping, coordination of tournaments and special events.

Teaching Professional/Shop Assistant   1988 to 1989
- Counter sales clerk, starter, and teaching.

Villa de Paz Golf Course, Anyplace, USA   1988
Position: Teaching Professional
- Acted as a strictly Independent Instructor.

Southern Hills Country Club, Anyplace, USA   1980 to 1987
Position: General Manager/Head Golf Professional
- Managed and supervised all golf services and club functions.
- Administered and directed tournaments, special events, hired and trained support staff, sourced and selected vendors, coordinated ownership and management operation of golf shop, snackbar and lounge.
- Conducted golf instructions and player development, dynamic custom club-fitting/building and repair programs.
- Worked closely with superintendent, Board of Directors, and Men's and Ladies Golf Associations.

Henry Griffitts Precision Fit Golf Club Co., Anyplace, USA   1985 to 1986
Position: Master Professional Golf Club Fitter
- Lead golf club fitter and salesman for this large golf club distributor that winter in Sun City, Arizona at the Lakes West Golf Club.

Lochland Country Club, Anyplace, USA   1973 to 1979
Position: Head Golf Professional
- Participated in the overall operations of this large upscale country club
- Managed the operations of the golf shop, with it's member and client services as a priority.

EDUCATION

Associate of Arts Degree in Business Administration - Anyplace Community College
Emphasis on Management and Business Education

REFERENCES FURNISHED UPON REQUEST

the writer. The client, who had been down on himself, found the courage to send out this resume. In a short time he got a job as a golf pro. (A true story about Bernie, this client, and this resume.)

John R. Sharp

. . . is looking for trouble

555 Maple Avenue
Anywhere, NC 00000
704/254-7893

Problem-Solving Expertise

People-oriented, machine-friendly individual who is at his best with a problem in front of him seeks position of service. Can learn quickly and teach effectively. Logical; adaptable; team player. Dedicated--will do what is necessary to get the job done.

Capable

- Customer Relations
- Personnel Scheduling and Training
- Computer Training & Operation (software includes Lotus 1-2-3, WordPerfect, Internet)
- Inventory Control and Analysis
- Financial and Cost Control, Analysis, and Reporting (Invoicing, P&L, Expenses, etc.)
- Facility Maintenance

Educated

A.A., Computer Science/Business Administration, 1994
A-Z Technical College, Anywhere, NC

Coursework included Computer Maintenance and Repair, Business Management

Additional training: Customer Service Seminars, Computer Instruction Seminars

Experienced

ABC THEATERS, Anywhere, NC (1990-Present)
Assistant Manager of multi-location franchise serving up to 6,000 people per day. Daily responsibilities of customer service, inventory, bookkeeping, and personnel training and scheduling; also recruited at Computer Trainer for all regional facilities--sent to a variety of software training seminars in several states, then returned to train staff personnel.

Excellent References Available Upon Request

192

Combination. *Dayna Feist, Asheville, North Carolina*

An effective, original resume. The three staggered lines below the name are mirrored by the staggered headings below. The continuation ". . . is looking for trouble" is unique.

Military-to-Civilian Transition

Resumes at a Glance

RESUME NO.	LAST OR CURRENT OCCUPATION	GOAL	PAGE
193.	Field Representative	Not specified	299
194.	Electronics Technician (USAF)	Not specified	300
195.	Leading Chief Petty Officer (U.S. Navy)	Not specified	302
196.	Propulsion Maintenance Facility Manager (USAF)	Not specified	303
197.	Auto Body Painter	Manager of painting operations for auto body shop	304
198.	Machinery Technician (U.S. Coast Guard)	Position in law enforcement	305
199.	Statehouse Reporter/City Editor	Not specified	306
200.	Assistant Clinical Division Officer (U.S. Navy)	Not specified	308

Jeffrey J. Catanya

One Park Place, #10 ■ Chicago, Illinois 60000
(555) 555-8800

SUMMARY	Seven years experience in computer/electronic systems support, data communications, and electro-mechanical devices. Background and specialized training in hardware/software installation and troubleshooting. Demonstrated record of success in positions of responsibility, including supervisory experience.
STRENGTHS	■ Frequently recognized for outstanding performance and attentiveness to detail. ■ Able to pinpoint problems and initiate creative solutions. ■ Quick and eager learner; able to master new systems and equipment in timely manner. ■ Strong leadership, communication, and negotiating skills.

PROFESSIONAL EXPERIENCE

Field Representative 1993 - Present
FORD MEDIA SERVICES, Conway, Wisconsin

Contact and service 100+ households annually in Chicago area for national media research firm. Supervise installation and maintenance of computer monitoring systems. Program hardware, software; install upgrades. Verify recording accuracy of data; perform on-call inspection and troubleshooting of computer and electronic equipment.

Maintenance Scheduler / Supply Technician 1990 - 1993
U.S. AIR FORCE

Scheduled maintenance for powered and non-powered ground equipment for aircraft fleet. Negotiated contracts, challenged overpricing, and secured all parts, equipment, and personnel for operations and maintenance. Utilized computerized database system, PC hardware/software, and CD ROM technology.

Aerospace Ground Equipment Mechanic 1988 - 1990
U.S. AIR FORCE

Member of team charged with operation and repair of 600 pieces of power-generating equipment to support airlift squad. Inspected, performed diagnostics, and repaired mechanical and hydraulic support equipment. Analyzed and repaired electronic circuitry, small engines, and control devices. Used and maintained various electronic tools and testing equipment.

EDUCATION

Associate of Electronics Technology 1992
CLOVER PARK TECHNICAL COLLEGE, Tacoma, WA

Associate of Applied Science 1992
COMMUNITY COLLEGE OF THE AIR FORCE

Aerospace Ground Equipment Mechanic School 1988
U.S. AIR FORCE

HONORS & AWARDS

Air Force Good Conduct Medal
Airman of the Month (May 1990)
Outstanding Unit Citation (1990)

193

Combination. *Carla Culp Coury, Glen Carbon, Illinois*

For a transfer from military to civilian life, "military" information needed to be softened. The decorative font for the name offers some relief from the lines and squares of the resume.

John J. Jameson

0000 N. West Avenue
Anywhere, USA
(000) 000-0000

Experience Summary

EXPERIENCED ELECTRONICS TECHNICIAN -- Ten-year career in the overhaul, repair, modification, calibration, certification, and quality control of advanced test measurement and diagnostic equipment traceable to the National Bureau of Standards. Advanced skills in the areas of:

- Voltage
- Current
- Power Impedance

- Frequency
- Microwave
- Temperature

- Physical
- Dimensional
- Radiac Measurements

Professional Experience

Advanced through increasingly responsible technical, quality assurance, and supervisory roles during tenure with the United States Air Force. Assignments included: 5/84-7/96

■ **Precision Measurement Equipment Laboratory Supervisor** (4/93-7/96)

Supervised, trained, and monitored production of 23 technicians in a Precision Measurement Equipment Laboratory (PMEL). Repaired, troubleshot, aligned, modified, overhauled, calibrated, and certified complex test, measurement, and diagnostic equipment supporting an inventory of over 3,500 items.

- Selected from 1,100 peers as President's Circle award winner for excellence in the maintenance technician specialist category.

- Maintained 100% pass rate on quality verification inspections; produced over 40 quality items per month; led team effort in reducing items in maintenance by 30%.

- Drew plans on off-duty time and implemented reconfiguration of laboratory to maximize accessibility and increase man-hour productivity.

- Volunteered weekend time to assist civilian expert in repair of aircraft stabilizer malfunction; taught an alternate troubleshooting method that quickly identified the problem.

- Commended by Radiation Safety Officer for Radiation Safety Program ... evaluator's comments included "best seen to date."

■ **Precision Measurement Equipment Laboratory Technician / Supervisor** (4/90-3/93)

Performed calibration, maintenance, repair, and circuit analysis of test, measurement, and diagnostic equipment (counters, generators, TACAN and IFF test sets, oscilloscopes). Used diagrams, schematics, and drawings to trace and determine malfunctions. Researched technical information to ensure repair compliance and to requisition parts. Performed duties as Quality Assurance Inspector.

- Calibrated and/or repaired over 25 items monthly; maintained a flawless quality assurance record which contributed to a perfect calibration audit and placement on the prestigious Aerospace Guidance and Metrology Center's Honor Roll.

- Selected for team which developed guidelines for and evaluated laboratory's new quality assurance program.

- Established and conducted a weekly training class on transistor theory that significantly improved the troubleshooting skills of other laboratory technicians.

- Selected as first military representative to attend American Science and Engineering, Inc.'s Micro-Dose X-Ray Inspection System Training; quickly repaired a critical micro-dose x-ray inspection system.

- Total Quality Management inputs contributed to a 60% decrease in laboratory's average backlog.

- Saved $3,500 in contract maintenance costs through repair of complex spectrum analyzer.

194

Combination. *Susan Britton Whitcomb, Fresno, California*

Arranging skill areas in three columns is yet another way to help a reader grasp information in a resume section, such as here in the Experience Summary. Square bullets before the side

PROFESSIONAL EXPERIENCE (cont.)

■ **Quality Assurance Evaluator** (6/88-3/90)

Assured quality, reliability, and serviceability of all test, measurement, and diagnostic equipment for a variety of systems. Utilized a multi-level continuous flow sampling system coupled with 100% outgoing inspection to ensure equipment condition. Evaluated technician, trainer, and supervisory proficiency. Evaluated and validated proposed technical data changes. Maintained an inventory of 200+ line items.

▸ Devised a method to keep laboratory's 1295 Attenuation Measurement standard fully operational while internal assemblies were awaiting parts.

▸ Provided quality verification with minimal turnaround time on systems which provided intelligence products viewed daily by National Command Authorities.

■ **Test Measurement and Diagnostic Equipment Specialist** (7/86-6/88)

Used advanced principles of metrology and calibration in frequency generation and microwave areas of laboratory.

▸ Contributed to reduction in backlog time from 5 to 2.5 days.

▸ Quickly learned intricacies of new Transportable Field Calibration Unit; cut two weeks from a 12-week temporary duty, saving the operation thousands of dollars.

▸ Promoted through prior positions as Precision Measurement Equipment Specialist (7/85-7/86) and Precision Measurement Apprentice (5/84-7/85).

TECHNICAL TRAINING

Electronics Major, Community College of the Air Force, 63 units
Micro-Dose X-Ray Inspection System (AS&E 101 Series), 1993
Honor Graduate -- Microwave Measurement & Calibration, 1993
Navigational Aids and IFF Diagnostics, 1992
Radiac Instrument Repair and Calibration, 1991
Advanced Electronic Diagnostics, 1989

LEADERSHIP TRAINING

Total Quality Management, 1993
Training the Trainer, 1992
NCO Leadership School, 1991
Trainer/Supervisor Skills, 1990

AWARDS

Master Technician Award, European Air Force Command, for sustained exceptional performance
Master Technician Award, Strategic Air Command, for sustained exceptional performance
Certification of Recognition, **Sustained Quality Production**, PMEL Quality Verification System
Journeyman Technician Award, Certificate of Recognition
Air Force Achievement Medal for Outstanding Achievement (10/91-9/92)
Air Force Achievement Medal for Meritorious Service (11/86-7/88)
Air Force Commendation Medal for Meritorious Service (8/91-8/93)
Air Force Commendation Medal for Meritorious Service (8/88-8/91)

■ ■ ■

subheadings and the underlining of these subheadings help tie together the two pages. Similarly, small caps link visually the individual's name in the contact information and the section headings. Awards at the end of the resume make the ending strong.

Charles G. Hamilton

5236 Big Road
Charles, VA 65313
(504) 555-9146

Qualifications Summary

❑ Ten years middle management experience in operating and maintaining electronic systems
❑ Prioritized, scheduled, and directed the activities of up to 23 team members
❑ Budgeting experience and cost control accountability for five work centers
❑ Saved $50,000 quarterly through proper identification of repairable versus replaceable items
❑ Strong verbal communication skills and a reputation as an extremely productive team leader
❑ Hands-on background in circuit board troubleshooting, component-level PC maintenance, and digital computer repair, including a full range of computer peripherals
❑ Extensive training in electronic systems, microwave technology, radio communications, power supplies, and computer operations
❑ Testing equipment knowledge includes voltmeters, oscilloscopes, and signal generators

Project Management Philosophy

❑ The supervisor is not above the team, he or she is a member of the team, working alongside technicians as a coach, ensuring deadlines are met and problems are anticipated and avoided. Open, two-way communication is a key factor in success. All team members should share in both accountability for failure and commendation for success.

United States Navy Experience – 1976 to 1995

❑ **Leading Chief Petty Officer** - USS Moosbrugger - 1992 to 1995
  » Coordinated operations and maintenance for five major weapon and radar systems
  » Managed team of 19 technicians, prioritizing, scheduling, and directing daily activities
❑ **Training Officer** - Naval Reserve Center, Charles, VA - 1989 to 1992
  » Allocated funding, scheduled training, and oversaw arrangements for 500 reserves
  » Responsible for initiating military orders and maintaining up-to-date training records
❑ **Leading petty Officer** - USS Spruance - 1985 to 1989
  » Coordinated operations and maintenance for five major weapon and radar systems
  » Managed team of 23 and served as liaison for the division to the department head
❑ **Shift Supervisor** - Naval Air Station, Oceana, Virginia - 1978 to 1984
  Fleet Aviation Specialized Organizational Training Group - Atlantic Fleet
  » Involved with total construction, maintenance, and operation of state-of-the-art flight simulators, including the installation of electronics, hydraulics, pneumatics, and all mechanical systems
❑ **Aviation Structural Mechanic** - Naval Air Station, Oceana, Virginia - 1976-1978
  » Maintained liquid oxygen, air conditioning, and ejection systems for F4 fighter aircraft

Education & Training

❑ Associate of Arts Degree in Accounting, St. Leo's College, St. Leo, Florida, 1981
❑ Successfully completed over 100 advanced military training courses, including

» Generators & Motors	» FORTRAN & Computing Overview
» Radio Principles	» Modulation Principles
» Transmission Lines and Antennas	» Micro Electronics
» Circuit Protection, Control, & Measurement	» Digital Computer Technology

195

Combination. *Barbie Dallmann, Charleston, West Virginia*

An inviting resume because of the extra large initial, the use of a font to approximate the type style of the initial, the hollow bullets (shadow check boxes), and the chevrons.

ANTHONY W. KRAFT
111 S. Pinella
Emmitt, Arkansas 00000
(000) 000-0000

SUMMARY
Nineteen years of steadily progressive assignments in the U.S. Air Force, including over 12 years of successful supervisory experience. Most recently supervised a staff of 62, with consistently high quality control results and measurable reductions in production costs. Trained in OSHA and EPA regulation compliance, Total Quality Management and quality control.

PROFESSIONAL EXPERIENCE -- United States Air Force (Honorably discharged March, 1994)
Propulsion Maintenance Facility Manager, Gary, Indiana   1988-1994
- Supervised 62 personnel providing aircraft engine production for seven customers worldwide.
- Implemented cost control measures, reducing production costs to 24% less than closest competitor.
- Introduced Total Quality Management program, producing first year results of a 5% reduction in engine maintenance flowtime and a 75% reduction in customer complaints.
- Led facility to a 96.1% annual quality control rating, exceeding the command standard by 16%.

Special Supervisory Assignment, Osaka Air Force Base, Osaka, Japan   1987-1988
- Selected to manage the operation of the base Aircraft Test Facility and Engine Maintenance Shop.

Maintenance Standardization and Evaluation Technician, Trane, New York   1984-1987
- Member of a team charged with evaluating the quality of maintenance work performed by assigned Air Force maintenance units worldwide.
- Directly observed each unit's maintenance procedures, inspected and followed-up on work performed, and tested the accuracy of internal quality assurance checks.
- Monitored and enforced compliance with all applicable OSHA and EPA regulations.
- Prepared technical reports for the ultimate use of the Headquarters' Director of Aircraft Maintenance.

Shift Supervisor, Morlon Air Force Base, Wyoming   1980-1984
- Supervised a staff of 40 comprising the first maintenance unit to receive an outstanding rating by the maintenance standardization and evaluation team.

Mechanic, promoted to Supervisor, Barnsworth Air Force Base, Nebraska   1974-1980
- Promoted to Supervisory Position within just 3 1/2 years.

EDUCATION
State College, Gary, Indiana
Completed over 70 hours of courses toward a B.A. in Elementary Education, 1992-1994.

U.S. Air Force Middle Managers School, Gopher Air Force Base, Alaska
Nine-week intensive training in personnel management, team building, and basic TQM, 1993.
Preceded by Basic (4 weeks) and Intermediate (6 weeks) Managers School.

Community College of the Air Force, Marks, Texas
Associates of Applied Science Degree in Aircraft Powerplant Technology, 1986.

ADDITIONAL LEADERSHIP ACTIVITIES
Co-Founder and Treasurer (3 years), Air Force Unit's Social Organization
- Oversaw set-up, budgeting, record-keeping, and fund-raising of approximately 85 person association.

196

Combination. *Laura C. Karlak, Bartlesville, Oklahoma*

The challenge for the writer was translating military experience into civilian business language. The readability of this resume shows that the writer was successful.

SAM D. FINCH

□ □ □ □ □ □ □ □ □ □

27-A Burton Road
Raleigh, NC 55555

(000) 000-0000

Objective: To manage painting operations for an auto body shop needing to increase efficiency and profitability in this area without jeopardizing quality.

Strengths & Skills:

- □ Extensive knowledge of urethane paint systems, including computerized mixing to produce customized colors.
- □ Expertise in precise color matching and blending in exact quantities needed to avoid waste.
- □ Good working knowledge of all modern techniques and equipment including downdraft spray booths, filters, lights, and oil or gas fired burners.
- □ Able to establish beneficial relationships with jobbers and regional suppliers of Sikkens, Spies-Hecker, Glasurit, DuPont and PPG paint lines to support shops' needs quickly and efficiently.
- □ Perform all painting operations neatly and in strict compliance with all safety and environmental standards.
- □ Self-motivated and productive in a heavy volume environment.
- □ Passed all drug testing and bonding requirements.

Related Experience:

1994 - Present **Auto Body Painter** — Triangle Buick & Mazda, Clayton, NC (Body shop sales of $1 million in 1994)
- □ Work alone at night on a commission basis, producing an average of 100-140 paint/labor billable hours a week.
- □ Entrusted with full responsibility for physical building security at end of shift.

1992 - 1994 **Auto Body Painting Subcontractor** (self-employed)
- □ Classic Auto Restoration, Cary, NC
- □ George's Auto Body, Durham, NC
- □ Wilson Collision Works, Raleigh, NC

1989 - 1990 **Auto Body Painter** — Square Deal Toyota, Roxbury, NJ

1986 - 1989 **Auto Body Painter** advancing to **Lead Painter** — Olafsen Auto Restoration, Dover, NJ

Other Employment:

1991 **Over-the-Road Truck Driver** (self-employed)

1986 **Administrative Assistant** — Commercial Mortgage Co., Pequannock, NJ

Military Experience:

1986 - 1990 **United Stated Navy** — Active duty at San Diego Naval Amphibious Base, Coronado, CA
- □ STG "A" Service School — Received training in surface sonar (submarine tracking), explosive ordnance disposal and marine mammal systems.
- □ Assigned to hazardous material control unit with responsibility for the proper storage of caustic and corrosive materials and coordination of Material Safety Data Sheets (MSDS).

Education:

1994 PPG Paint School — Refinish Training Course

1985 - 1986 County College of Morris, Randolph, NJ — Math and business courses.

1984 Morris County Vo-Tech, Adult Night School — Auto Body Repair course with on-the-job training at Olafsen Auto Restoration.

Additional Credentials:

- □ ASE Certified — Recertified in 1994.
- □ Class "A" Commercial Driver's License with hazardous materials endorsement.

197

Combination. *Melanie A. Noonan, West Paterson, New Jersey*

Another superb resume by this writer whose printer enables her to lower the point size of her type without a sacrifice of clarity. The selling occurs in the Strengths & Skills section.

Michael Arrowsmith
25 Harpers Lane
Governors Island, NY 11111
(212) 555-5555

PROFILE   Extremely disciplined professional offering a strong practical and educational foundation in law enforcement. Proven decision-making skills in what are often high-pressure and volatile situations. Recognized for dedication to service, maintaining wellness, and working effectively within team framework. Enthusiastic and motivated; adapt quickly to new tasks and environments.

ACCOMPLISHMENTS

◆ Received ***Commandant's Letter of Commendation*** for discovering 2498 kilos of cocaine (with a street value of $50 million) on the motor vessel *Gladiador*, during drug patrols in the Bahamas. Participated in over forty boardings capturing two wanted felons in addition to seizure of drugs and weapons.

◆ Participated in the interception of a Korean/Honduran vessel transporting 300 illegal Chinese immigrants. Provided security on the vessel for six days, maintaining crowd control, patrolling, rationing food, and confiscating weapons.

◆ As part of *"Operation Able Manner"* in Haiti, boarded small and large vessels in search of refugees who were then transported to Guantanamo Bay, Cuba or returned to Port-A-Prince, Haiti. Searched refugees for drugs, weapons, needles and other contraband.

◆ Training as a Machinery Technician facilitated ability to perform successfully as a Boarding Engineer, resulting in the above accomplishments.

◆ ***Certified Expert*** in 9mm handguns, M16 rifles and riot shotguns. Also proficient in the use of retractable batons.

◆ *President* of the Orleans County Sheriff's Department *"Explorers Post"*, 1989.

HISTORY   **United States Coast Guard** (Rank E4)   **11/91 - Present**
Machinery Technician, 3rd Class (3/94-Present)
Fireman (11/91-3/94)
★ Received several ***Citations and Awards***

Acme Manufacturing, Medina, NY   **9/90 - 11/91**
Shipping & Receiving

Darien Lake, Darien, NY   **Summers '90 & '91**
Security Officer

EDUCATION   **United States Coast Guard**
Trained at U.S. Customs and the Maritime Law Enforcement School: *Open Hand Combat; Search & Seizure; Self-Defense; Narcotics Identification; Drug Interdiction; Migrant Interception; Report Writing; Weaponry; and Boat Safety.*

Niagara County Community College
Criminal Justice, Fall 1989

SKILLS   ◆ PC literate; E-Mail; spreadsheets; document designer

198

Combination. *Judith Friedler, New York, New York*

The prominent area of this resume is Accomplishments with its eye-catching diamond bullets. What matters most is that the accomplishments are fascinating to read!

Collin Kasler

1 North Lancaster
Athens, Ohio 45701
(614) 592-3993

Consistently achieves superior results. He has my trust in all public relations matters.
Outstanding writer. Our best and brightest. The number one journalist in the fleet.
Understands the fine art of public relations. Knows public relations opportunities
and takes maximum advantage of every occasion to cast the Navy in a positive light.

— A.B. Military, Commander, USS Kory Kasler

PROFILE

Very successful military career and educational background in public relations and journalism; extensive knowledge of all areas of these fields. Extremely conscientious individual; possess initiative and ability to complete the most difficult assignments successfully. Seeking a position in public relations or as a reporter/editor which will utilize this background and extensive experience.

COMPETENCIES

- Comprehensive background in dealing with media from small newspapers to well-known magazines to internationally-recognized network news programs
- Extensive public relations and media liaison experience throughout naval career
- Proven leadership, planning, organizational, management and motivational skills
- Ability to work well with all levels of personnel from entry-level to senior management
- Extensive foreign travel and liaison with foreign news correspondents
- On-scene coordinator for various video documentary production crews
- Experience with Ampex ACE-25 and Sony BMV-3000 video editing and production equipment
- Extensive experience with WordPerfect, Microsoft Word, Aldus Pagemaker, Quark-X-Press, Internet and Aldus Photoshop
- Outstanding broadcast operations specialist, writer, editor and photographer
- Trustworthy; received Top Secret military clearance
- Consistently assigned to tasks normally performed by officers including instruction of naval officers

EDUCATION & TRAINING

OHIO UNIVERSITY, E.W. Scripps School of Journalism, Athens, Ohio
Candidate for Bachelor of Science in Journalism, June 1996

Additional Training
Editorial Experts, Washington, DC, 1995
- Training in various writing and editing techniques

TQL (Total Quality Leadership) Instructor Course, US Navy, Athens, OH, 1993
- Training in teaching TQL skills

Drug & Alcohol Program, US Navy, Athens, OH, 1993
- Training in drug abuse detection, treatment and counseling of substance abusers

Career Counselor, US Navy, Athens, OH, 1993
- Training focused on retention and providing information on opportunities within the Navy

MILITARY

UNITED STATES NAVY, Honorable Discharge, 1987-1994
Enlisted in 1987 and received rapid promotions to Leading Petty Officer

199

Combination. *Melissa L. Kasler, Athens, Ohio*

The opening testimonial, enclosed within lines and center-justified, not only captures the reader's attention but also sells the reader on the applicant before any part of the rest of

Collin Kasler   **Page 2**

RELATED EXPERIENCE

Statehouse Reporter/City Editor   1/95-present
THE PAPER, Ohio University's student-run newspaper, Athens, Ohio
- Handled all news coverage at the Ohio Statehouse for two quarters; promoted to Nelsonville City Editor for 1995-96 school year
- Developed, hired, trained and supervised four staff writers covering Hocking College and Nelsonville city government
- Responsible for copy, photos and layout of Nelsonville city's new dedicated edition of The Post

Information Specialist/Writer   3/95-present
OHIO UNIVERSITY NEWS SERVICES & PERIODICALS, Athens, Ohio
- Gather information and write feature articles for various public relations publications
- Author grant and public announcement articles for news releases and house publications
- Gaining valuable insight into various aspects of public relations in the civilian arena

Assistant Editor/Photojournalist/Leading Petty Officer/
Assistant Duty Officer at CHINFO in the Pentagon   5/94-12/94
US NAVY — MILITARY MAGAZINE, Washington, DC
- Oversaw aa staff of five photojournalists and two civilian graphic artists in the production of a monthly 48-page, 4-color magazine distributed to DOD personnel worldwide
- Responsible for story and photo selection and editing, travel requirements, layout and design and assuring print quality of magazine
- Answered media queries of national military affairs correspondents covering the Pentagon

Public Affairs Officer/ Leading Petty Officer/Editor   2/93-4/94
USS RHODES PUBLIC AFFAIRS OFFICE, Athens, OH
Third in command on 3,500 man aircraft carrier as an enlisted man
- Supervised Public Affairs Office and its programs aboard USS Rhodes
- Acted as primary media liaison for commanding officer of the 4,000 man ship
- Oversaw $14 million renovation of public affairs areas including closed circuit TV system
- Instructed 200 officers in TQL (Total Quality Leadership) as an enlisted man
- Editor of ship's weekly newspaper and monthly magazine distributed to crew and families

Public Affairs Officer   11/90-1/93
USS KORY KASLER, Athens, OH
- Solely responsible for all publicity for the Navy's largest procurement program into the 21st century—a $50 billion shipbuilding program; hand-picked for this extremely demanding position by the Pentagon over 400 competing Navy journalist
- Purpose of publicity efforts was to convince Congress, the Pentagon and citizens of the United States on the need for spending tax money on this program; efforts were very successful as 47 of these ships are scheduled to be built

Journalist/Public Affairs Assistant   6/87-11/90
US NAVAL BASE, Shade, OH
- Served as direct special assistant for public affairs to the commanding officer, a one-star admiral; also wrote speeches for this admiral
- Acted as media liaison during activation of reservists for Gulf War
- Voluntarily assisted civilian personnel in set-up and operation of a TV studio—served as cameraman, video editor and anchorman for daily newscasts covering DOD and Navy news
- Worked as writer, photographer and editor of a monthly magazine for 6,000 naval reservists

MILITARY HONORS & AWARDS
- 1993 Navy Chief of Information Merit Award for editorial excellence
- 1993 Ohio Governor's Award for Volunteering Excellence & 1993 JC Penney Golden Rule Award for coordinating Conflict Manager's Program in Athens, OH, while stationed aboard USS Kasler
- 1991 Sailor of the Year while assigned to Naval Base, Shade, OH
- Numerous campaign badges and military decorations for meritorious achievement

the resume is read. After the testimonial the hiring question is no longer whether but when. Any lingering doubt is erased by the Profile and the Competencies section. Note in the rest of the resume the use of boldfacing, uppercase letters, and italic to support the testimonial.

FRED CASAS

165 E. HOBART CIRCLE
MESA, ARIZONA 87220

602-646-2464

PROFESSIONAL PROFILE	Combines University Degree and extensive additional training with more than 20 years hands-on experience in positions of critical responsibility demanding a high level of proficiency in the following:

Direct Patient Care	**Medical Terminology**
TQM	**Medical Administration**
Physical Therapy	**Hospital Procedures**
Physician Liaison	**ICD-9 Coding**
Patient Education	**Patient Relations**

- Adept at a variety of medical procedures including, but not limited to: **casting; blood draws, nutritional/wellness counseling, front and back office, record keeping, mental health evaluation, exercise/ Orthopedic therapy, Acute/Trauma care.**
- Bilingual: **English** and **Spanish**.
- Computer literate: **Windows, Lotus 1-2-3, WordPerfect, Harvard Graphics.**

EXPERIENCE 1976 - xxxx	*United States Navy* Honorable Discharge

United States Navy Outstanding performance in a variety of medical positions and assignments resulted in advancement and numerous commendations/awards. Highlights below:

ASSISTANT CLINICAL DIVISION OFFICER
Previously served as *Medical Department Representative, Senior Enlisted Advisor* and other *Medical Administration* positions.

- Background encompasses a broad range of medical procedures and administrative functions including assistance with minor surgeries, direct patient care, physical therapy, counseling, patient education and more. Entrusted with diagnosis and treatment.

- Supervised up to 16 medical personnel and health care providers; implemented treatment plans; patient care prioritization; clinical administration.

- Recipient of *Achievement Award* for hospital screening program involving training of medical personnel in diagnostic and procedural techniques.

- Selected as Instructor for the first EMT-Defibrillator training course.

- Decreased patient waiting time and increased physician productivity by initiating highly successful appointment system.

- As *Medical Department Representative* was the sole provider of direct medical care and treatment to 130 personnel. Additionally, served as *Radiation Health Officer* providing training in Haz-Mat procedures, safety and environmental issues

- In the capacity of *Senior Enlisted Advisor* coordinated medical department activities and performed duties of *Medical Supply* and *Medical Administration* personnel. As sole medical provider, utilized broad-based pharmaceutical knowledge to dispense approximately 500 prescriptions, with use counseling, a day.

EDUCATION	*University of Southern Arizona Extension* **AS Degree**	San Diego, California
Additional Training	Medical Technician School (52 Weeks); Medical Service & Hospital Courses	
PERSONAL	References and supplemental information available upon request.	

200

Combination. *Brooke Andrews, Chandler, Arizona*

Twenty-four years of military experience needed translating into "Civilian-ese." That was true especially in the Experience section. The result is successful, aided by small bullets.

Sales and Marketing

Resumes at a Glance

RESUME NO.	LAST OR CURRENT OCCUPATION	GOAL	PAGE
201.	Sales Associate	Position in business administration	311
202.	Auto Part Sales Manager	Not specified	312
203.	Sales Associate	Not specified	313
204.	Sales Representative	Not specified	314
205.	Service Coordinator	Dental Sales Representative	316
206.	Account Representative	Sales/Marketing representative in music industry	317
207.	Senior Collector	Sales position	318
208.	Independent Beauty Consultant	Sales position	320
209.	Position in advertising sales/collections	Position in advertising or marketing	321
210.	Account Executive	Not specified	322
211.	Production Supervisor	Position in marketing services or marketing communications	323
212.	Quality Assurance Specialist	Position in sales and customer service	324
213.	Sales Counselor	Position in sales/marketing	326
214.	Professional Sales Representative	Not specified	327
215.	Director of Sales	Not specified	328
216.	Director of Sales	Not specified	329
217.	IMG Marketing Specialist	Position in software sales	330
218.	Manager of Business Operations	Position in sales/management	332
219.	Manager	Sales-management position	333
220.	Consultant/Owner	Not specified	334
221.	Sales Manager	Not specified	335
222.	Vice President of a communications and systems company	Not specified	336

RESUME NO.	LAST OR CURRENT OCCUPATION	GOAL	PAGE
223.	Consultant	Not specified	338
224.	General Insurance Agent	Not specified	340
225.	Implementation Manager	Position in senior sales/ sales management	342

Robin B. Bentley

0000 North West
Anywhere, USA
(000) 000-0000

◆ Emphasis: Business Administration ◆

Education

A.S. -- Business Institute of America, Anywhere, USA (6/95)
Major: Business Administration

Related Experiences, Strengths

Business Coursework

- Representative coursework included the following disciplines: Sales, Marketing, Business Organization, Economic Analysis, Credit & Finance, Multi-Cultural Labor Relations, and Appraisal.
- Gained thorough knowledge of business management theory in hypothetical and actual business environments, working independently and in team settings.
- Selected by a Professor as Teacher's Aide for two semesters.

Employment Experiences

- Experienced Sales Associate in retail environments; sales skills include asking open-ended questions, analyzing clients' needs, presenting product features and benefits, and closing techniques.
- Worked as Tour Guide in Yellowstone and Big Bend National Park; entrusted with care and safety of 20-30 guests on week-long pack trips in rugged back country.
- Served as Assistant for public relations firm; assisted with various facets of a stop smoking campaign.

Accomplishment, Awards

- Completed **Outward Bound** Program in Alaska; learned wildlife survival, rock climbing, and team building.
- Awards: Coaches Award in Soccer; finalist in Rotary International Student Speaker Contest.
- Language: Three years high school Spanish.

Employment Summary

Financed approximately 75% of education through part-time and seasonal employment:

Sales Associate -- The Sports Store, Anywhere, USA	9/94-Present
Tour Guide -- Yellowstone National Park	Summers 1992-1993
Sales Associate/Stocker -- The Retailers, Anywhere, USA	Christmas 1984-1991
Public Relations Assistant -- McCann Ericson, Anywhere, USA	9/92-12/93

Activities, Interests

College Activities: Sigma Delta Gamma (business management fraternity), Alpha Delta Zeta (community service fraternity).
High School Activities: Varsity Soccer, Varsity Volleyball, Forensics
Interests: Outdoor Activities, Fishing, Horses, Golf

◆ ◆ ◆

201

Combination. *Susan Britton Whitcomb, Fresno, California*

The writer chose not to use a chronological format because the individual's positions were not specifically related to the job goal. The format of the Strengths section is impressive.

Mr. X
11 William Rd
Kingsland, Georgia 55500
(900) 555-5555

Education

Altaha Technical Institute, Jessup Georgia
Presently taking a course in Air Conditioning and Repair (Home & Commercial)

Military Schools

Propulsion and Engineering Plant   Diesel Mechanic I
Fairbanks Morse Diesel Engines   Basic Fire Firefighting
General Motors Diesel Technician   Material Maintenance Manager
Leadership Management Training   Diesel Mechanic II
Level 1 Sub-Safe Manager   Submarine Equipment Repair

Correspondence Courses

Basic Hardtools   Engineering Administration
Standard First Aid Training   Shipboard Accident Prevention
Fluid Power   Blueprint Reading and Sketching

WORK EXPERIENCE

Autozone, Brunswick, Georgia, January 1994 - Present:

Auto Part Sales Manager - One of four store managers; managed 5 to 6 employees; duties consist of computer operations; customer service; scheduling employees; handling customer complaints; maintaining appearance of the store; in charge of opening /closing paperwork and procedures for the store; give recommendations to store manager for employee review.

EMPLOYMENT HIGHLIGHTS

28 years of submarine service with the United States Navy. Retired as a Master Chief Machinist Mate (E-9).

Machinist Mate - Identified deficiencies of equipment and machinery, prepared directives and instructions for attaining organization objectives, established and implemented a program for interviewing, evaluating and assigning personnel to assure maximum utilization, trained and supervised personnel, organized schedules training programs; administered a long-range maintenance program.

Auxiliary Equipment Technician - Operated and performed preventive maintenance on high pressure air compressors, hydraulic systems, hydrogen burners, high pressure air systems; performed preventive, corrective and overhaul maintenance on refrigeration plants, carbon dioxide scrubbers, and miscellaneous pumps.

Engineman - inspected, repaired, tested and maintained auxiliary boilers; determined diesel engine malfunction and corrective action; supervised a damage control party; repaired engineroom and auxiliary equipment, refrigeration and air conditioning equipment.

Division Officer and Instructor - assigned in the Human Resource Management Training Division which provides leadership and management training and overseas Duty Support Coordinator Training; implemented the Navy's Petty Officer Indoctrination course.

REFERENCES AVAILABLE UPON REQUEST

202

Combination. *Rose Montgomery, Charlotte, North Carolina*

The educational sections are put first, but they are toned down by keeping the size of the side headings small. The horizontal lines help to separate the sections visually.

Sara Vilempa

37891 Windwood • Farmington Hills, Michigan 48335 • 248.555.6474

EDUCATION

LOYOLA UNIVERSITY CHICAGO   Chicago, Illinois
Associate of Science Degree – Biology

TRITON COMMUNITY COLLEGE   River Grove, Illinois
Major: 2-Year Pre-Health Professional Studies

Major Courses:

Biology I & II w/Lab	Chemistry I & II w/Lab	Physics I & II w/Lab
Anatomy w/Lab	Ecology w/Lab	Histology w/Lab
Organic Chemistry	Philosophy	Ethics
Genetics	Economics	Calculus

RESEARCH EXPERIENCE

Lab Assistant at **Loyola University Chicago**
    Worked with *Dr. Jones* (Anatomy and Physiology Professor)
        Responsibilities included: making solutions, sterilization of laboratory
        instruments, setting up for laboratory classes
Lab Assistant at **Community Labs in Dearborn, Michigan**
    Worked with *Dr. Paul Singh*
        Responsibilities included: typing lab reports, making throat and urine cultures,
        testing blood samples

WORK EXPERIENCE

SEARS, ROEBUCK & COMPANY (xxxx)   Novi, Michigan
CARSONS PIERRE SCOTT (xxxx)   North Riverside, Illinois
    Sales Associate
        Provided service to customers and interacted positively with co-workers and
        managers and maintained high company standards.

LOYOLA UNIVERSITY MEDICAL CENTER   Maywood, Illinois
    Clerk   xxxx
        Entered data of patients health insurance, called patients and verified
        information, filing and typing.

LOYOLA UNIVERSITY CHICAGO   Chicago, Illinois
    Telemarketing
        Contacted Alumni in fundraising efforts.

VOLUNTEER EXPERIENCE

Cambodian Association – Tutored Cambodian children who did not understand English
Loyola University – Soup Kitchen Program
Chicago House – AIDS awareness program speaker at inner-city schools

AFFILIATIONS

Member of *Preprofessional Society*   Member of *Amnesty International*

OF SPECIAL NOTE

Fluent in *Hindi*

203

Combination. *Lorie Lebert, Novi, Michigan*

The unusual table of Major Courses is striking because of the shading of alternate cells. The
three categories of experience—research, work, and volunteer—provide a useful scheme.

WILLIAM B. CHASE

(555) 555-5555

555 S. Peters Avenue
Orange City, Florida 55555

PROFILE

Top-performing sales professional with persuasive presentation, negotiation, and sales closing skills. Consistently successful in increasing revenues and capturing key accounts.

EXPERIENCE

ABC TECHNOLOGIES, INC., Orange City, FL   7/93 to Present
Sales Representative
- Promote sales throughout the state of Florida for the 4th largest private pay phone company in the U.S., providing high-tech internal systems to over 9,000 phones.
- As the result of extensive telecommunications background, was selected to present weekly training classes to sales representatives, incorporating both sales techniques and technical product knowledge.
- Began with company as a Service Technician and was promoted to Sales Representative within six months.

Achievements
- "#1 Salesman of the Quarter," out of 30 sales representatives throughout the U.S., for the past two quarters.
- Landed two major accounts with multimillion dollar corporate oil companies.

CABLE VISION INDUSTRIES, DeLand, FL   8/94 to 2/95
Sales Representative
- Sold cable television services to residences throughout Central Florida through cold calling and referrals on weekends and evenings.

Achievements
- Received several bonuses based on volume of sales produced.
- Ranked #1 sales representative out of 10.

BIZ TEL COMMUNICATIONS, Orlando, FL   1/93 to 6/93
Sales Representative
- Sold long distance telephone communication services for the 3rd largest business long distance carrier in the U.S.

Achievements
- #2 Salesman in Central Florida for 2 consecutive months.
- Won expense-paid vacation based on sales volume produced.

COMMUNICATION CENTRAL, INC., Rosewell, GA   9/91 to 3/93
Field Service Technician
- Served Protel and Elcotel pay phones throughout Central and South Florida.

Achievements
- Awarded "Employee of the Quarter" four times.
- Increased coin revenues by 80% and OSP carrier service by 68%, elevating area to #2 profit center in the country.

204

Combination. *Beverly Harvey, Pierson, Florida*

Without the Profile, which refers to the individual's skills, the resume would be a
chronological resume. Indicating achievements for almost all of the positions is a strong

WILLIAM B. CHASE   2

NEWPORT HOSTPITAL, Newport, RI   9/82 to 11/86
Orthopedic Technician / EMT
- Provided emergency medical services throughout the entire hospital, primarily in the Emergency Room with direct involvement in patients' health care.
- Responsibilities included accountability for all orthopedic supplies including inventory control, as well as assembly and set-up of traction equipment for patients.

MILITARY
UNITED STATES ARMY   1986 to 1991
Tactical Satellite Digital Microwave Systems Operator & Repair
- Operated and repaired multichannel communications systems.
- Installed, operated, and maintained satellite and multiplexing equipment.
- Troubleshot and repaired communication security devices.
- Developed radio support system for specific satellites.

Achievements
- Two achievement medals for outstanding performance in the field.
- Commendation medal for performance above and beyond call of duty.
- Overseas ribbon for recognized achievements.

EDUCATION
COMMUNITY COLLEGE OF RHODE ISLAND, RI
A. S. DEGREE – BUSINESS – 1982

feature of this two-page resume. The Achievements subheading becomes something to look for with interest. A review of the individual's career path shows that his transition from a technical military career to civilian sales has been very successful without a four-year degree.

JENNIFER ANNE LUKINS

1234 5th Avenue ▫ Anytown, USA ▫ 555/555-5555

OBJECTIVE

Dental Sales Representative where skills in prospecting and closing and an expertise in dental office operation can establish key referral accounts, gain a competitive edge, and increase market share.

PROFILE

A highly energetic, motivated, and productive optimist with strong persuasive and negotiation abilities refined through 10 years of sales experience in the fitness and training industry. Exceptionally talented in customer development; able to establish rapport and trust with a diverse clientele. Extremely persistent. Work best under pressure in a fast-paced environment. Bottom line-oriented with proven record of exceeding standards and expectations.

EDUCATION

▫ Price College
  Currently pursuing Associate Degree–Business Administration for Transfer
  3.89 GPA

▫ Park West Technical College, 1992
  Completed 2,370-hour Dental Assistant Program, including 180 hours of OSHA/OISHA training.

EXPERIENCE

TOP-NOTCH HEALTH CLUB, Anytown   1986 to Present

Service Coordinator (1990 to Present)
Sales Representative (1990 to Present)
Personal Trainer (1986 to Present)
Pro Shop Sales (1986 to 1990)

▫ Maintain full university class schedule with a 3.89 GPA while working a 72-hour week.
▫ Train receptionists on contract content, program availability, and gross profit reports.
▫ Generate daily adjusted gross reports.
▫ Train personal trainers on equipment use, first workout techniques, nutritional methods.
▫ Teach up to 15 aerobic classes per week.
▫ Supervise up to 10 receptionists.
▫ Audit 320 contracts a week to insure win-win situations for company and clients.
▫ Handle customer complaints, resolving disputes ranging from equipment usage to contract problems.
▫ Rotate among 7 clubs assisting sales and personal training as needed.

GENERIC COMPANY, Anytown   1992 to 1995
Print Services Specialist

▫ Coordinated the sending and receiving of up to 30 international facsimile transmissions a day.
▫ Managed organization of CAD drawing distribution procedures:
  ▪ Received up to 30 CAD drawings a day
  ▪ Interpreted drawings to insure appropriate measurements.
  ▪ Input information into computer system for parts ordering.
  ▪ Converted data to microfiche, generated prints from microfiche, and distributed to appropriate departments and world headquarters in Geneva.

205

Combination. *Carole S. Barns, Woodinville, Washington*

This individual decided that she wanted to sell dental equipment. Her education is preparation for that goal. To see how she keeps busy, read her Experience section!

ART STORMAN JR.

120 N. Jefferson
Trenton, IL 62293
(618) 555-0330

OBJECTIVE

Sales/Marketing Representative in the music industry

HIGHLIGHTS OF QUALIFICATIONS

- Dynamic Sales Representative generating nearly $750,000 annually in sale of instruments, accessories and sound reinforcement equipment.
- Guitar training specialist and leading inside salesperson for Vester guitars.
- Expertise in technical and acoustic principles of musical equipment.
- In-depth knowledge of competitive and copy brands manufactured in U.S. and abroad.
- Interest in organizing promotional events or marketing products on a national level.

PROFESSIONAL EXPERIENCE

Account Representative   1992-Present
MIDCO International, Effingham, IL
- Manage 450 accounts in eight states, representing $1.3 million in annual sales (MN, WI, ND, IL, MO, IN, CA, NV).
- Ranked #1 Vester guitar salesman without benefit of national ad campaign.
- Rewrote product knowledge and sales training tests to include competitive brands and sales tactics.

Retail Sales Representative   1993-Present
Uncle Bob's Music, Belleville, IL
- Sell and service guitars, amps, bowed instruments, and accessories.

Account Executive   1991-1992
Beltone Hearing Aids, O'Fallon, IL
- Completed state audiometry/acoustics training certification.

Self-employed Musician   1986-1991
- Lead guitarist and singer for local bands.

EDUCATION/TRAINING

- **A.A. Degree, Marketing/Music**, Kaskaskia Community College, Centralia, IL
- Retail/Wholesale Sales, Winter NAMM Show, 1993
- Sales Training, Beltone, O'Fallon, IL

REFERENCES AVAILABLE UPON REQUEST

206

Combination. *John A. Suarez, location unknown*

This resume received strong praise for its powerful presentation of this person's skills. The music graphic is eye-catching—particularly to those who read music.

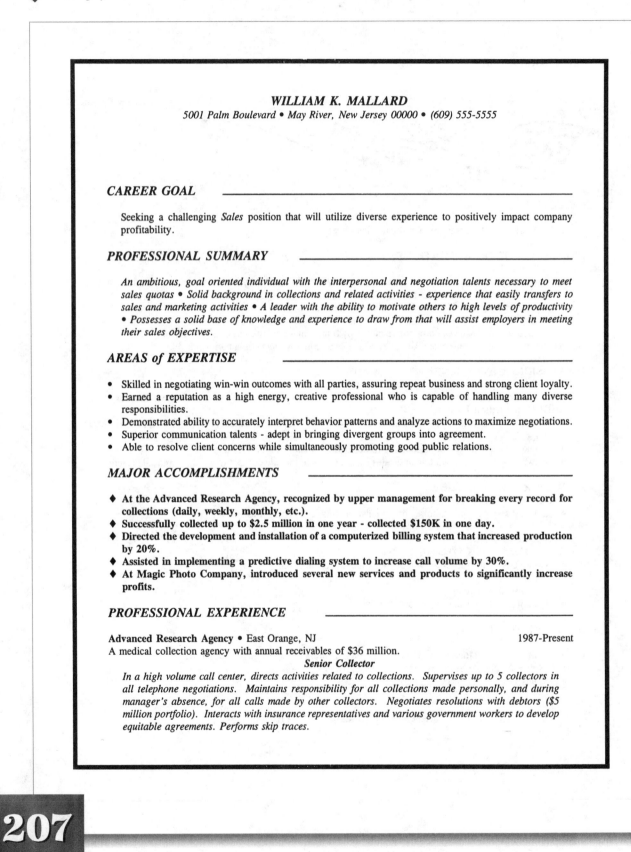

WILLIAM K. MALLARD
5001 Palm Boulevard • May River, New Jersey 00000 • (609) 555-5555

CAREER GOAL

Seeking a challenging *Sales* position that will utilize diverse experience to positively impact company profitability.

PROFESSIONAL SUMMARY

An ambitious, goal oriented individual with the interpersonal and negotiation talents necessary to meet sales quotas • Solid background in collections and related activities - experience that easily transfers to sales and marketing activities • A leader with the ability to motivate others to high levels of productivity • Possesses a solid base of knowledge and experience to draw from that will assist employers in meeting their sales objectives.

AREAS of EXPERTISE

- Skilled in negotiating win-win outcomes with all parties, assuring repeat business and strong client loyalty.
- Earned a reputation as a high energy, creative professional who is capable of handling many diverse responsibilities.
- Demonstrated ability to accurately interpret behavior patterns and analyze actions to maximize negotiations.
- Superior communication talents - adept in bringing divergent groups into agreement.
- Able to resolve client concerns while simultaneously promoting good public relations.

MAJOR ACCOMPLISHMENTS

- ♦ **At the Advanced Research Agency, recognized by upper management for breaking every record for collections (daily, weekly, monthly, etc.).**
- ♦ **Successfully collected up to $2.5 million in one year - collected $150K in one day.**
- ♦ **Directed the development and installation of a computerized billing system that increased production by 20%.**
- ♦ **Assisted in implementing a predictive dialing system to increase call volume by 30%.**
- ♦ **At Magic Photo Company, introduced several new services and products to significantly increase profits.**

PROFESSIONAL EXPERIENCE

Advanced Research Agency • East Orange, NJ   1987-Present
A medical collection agency with annual receivables of $36 million.
Senior Collector
In a high volume call center, directs activities related to collections. Supervises up to 5 collectors in all telephone negotiations. Maintains responsibility for all collections made personally, and during manager's absence, for all calls made by other collectors. Negotiates resolutions with debtors ($5 million portfolio). Interacts with insurance representatives and various government workers to develop equitable agreements. Performs skip traces.

207

Combination. *Alesia Benedict, Rochelle Park, New Jersey*

To appreciate the many features of this resume, notice its use of italic, horizontal lines, bullets, page borders, indentation, right-alignment (for the years), and boldfacing.

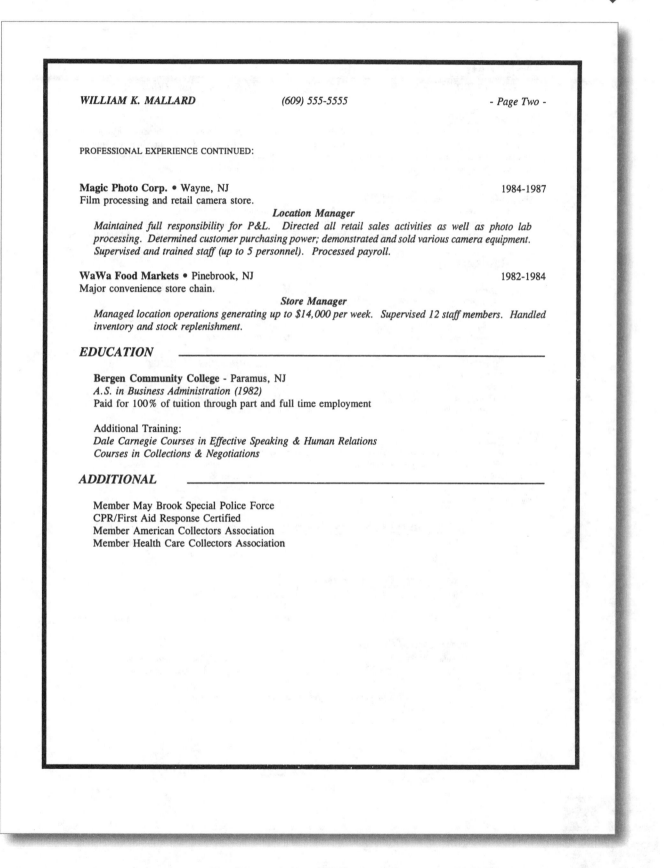

WILLIAM K. MALLARD   *(609) 555-5555*   *- Page Two -*

PROFESSIONAL EXPERIENCE CONTINUED:

Magic Photo Corp. • Wayne, NJ   1984-1987
Film processing and retail camera store.

Location Manager

Maintained full responsibility for P&L. Directed all retail sales activities as well as photo lab processing. Determined customer purchasing power; demonstrated and sold various camera equipment. Supervised and trained staff (up to 5 personnel). Processed payroll.

WaWa Food Markets • Pinebrook, NJ   1982-1984
Major convenience store chain.

Store Manager

Managed location operations generating up to $14,000 per week. Supervised 12 staff members. Handled inventory and stock replenishment.

EDUCATION _____

Bergen Community College - Paramus, NJ
A.S. in Business Administration (1982)
Paid for 100% of tuition through part and full time employment

Additional Training:
Dale Carnegie Courses in Effective Speaking & Human Relations
Courses in Collections & Negotiations

ADDITIONAL _____

Member May Brook Special Police Force
CPR/First Aid Response Certified
Member American Collectors Association
Member Health Care Collectors Association

Notice, too, how the positions are indicated in this resume: not near or just under the name of each firm but centered, in italic, and over the italic descriptions of duties and achievements. Education beyond a two-year degree is listed as additional training.

Deborah K. Bloomquist

9832 89t Avenue, P.O. Box 67, Hopkins, MI 57000, 555-000-2222

Summary Profile

Enthusiastic self-starter ready for a take-charge position requiring an individual who can make decisions, handle own responsibilities, and adapt to any job or situation. Offering over 18 years of extensive and diversified service within the community. Personal qualities include the ability to inspire organizational cooperation, recognize and resolve problems, and develop the means to achieve organizational goals on a prompt and efficient basis.

Highlights of Qualifications

- Extremely motivated and focused. Proven successful sales leader, trainer, and motivator.
- Enjoy heavy interaction with people. Performance-driven. Proven ability to adapt quickly to a challenge.
- Excellent speaking and communication skills. Experience in coordinating projects involving people and activities.

Skill Areas

Public Relations
- *Customer/client services*
- *Community involvement*
- *Volunteer experience*
- *special events promotion*

Health-Related Knowledge
- *Disease awareness*
- *Medical evaluation & response*
- *Staff assistance*
- *Patient awareness*

Sales
- *Customer needs analysis*
- *Sales presentations*
- *Overcoming objections*
- *Post-sale follow-up*

Organization and Planning
- *Program development*
- *Appointment/agenda setting*
- *Marketing and advertising*
- *Record keeping*

Career History

1990 - Pres.	Independent Beauty Consultant	Susan Shay Cosmetics, Hopkins, MI
1983 - 1993	Medical Receptionist/Ombudsman	Covert County Health Department, Covert, MI
1881 - 1983	Waitress	Marsha's Kitchen, South Haven, MI
1979 - 1981	Waitress	Coffee Pot Restaurant, Wayland, MI
1976 - 1994	Licensed Real Estate Agent	William Tobey, Fennville, MI

Community/Area Involvement

1995	Graduate: John Casablanca Modeling School
1986 - 1988	Township Clerk, Ross Township

Volunteer Experience

1994 - 1995	United Way, Ross Township
1994	Red Cross Blood Drive, Lee Township
1993 - 1994	Prevention of Child Abuse/Neglect (CAN), Allegan County

Education/Training

Graduate: 1994	Parkwood Business College, Grand Rapids, MI. 2 years.
1986	Certified Emergency Medical Technician

- *Excellent professional references available upon request.*

208

Combination. *Randy Clair, location unknown*

Double-underlining is a distinctive feature, calling attention to the individual's name and most headings and subheadings. The clustering of skill areas into four groups is another.

GUY GARRISON

EMPHASIS ■ INTERESTS

Advertising: Account Executive, Creative Support
Marketing: Business Development, Account Retention

EDUCATION

A.A., Journalism/Advertising -- The Advertising Institute   12/95
Minor in **Business Marketing**

ADVERTISING AWARD: Wrote major components and designed visuals for Advertising Plan that won 1st place in American Advertising Federation regional competition and 2nd place at nationals.

EXPERIENCE SUMMARY

Managed 2-3 part-time positions while carrying full courseload:

Advertising Sales / Collections   1/92-Present
The Collegian Newspaper
   Generated sales of advertising for college's weekly newspaper. Developed new business through cold calling, telemarketing, and networking. Designed ads and wrote copy. Cleaned up 100% of overdue accounts; diplomatically handled customer relations in anticipation of future sales.

Property Management   1992-1995
The Property Company and Property Managers, Inc.
   Performed property management and maintenance services for commercial investment properties and regional shopping center.

Telemarketer   1992-1993
The Best Real Estate Company
   Generated leads for top sales agent with area's most prestigious brokerage. Qualified prospective sellers and buyers.

Warehouse Supervisor   1991-1992
Solutions by Design
   Managed shipping and receiving functions for advertising firm.

COMPUTER SKILLS

Graphic Design • Newspaper Editing • Word Processing (WordPerfect)

ADDITIONAL DATA

Junior Olympic Team: Won Olympic Gold Medal as member of Junior
   Olympic Volleyball Team; competed in Japan.
Travel: Backpacked four months throughout Europe.

CONTACT

(000) 000-0000 • 0000 North West Avenue • Anywhere, USA

209

Combination. *Susan Britton Whitcomb, Fresno, California*

Although this type of format is seen from time to time, it is a nontraditional format and appropriate for this recent graduate who wanted to work in advertising or marketing.

BEVERLY A. ROBERTS, R.N.

(904) 775-0916 • 815 Volusia Ave. • Orange City, FL 32763

PROFILE: Career minded **Sales Professional** with strong background encompassing:

- Sales & Marketing
- Healthcare
- Networking
- Strategic Marketing Plans
- Market Penetration
- Revenue Growth Strategies

- Major Client Development
- Competitive Maneuvering
- Contract Negotiations
- New Product Development/Pricing
- In-Service Programs
- Strong Presentation Skills

SUMMARY OF QUALIFICATIONS:

- Developed major managed-care accounts including PCA Century Plan, Community Health Choice, Premier Accountable Health Plan, Hospice of Central Florida and Humana.
- Successfully utilized prior contacts to develop leads and referrals.
- Coordinated and presented in-service programs to major accounts
- Instituted plan utilizing research strategies to target and developed new accounts for start-up of women's health program.
- Successfully identified and developed client base and delivered effective sales presentations.
- Developed, marketed and presented comprehensive contracts to managed care companies, nursing home facilities and nursing associations.
- Conducted high-energy cold calling campaign on a daily basis continually opening up new sales territory.
- Built account base through assertive sales campaign and consistent follow-up.
- Provided social, psychological support; acted as liaison between patients, physicians, and case managers.
- Trained patients and family in administration of medications, use of home medical equipment, and signs and symptoms of medical complications associated with patient's medical problem.

EXPERIENCE:

Coram Healthcare, Orlando, FL – 1993-1995	*Account Executive*
Florida Hospital, Orlando, FL – 1989-1992	*Registered Nurse III*
Memorial Mission Hospital, Asheville, NC – 1988	*Registered Nurse*
Florida Hospital, Orlando, FL – 1987	*Registered Nurse III*
Central Florida Regional Hospital, Sanford, FL – 1986	*Registered Nurse*
Florida Hospital Central Nursing, Orlando, FL – 1985	*Nurse Technician*
Pineapple Club, Islamorada, FL – 1983-1984	*Promotional Manager*
Mr. S's Men's Wear, Tavernier, FL – 1978-1979	*Manager*
Keys Community Hospital Tavernier, FL – 1978	*Nursing Assistant*

EDUCATION:

Southern College Of Seventh Day Adventists, Orlando, FL
Associates of Science – Nursing Degree

Miami Dade Junior College, Miami, FL
General Studies

210

Combination. *Beverly Harvey, Pierson, Florida*

A practical layout for much information. The arrangement of the Experience section lets you see at a glance a person's promotions or ascent on a career ladder.

CATHERINE A. MAY

555 Sunsweet Drive
Jaunty, New York 55555
Home: (555) 555-5555

CAREER OBJECTIVE:

A challenging position in **Marketing Services** or **Marketing Communications**, offering an opportunity for further professional growth and career advancement.

PROFILE SUMMARY:

A results-oriented individual with extensive experience in many phases of graphic design and advertising; proficient in project management, packaging development and customer relations. Strong administrative skills.

EXPERIENCE:

JAUNTY PRODUCTS COMPANY   1993 to Present
(Wholly-Owned Subsidiary of Jaunty, Inc.), Jaunty, NY
Production Supervisor - Packaging Design Department
- Directing and managing packaging projects with design firms, photographers, separators and printers
- Monitoring and controlling the costs and scheduling objectives for packaging projects
- Photography art direction and photo selection
- Reviewing and approving cromalins/matchprints from separators
- Press approvals on location at printers
- Hiring, training and supervising support staff

JAUNTY GRAPHIC ASSOCIATES, INC., Jaunty, NY   1990 to 1993
(Advertising/Design Firm)
Account Executive/Production Supervisor
Customer service and sales, supervising the design and production of brochures, ads, catalogs, inserts, package design, exhibits, direct mail and textbook programs
- Purchasing - printing, photography, illustration and copy writing services
- Supervising staff, organizing, scheduling and coordinating projects, accustomed to meeting strict deadlines
- Budgeting, estimating and invoicing - awareness of cost
- Knowledge of design, paste-up, layout and typography
- Knowledge of electronic design and production capabilities on the Macintosh

EDUCATION:

JAUNTY COLLEGE OF TECHNOLOGY, Jaunty, NY
A.S. in Business Management - 1990

BROOKDALE COMMUNITY COLLEGE, Lincroft, NJ
Retailing and Fashion Merchandising - 1988-1990

Graduate, 1986 - JAUNTY AREA HIGH SCHOOL, Jaunty, NY

REFERENCES AVAILABLE UPON REQUEST

211

Combination. *Betty Geller, Elmira, New York*

This individual was not a recent graduate, so the Education section was put last on the resume. The use of boldfacing is effective in all three sections.

SCOTT R. PETERS
507 Gorman Street ■ Alton, Illinois 60532
(800) 555-1212

OBJECTIVE	■ ■ ■ Position in sales and customer service ■ ■ ■

PROFILE

- Over 10 years' experience in sales, customer service and account management.
- Confident and effective in product presentations, negotiations and closings.
- Quick to establish good relations. Gain customer confidence based on thorough product knowledge and commitment to service after the sale.
- Work well with personnel and customers at all levels. Diplomatic and tactful in resolving difficult situations.

EXPERIENCE

PERMA-PROOF, INC. ■ Salter, Wisconsin   1992 — Present
Quality Assurance Specialist - Wisconsin & Northern Illinois territory
Set own schedule, appointments and travel plans for commercial roof inspection and warranty work. Deal directly with authorized contractors and their customers (building owners). Evaluate and troubleshoot roofing problems to ensure customer satisfaction. Train new contractors and inspectors in product application to meet strict Perma-Proof standards and warranty (15-year guarantee materials & labor, $12 million liability).

- On personal initiative and time, presented sales proposal to business owner which resulted in 106,000 sq. ft. project.
- Saved a national account by resolving contractor dispute.
- Achieved the highest efficiency rating within 30-man department in 1994 (based on quality and quantity of work and territory coverage).
- One of only two inspectors in company history to inspect two million sq. ft in one year (1994).

DURACLAD, INC. ■ Alton, Illinois   1990 — 1992
Outside Sales Representative
Made cold-call presentations to homeowners, promoting sales of window and door products (seven lines) for new construction and rehab projects. Generated on-site quotations.

- Achieved 40-60% closing rate.

PETERSON TOOL CORPORATION ■ Alton, Illinois   1988 — 1990
Purchasing Agent
Directed purchasing operations for material, tooling and subcontract services for entire company ($1.5 million annually). Interviewed salespeople and negotiated contracts. Requested and processed quotations. Expedited orders and subcontract work to meet production deadlines. Verified accuracy of packing list and invoices.

- Located and evaluated new vendors on site; rated quality, availability and price.
- Started development of cost reduction program. Consulted with individual departments to identify target areas for cost control.

212

Combination. *Robin Folsom, location unknown*

The challenge was to make the most of the individual's sales experience, which was limited, and to stress customer service and negotiating skills. Note the dual roles of square bullets as

EXPERIENCE (cont'd)

HENTLEY STRUCTURES, INC. ■ Oakridge, Illinois   1985 — 1988
Superintendent
Coordinated all aspects of construction projects and managed 8-man crew in commercial
developments in New Jersey, Washington, D.C., Chicago and Milwaukee.

- Secured subcontractors for new projects: located contractors, researched company
  reputation and evaluated competitive bids.

- Dealt extensively with EPA officials and Washington, D.C. Fire Marshall in complying
  with regulations and resolving problems at a project with pre-existing site contamination.

EDUCATION

ALTON COMMUNITY COLLEGE ■ Alton, Illinois   1990
Associate Degree - Business Management

Effective Negotiating - Seminar by Charles Renault   1992

AFFILIATION

National Association of Purchasing Managers

References Available Upon Request

ellipses in the Objective and as bullets pointing to achievements in the Experience section.
Activities and responsibilities are presented in the paragraph immediately after each job
position.

MARTY M. MATLIN

0000 North West
Anywhere, USA
(000) 000-0000

PROFESSIONAL GOAL

Sales/Marketing career, impacting your organization's sales and profits through proven skills in business development, account management, and customer retention.

EDUCATION

- **A.S., Marketing** -- Atlinger Junior College, Anywhere, USA   8/95

- **Coursework Emphasis** -- Marketing coursework included Channels of Distribution, Consumer Behavior, Retail Merchandising, Marketing Research, Marketing Strategy, and Sales & Persuasion Techniques.

- **London Semester** -- Studies abroad centered around International Politics and also included British Art, British History, and British Theater. Semester culminated in European travel.

COURSEWORK EXPERIENCE

- <u>**Marketing Projects**</u> -- Gained hands-on experience in application of marketing principles through senior projects:
  - Researched channels of distribution which propelled local manufacturer from regional to national penetration.
  - Developed and presented comprehensive marketing program for insurance product; project earned "100%" rating by professor and "best in class" by peers.

EXPERIENCE

Financed majority of expenses through sales employment while completing degree. Highlights include:

- <u>**Sales Counselor**</u> -- Wireless of America, Anywhere, USA   5/93-Present
  Experienced in commission sales (wireless communications). Earned recognition for quality of gross margin, percentage of extended service policies sold, installation penetration, and low return percentage.
  - Earned membership in "President's Club" and honored as "Sales Counselor of the Month" (among staff of 60) two times in a 10-month period.
  - Generated highest part-time sales production in department; recognized by corporate for outstanding customer service.

- <u>**Route Sales/Merchandiser**</u> -- ABC Company, Anywhere, USA   1990-1991
  Developed commission sales route in southern Florida territory. Sold to and serviced independent grocers and national chains. Managed as many as 30 calls on a 300-mile round trip.
  - Doubled sales in coastal area; established relationships and secured long-term business with previously "no see" customers which developed into key accounts.
  - Trained distributors with history of poor performance, developing several to status as top producers in company.

INTERESTS

Competed in tri-athlons during high school ... taught archery, horsemanship ... downhill ski instructor.

♦ ♦ ♦

213

Combination. *Susan Britton Whitcomb, Fresno, California*

A Coursework Experience section calls special attention to the individual's marketing experience. The (part-time) Experience section shows good field-related accomplishments.

GARY R. VICTORY

0000 Competition Dr. • Los Angeles, CA 00000 • (000) 000-0000

SUMMARY

- ◆ Over 15 Years Dedicated to Professional Sales & Client Services
- ◆ Generated in Excess of $500,000 in Revenue on an Annual Basis
- ◆ Developed and Maintained Over 1400 Repetitive Clients through Individualized Client Relations
- ◆ Recipient of *The Summit Award* as being 1 of the Top 50 Customer Satisfaction Sales Professionals within the Los Angeles Region

PROFESSIONAL HIGHLIGHTS

MAIN TRANSPORTATION   Los Angeles, CA
Professional Sales Representative   February 1990 - Present

SALES / MARKETING
- Implement professional sales techniques in the promotion of company products and services to existing and potential clients
- Provide assistance in the selection and recommendation of products which will be best suited to the individual client needs
- Execute refined negotiation techniques which results in closing of sale

CLIENT RELATIONS
- Provide professional service to over 400 existing clients
- Coordinate and provide service maintenance for clients while at their place of employment
- Maintain close contact with clients through follow-up and obtaining referrals

SERVICE LIAISON
- Act as liaison between clients and Service Department in scheduling and obtaining optimum service in a timely manner

LEASING CONSULTANT
- Thoroughly explain all options and benefits available to client prior to purchase
- Notify clients of expiration contract and options available to best suit their needs

ADMINISTRATIVE
- Meet within a team environment on a daily basis to discuss company goals, objectives, client relations, marketing strategies, and overall performance

SUNSHINE AUTOMOTIVES   Los Angeles, CA
Professional Sales Representative   August 1982 - February 1990

EDUCATIONAL BACKGROUND

Excellence in Selling
Brian Tracy Seminar • 1994

A.S., Business Administration
Sunshine College • Sunshine, CA • 1980
Emphasis: Business Communications

References Available Upon Request

214

Combination. *Betty Callahan, location unknown*

Horizontal lines appearing under the individual's name, under the section headings, and at the end make the resume's sections easy to see. Underlining highlights areas of experience.

MARY SMITH ▪ 555 E. 55th Street, Apt. 55 ▪ New York, NY 55555 ▪ (555) 555-5555

Profile

Eighteen years of dedicated experience in all facets of Direct Marketing from Sales and Marketing to Product Development and Production. Excellent product knowledge of list information and sources. Successful in generating new business and increasing sales volume. Ability to devise new procedures to expedite operations. Proven leadership and team-building abilities.

Experience

1955 to Present

Major Mailing List Company, New York, NY
Director of Sales - Report to President
Developed and built up Trade Division servicing major list brokers and direct marketing firms.

- Motivate sales staff through weekly meetings and sales incentives.
- Generate new business and oversee top 30 accounts.
- Ensure that production schedules are met within tight timetables.
- Consult and advise clients on marketing and list strategies.
- Compile in-house and customized lists for clients. Research lists from outside vendors.
- Represent company at major industry trade shows.

Achievements

- Reorganized Division and increased revenues by 200%.
- Developed new forms and procedures to expedite production and operations.
- Created new promotional material to market company to clients.
- Planned and implemented detailed reports for improved sales tracking.
- Devised a pricing system for large volume discounts.

1955 to 1955

Worldwide Marketing Company, New York, NY
Account Executive
Supervised and maintained accounts for leading ad agencies, publishers and non-profit organizations.

- Coordinated and supervised production, overseeing quality control and scheduling.
- Instrumental in closing many difficult sales by effectively overcoming objections.

1955 to 1955

Leon Grey, Inc., New York, NY
Director of Sales - Reported to Vice President
Represented leading direct mail marketing firm at trade shows, conventions and seminars in major U.S. cities.

- Acquired new and substantial accounts including Coke and The Gap, while maintaining existing accounts.
- Produced highest yearly individual sales volume for five consecutive years.
- Won various sales contests and incentives.

Education

Nassau Community College, 1955 - 1955
Business Courses

New York Center for Acting
Graduated 1955

Major University - School of Continuing Education
Marketing and Sales Courses, 1955 - 1955

Hal Shoner Course, Graduated 1955

Affiliations

Vice President - **Mailing List Association**
Member - **Another Mailing List Association**

215

Combination. *Etta Barmann, New York, New York*

A resume with ample white space ensured by noticeable space between the side headings and the body of information. Many blank lines also prevent crowding or a cramped look.

Thomas A. Miller

1712 E. Capital Drive
Appleton, Wisconsin 54911

Work — 414 / 784-8514
Home — 414 / 788-1847

■ ■

■ Summary of Qualifications

- Self-motivated professional capable of implementing change and achieving goals.

- Proven performance record in progressively responsible positions. Consistently increase productivity and sales revenues.

- Excellent communication and interpersonal skills. Successfully manage and motivate employees, stimulate maximum levels of sales achievement, and provide high standards of service to clients.

- Well-developed analytical and organizational abilities.

■ Professional Experience

Food Corporation of America, Chicago, Illinois

May 1986—Present

Director of Sales, Northeast Wisconsin (1988-Present)
- Develop, motivate, and direct sales force to attain corporate sales and retention goals.
- Establish annual sales goals and expense budget; monitor on a monthly basis.
- Develop and implement promotional campaigns and pricing strategies.

Account Manager, Milwaukee, Wisconsin (1986-1988)
- Accountable for the sale of new business, retention of existing accounts, and development of assigned territory in accordance with corporate standards.

Accomplishments:
- Consistently achieved a dollar volume increase ranging from 12-33% annually.
- Expense rate for assigned territory ranked top for efficiency on a national level.
- President's Club Award, 1987 and 1992 (top sales award within company).

Our Town Grocery, Appleton, Wisconsin

1976—1986

Assistant Store Manager (1981–1986)
- Diverse responsibilities included supervising staff, interacting with vendors, balancing registers, handling bank transactions, and opening/closing store.

Department Manager (1979–1981)
Managed Frozen Food and Dairy Departments for two stores.

Stocker — part–time while in high school (1976–1979)

■ Education

Fox Valley Technical College, Appleton, Wisconsin
Associate Degree — Sales & Marketing

May 1980

216

Combination. *Kathy Keshemberg, Appleton, Wisconsin*

The striking design feature is the row of spaced square bullets after the contact information at the top of the resume. These make the square bullets at the left margin stand out.

JANE P. WEIS
74 Fourth Street
Northboro, Massachusetts 00000
(508) 555-5555

CAREER OBJECTIVE:

RESULTS-ORIENTED software sales professional seeks a position with advancement opportunities that will utilize a proactive approach to increase company profitability.

PROFILE SUMMARY:

A dynamic and successful team player with a proven record of aggressively developing a profitable client base. Possesses outstanding oral and written skills. Easily develops rapport with customers. Areas of concentration include:

UNIX • CLIENT SERVER • APPLICATION DEVELOPMENT

STRENGTHS:

- Thorough understanding of sales and marketing in highly competitive environments with the ability to consistently meet and exceed quotas.
- Proven creative sales techniques that have resulted in progressive growth through unstable and regressive market conditions.
- Demonstrated talent for building an account base and establishing long term relationships.

ACHIEVEMENTS:

- ◆ *Consistently meets or exceeds sales quotas through development and implementation of strategic sales and marketing strategies.*
- ◆ *Inducted into the Compass Club, indicating attainment of 100% quota.*
- ◆ *Ranked #1 in the country for Business Partner Sales.*

PROFESSIONAL EXPERIENCE:

COMPUTER APPLICATION GROUP   **1992 - Present**

IMG MARKETING SPECIALIST • Culver City, CA (1990 - Present)

- Aggressively markets application development tools and related product line to clients throughout the highly competitive Los Angeles territory.
- Successfully sells databases for all platforms (Unix) to new prospects and existing customers.
- Manages an account base generating over $2 million.
- Devises innovative marketing plans and forecasting strategies to ensure organizational goals are obtained.

(continued…)

217

Combination. *Alesia Benedict, Rochelle Park, New Jersey*

Shaded centered headings, together with two-line page borders, make this resume eye-catching. Notice also the use of boldface, all-uppercase letters, italic, and bullets.

JANE P. WEIS   (508) 555-5555   - Page Two -

PROFESSIONAL EXPERIENCE continued...

__COMPUTER APPLICATION GROUP__ experience continued

BUSINESS PARTNER • Reston, VA (1991 - 1994)

- Managed Value Added Resellers Sales (VARS).
- Established 10 - 15 appointments weekly.
- Successfully recruited new VARS.
- Conducted seminars and served as a company representative at major trade shows including FOSE.
- Kept channel stocked on products and new releases/enhancement updates.

EDUCATIONAL SALES REPRESENTATIVE • Fort Lee, NJ (1990 - 1991)

- Provided training and educational information to existing clients.
- Telemarketed Computer Associates product line and educational training to clients.

COMPUTER PROFICIENCY:

Mainframes • Midrange • PC's

EDUCATIONAL BACKGROUND:

Boston Community College • Boston, Massachusetts
A.S. in Business Administration

Regularly attends advanced training through sales and marketing seminars.

PROFESSIONAL MEMBERSHIPS:

IDMS Northeast User Group • INGRES User Group • DATACOM User Group

Besides these visual elements, the resume is distinctive in having additional sections for Strengths, Acheivements, Computer Proficiency, and Professional Memberships. The horizontal line under the contact information is repeated with the header on page 2.

SANDRA PLUMITTER
000 Douth Street
Stongnear, IN 000000
(000) 000-0000

JOB TARGET • SALES / MANAGEMENT

EDUCATION

Value Community College
Associate of Science Degree
Major: General Business Management
January 1993

COMPUTER BACKGROUND

Microsoft Word 5.1
Microsoft Windows 4.0
PageMaker 5.0
Excel
Quicken

ACADEMIC EMPHASIS

Sales & Marketing Techniques
Business Etiquette
Customer Relations
Business Law
Communication Through Effective Writing
Negotiation Skills
Computers for the Future
Effective Time Management for Life

EXPERIENCE

Managing Business Operations
QQQ Company, Town, AZ, 1993 - Present
Sell building materials, estimate projects, answer
telephones, assist with customer service, and set up
deliveries.

Leasing Agent
Your Town Apartments, Union, SC
Prepared lease agreements, answered multi-line
telephones, and scheduled service requests.

Sales Associate
Personal Care Services, Scotchville, IL
Sold personal care services through professional
sales techniques, consulted with clients on
determining needs, and distributed flyers to potential
clients.

REFERENCES

Available Upon Request

218

Combination. *Betty Callahan, location unknown*

Evident white space is provided by the narrowness of the right column. The Computer
Background subsection and the Academic Emphasis section, in effect, display skills.

HERMIONE A. BRIDGER

638A Jagger Drive ◆ Epsom, Ohio ◆ 45999
(123) 456-7890

OBJECTIVE:
Progressive sales-management position with a growth-oriented organization in which I can immediately apply my knowledge, experience, and interpersonal / leadership skills, while continuing to develop them to their full potential.

KEY SKILLS PROFILE:
- Top-rank communicator with ability to disseminate ideas and generate action throughout an organization.
- Function effectively both as an autonomous, self-motivated individual and as an active, contributing team member.
- Experienced in identifying corporate needs, then interviewing, assessing, recruiting & training appropriate new staff.
- Able to bring together diverse individuals to form a cohesive team, and motivate them to identify personally with key objectives. Exceptional ability to identify potential interpersonal barriers and communication problems, and take the steps necessary to circumvent them. An innate leader, with the capacity to train, mentor and develop both new and established team members.
- Customer-oriented, with demonstrated ability to develop an instant rapport and build lasting relationships with new and existing clients, through maximum attention to total quality, complete customer satisfaction – and service beyond expectation – based on consistent and comprehensive follow-through by telephone, or by letter.
- Experienced in planning and delivering informational and promotional presentations to diverse audiences, using a full spectrum of presentation media; adept at planning and executing innovative marketing campaigns.
- Strong advocate of the need to develop and continuously enhance knowledge of product, processes, and market.

EXPERIENCE PROFILE:

BLASÉ, Dayton, Ohio   **October 1994 - Present**
Manager
- Recruited and trained two assistant managers and two sales associates; recognized as top sales manager in the store.
- Conceptualized, developed and introduced a comprehensive plan to revitalize operations and reduce staff turnover.

FULL TIME MOTHERS, INC., Dayton, Ohio   **February 1994 - October 1994**
Area Manager
- Recruited by this company with a view to advancement to District Manager.
- Personally managed complete operation of one store, supervised two other existing retail stores; in July 1994, opened and supervised one additional new store.
- Developed and implemented a customer profile base and an associated follow-up and retention program.

A BUN IN THE OVEN, Dayton, Ohio   **May 1993 - February 1994**
Manager
- Was head-hunted to recruit and train all staff for the first Dayton branch of this maternity specialty store; assisted in recruiting / training personnel and making overall preparations for opening of new location in Indiana.
- Developed and implemented marketing strategies which successfully attracted a large new client base.

SEPTEMBER LEAVES, Columbus, Ohio   **October 1992 - May 1993**
[A Division of U.S. Shoe Corporation]
Manager
- Recruited to restore under-performing store to successful operation through team building, training, and motivation.
- Reassigned to larger volume store to oversee total store operations.

SQUARE GARDEN, Columbus, Ohio   **November 1989 - October 1992**
Manager
- Promoted to position after 9 months as Assistant Manager and 11 months as Training Manager.
- Selected, hired, and trained two Assistant Managers and 13 staff; directed sales training; supervised new store openings; promoted fashion shows and in-store promotions.
- Increased productivity and staff retention through team training and motivation, and building a preferred client base.
- Provided timely feedback to corporate buyers regarding optimal merchandise assortment.

EDUCATION:
- PETERHOUSE COMMUNITY COLLEGE, Dayton, Ohio. Associates Degree – *Marketing Management*. 1986
- *Dale Carnegie Public Speaking Course*, August – September, 1987.

EXCELLENT REFERENCES AVAILABLE UPON REQUEST

219

Combination. *Barry Hunt, location unknown*

Because of consistent use of font enhancements, the eye can sort out the various firms, location, dates, jobs, and so on. Hanging indentation makes the headings easy to see.

GEORGE W. SMITH
123 Main Street
Los Angeles, CA, 00000
(000) 000-0000

SUMMARY:
- Nine years management/sales experience in skin care/cosmetics retailing; product knowledge includes many industry leaders
- Consistent sales leader
- Expertise in product development and marketing, long- and short-term planning, personnel, supervision, and project management

EXPERIENCE:

Consultant/Owner, B. A. Body Shop   Los Angeles, CA, 1993–present
Operate retail marketing consultancy emphasizing point-of-purchase and other in-store marketing/merchandising/product promotion, including overall store layout and concept, motivational aids, informational materials, etc. Also consult on expansion: new locations, new venture into mail order, etc.; full responsibility to develop initial mail-order catalog, including product selection, vendor negotiation, layout, writing, and photography. Manage multiple and substantial accounts. Major accounts include:
- Captivating Concepts, Beverly Hills, CA (point-of-purchase restaurant marketing specialist)
- Bathworks, Santa Monica, CA (personal care/toiletry store)

Manager, Horticulture Haven   Los Angeles, CA, 1993
Trained and supervised sales staff. Coordinated in-store merchandising. Handled public relations/media contact/promotional writing. Ensured accurate accounting (including cash handling as well as monitoring testers and damaged goods), store security, etc.
- Consistently led store in sales

Assistant Manager, Bathing Beautiful   Santa Monica, CA, 1991–93
Similar duties, with emphasis on marketing/merchandising. Extensive sales force motivation. Wrote numerous promotional and informational materials. Coordinated marketing strategies with corporate headquarters.
- Consistently led store in sales

Sales Advisor, B.C. Body Works   San Diego, CA, 1988–91
Also significant responsibility for quality control, inventory/ordering, and staff training. Instructed make-up artistry.
- Top sales performer at one of the Top Ten locations nationwide

Sales Representative, GGB's   La Jolla, CA, 1989–90
- Consistently led store in sales

Sales Associate, Perfume Department, Macy's   San Diego, CA, 1988–89
Strong sales performer at busy downtown location.
- Chosen for key sales position introducing Aramis Tuscany line for Christmas season

Shift Manager, Cormier Skin Care, Inc.   San Diego, CA, 1986–87
Strong sales performer with additional responsibilities including: opening and closing, inventory, merchandising, make-up and skin care consulting.

EDUCATION:

A.A., Liberal Arts, ABC Community College   San Diego, CA, 1991
- Editor-in-Chief, campus newspaper

REFERENCES:
Available upon request.

220

Combination. *Shel Horowitz, Northampton, Massachusetts*

Apart from the Summary, the format would be strictly chronological. Bullets are used judiciously to call attention to special information beyond duties. Boldfacing is effective.

David L. O'Connor

493 Crestwood Lane • Smithville, N. Y. 00000
(555) 555-5555

QUALIFICATIONS
- Self-motivated, aggressive individual experienced in business and public office with proven skills in the areas of sales, management, and finances
- Experienced in contract and labor negotiations
- Exceptional organizational, communication and problem-solving abilities,
- Able to work successfully with all levels of management and labor
- Have a talent for initiating essential projects and overseeing them to completion.

EMPLOYMENT

TEXAS REFINERY CORP., Ft. Worth, Texas
New York State Manager (out of Smithville, NY) — 1985 to Present
- Supervise and train 26 full- and part-time salespeople
- Involved in direct sales
- Conducted training seminars

D.L. O'CONNOR LUBE AND SUPPLY, INC., Smithville, NY
President and CEO — 1988 to Present

GENERAL MOTORS ACCEPTANCE CORP., Elmira and Rochester, NY
District Representative — 1976-1985
- Responsible for all aspects of credit and collections

WAVERLY POLICE DEPT., Waverly, NY
Patrolman (part-time) — 1977-1979

PUBLIC OFFICE

TOWN OF SMITHVILLE, NY
Supervisor and Chief Fiscal Officer — 1988-1989, 1992-1993
- Responsibilities included working as Budget Officer, Fixed Assets Officer, Chairman of Health Board, and Chairman of Economic Development Board
- Supervised 56 people in full-time, part-time, and appointed positions as well as various committees
- Negotiated economic development and natural gas contracts

SMITHVILLE FIRE DISTRICT, NY
President — 1993 to Present
Treasurer — 1988-1993

SMITHVILLE, NY
School Board Member — 1985-1987

COMMUNITY SERVICE
- Initiated and directed fund raising for the following (total raised over $23,000):
  — Family whose son had terminal heart problems and no health insurance
  — Steuben County Sheriff K-9 Division's Drug Dog and Equipment Fund.
- Scout Master for Troop #46
- Member of Jasper Fire Department and Ambulance Corp.
- Hold membership in several local groups and various lodges

EDUCATION

CORNING COMMUNITY COLLEGE, Corning, NY
A.A.S. in Criminal Justice — Graduated 1975

TRAINING
- Business and sales seminars through Texas Refinery Corp.
- Additional courses in crime scene investigation, first aid, and fire fighting

References available upon request.

221

Combination. *Catherine Seebald, Wellsville, New York*

This resume calls attention to the individual's wealth of experience in business, public office, and community service. Separate headings for these areas make them readily seen.

BRYANT W. BLACK

521 Gary's Lane • Paramus, New Jersey 00000 • (201) 555-5555

SUMMARY of QUALIFICATIONS —————————————————

- Successful executive level sales management experience with Profit & Loss responsibility.
- Proven ability to manage corporate marketing functions including product management, advertising/sales promotion, sales training, and telemarketing.
- Experienced with various channels of distribution including direct sales, distributors, dealers and telephone carriers.
- Product expertise includes facsimile equipment, cellular telephones, pagers and office systems.
- Excellent analytical, organizational, and interpersonal skills.
- Practical knowledge and understanding of Japanese management techniques.

PROFESSIONAL EXPERIENCE —————————————————

PANASONIC COMMUNICATIONS and SYSTEMS COMPANY - Secaucus, NJ   **1987 - Present**
An international, multi-billion dollar leader in office automation, office systems, consumer electronics, office equipment and communications equipment.

VICE PRESIDENT (1989-Present)

- Profit & Loss responsibility for an $150 million division in cellular telephone and paging equipment sales.
- Generated cellular telephone sales of $97 million in 1994.
- Achieved 105% of pager sales budget in 1994.
- Maintained divisional profitability in a volatile and competitive marketplace.
- Preserved market share despite declining economy and changing distribution patterns.
- Departmental productivity totals nearly $3 million per staff member vs. company standards of $1 million per employee.

GENERAL MANAGER - DIRECT SALES (1987-1989)

- Directed the functions of a $76 million direct sales organization in facsimile equipment sales, including staff management of 110 sales representatives.
- Achieved 120% of sales budget and 289% of profit budget for 1994.
- Increased sales rep productivity 18% within 2 years.
- Reduced sales rep turnover despite changing distribution patterns in the industry.
- Implemented a successful Major Account Program to insure the long term profitability of the direct sales organization.

RICOH CORPORATION - West Caldwell, New Jersey   **1977 - 1987**
A multi-billion dollar manufacturer of office equipment and camera products.

DIRECTOR of MARKETING - SYSTEMS PRODUCTS (1983-1987)
DIRECTOR of PRODUCT MARKETING (1979-1983)
DIRECTOR of MARKET PLANNING (1978-1979)
MARKETING SUPPORT MANAGER (1977-1978)

- Directed the planning and marketing of systems/office automation products. Promoted to position to direct the Company into new business/product areas.
- Responsible for the development and implementation of all phases of marketing in the data communications/office equipment field.
- Developed business, marketing and launch plans for facsimile products. Successfully introduced several major products which accounted for over 90% of the Group's sales.

222

Combination. *Alesia Benedict, Rochelle Park, New Jersey*

The eye sees first the shaded box, next the page border, and then the horizontal line after each main heading. This kind of eye movement creates interest before any word is read.

BRYANT W. BLACK————————————————————————————————————
                                    (201) 555-5555 • Page Two

PROFESSIONAL EXPERIENCE continued————————————————————————

<u>RICOH CORPORATION</u> experience continued...

- Accountable for the Group program/product management functions.
- Directed OEM sales of peripheral products.
- Developed and managed national account sales programs and successfully negotiated largest sales order in Company's history.
- Initiated and managed the Corporate Telemarketing Program which generated over $4 million in additional revenue.
- Constructed and activated the Sales Training Program which increased sales productivity 18% over two years.
- Directed the advertising, public relations and trade show functions resulting in increased measured brand awareness 20% and generated over 10,000 sales leads in one year.

<u>BURROUGHS CORPORATION</u> - Danbury, Connecticut   **1972 - 1977**
   A manufacturer of facsimile products with revenues of $100 million.

SALES DEVELOPMENT MANAGER (1975-1977)
STAFF MARKETING PLANNER (1973-1975)
SENIOR MARKETING ANALYST (1973)
MARKET PLANNING ANALYST (1971-1972)

- Developed strategic and profitable programs in sales support, sales development, market planning, and market research.
- Supervised and motivated staff to peak levels of performance.

EDUCATION——

   A.S. (Marketing), Bergen Community College - Paramus, New Jersey

The information for each company is presented consistently: a thumbnail description (in italic) of each country, position(s) held with dates, and bulleted accomplishments. Education, the weakest section, is put last without elaboration.

PATRICK D. SMITH
1016 NW Downey Street
Camas, Washington 98607
555-855-1111

CAREER PROFILE

Over 25 years of experience in retail sales. Supervision of 70 - 150 employees.
Directly responsible for budgeted profit/loss targets which include sales projections,
labor control, maintenance and supply expense. Responsible for upkeep of physical
plants as well inventory control and store presentation. Skilled in working with groups
of people; effective presenter and facilitator of small and large groups.

PROFESSIONAL ACCOMPLISHMENTS

Merchandising

- Achieved budgeted gross profit targets of approximately 35% quarterly.
- Designed and implemented seasonal and promotional product sets that are
  still being used today. Approximately 30 percent of sales were generated by
  seasonal promotional goods.

Store Management

- Consistently beat previous year's sales and met or exceeded targeted gross
  profit requirements.

Customer Service

- Maintained high standards while processing up to $1,000 per hour and 1,500
  customers per day at front end.

EMPLOYMENT EXPERIENCE

Procedural Consultants, Portland, Oregon   6/95 - present

Consultant. Design and implement labor scheduling and time management to retail
firms.

Supermarket Plus, Bellevue, Washington   2/95 - 6/95

Store Manager. Even though operating below the previous year's sales, increased
those sales by about 5 points. Brought customer count from a 15 point deficit to an
approximate 6 point deficit.

223

Combination. *Janette M. Campbell, Washougal, Washington*

The well-organized layout fits the individual well. Notice the subheadings in the Professional
Accomplishments section. Grouping achievements under such categories aids readability.

PATRICK D. SMITH   Page 2
555-855-1111

Alaska Supercenters. Alaska.   1989 to 1995 and 1972 to 1986

>   **Store Manager**. Seward, Alaska. (9/94 to 1/95)
>   **Store Manager**. Ketchikan, Alaska. (1/94 to 9/94)
>   **Store Manager**. Homer, Alaska. (6/90 to 1/94)
>   **2nd Assistant Manager**. (1/90 to 6/90). Training.
>
>   **Assistant to Director of Management, Planning and Training**. (9/89 to 1/90).
>   Updated and developed new front end labor scheduling program.
>
>   **General Merchandise Supervisor**. (1/83 to 1/86). Responsible for merchandising
>   non-food departments in 13 stores including personnel requirements, inventory
>   control, gross profit requirements, coordinating major remodels and opening new
>   stores. Multi-unit supervision; directly supervised 40 people.
>
>   **Assistant to Director of Management, Planning and Training**. (2/81 to 1/83).
>   Maintained and updated time management program.
>
>   **Department Manager**. (6/79 to 2/81) Trained all subordinates in departmental
>   operations; delegated daily work activities.

Smith's Family Market, Veneta Feed and Seed, Veneta, Oregon   3/86 to 8/89

>   **Owner** of convenience store: fuel, hot deli foods, dry grocery, general merchandise,
>   animal feed, fertilizer, and seed. Began with daily sales of $500; within 12 months,
>   daily sales were $1,500.
>
>   **Previous experience** included licensed real estate agent (Oregon) specializing in
>   business brokerage.

EDUCATION

>   Associates of Arts Degree. Electronics Technology. Anchorage Community College,
>   Anchorage, Alaska.

PROFESSIONAL AND COMMUNITY AFFILIATIONS

>   President, Homer Chamber of Commerce, 1992.
>   Commissioner, Homer Economic Development Commission, 1992-93.
>   Member, Board of Directors, South Peninsula Hospital, Inc. 1991-93.
>   President, Fern Ridge Development Commission, 1988-89.
>   Vice President, West Lane Chamber of Commerce, Veneta, Oregon, 1987-88.

References Provided Upon Request

Month and year dates in parentheses specify positions, locations, and periods in working for
the same company. Boldfacing helps the reader spot the different positions. Education is
placed without fanfare near the end.

NAME
Address
City, State Zip Code
Telephone - No parenthesis

KEYWORD SUMMARY: Experienced Manager. Sales. District Manager. Insurance. Real Estate. Supervisor. 28 Staff. Exceeded All Sales Goals. Quotas. Competitive. Aggressive. Self Motivated. Strong Work Ethic. Committed. Team Player. Planning. Business Development. Hiring. Staff Development. Agent of Year (4 Times). Attended All Conferences. Life and Health. Property. Casualty. Associate of Business. AAB. LUTCF. Life Underwriter Training Counsel Fellow. Marathon Runner.

PROFESSIONAL HIGHLIGHTS:
* 15 Years of managerial experience.
* Exceptional interpersonal and communication skills.
* Proven record in sales.
* Effective team developer and positive motivator.

OBJECTIVE: A position in sales or as a team manager for a progressive business in the Southwestern Virginia Area.

EMPLOYMENT: **General Agent**, Independent Insurance Companies. Pulaski, Montgomery, and Giles Counties in Virginia. 1994 to Present.

Represent 7 insurance companies in three county district marketing to a client base of 1,000 insurers.
* Handled competitive insurance packages for life, auto, homeowners, health, annuities, and commercial needs of customers.
* Demonstrated ability in business development, sales, and customer service.

District Agent, Wise Financial Services. New River Valley, Virginia. 1991-1994.

Successfully marketed a full range of products for the company and was awarded, "Rookie of the Year" in 1991 from a field of 200 agents.
* Responsibilities included selling to new clients, servicing, and maintaining existing accounts, in the New River Valley Area.

224

Combination. *Kathryn Jordan, Blacksburg, Virginia*

A resume with keywords for scanning and storage of information in a computer database. For retrieval, nouns as keywords are better than strong verbs. Nouns are specific; verbs are

District Manager, East Coast Insurance. Pulaski, Virginia.
1973-1990.

Began as a Sales Agent and moved into Sales Manager position.
Supervised territory and 7 agents for 5 years. Promoted to
assistant District Manager for 1 year and then served as District
Manager for 8 years.
* Demonstrated ability to recruit staff and develop them into
  successful insurance agents.
* Served as team motivator capable of encouraging people to
  perform to capacity.
* Met and exceeded all personal and district sales objectives and
  goals.

EDUCATION: **A.A.B.**, National Business College. Roanoke, Virginia. 1975.

Major: Business.

OTHER: **Lions Club**: 1982-Present.
* Served in numerous leadership capacities.

Marathon Runner.
* Demonstrates discipline to train, capacity to be self motivated,
  and competitiveness to participate in the sport.

less so. After stored information has been retrieved, an interested potential employer may
want to see an image of the original resume. Resumes for scanning, therefore, need to look
like resumes in general.

Benjamin Michaels

123 Fourth Street ▪ Chicago, Illinois 62000 ▪ home (555) 555-0987 ▪ office (555) 555-8765

SENIOR SALES / SALES MANAGEMENT
Wholesale & Retail

Top producing Senior Sales Manager with 12 years professional experience building and leading high-caliber sales, marketing strategies, and major account management for country's largest wholesale bread and cake baker. Expertise in developing sales and marketing management plans; recruiting, training and directing sales team. Record of consistent achievement and positive corporate growth through increased profitability and analysis/development of sales territories and personnel. Outstanding analytical, presentation, negotiation, and team leadership qualifications.

PROFESSIONAL EXPERIENCE

WONDER BAKING COMPANY, Chicago, Illinois   1983 - Present

▪ **RASS/DEX Implementation Manager** (1992 - Present)
Route Accounting Support Systems (RASS) and Direct Exchange (DEX/USC)

Provide direction, support and management for fast-paced national rollout of RASS system, converting approximately 4500 (over 65%) routes from manual accounting to Norand hand-held computer system. Train, manage and support RASS coordinators and route sales representatives in over 22 sales trade areas nationwide, developing training materials and user documentation for sales reps, district sales manager, zone/general managers, and technical support for 24-hour hotline.

Introduce of Wonder's DEX/UCS system to major grocery accounts allowing direct exchange of invoices, delivery acknowledgements, and product and price information between hand-held computers and retailer back-door receiving stations minimizing paper handling and manual errors.

▪ **Zone Sales Manager** ▪ 1988 - 1992

Directed, supervised and trained district sales managers and supervisors encompassing 5 branch locations and 50 route sales reps in 5-state area. Called on major retailers, managers, and buyers to develop working partnerships and sales plans to build profitable sales. Participated in special assignments in training, identifying and developing DSMs for expanded market areas. Worked with consulting firm in job description, schedule of events, and priorities for DSMs during development through implementation of functional management.

▪ **Branch Sales Manager** ▪ 1983 - 1988 ▪ Lincoln, Nebraska; Norfolk, Nebraska

Progressively managed 7 to 14 routes, including multiple thrift store locations, clerks, loaders, and garage mechanics. Supervised construction and completion of new branch facility, including offices, thrift store and garage; instrumental in increasing 2-route branch to 6, and adding one thrift store operation. Managed customer relations, manpower and sales, safety and security training, merchandising, special promotions, and daily operations.

MICHAELS DISTRIBUTING, Rushville, Nebraska

▪ **Owner** ▪ 1977 - 1983

Provided independent distribution services to WBC. Developed profitable sales base; ordered, merchandised and delivered products; and maintained outstanding customer service record.

EDUCATION

A.S. General Business, LEWISTON COMMUNITY COLLEGE, Lewiston, Nebraska

Numerous continuing education courses, management workshops, seminars, and practical training, including computers (Lotus Smart Suite, Windows, Harvard Graphics, Microsoft Project, Freelance Graphics, Compel, DEXdemo), handheld computers, and multimedia LCD projection systems.

225

Combination. *Carla Culp Coury, Glen Carbon, Illinois*

This person lost his job because of a company buyout. He had to apply for his old job with the new company. The new president liked especially *this* resume. The person was rehired.

Social Service

Resumes at a Glance

RESUME NO.	LAST OR CURRENT OCCUPATION	GOAL	PAGE
226.	Development Assistant	Position serving people with developmental disabilities	345
227.	Assistant, funeral home	Intern, funeral home	346
228.	Resident Counselor	Not specified	347
229.	Occupational Therapy Assistant (Intern)	Not specified	348

Angel Friel

OBJECTIVE
I am seeking a challenging position, in which to serve people with developmental disabilities, within a progressive organization offering opportunities for continued personal and professional growth.

EXPERIENCE
Troy County Association for Retarded Citizens, Inc. Indianapolis, IN: 0000-0000
Developmental Assistant

Provide assistance to Community Living Instructors including: therapeutic needs; training and supervision of residents; transportation; and operation, usage, and maintenance of resident's life support devices. Maintain resident's charts and perform record keeping tasks, charting behavior and medication. Train residents in personal hygiene and dress, appropriate manners and conduct, housekeeping, laundry, shopping, and meal preparation responsibilities. Provide input and assist with implementation of Individual Habilitation Plan objectives, goals, and behavior plans. Document daily and special resident contacts, including family, peers, and friends. Attend and participate in monthly Group Home and In-Service Meetings, and yearly Resident Case Conferences. Trained in CPR, CORE A and B and First Aid.

- Creative, instinctively able to stimulate residents to participate in activities and to achieve positive behavioral goals. Understanding, respond readily to resident's needs.
- Monitor resident's medications including seizure and/or special needs supervision.
- Special Olympics supervisory participant, 0000-0000.
- Provide time management instruction and encourage quality leisure-time activities of residents.
- Participate as a professional member of the Interdisciplinary Team to develop Individual Habilitation, and Facility Service plans.
- Assume Community Living instructor's duties as necessary.

PROFILE
A straight-forward, cooperative team member who is industrious, intuitive, reliable and outgoing.

EDUCATION/SEMINARS
Jones University. Jones, Iowa: 0000
A. S. Degree in Psychology
- Peer tutor for disabled young teens.

00 South 5th Street, Jones, Iowa 00000   (000) 000-0000

226

Combination. *Colleen S. Jaracz, Vincennes, Indiana*

A different feature is the placement of the individual's address and phone number *below* the lines at the bottom of the page. These lines balance those at the top.

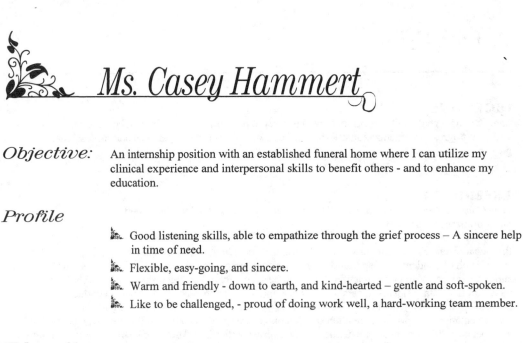

Ms. Casey Hammert

Objective: An internship position with an established funeral home where I can utilize my clinical experience and interpersonal skills to benefit others - and to enhance my education.

Profile

- Good listening skills, able to empathize through the grief process – A sincere help in time of need.
- Flexible, easy-going, and sincere.
- Warm and friendly - down to earth, and kind-hearted – gentle and soft-spoken.
- Like to be challenged, - proud of doing work well, a hard-working team member.

Education

Associate Degree of Science (Funeral Service Education) → May, 2000
(National Boards → May, 2000). *Somewhere University*. Somme, IN: 1997-2000

- Member of Sigma Phi Sigma (Funeral Service Organization)

Coursework: Funeral Service (Law, Merchandising, Operations), Clinical Orientation, Funeral Directing Concepts, Restorative Art, Embalming (three classes), Counseling, Mortuary Administration and Funeral Management, Psychology Aspects of Grief and Death, Organic/Biochemistry, Anatomy and Physiology, Psychology, and Sociology.

Employment

Boss & Sons Funeral Home. Somewhere, IN: Summer 1999 and Christmas Break 1999-2000.
Observed families in decision-making process. Observed embalming, and presentation procedures. Insured orderliness of premises. Facilitated death certificate and memorial handling. Assisted in writing obituaries.

Captain D's. Somewhere, IN: 1997-Present

JC Penney. Somewhere, IN: 0000-0000

000 Lee Blvd.
Somme, IN 00000
(812) 000-0000

227

Combination. *Colleen S. Jaracz, Vincennes, Indiana*

Ornate floral graphics in opposite corners and as bullets are fitting for the work goal: an internship at a funeral home. Italic and the curl at the end of the line match the graphics.

David L. O'Connor

493 Crestwood Lane • Smithville, N. Y. 00000
(555) 555-5555

QUALIFICATIONS
- Experienced in areas of resident counselling and therapeutic foster care of infants, young children and adolescents. Trained to deal with their emotional problems, as well as to provide a safe environment and structure that allows them to become self-sufficient.
- Have experience working with the Department of Social Services and other state organizations coordinating children's care, and preparing required reports describing care and progress of children.
- Cleared through the New York State Central Registry on Child Abuse.
- Completed and cleared background check through Steuben County Sheriff's Department.

RELATED EXPERIENCE
Kinship Family & Youth Services, Anderson, NY — 1994 to Present
Resident Counselor for the Kennedy House
  Group home for boys ages 12–18 classified as delinquent, abused, etc. and placed in home by court order

Therapeutic Foster Care — 1992 to Present
- Certified from newborn to 18 years

EDUCATION & TRAINING
The following courses were completed in conjunction with work as Resident Counselor and foster care:
- Mandated Reporting
- Suicide
- Criminal Justice System
- Life Books and Life Packs
- Permanency Planning
- Therapeutic Crisis Intervention Training (biannual)
- Child Abuse
- Drug Addiction/HIV
- First Aid
- Behavioral Emergencies
- Cultural Sensitivity

Corning Community College, Corning, NY
A.A.S. in Criminal Justice — Graduated 1975

OTHER EXPERIENCE
New York State Manager (out of Smithville, NY) — 1985 to Present
Texas Refinery Corp., Ft. Worth, Texas

President and CEO — 1988 to Present
D.L. O'Connor Lube and Supply, Inc., Smithville, NY

District Representative — 1976-1985
General Motors Acceptance Corp., Elmira and Rochester, NY

Patrolman (part-time), Waverly Police Dept., Waverly, NY — 1977-1979

PUBLIC OFFICE
Wayne, NY, Supervisor and Chief Fiscal Officer — 1988-1989, 1992-1993
Wayne Fire District, NY, President — 1993 to Present; Treasurer — 1988-1993
Wayne, NY, School Board Member — 1985-1987

COMMUNITY SERVICE
- Initiated and directed fund raising for the following (total raised over $23,000):
  — Family whose son had terminal heart problems and no health insurance
  — Steuben County Sheriff K-9 Division's Drug Dog and Equipment Fund.
- Scout Master for Troop #46
- Member of Wayne Fire Department and Ambulance Corp.

228

Combination. *Catherine Seebald, Wellsville, New York*

A resume for a career change for a highly experienced, mature, and community-minded individual. The Other Experience section displays an impressive list of varied positions.

JOHN R. FITZMAURICE
48 Armstrong Street
Newton, MA 00000
(000) 000–0000

EDUCATION:
A.S. with Highest Honors as an Occupational Therapy Assistant, Newton College, Newton, MA, May 1995.
- **GPA:** 3.89
- **Honors:** Phi Theta Kappa National Honor Society; Non-traditional Student Award for Outstanding Contributions to the College; Program of Study Award for Outstanding Academic Achievement; D. Llewellyn Evans Scholarship for Outstanding Academic Achievement
- Occupational Therapy Observer/Assistant, Pediatrics and Geriatrics, Arlington Nursing Home, Arlington, MA, 1994

Certified Nurses Aide, American Red Cross, 1993.

EXPERIENCE:
Occupational Therapy Assistant (Intern)
- Pickering Center for Rehabilitation at Crossroads Hospital, Cambridge, MA, Spring, 1995. Provided physical therapeutic exercises, taught functional mobility and safety, as well as functional ADL. Assisted in treatment planning and implementation. Maintained progress notes and other paperwork. Led/co-led community re-entry groups for head injury, stroke, RA, and amputee patients. Provided weekly reports to multidisciplinary team on patients' goals and accomplishments.

- Acute Psychiatric Care Unit, University Medical Center, Boston, MA, Winter 1995. Ran motivation/self-esteem/life skills groups, as well as craft-based activities for assessment (e.g., leather, ceramics, woodworking). Assisted in treatment planning and implementation. Extensive documentation of patient progress, including frequent updates of patients' individual Allen Cognitive Level of Functioning.

Personal Care Attendant for head-injured client, 1993–94.

Certified Nurses Aide
- Harper Nursing Home, Boston, MA, 1993

- Exeter Extended Care Center for Children, Andover, MA, 1991–93 (Promoted from original position in food service, May 1992).

ADDITIONAL SKILLS:
- Considerable knowledge of substance abuse issues and treatment
- Knowledge of alternative stress-reduction modalities
- Computer-literate, including WordPerfect and medical billing program

References available upon request.

229

Combination. *Shel Horowitz, Northampton, Massachusetts*

Larger type and boldfacing make this resume easy to read. Honors in the Education section are impressive because they are field-related. Skills strengthen the ending.

3

P·A·R·T

Best Cover Letter Tips

Best Cover Letter Tips at a Glance

Best Cover Letter Writing Tips 351

   Myths about Cover Letters 351

   Tips for Polishing Cover Letters 352

      ■ Using Good Strategies for Letters 352

      ■ Using Pronouns Correctly 353

      ■ Using Verb Forms Correctly 354

      ■ Using Punctuation Correctly 355

      ■ Using Words Correctly 358

   Exhibit of Cover Letters 360

Best Cover Letter Writing Tips

In an active job search, your cover letter and resume should complement one another. Both are tailored to a particular reader you have contacted or to a specific job target. To help you create the "best" cover letters for your resumes, this part of the book mentions some common myths about cover letters and presents tips for polishing the letters you write.

Myths about Cover Letters

1. **Resumes and cover letters are two separate documents that have little relation to each other.** The resume and cover letter work together in presenting you effectively to a prospective employer. The cover letter should mention the resume and call attention to some important aspect of it.

2. **The main purpose of the cover letter is to establish friendly rapport with the reader.** Resumes show that you *can* do the work required. Cover letters express that you *want* to do the work required. But it doesn't hurt to display enthusiasm in your resumes and refer to your abilities in your cover letters.

3. **You can use the same cover letter for each reader of your resume.** Modify your cover letter for each reader so that it sounds fresh rather than canned. Chances are that in an active job search, you have already talked with the person who will interview you. Your cover letter should reflect that conversation and build on it.

4. **In a cover letter, you should mention any negative things about your education, work experience, life experience, or health to prepare the reader in advance of an interview.** This is not the purpose of the cover letter. You might bring up these topics in the first or second interview, but only after the interviewer has shown interest in you or offered you a job. Even then, if you feel that you must mention something negative about your past, present it in a positive way, perhaps by saying how that experience has strengthened your will to work hard at any new job.

5. **It is more important to remove errors from a resume than from a cover letter, because the resume is more important than the cover letter.** Both your resume and your cover letter should be free of errors. The cover letter is usually the first document a prospective employer sees. The first impression is often the most important one. If your cover letter has an embarrassing error in it, the chances are good that the reader may not bother to read your resume or may read it with less interest.

6. **To make certain that your cover letter has no errors, all you need to do is proofread it or ask a friend to "proof" it.** Trying to proofread your own cover letter is risky, even if you are good at grammar and writing. Once a document is typewritten or printed, it has an aura about it that may make it

seem better written than it is. For this reason, you are likely to miss typos or other kinds of errors.

Relying on someone else is risky too. If your friend is not good at grammar and writing, that person may not see any mistakes either. Try to find a proofreader, a professional editor, an English teacher, a professional writer, or an experienced secretary who can point out any errors you may have missed.

7.   **After someone has proofread your letter, you can make a few changes to it and not have it looked at again.** More errors creep into a document this way than you would think possible. The reason is that such changes are often done hastily, and haste can waste an error-free document. If you make *any* change to a document, ask someone to proofread it a final time just to make sure that you haven't introduced an error during the last stage of composition. If you can't find someone to help you, the next section gives you advice on how to eliminate common mistakes in cover letters.

Tips for Polishing Cover Letters

You might spend several days working on your resume, getting it "just right" and free of errors. But if you send it with a cover letter that is written quickly and contains even one conspicuous error, all of your good effort may be wasted. That error could be just the kind of mistake the reader is looking for to screen you out.

You can prevent this kind of tragedy by polishing your cover letter so that it is free of all errors. The following tips can help you avoid or eliminate common errors in cover letters. If you become aware of these kinds of errors and know how to fix them, you can be more confident about the cover letters you send with your resumes.

Using Good Strategies for Letters

1.   **Use the postal abbreviation for the state in your mailing address.** See resume writing strategy 1 in Part 1.

2.   **Make certain that the letter is addressed to a specific person and that you use this person's name in the salutation.** Avoid using such general salutations as Dear Sir or Madam, To Whom It May Concern, Dear Administrator, Dear Prospective Employer, and Dear Committee. In an active job search, you should do everything possible to send your cover letter and resume to a particular individual, preferably someone you've already talked with in person or by phone, and with whom you have arranged an interview. If you have not been able to make a personal contact, at least do everything possible to find out the name of the person who will read your letter and resume. Then address the letter to that person.

3.   **Adjust the margins for a short letter.** If your cover letter is 300 words or longer, use left, right, top, and bottom margins of one inch. If the letter is shorter, the width of the margins should increase. How much they increase is a matter of personal taste. One way to take care of the width of the top and bottom margins is to center a shorter letter vertically on the page. A maximum width for a short cover letter of 100 words or fewer might be two-inch left and right margins. As the number of words increases by 50 words, you might decrease the width of the left and right margins by two-tenths of an inch.

4. **If you write your letter with word processing or desktop publishing software, use left-justification to ensure that the lines of text are readable with fixed spacing between words.** The letter will have a "ragged right" look along the right margin, but the words will be evenly spaced horizontally. Don't use justification in an attempt to give a letter a printed look. Unless you do other typesetting procedures, like kerning and hyphenating words at the end of some lines, full justification can make your letter look worse with some extra wide spaces between words.

Using Pronouns Correctly

5. **Use *I* and *My* sparingly.** When most of the sentences in a cover letter begin with *I* or *My*, the writer may appear self-absorbed, self-centered, or egotistical. If the reader of the letter is turned off by this kind of impression (even if it is a false one for you), you could be screened out without ever having an interview. Of course, you will need to use these first-person pronouns because most of the information you put in your cover letter will be personal. But try to avoid using *I* and *My* at the beginnings of sentences and paragraphs.

6. **Refer to a business, company, corporation, or organization as "it" rather than "they."** Members of the Board may be referred to as "they," but a company is a singular subject requiring a singular verb. Note this example:

    New Products, Inc., was established in 1980. It grossed over a million dollars in sales during its first year.

7. **If you start a sentence with *This*, be sure that what *This* refers to is clear.** If the reference is not clear, insert some word or phrase to clarify what *This* means. Compare the following lines:

    My revised application for the new position will be faxed to you by noon on Friday. *This* should be acceptable to you.

    My revised application for the new position will be faxed to you by noon on Friday. This *method of sending the application* should be acceptable to you.

    A reader of the first sentence wouldn't know what *This* refers to. Friday? By noon on Friday? The revised application for the new position? The insertion after *This* in the second sentence, however, tells the reader that *This* refers to the use of faxing.

8. **Use *as follows* after a singular subject.** Literally, *as follows* means *as it follows*, so the phrase is illogical after a plural subject. Compare the following lines:

Incorrect:	My plans for the day of the interview are as follows:
Fixed:	My plans for the day of the interview are these:
Correct:	My plan for the day of the interview is as follows:
Better:	Here is my plan for the day of the interview:

    In the second set, the improved version avoids a hidden reference problem—the possible association of the silent "it" with *interview*. Whenever you want to use *as follows*, check to see whether the subject that precedes *as follows* is plural. If it is, don't use this phrase.

Using Verb Forms Correctly

9. **Make certain that subjects and verbs agree in number.** Plural subjects require plural forms of verbs. Singular subjects require singular verb forms. Most writers know these things, but problems arise when subject and verb agreement gets tricky. Compare the following lines:

   Incorrect: My education and experience has prepared me . . . .

   Correct: My education and experience have prepared me . . . .

   Incorrect: Making plans plus scheduling conferences were . . . .

   Correct: Making plans plus scheduling conferences was . . . .

   In the first set, *education* and *experience* are two things (you can have one without the other) and require a plural verb. A hasty writer might lump them together and use a singular verb. When you reread what you have written, look out for this kind of improper agreement between a plural subject and a singular verb.

   In the second set, *making plans* is the subject. It is singular, so the verb must be singular. The misleading part of this sentence is the phrase *plus scheduling conferences*. It may seem to make the subject plural, but it doesn't. In English, phrases that begin with such words as *plus*, *together with*, *in addition to*, *along with*, and *as well as* usually don't make a singular subject plural.

10. **Whenever possible, use active forms of verbs rather than passive forms.** Compare these lines:

    Passive: My report will be sent by my assistant tomorrow.

    Active: My assistant will send my report tomorrow.

    Passive: Your interest is appreciated.

    Active: I appreciate your interest.

    Passive: Your letter was received yesterday.

    Active: I received your letter yesterday.

   Sentences with passive verbs are usually longer and clumsier than sentences with active verbs. Spot passive verbs by looking for some form of the verb *to be* (such as *be*, *will be*, *have been*, *is*, *was*, and *were*) used with another verb.

   A trade-off in using active verbs is the frequent introduction of the pronouns *I* and *My*. To solve one problem, you might create another (see Tip 5 in this list). The task then becomes one of finding some other way to start a sentence.

11. **Be sure that present and past participles are grammatically parallel in a list.** See Tip 49 in Part 1. What is true about parallel forms in resumes is true also in cover letters. Present participles are action words ending in *-ing*, such as *creating*, *testing*, and *implementing*. Past participles are action words usually ending in *-ed*, such as *created*, *tested*, and *implemented*. These are called *verbals* because they are derived from verbs but are not strong enough to function as verbs in a sentence. When you use a string of verbals, control them by keeping them parallel.

12. **Use split infinitives only when *not* splitting them is misleading or awkward.** An *infinitive* is a verb preceded by the preposition *to*, as in *to create*, *to test*, and *to implement*. You split an infinitive when you insert an adverb

between the preposition and the verb, as in *to quickly create, to repeatedly test,* and *to slowly implement.* About 50 years ago, split infinitives were considered grammatical errors, but opinion about them has changed. Many grammar handbooks now recommend that you split your infinitives to avoid awkward or misleading sentences. Compare the following lines:

Split infinitive:	I plan to periodically send updated reports on my progress in school.
Misleading:	I plan periodically to send updated reports on my progress in school.
Misleading:	I plan to send periodically updated reports on my progress in school.

The first example is clear enough, but the second and third examples may be misleading. If you are uncomfortable with split infinitives, one solution is to move *periodically* further into the sentence: "I plan to send updated reports periodically on my progress in school."

Most handbooks that allow split infinitives also recommend that they not be split by more than one word, as in *to quickly and easily write.* A gold medal for splitting an infinitive should go to Lowell Schmalz, an Archie Bunker prototype in "The Man Who Knew Coolidge" by Sinclair Lewis. Schmalz, who thought that Coolidge was one of America's greatest presidents, split an infinitive this way: "*to instantly and without the least loss of time or effort find.* . . ."[1]

Using Punctuation Correctly

13. **Punctuate a compound sentence with a comma.** A compound sentence is one that contains two main clauses joined by one of seven conjunctions (*and, but, or, nor, for, yet,* and *so*). In English, a comma is customarily put before the conjunction if the sentence isn't unusually short. Here is an example of a compound sentence punctuated correctly:

    I plan to arrive at O'Hare at 9:35 a.m. on Thursday, and my trip by cab to your office should take no longer than 40 minutes.

    The comma is important because it signals that a new grammatical subject (*trip,* the subject of the second main clause) is about to be expressed. If you use this kind of comma consistently, the reader will rely on your punctuation and be on the lookout for the next subject in a compound sentence.

14. **Be certain not to put a comma between compound verbs.** When a sentence has two verbs joined by the conjunction *and,* these verbs are called *compound verbs.* Usually, they should not be separated by a comma before the conjunction. Note the following examples:

    I *started* the letter last night *and finished* it this morning.

    I *am sending* my resume separately *and would like* you to keep the information confidential.

---

[1] Sinclair Lewis, "The Man Who Knew Coolidge," *The Man Who Knew Coolidge* (New York: Books for Libraries Press, 1956), p. 29.

Both examples are simple sentences containing compound verbs. Therefore, no comma appears before *and*. In either case, a comma would send a wrong signal that a new subject in another main clause is coming, but no such subject exists.

Note: In a sentence with a series of three or more verbs, use commas between the verbs. The comma before the last verb is called the *serial comma*.

15. **Avoid using *as well as* for *and* in a series.** Compare the following lines:

Incorrect:	Your company is impressive because it has offices in Canada, Mexico, as well as the United States.
Correct:	Your company is impressive because it has offices in Canada and Mexico, as well as in the United States.

Usually, what is considered exceptional precedes *as well as*, and what is considered customary follows it. Note this example:

Your company is impressive because its managerial openings are filled by women as well as men.

16. **Put a comma after the year when it appears after the month.** Similarly, put a comma after the state when it appears after the city. Compare the following pairs of lines:

Incorrect:	In January, 1994 I was promoted to senior analyst.
Correct:	In January, 1994, I was promoted to senior analyst.

Incorrect:	I worked in Chicago, Illinois before moving to Dallas.
Correct:	I worked in Chicago, Illinois, before moving to Dallas.

17. **Put a comma after an opening dependent clause.** Compare the following lines:

Incorrect:	If you have any questions you may contact me by phone or fax.
Correct:	If you have any questions, you may contact me by phone or fax.

Actually, many writers of fiction and nonfiction don't use this kind of comma. The comma is useful, though, because it signals where the main clause begins. If you glance at the example with the comma, you can tell where the main clause is without even reading the opening clause. For a step up in clarity and readability, use this comma. It can give you a "feel" for a sentence even before you begin to read the words.

18. **Use semicolons when they are needed.** Semicolons are used also to separate main clauses when the second clause starts with a *conjunctive adverb* like *however*, *moreover*, and *therefore*. Compare the following lines:

Incorrect:	Your position in sales looks interesting, however, I would like more information about it.
Correct:	Your position in sales looks interesting; however, I would like more information about it.

The first example is incorrect because the comma before *however* is a *comma splice*, which is a comma that joins two sentences. It's like putting a comma instead of a period at the end of the first sentence and then starting the second sentence. A comma may be a small punctuation mark, but a comma splice is a huge grammatical mistake. What are your chances for getting hired if your cover

letter tells your reader that you don't recognize where a sentence ends, especially if a requirement for the job is good communication skills? Yes, you could
be screened out because of one little comma!

19. **Avoid putting a colon after a verb or a preposition to introduce information.** The reason is that the colon interrupts a continuing clause. Compare the
following lines:

  Incorrect: My interests in your company *are:* its reputation, the review
  of salary after six months, and your personal desire to hire
  handicapped persons.

  Correct: My interests in your company *are these:* its reputation, the
  review of salary after six months, and your personal desire to
  hire handicapped persons.

  Incorrect: In my interview with you, I would like *to:* learn how your
  company was started, get your reaction to my updated
  portfolio, and discuss your department's plans to move to a
  new building.

  Correct: In my interview with you, I would like to discuss *these issues:*
  how your company was started, what you think of my
  updated portfolio, and when your department may move to a
  new building.

Although some people may say that it is OK to put a colon after a verb like
include if the list of information is long, it is better to be consistent and avoid
colons after verbs altogether.

20. **Understand colons clearly.** People often associate colons with semicolons
because they sound alike, but colons and semicolons have nothing to do with
each other. Colons are the opposite of dashes. Dashes look backward, and colons
usually look forward to information about to be delivered. One common use of
the colon does look backward, however. Here are two examples:

  My experience with computers is limited: I have had only one course on
  programming, and I don't own a computer.

  I must make a decision by Monday: that is the deadline for renewing the
  lease for my apartment.

In each example, what follows the colon explains what was said before the
colon. Using a colon this way in a cover letter can impress a knowledgeable
reader who is looking for evidence of writing skills.

21. **Use slashes correctly.** Information about slashes is sometimes hard to find
because *slash* often is listed under a different name, such as *virgule* or *solidus*. If
you are not familiar with these terms, your hunt for advice on slashes may lead
to nothing.

At least know that one important meaning of a slash is *or*. For this reason, you often
see a slash in an expression like ON/OFF. This means that a condition or state, like
that of electricity activated by a switch, is either ON or OFF but never ON and OFF
at the same time. This condition may be one in which a change means going from
the current state to the opposite (or alternate) state. If the current state is ON and
there is a change, the next state will be OFF, and vice versa. With this understanding, you can recognize the logic behind the following examples:

Incorrect:	ON-OFF switch (on and off at the same time!)
Correct:	ON/OFF switch (on or off at any time)

Correct:	his-her clothes (unisex clothes, worn by both sexes)
Correct:	his/her clothes (each sex had different clothes)

Note: Although the slash is correct in *his/her* and is one way to avoid sexism, many people consider this expression clumsy. Consider some other wording, such as "clothes that both men and women wear" or "unisex clothes."

22. **Think twice about using *and/or*.** This stilted expression is commonly misunderstood to mean *two* alternatives, but it literally means *three*. Look at the following example:

    If you don't hear from me by Friday, please phone and/or fax me the information on Monday.

    What is the person at the other end to do? The sentence really states three alternatives: just phone, just fax, or phone *and* fax the information by Monday. For better clarity, use the connectives *and* or *or* whenever possible.

23. **Use punctuation correctly with quotation marks.** A common misconception is that commas and periods should be placed outside closing quotation marks, but the opposite is true. Compare the following lines:

Incorrect:	Your company certainly has the "leading edge", which means that its razor blades are the best on the market.
Correct:	Your company certainly has the "leading edge," which means that its razor blades are the best on the market.

Incorrect:	In the engineering department, my classmates referred to me as "the guru in pigtails". I was the youngest expert in programming languages on campus.
Correct:	In the engineering department, my classmates referred to me as "the guru in pigtails." I was the youngest expert in programming languages on campus.

    Unlike commas and periods, colons and semicolons go *outside* double quotation marks.

Using Words Correctly

24. **Avoid using lofty language in your cover letter.** A real turn-off in a cover letter is the use of elevated diction (high-sounding words and phrases) as a bid to seem important. Note the following examples, along with their straight-talk translations:

Elevated:	My background has afforded me experience in. . . .
Better:	In my previous jobs, I. . . .

Elevated:	Prior to that term of employment. . . .
Better:	Before I worked at. . . .

Elevated:	I am someone with a results-driven profit orientation.
Better:	I want to make your company more profitable.

Elevated: I hope to utilize my qualifications. . . .

Better: I want to use my skills. . . .

In letter writing, the shortest distance between the writer and the reader is the most direct idea.

25. **Check your sentences for an excessive use of compounds joined by *and*.** A cheap way to make your letters longer is to join words with *and* and do this repeatedly. Note the following wordy sentence:

> Because of my background and preparation for work and advancement with your company and new enterprise, I have a concern and commitment to implement and put into effect my skills and abilities for new solutions and achievements above and beyond your dreams and expectations. [44 words]

Just one inflated sentence like that would drive a reader to say, "No way!" The writer of the inflated sentence has said only this:

> Because of my background and skills, I want to contribute to your new venture. [14 words]

If, during rereading, you eliminate the wordiness caused by this common writing weakness, your letter will have a better chance of being read completely.

26. **Avoid using abstract nouns excessively.** Look again at the inflated sentence of the preceding tip, but this time with the abstract nouns in italic:

> Because of my *background* and *preparation* for *work* and *advancement* with your *company* and new *enterprise*, I have a *concern* and *commitment* to implement and put into *effect* my *skills* and *abilities* for new *solutions* and *achievements* above and beyond your *dreams* and *expectations*.

Try picturing in your mind any of the words in italic. You can't because they are *abstract nouns*, which means that they are ideas and not images of things you can see, taste, hear, smell, or touch. One certain way to turn off the reader of your cover letter is to load it with abstract nouns. The following sentence, containing some images, has a better chance of capturing the reader's attention:

> Having created seven multimedia tutorials with my videocamera and Gateway Pentium computer, I now want to create some breakthrough adult-learning packages so that your company, New Century Instructional Technologies, Inc., will exceed $50,000,000 in contracts by 1995.

Compare this sentence with the one loaded with abstract nouns. The one with images is obviously the better attention grabber.

27. **Avoid wordy expressions in your cover letters.** Note the following examples:

> at the location of (at)
> for the reason that (because)
> in a short time (soon)
> in a timely manner (on time)
> in spite of everything to the contrary (nevertheless)
> in the event of (if)
> in the proximity of (near)
> now and then (occasionally)
> on a daily basis (daily)
> on a regular basis (regularly)

on account of (because)
one day from now (tomorrow)
would you be so kind as to (please)

After each of these phrases is a suitable substitute in parentheses. Trim the fat wherever you can, and your reader will appreciate the leanness of your cover letter.

28. **At the end of your cover letter, don't make a statement that the reader can use to reject you.** For example, suppose that you close your letter with this statement:

> If you wish to discuss this matter further, please call me at (555) 555-5555.

This statement gives the reader a chance to think, "I don't wish it, so I don't have to call." Here is another example:

> If you know of the right opportunity for me, please call me at (555) 555-5555.

The reader may think, "I don't know of any such opportunity. How would I know what is right for you?" Avoid questions that prompt yes or no answers, such as, "Do you want to discuss this matter further?" If you ask this kind of question, you give the reader a chance to say no. Instead, make a closing statement that indicates your optimism about a positive response from the reader. Such a statement might begin with one of the following:

I am confident that . . . .
I look forward to . . . .

In this way, you invite the reader to say yes to further consideration.

Exhibit of Cover Letters

The following Exhibit contains sample cover letters that were prepared by professional resume writers to accompany resumes submitted for this book. In most cases, the names, addresses, and facts have been changed to ensure the confidentiality of the original sender and receiver of the letter. For each letter, however, the essential substance of the original remains intact.

If a cover letter was written for a resume displayed in the Gallery, the resume number is indicated along with the name of the resume writer. If the letter was written for a resume not included in the Gallery, only the name of the writer is given.

Use the Exhibit of Cover Letters as a reference whenever you need to write a cover letter for your resume. If you have trouble starting and ending letters, look at the beginnings and ends of the letters. If you need help on writing about your work experience, describing your abilities and skills, or mentioning some of your best achievements, look at the middle paragraph(s). Search for features that will give you ideas for making your own cover letters more effective. After you have examined the cover letters in the Exhibit, you will be better able to write an attention-getting letter—one that leads the reader to your resume and to scheduling an interview with you.

SANDRA L. COLLECTOR
52 Standing Bridge Road
Thomas, GA 19207
(555) 555-0000

Local Large Hospital
203 South Curve St.
Small city, SX 00000

I am exploring the possibility that you need someone with my qualifications.

As you can see by the enclosed resume, I have been able to successfully improve my employers' insurance collection rates by a significant amount - and I have enjoyed the challenge!

Today's private insurance and the government's Medicare insurance collection has become a major hurdle for physicians' offices to overcome. The life of a practice is, of course, dependent on being reimbursed for its services – the success of that practice is dependent on the medical care given to its patients. I am able to significantly contribute to the life of the practice so that the physician can care for his patients and contribute to the success of the practice.

I am currently working part time in Thomas and would like to reduce my time away from home. Your reputation as an excellent practice and place to work is the reason for this inquiry.

Sincerely,

Sandra L. Collector

Enclosure

For Resume 126. *Karen Swann, Clemson, South Carolina*

This letter is a probe to see what interest the reader may have in the applicant's skills. As a cover letter, it refers to the resume and appeals to the reader's economic interests.

EXPERT N. CREDIT

405 West Check Way, #111
Suburban Township, USA 99999
(555) 999-9999

September 11, XXXX

Mr. Tom N. Charge
Corporate Credit Manager
Great Tasting Foods Company
1000 Yum Yum Road
Big Town, USA 99999

Dear Mr. Charge:

It was a pleasure meeting you last Friday to discuss the credit position at Great Tasting Foods. I greatly appreciate the time you spent with me and the valuable information you offered about the position's various duties and responsibilities. It was a most informative and interesting interview.

Upon reflection of our discussion, I feel confident that my background and qualifications would make a positive contribution to your company. My experiences and accomplishments in credit and credit management closely parallel the defined objectives and expectations of this position. The international aspect of the business is of particular interest to me as I strive for continued professional growth and to expand my knowledge base.

I hope that my response to your concerns and my credentials relative to the job requirements are satisfactory and that a mutually beneficial working relationship will result. I look forward to hearing from you in the near future.

Thank you again for your time and consideration!

Sincerely,

Expert N. Credit

For Resume 171. *Cathleen M. Hunt, Chicago, Illinois*

An interview follow-up letter that expresses appreciation for the interview and focuses on how the person might benefit the company and what aspect is of special interest.

Chris Venture

OOO Dogwood Lane, Apartment 9 ◇ Castlewin, IN 00000
(000) 000-0000

January 1, 2000

Mr. Nick Karathus
Karathus Funeral Home, Inc.
000 Pine Street
Cliffton, Iowa 00000

Dear Mr. Karathus,

I recently graduated from Castlewin University with an Associates Degree in Science (Funeral Service Education). I am registered with the Indiana State Licensing Boards of Funeral Service and will be completing my internship in June of 1999. I am seeking a career opportunity as a Funeral Director with Karathus Funeral Home.

My professional goal is the determination to take all appropriate steps to meet the wishes of family members during the time of stress involved in the funeral process, dealing effectively with every difficulty that may arise. Dedicated and dependable, I enjoy turning negative situations into positives. During my career in this field I have developed a heart-felt desire to contribute to my profession in a positive, caring manner. I enjoy all age groups and am able to project a calm, controlled demeanor while dealing with challenging situations.

You will find me to be a willing, goal-oriented team member who appreciates the professional bonding associated with funeral services management. The experience I have gained would make me an asset to your facility and I would appreciate the opportunity to speak with you should you have need of my services.

Sincerely,

Chris Venture

3

For Resume 186. *Colleen S. Jaracz, Vincennes, Indiana*

After indicating the goal of the letter, the person carefully and tactfully expresses interest in funeral work because it offers opportunities for helping clients get through difficult times.

H **Charles G. Hamilton**

5236 Big Road
Charles, VA 65313
(504) 555-9146

November 4, XXXX

Jim Moore
Digital Paging
1234 Watson Drive
Charles, VA 65313

Dear Mr. Moore:

How would your company like an opportunity to benefit firsthand from the thousands of tax dollars it pays annually? As you know, a large percentage of federal tax spending is directed toward the military, and for the last 20 years, the U.S. Navy has been investing your money in my growth and training. The Navy provided me a dynamic, hands-on background in electronic systems operations and maintenance, as well as a decade of increasingly responsible supervisory experience. The end product of your tax dollars at work: A hard-working, experienced employee ready to put his training to work for your company.

From the Midwest originally, I served for three years at the Naval Reserve Center in Charles between 1989 and 1992. As I struggled with a loaded U-Haul through the traffic-clogged streets of Cross Lanes, I was stunned to find a friendly motorist holding up a line of cars to let me through. It was then I knew that I wanted to make Virginia my permanent home after retirement from the military.

My background, training, and qualifications are summarized on the attached résumé. I would appreciate the opportunity to talk with you personally about a career position within your organization.

Sincerely,

Charles G. Hamilton

Enclosure

4

For Resume 195. *Barbie Dallman, Charleston, West Virginia*

The original initial in the upper-left corner resembled stamped gold leaf. The first paragraph, in which the applicant playfully presents an argument for being hired, is novel.

Melanie Stone, CRNA
1555 Main Street • Charleston, WV 25302 • (304) 555-5555

November 4, XXXX

Roger Cummings, MD
Pleasants Hospital
411 Pleasants Drive
Boston, MA 55555

Dear Dr. Cummings:

For the last several years, whenever I've thought about New England—Boston in particular—I've found myself musing about its opportunities for professional growth and continuing education. Boston is the heart of medicine in America. Its reputation for significant research and professional excellence is world renown. More than anything, I want to make myself a valuable member of Boston's medical community.

As a CRNA with four years' experience at a busy teaching hospital, I am proud of my reputation for outstanding clinical performance. I can offer top-notch skills as well as clinical instructor experience and a balanced background that includes both nursing and fine arts. Because I love my career, you'll find me eager to be an involved employee, serving on committees and assisting in any area where I can be effective. Locally, I have played an active role in maintaining CRNA professional standards and expanding our scope of practice.

My résumé is enclosed for your consideration. I would appreciate the chance to talk with you personally regarding opportunities within your facility. I'll follow up next week to see if there's an interest. In the meantime, please feel free to call me at the number listed above.

Respectfully,

Melanie Stone

Enclosure

5

Provided by: *Barbie Dallman, Charleston, West Virginia*

An interesting letter because the first two paragraphs are fresh without any cliché commonly found in cover letters. The first paragraph begins as a narrative.

OPTIONS GALORE
123 X Street • Anywhere, America 00000 • (000) 000-0000 • optionsgalore@aol.com

Date

Mr. Contact Person
Sales Manager - Eastern Sales
XYZ Printers
City
State

Re: Account Executive position

Dear Mr. Person:

I am taking the liberty of writing because I believe that you may be interested in a candidate with my credentials.

I am specifically interested in exploring sales opportunities with XYZ Printing Company. Here's why: having been exposed to the industry all my life, and with printing and sales in my blood, I am ready for greater challenges. I'm currently searching to work for a company with the capacity to handle national accounts and larger prospects than Your Printing Company, to enable me to maximize my sales potential. I have trained well for this position, including a year spent apprenticing in each department of the company, learning the technical details and fine points of the business.

With innate sales savvy and a keen understanding of the technical ingredients of commercial printing, I am able to reach the principal decision-makers of target companies, present practical, efficient methods to manufacture the client's products, and offer total printing solutions. I am committed to building partnerships/customer loyalty, and pride myself on keeping up-to-date on the constant changes in industry technology.

If you are seeking a consultant in the trade who can provide total printing solutions, I would welcome a personal interview to discuss the ways in which my expertise will help you accomplish your goals. Thank you for your consideration. I look forward to meeting with you.

Sincerely,

Options Galore

For Resume 18. *Beverley Kagan, North Miami Beach, Florida*

This person wants to know what interest the reader may have in someone with the person's skills. The letter freely indicates an ability to be successful in sales and the will to do so.

Don Saltman

0000 Elbert Drive
Somewhere, IN 47591

(812) 888-0000
e-mail: @somewhere.net

January 1, 2000

Mr. Larry Whatever
Thais Manufacturing Company
0000 Bayou
Somewhere, Louisiana 00000

Dear Mr. Whatever,

Unfortunately, I find myself in the position of searching for a **MRO/Buyer** position with your company. I say 'unfortunately' because I enjoyed my work at BRG Industries very much and was sorry that the company elected to close the Somewhere facility.

I have extensive experience in the Metal Working Industry and could immediately contribute to the effectiveness of your organization in this capacity. You will find me to be a candidate with excellent credentials and, should you offer me the opportunity, an employee with the willingness to put all my energies into effectively administering my duties.

Should you desire more information, please contact me. I look forward to hearing from you soon.

Sincerely,

Don Saltman

For Resume 73. *Colleen S. Jaracz, Vincennes, Indiana*

The opening of the letter is an attempt to catch the attention of the reader through an unexpected statement that calls for an explanation. Look for a hook to grab attention.

Gina J. Browne, RHIT, CMT

43 Vintage Road
Bayview, Maine XXXXX
(207) xxx-xxxx

March 7, 20XX

Northeast Medical Transcription
30 Savannah Street
Suite One
Bayview, Maine XXXXX

Dear Sir or Madam:

I am very interested in being considered for the **Office Manager** position which was recently advertised in the *Bayview Daily News*. I can offer you more than twenty years of professional office experience.

As you can see from the enclosed resume, I have worked at Downeast Maine Medical Center for the past thirty-three years, with most of those years devoted to the Medical Records Department. Throughout my career I have had the opportunity to develop my skills and expertise in the areas of medical records management, transcription, office management, staff supervision and training. Although I am still employed at DMMC, my position in the Medical Records Department was eliminated late last year. During the past year DMMC decided to outsource its transcription service, which resulted in my position elimination.

I have always enjoyed my work and look forward to continuing my career in the healthcare field. I have a high degree of motivation, am detail-oriented and have excellent organizational and communication skills.

I am very excited about this opportunity and would like to meet with you to discuss your needs and my qualifications in more depth. To set up an interview, you may reach me at (207) XXX-XXXX.

Thank you for your consideration.

Sincerely,

Gina J. Browne, RHIT, CMT

Enclosure

8

For Resume 128. *Joan M. Roberts, Bangor, Maine*

In seeking a new position, the individual has more experience to offer than a record of education. The letter plays up the applicant's experience, skills, and motivation.

Scott Bodarmel
0000 Harrison Street - Somewhere, IN 00000
(000) 000-0000

January 22, 2000

Tharson Enterprises, Inc.
P. O. Box 0000
Farguson, ND 00000

Good morning,

I recently graduated from Somewhere University with an Associate of Science degree in **Business Administration - Management Information Systems** and I am interested in applying my skills toward becoming a quality team member within your organization.

I have given my time and attention to developing the very best talents I have for my future employer. I am enthusiastic and positive about my career potential, looking forward to the challenges ahead and excited about the possibilities. I uphold the highest standards of integrity in my work and believe in the establishment of a loyal, long-term relationship with the company where I will be employed.

◆ I am willing to relocate. My wife is a nurse and we presently have no children. We anticipate developing our careers and establishing our future home together.

◆ As an older graduate (26) I feel that I can offer my employer a maturity and confidence that will make me an effective employee. I realize the importance of my education and will actively pursue all continuing educational opportunities within your industry, as they present themselves.

I would like the opportunity to discuss the ways my background and skills might be of benefit to you. Also, I would like to demonstrate that, along with my credentials, I have the personality that would make me a successful addition to the management team.

Sincerely,

Scott Bodarmel

9

For Resume 28. *Colleen S. Jaracz, Vincennes, Indiana*

Boldfacing makes the applicant's degree area stand out. Large diamond bullets point to major selling points about the candidate. The writer is upbeat and enthusiastic throughout.

MARTY M. MATLIN
0000 North West
Anywhere, USA
(000) 000-0000

Initiative, intelligence, and a personality that is conducive to a successful career in sales are among the qualifications I can offer an employer. As an honors student anticipating graduation this summer, I am interested in exploring opportunities that will make use of my skills, education, and experience. The enclosed résumé outlines my qualifications, which include:

♦ **Academic Preparation:** A.S. in Marketing from Atlinger Junior College ... coursework emphasis in Marketing included Consumer Behavior, Marketing Research, and Channels of Distribution (partial list).

♦ **Sales Experience:** Successful commission sales experience in a variety of wholesale and retail environments ... doubled my territory volume as a route salesman/merchandiser and earned numerous local sales awards and regional recognition as a retail sales associate.

♦ **Personal Profile:** Self-starter--supported myself through school by working as many as three jobs concurrently ... involvement in co-curricular activities developed leadership skills and expanded my decision-making and management skills.

Should your organization be in need of an individual with my potential, I would welcome the opportunity to meet with you. I recognize that tangible achievements require commitment, intelligence, and hard work. I believe my early successes in sales indicate a strong future, and I am committed to generating bottom-line profits for your company.

Your schedule is undoubtedly busy. I can be available for a telephone interview at your convenience and am anxious to meet and explore our mutual interests. In advance, thank you for your time and consideration.

Sincerely,

Marty M. Matlin

Enclosure

10

For Resume 213. *Susan Britton Whitcomb, Fresno, California*

This letter not only refers to the resume but mentions specifically three key areas. By putting diamond bullets before them and boldfacing them, the writer has made them clearly visible.

Rhonda Nilson, R.N.

10 Langford Avenue, Elliot, NJ 00000 • (555) 555-5555 • Willing to Relocate

July 16, XXXX

Wecare Behavioral Health Center
35 Edge Way
Elliot NJ 00000

Attention: Nurse Recruiter

Dear Nurse Recruiter:

I am interested in pursuing the nursing position recently advertised in the *Elliot Tribune*. I am confident that my strong clinical and human relations skills, conscientiousness, and ability to work effectively under pressure will make me a valuable addition to your nursing staff.

I recently graduated summa cum laude from Elliot Community College, and received an award for academic excellence and outstanding achievement in nursing practice. My classmates frequently relied on me to assist them with their studies, and I often led tutoring sessions.

My life experiences prior to nursing school will strengthen my abilities as a nurse. After earning my B.A. degree from Midland State College, I pursued an acting career in Manhattan. In trying to launch this career, I held numerous positions requiring strong interpersonal, communication and presentation skills, and the ability to think and respond quickly. These experiences have also helped me to relate easily and comfortably with all types of people and to appreciate each person's uniqueness.

If your facility is in need of a competent, energetic registered nurse with a mature attitude, please contact me at (555) 555-5555. My schedule is extremely flexible, and I am available to work whatever hours or days you require.

Sincerely,

Rhonda Nilson, R.N.

Enclosure

Provided by: *Rhoda Kopy, Toms River, New Jersey*

A strong, convincing letter that displays interest, confidence, academic excellence, people skills, maturity, and humility in the willingness to work any hours or days.

ANTHONY W. KRAFT
111 S. Pinella
Emmitt, Arkansas 00000
(000) 000-0000

September 12, XXXX

Mr. Robert Jones
President
Powerplant, Inc.
2222 Main Street
Emmitt, Arkansas 00000

Dear Mr. Jones:

I am enclosing my résumé for your consideration in response to the advertised opening for **Operations Manager** of the Plastics Manufacturing Facility. I was extremely interested to read of this opportunity, as my background of over 12 years of supervisory experience matches the skills which you require for this position.

I recently relocated in Emmitt after nineteen years of service in the U.S. Air Force. As you can see from my résumé, my last assignment involved supervision of more that 60 persons in the operation of a full service aircraft maintenance facility. During my five-year assignment, I implemented procedures which measurably cut costs and production flowtime while reducing consumer complaints and exceeding quality control goals.

Additionally, my prior experience as a team member evaluating the quality of maintenance units located worldwide enhanced my ability to critically analyze and document existing procedures and recommend production changes, and gave me a working knowledge of OSHA and EPA regulations. I also have received formal training in management principles, communication skills, team building and leadership. I believe these skills would prove an asset to your company.

I look forward to speaking to you in the near future to schedule an interview at your convenience, during which I hope to share with you in detail how my skills could contribute to your organization.

Sincerely,

Anthony W. Kraft

Enclosure

12

For Resume 196. *Laura C. Karlak, Bartlesville, Oklahoma*

Putting the position in boldface is useful when a company has placed ads for several different positions. The reader can see at a glance which ad the applicant is responding to.

David L. O'Connor

493 Crestwood Lane • Smithville, NY 00000
(555) 555-5555

November 7, 20XX

Mr. Anthony Dunbar, Executive Director
Human Services Institute
9 Chestnut Dr.
Garland, NY 00000

Dear Mr. Dunbar:

Enclosed you will find my resume in response to your advertisement in the *Evening Tribune* for a Project Director.

In regard to our telephone conversation on Nov. 1st, I have reviewed the information you faxed to me that day. As you can see on my resume, I am very strong in the qualifications for this position. I am a self-motivated individual who started and runs my own business. Every position I have held in business and public office has required a nonjudgmental attitude in dealing wih the many different people and situations that arise. I am a very organized person with exceptional communications abilities and excellent personal and working relationships.

I have worked as state manager for Texas Refinery since 1985, and in my capacity as Town Supervisor am currently negotiating economic development contracts for the Town of Smithville. My experience has given me an increased awareness of the needs of the surrounding areas in Sullivan County and a desire to see those needs met and to be a part of the resulting growth. In addition, I was a school board member for three years, and I am *very* familiar with the Byron School District since I have lived almost my entire life in the Smithville/Sullivan Country area.

I will contact you within 5 days to confirm your receipt of my resume and to arrange a convenient time for an interview. I feel confident that an in-person discussion would be time well spent and am looking forward to meeting with you. If you have any questions or require additional information, I can be reached at (555) 555-5555.

Sincerely yours,

David L. O'Connor

enclosure

13

For Resume 228. *Catherine Seebald, Wellsville, New York*

A strong letter. Instead of merely sending a resume and cover letter in response to an ad, the applicant has talked with the reader over the phone to establish rapport and interest.

CHRISTINE JONES
974 North Stanley • Coopersville, Illinois 60000
(555) 555-1234

November 15, 20XX

James Lowden
Department of Human Resources
Saint Joseph University Health Services Center
3 Saint Joseph Plaza
Kansas City, MO 60000

Dear Robin:

An acquaintance of mine, Dr. Cory Greene, Professor of Biostatistics at Saint Joseph University, spoke to me recently of your need for a Facility Manager, Gift Shop at Saint Joseph University Hospital. With a strong background in department management and customer service, I am most interested in this position. My resume is enclosed for your review.

I am currently the Assistant Manager of Textbook Services, a division of the University Bookstore, at Eastern Illinois University. I interact daily with hundreds of students, faculty, and administrative staff and am proud of the high standard of customer service our department has established. My job is to manage the staff and distribution system for making this one of the most efficiently run operations on campus.

Although I have found this work satisfying, I am looking for an opportunity to refocus my career and move ahead into retail management. I am confident my background and skills in customer service, administration, staff supervision, and product distribution would transition well into a retail environment, and my understanding of the university and institutional culture would make me a good fit with your staffing needs.

I look forward to meeting with you and other staff to discuss my qualifications in further detail and to learn more about your Gift Shop operations. Once a mutual interest has been established, I would be happy to provide you with references and other credentials. Your cooperation in keeping this employment inquiry confidential, at this time, would be appreciated. Thank you for your consideration.

Sincerely,

Christine Jones

14

For Resume 181. *Carla Culp Coury, Glen Carbon, Illinois*

The reference to an acquaintance as the source of information about the opening shifts the status of the writer from outsider to insider, providing a powerful advantage in job seeking.

Priscilla Hagan

936 Hedgemont Street
San Francisco, California 99592
(767) 498-5322

Dear Hiring Manager:

I would like to discuss the possibility of working with your organization in a position that would benefit from my ability to work effectively with both children and adults. Details on my background are enclosed in this letter.

You can count on me to build trust, stay calm in a crisis, and produce effectively under stress when I am helping people in different types of healing situations.

Here are a few of my qualifications:

- RMT national designation
- Medical Technology experience at Stanford University Hospital, San Diego State Hospital and Seattle General Hospital
- B.S. degree in Medical Technology from San Francisco State College
- Certification in Herbology
- Sales experience at The Toy Shoppe and Herbal Green in Bellevue, Washington

Volunteer work that may be of benefit to you includes designing and presenting a three-part course on different types of handicaps to sixth graders in the public school system, and coauthoring a play for children to help them cope with admission to a hospital.

My strong interpersonal skills and nonthreatening style carry me through in all phases of my life, and, of course, I am a team player.

It is now time to return to the work I love after having raised children to school age.

If you see a potential fit between your needs and my abilities, I would appreciate speaking with you at a personal interview. At that time I would hope to show you how I can contribute to the continued growth and success of your organization.

I will be in the city on February 20th and would like to meet with you then, if that would be convenient for you. I look forward to hearing from you.

Sincerely,

Priscilla Hagan

PH/pf

15

Provided by: *Phyllis Fern, Cranston, Rhode Island*

A cover letter that serves also as a resume. The opening paragraph expresses the applicant's goal. The second paragraph is like a profile, and the third summarizes qualifications.

LAWRENCE D. ENFORCER

88 Safeway Lane, Crimefree, NJ • Willing to Relocate   **(555) 555-5555**

August 16, XXXX

Carl D. Atkinson
Chief of Police
North Kinlan Police Department
North Kinlan, NJ 00000

Dear Chief Atkinson:

I am interested in pursuing a law enforcement position with your department and have enclosed my resume for your review.

With a background in the security field and in emergency medical care, I have had a great deal of experience in protecting the public's safety and welfare. In tense situations I remain calm and poised, and confidently take control. My ability to quickly assess and effectively react to crises has led to several promotions and increased job responsibilities.

My work-related accomplishments include the following:

- Supervised up to 15 security officers responsible for the safety of 20,000 to 45,000 amusement park guests daily; handled diverse security emergencies, including those related to drugs, drinking, fighting, and lost children.

- Deterred internal and external theft at a major department store; apprehended over 70 shoplifters in a two-year period and was selected to monitor employees suspected of theft.

- Managed a wide range of medical emergencies, working cooperatively with law enforcement officers and paramedics.

- Oriented new employees to their positions and clarified company policies and procedures.

- Documented all security/medical incidents thoroughly and accurately.

If you are in need of a law enforcement officer with a strong sense of community, the desire to work toward a safe, crime-free environment, and an academic background in criminal justice, please contact me for an interview. I am confident that I will be an asset to your department.

Sincerely,

Lawrence D. Enforcer

Enclosure

16

For Resume 148. *Rhoda Kopy, Toms River, New Jersey*

Acccomplishments are specified in the letter to ensure that they will be seen by the reader. Listing the accomplishments with bullets and line spacing gives them additional impact.

Jane T. Watkins

520 Bournemouth Road
Wilmington, North Carolina 28401
(910) 123-456

Dear Employer:

If your financial institution is currently seeking candidates for Teller positions, I would appreciate your consideration of my qualifications.

My experience includes a great deal of responsibility in handling financial matters. As the owner of my own business, which I have recently sold, I handled all banking transactions, preparation of tax reports, and all accounts payable. I am a very detail-oriented person and feel confident that I would be able to learn the duties of a teller very quickly.

In addition to my financial skills, working with the public is an area where I excel. I have successfully handled all aspects of customer service including assisting customers in a fast-paced environment, resolving problems, and working with customers from a wide range of backgrounds. With my skills in this area combined with my ability to handle to financial matters and my desire to excel in a banking career, I believe I would be an asset to your staff.

Thank you for taking the time to review my enclosed resume. I will contact you in the near future and will be glad to provide any additional information you require.

I look forward to talking with you soon and learning more about opportunities with you company.

Sincerely,

Jane T. Watkins

Enclosure

17

For Resume 183. *Sandy Adcox Saburn, Wilmington, North Carolina*

A straightforward letter in which the writer displays interest, experience, people skills, confidence, excellence, gratitude, a resolve to follow up, cooperativeness, and anticipation.

Glen L. Holt

1902 Coachman's Trail • South Bend, Indiana 46637
(219) 243-0296

Dear Prospective Employer:

Please accept this letter and accompanying résumé as my expressed interest in joining your company as a **Systems Programmer**. At this point in my career I am researching opportunities.

I am detail-oriented, and possess the ability to understand technical aspects of various PC computers and associated equipment. At my current job I am responsible for setting my own schedule, performing numerous in-house and on-site assignments, and rendering appropriate customer follow-up service.

I am able to identify and solve customer problems effectively. I especially enjoy challenges, diversity in daily tasks, and working with people. My personal characteristics include ... a high level of dedication to my work...excellent technical training...strong values of integrity and honesty. In addition I realize the importance of teaching PC owners how to use their systems effectively.

Thank you for your time and courtesy in reviewing these materials. I welcome the opportunity to meet with you and discuss your company's need in greater depth.

Should you wish to arrange an interview, I can be reached at the telephone number listed above after 5:00 p.m. I look forward to hearing from you.

Sincerely,

Glen L. Holt

18

For Resume 23. *Patricia Strefling, Niles, Michigan*

A series of five short paragraphs makes this exploratory letter easy to read. The paragraph sequence is purpose, skills, worker traits, thanks and interest, and interview details.

15 Anderson Street
Elizabeth, NJ 55555

PAUL DRISCOLL

(000) 000-0000

January 2, 20XX

Farnsworth College
Human Resources Department
Route 577
Scotch Plains, NJ 07076

Dear Human Resources Manager:

Please accept this letter and attached resume as an expression of my interest in the position of College Recruiter for Farnsworth College, as advertised in Sunday's Star-Ledger.

I feel I have the skills you require to interest high school students in your various programs and campus activities, both academic and non-academic. Much of my present career in law enforcement has centered around youth programs, and there have been many occasions when I visited local high schools to address assemblies on matters of social concern.

On a personal level, I am considered a good judge of character and can relate easily to many different types of people. This would enable me to identify students most likely to fit in with the character of the university and enhance its image of competency as an academic institution.

As a recent retiree from the Elizabeth Police force, having been a civil servant for the past 25 years (since my teens), I have been preparing for a second career by obtaining my A.A. degree in Social Sciences. Your opportunity for a College Recruiter sounds like the type of position that would allow me to make use of my education and social services background to make a significant contribution to your staff. The travel requirement would not present a problem for me.

I would appreciate an interview to further discuss the details of this position and will call you next week to see if such a meeting can be arranged. Thank you for your consideration.

Sincerely,

Paul Driscoll
Enclosure

19

For Resume 150. *Melanie A. Noonan, West Paterson, New Jersey*

A letter by a mature individual who has just retired from one career and is at the threshold of another. The tone is mature throughout and shows genuine interest in an interview.

KEITH M. DAIGLE

7 Hapworth Street   Winter, ME 04432   **(555) 989-3251**

June 7, 20XX

Sam Connor
Plant Controller
Industrial Paper Corporation
Winter, ME 04432

Dear Mr. Connor:

At your suggestion made during a conversation we had at Dover College in 1994, I am enclosing a résumé for you to review. Perhaps you'll remember me as a student in your Business Finance class. Now that I have completed my A.S. degree, I want to secure an accounting position. preferably with a manufacturing company.

I have been highly successful in my academic endeavors attaining a 3.8 GPA in all of my accounting coursework. This field is exciting to me and one where I feel much of my acquired experience would be useful. As the summary of qualifications of my résumé states, I have accumulated computer, analytical, organizational, and interpersonal skills which, as you know, are very important in an accounting position.

What I *do* have in terms of enthusiasm and commitment to a career in accounting makes up for my lack of actual accounting work experience. The jobs I have held provided many opportunities to interact with the public, lead a team of workers and complete various administrative tasks (writing reports, planning daily activities and resolving problems).

My future plans are to pursue my Bachelor's degree and to learn all I can about the accounting field, so I can be a valuable employee with a strong educational and experiential foundation.

Please feel free to give one of the enclosed résumés to anyone in or outside of Industrial Paper Corporation who you feel might be able to assist me in my career search. *Thank you* for your time and assistance.

Sincerely,

Keith M. DAIGLE
Enclosures

20

For Resume 3. *Elizabeth (Lisa) M. Carey, Waterville, Maine*

The writer builds on a previous conversation with the reader, and this is a strong start for the letter. The end is strong, too, as it asks that enclosed resumes be passed on to others.

WILL CASE
1234 - Totem Avenue SE
Mytown, USA 99999
555/555-5555

May 1, 20XX

Mr. Jackson Lee
789 East Drive
Another City, USA 99999

Dear Mr. Lee:

This is in response to your request for commercial divers sent to Harry Smith of the Divers Institute, from which I will graduate next month. Your proposal is of particular interest to me because of its hazardous materials component. My primary interest in the commercial diving industry has always been in hazardous materials, an interest which was strongly confirmed during that segment of the Institute's training. I not only performed very well, I performed with both a high level of confidence and an appreciation of the potential dangers. Coupled with my commitment to safety and training in diving medicine, I believe I am an excellent candidate for your project.

YOUR REQUIREMENTS	MY QUALIFICATIONS
◆ 40-Hour 29 CFR 1910.120 hazardous materials course.	◆ 80 hours of hazardous materials course training (29 CFR 1910.120).
◆ Proof of diver training.	◆ Graduating on June 2, 20XX, from the Divers Institute, with certificates in hazardous materials, advanced scuba, nondestructive testing, and rigger certification.
◆ Experience in diving/tending and handling work involving hazardous materials.	◆ Upon graduation will have 38 – 40 hours of dive time, plus 20 – 30 hours of repair and maintenance work on underwater television cameras, photo equipment, and ROVs.
	I have made a 20-foot hazardous materials dive into a 150-foot horizontal sewer overflow pipe in a 68-inch culvert to inspect the pipe. I used a Superlite 27 with a vulcanized dry suit.
	As a member of the State National Guard, I had NBC (nuclear/biological/chemical) training.

I look forward to talking to you and discussing in further detail how I can successfully contribute to your project to recover submerged discarded batteries.

Sincerely,

Will Case

Enclosure

21

For Resume 89. *Carole S. Barns, Woodinville, Washington*

A distinctive letter that features a table in which the writer shows with diamond bullets that the reader's requirements are more than adequately met by the applicant's qualifications.

LORETTA L. LIERHOST

0000 Independence Blvd., #000
Parma Heights, Ohio 55555
555.555.5555

sec|re|tary (sek´re ter´é), *n, pl.* -tar|ies. **1** a person who writes letters and keeps records for a person, company, club, committee, or the like: *a private secretary. Our club has a secretary who keeps the minutes of the meeting.* **SYN:** clerk. **2** an official who has charge of a department of the government or similar organization. The Secretary of the Treasury is the head of the Treasury Department. **3** a diplomatic agent, usually of a lower rank in an embassy or legation, often designated at first secretary, second secretary, and so on. *Abbr:* sec. **4** a writing desk with a set of drawers and often with shelves for books [<Late Latin *sécrétárius* confidential officer < Latin *sécrétum* a secret, neuter of *sécrétus*; see etym. Under secret][1]

[1]*The World Book Dictionary*; Volume two L-Z: 1989 Edition, p. 1880

The above is *one* description of a secretary. Please allow me to give you my *personal* description:

A knowledgeable, dedicated and self-motivated individual who utilizes their skills efficiently to direct office operations, communicate on a professional level and perform with confidence and competence. Add over thirty years of experience, and you have Loretta L. Lierhost.

Enclosed is my résumé, outlining professional experience and qualifications. I feel that with my credentials, I will serve as an asset to your company or business. Please consider this information and feel free to call with questions or to set up a personal interview to discuss your requirements.

Thank you very much for your time in review of my résumé and for consideration of future employment. I hope to hear from you soon.

Sincerely,

Loretta L. Lierhost

Enclosure: Professional Résumé

22

For **Resume 12.** *Lorie Lebert, Novi, Michigan*

Another distinctive cover letter, showing originality, daring (to be different), and cleverness. Overall, this letter is a novel way to call attention to the enclosed resume.

LAURA CONNERS
4130 Greenville Parkway
Marietta, Georgia 30007
℘ [770] 555-5555 — [770] 555- 6666 (fax) — conner124@email.com

September 15, XXXX

Ms. Sherry Withers
Assistant Manager
Cratchett & Company
1000 Pleasant Hill Road
Duluth, Georgia 30000

Dear Ms. Withers:

I want to join the Cratchett & Company team as you launch your very visible Mall of Georgia store. A work ethic that comes from my years as an entrepreneur and an in-depth knowledge of the book business could make us a perfect match.

My résumé can help you learn more about me. It may not look like others you have seen. I have not provided the usual, sterile lists of responsibilities. In their place are nearly a half dozen contributions that advanced my organizations' missions, bottom line, or both.

There is no magic in what I do. My love of every kind of book lets me discern and satisfy readers' needs. Beyond that, I mastered every task in the business, from designing displays to arranging for book signings.

Now that my family needs less of my time, I want to return to my first love—bookselling. However, words on paper are no substitute for hearing about your requirements at first hand. May I call in few days to arrange an interview?

Sincerely,

Laura Conners

Encl.: Résumé

23

Provided by: *Donald Orlando, Montgomery, Alabama*

This writer makes every attempt to avoid clichés and to find new expressions in job search documents. Study each paragraph to see how he has steered clear of typical remarks.

DAVID DANTON
265 Charlotte Street
Asheville, NC 28801
828/555-1212

Dear Sir or Madam:

I'll be blunt. I'm looking for a "9 to 5" position that will allow me to come home to my family at night with a decent but not astronomical paycheck. I've got collections, fund-raising, and accounting experience—lots of it. I know how to do payroll, corporate and individual tax returns, general ledger, A/R, A/P, all types of bookkeeping.

I know—I'm overqualified. You're thinking, "He'll be bored. He won't last six months." Wrong. I sold my business in November for a tidy profit, my wife is a registered nurse with an excellent position she wants to keep, and I just spent a summer at home with my three children. I am not looking for inspiration from my job; my family gives me that. I *am* looking for a job that will leave me with time and energy for my family. And I *like* bookkeeping.

If we find that we work comfortably together, I will stay for the next 14 years until I retire. You get what you pay for, but in my case you'll get more than you pay for. Give me a try.

May we talk? I look forward to your response, and thank you for your time.

Best regards,

David Danton

enc.

24

Provided by: *Dayna Feist, Asheville, North Carolina*

A direct letter in which the applicant wants to dispense with formalities, play no games, be frank, speak shoulder to shoulder, be vital, and "tell it like it is."

Robert L. Bachman

000 Magnolia Court ■ Hendersonville, Tennessee 37075   (615) 000-0000

November 10, XXXX

PO Box 00000
Nashville, TN 00000-0000

Dear Hiring Manager:

The position of **Multi-Line Adjuster** advertised in the November 2nd edition of *The Tennessean* is of particular interest to me, and I have enclosed a summary of my experience and qualifications for your review.

Your ad states a preference for someone with experience in trucking claim adjusting. I have this necessary experience, having handled numerous bodily injury and damage claims for self-insured trucking companies while employed with Capitol & Company. In fact, of all the different types of claims I have handled during my career, negotiating and settling trucking claims has proven the most satisfactory both personally and professionally.

I am a highly productive yet thorough adjuster with a solid background in handling all types of claims, sales and marketing, and customer service. In addition, I am well organized, highly capable of researching and coordinating detailed data, and communicate effectively with policyholders, corporate management, and other professionals.

Should you agree that I am well qualified for the Multi-Line Adjuster position, I would look forward to the opportunity to meet with a company representative to discuss my qualifications and your specific needs in more detail. Thank you for your time and consideration.

Sincerely,

Robert L. Bachman

Enclosure

25

Provided by: *Carolyn S. Braden, Hendersonville, Tennessee*

A response to an ad. Lines enclosing the phone number make it easy to see, and boldfacing the job target makes it clearly visible. The letter shows how the person is right for the job.

DEBRA SUE CORDIAN
9000 Rockview
Tyler, Texas 75701
(903) 999-6666

November 13, xxxx

Mr. Dean Holbrook
Holbrook Advertising Company
P.O. Box 1000
Tyler, Texas 75700

Dear Mr. Holbrook:

As a highly organized and efficient professional with extensive experience and expertise in **sales and marketing management**, along with exceptional public relations, communication, and interpersonal skills, I am confident that I will be a valuable member of your sales and marketing team.

As a marketing assistant with a major insurance firm, I provided marketing assistance and administrative support to the agency manager and nineteen agents. Achievements included creating more efficient report forms; designing, composing, and creating a monthly newsletter, which I distributed to clients; and performing detailed marketing analysis. Developing an excellent rapport with the agency manager, territory sales manager, agents, and clients significantly improved continuity in operations and employee morale, which resulted in an increase in market share and sales revenues.

During my tenure with a manufacturer of hyperthermia equipment, I was accountable for all aspects of marketing and sales administration and a staff of seven. This position encompassed planning and coordinating international, national, and local meetings, training programs, trade shows, and symposiums. Additionally, I restructured, improved, and instructed training classes each quarter for sales representatives and customers.

Mr. Holbrook, I am excited about joining your advertising company and leading your sales team toward unsurpassed growth in the new millennium. So that we may discuss some ideas I have to accomplish this goal, I will call you next Wednesday to schedule a meeting at your convenience. Thank you for your time and consideration, and I look forward to visiting with you soon.

Sincerely,

DEBRA SUE CORDIAN

Enclosure

26

Provided by: *Ann Klint, Tyler, Texas*

The page border makes this letter different. The first paragraph is a strong start, and the second focuses on achievements. The third covers scope; and the fourth, motivation.

WENDY LILLIP

24 Hawkin Drive   Brick, New Jersey 08723   (632) 349-2224

Dear Superintendent:

As a New Jersey Certified Teacher of the Handicapped with more than seven years of experience, I can make a valuable contribution to your school system and a worthwhile impact on your students. Patience, empathy and structure are the hallmarks of my teaching technique.

Throughout my professional experience, I have brought energy and enthusiasm to the classroom, working to meet the specialized needs of students, both intellectually and emotionally. My skills have been tested in diversified environments. I have proven myself time and again to be a highly effective teacher, with a pure love for teaching.

As a Teacher of the Handicapped within your school system, I will once again prove my capabilities, as well as my commitment to education.

Since I have provided you with but a brief overview of my background, I look forward to the opportunity for a personal interview as the chance to provide you with further insight into my professional value.

Thank you for your consideration.

Yours truly,

Wendy Lillip
Enclosure

27

Provided by: *Lorie Lebert, Novi, Michigan*

The concern of this letter is to sell the applicant to the reader. Experience, skills, worker traits, motivation, commitment, interest in an interview, and thanks are the key issues.

NOREEN ANDERSON
6809 Strawberry Lane • Orchards, NJ 00000
555-555-5555

Dear Manager:

I am interested in pursuing a position with your bank as a Customer Service or New Account Representative. With nine years of experience in banking, a talent for promoting bank products, and a reputation for providing exceptional service, I am confident that I can be a valuable addition to your team. My resume is enclosed for your review.

My philosophy in relating with customers is to always be willing to go the extra mile, and I am flattered by the number of people who specifically requested my assistance. The banking industry is extremely competitive, so superior service is a key factor in winning and retaining customers.

I am familiar with a broad range of bank services and products, and experienced in describing them to customers. When account problems arise, I can swiftly troubleshoot them and clearly explain the situation.

Through intense CSR training, I strengthened my knowledge of bank products, promotion, troubleshooting, computer applications, client relations, transactions, and opening new accounts. I am extremely interested in furthering my education in banking.

If you are searching for a career-minded professional who is customer-focused, please contact me to arrange an interview. Thank you for your consideration.

Sincerely,

Noreen Anderson

Enclosure

28

Provided by: *Rhoda Kopy, Toms River, New Jersey*

This letter treats in turn the individual's profile, philosophy, knowledge and ability, training, and interest in an interview. Interest, experience, and service are recurrent themes.

Nancy Vaccaro
462 Summit Drive
Overlook, MT 00000
(555) 555-5555

March 1, 20XX

Louise Mullens
Regional Manager
Corps d'Sprit Fashions
1150 Merchant Highway
Boise, ID 00000

Dear Ms. Mullens:

I was informed by Christine Graham, a sales representative with Corps d'Sprit Fashions, that her position has become available because of her promotion within the company. In speaking with her recently, she thought that I had the necessary qualifications to fill this vacancy and encouraged me to apply for it. My resume is enclosed which details my coaching background and skills that can easily be transferred to a position in sales.

Before moving out of Hillcrest, MT last year, I was cheerleading coach at Holy Family School for a total of 12 years. Under my direction the team had a very impressive competitive record which included winning prestigious championships for the past three years. I feel that their professional appearance, outfitted in Corps d'Sprit Fashions, contributed greatly to their motivation to excel. Our school has been purchasing your products from Ms. Graham for several years and we have been very pleased with the quality of the teamwear and supplies as well as responsiveness of your service.

I would very much like to be considered for the sales opportunity in the South Montana area. I can be available for an interview at your convenience to learn more about the position and how I may be able to meet your goals. May I hear from you soon?

Sincerely,

Nnacy Vaccaro

Enclosure: Resume

29

Provided by: *Melanie A. Noonan, West Paterson, New Jersey*

Italic is used throughout to simulate handwriting and to make the letter different. The transition from cheerleading coach to sales rep is a tough one. Referral by a friend is key.

RANDI NARSINAKIS, R.N.
5280 No. Andover Avenue ◆ Millersville, NJ 00000
(555) 555-5555

Dear Nurse Recruiter:

If your organization is searching for a focused, empathic, and energetic Registered Nurse who thoroughly enjoys the challenges of health care, please contact me to arrange an interview. I have enclosed my resume for your review.

During my clinical rotations as a student nurse, I developed a reputation for being able to manage the care of patients with complex needs, and for my ability to handle a larger patient load than many other students. The evaluations I received were very positive.

I pride myself on being extremely alert and conscientious; as a student, I helped prevent a possible drug interaction in a patient. Good time management skills allow me to balance numerous responsibilities. It's important to me to present a personable, calm, and professional demeanor. My instructors have received compliments on the caring way I interact with patients and their families.

I am extremely enthusiastic about embarking on my nursing career, and hope to have the opportunity to convince you that I would be a valuable addition to your team.

Thank you for your time and consideration.

Sincerely,

Randi Narsinakis, R.N.

Enclosure

30

Provided by: Rhoda Kopy, Toms River, New Jersey

This individual was applying for an entry-level position after a two-year delay following her education to take care of serious family health problems and related responsibilities.

List of Contributors

List of Contributors

The following persons are the contributors of the resumes and cover letters in this book. All of the contributors are professional resume writers. To include in this appendix the names of these writers and information about their businesses is to acknowledge with appreciation their voluntary submissions and the insights expressed in the letters that accompanied the submissions. Resume and cover letter numbers after a writer's contact information are the *numbers of the writer's resumes and cover letters* included in the Gallery, not page numbers.

Alabama

Montgomery

Donald Orlando
The McLean Group
640 South McDonough
Montgomery, AL 36104
Phone: (334) 264-2020
Fax: (334) 264-9227
E-mail: orlandores@aol.com
Member: PARW
Certification: MBA, CPRW
Resume: 96
Cover letter: 23

Arizona

Chandler

Brooke Andrews
A New Beginning
521 N. Superstition Boulevard
Chandler, AZ 85225
Phone: (480) 786-1806
Fax: By arrangement–call first
E-mail: brooke@amug.org
Member: PARW, RWCA (Résumé
Writers Council of Arizona,
President)
Certification: CPRW
Resumes: 66, 200

California

Fresno

Susan Britton Whitcomb
Alpha Omega Services
757 E Hampton Way
Fresno, CA 93704
Phone: (559) 222-7474
Fax: (559) 222-9538
E-mail: topresume@aol.com
Web site: www.careerwriter.com
Member: NRWA, PARW
Certification: NCRW, CPRW
Resumes: 69, 194, 201, 209, 213
Cover letter: 10

Florida

North Miami Beach

Beverley Kagan
Beverley Kagan Resumes
633 NE 167th Street, Suite 607
North Miami Beach, FL 33162
Phone: (305) 653-7887
Toll-free: (888) 779-2171
Fax: (208) 728-4629
E-mail: bevkagan@gate.net
Web site: www.bevkagan.com
Member: PARW, NRWA
Certification: CPRW
Resumes: 18, 65
Cover letter: 6

Pierson

Beverly Harvey
Beverly Harvey Resume & Career Services
P.O. Box 750
Pierson, FL 32180
Phone: (904) 749-3111
E-mail: beverly@harveycareers.com
Web site: harveycareers.com
Member: PARW, NRWA
Certifications: CPRW, JCTC
Resumes: 42, 54, 83, 187, 204, 210

Tampa

M. Carol Heider
Heider's Resume Center
10014 North Dale Mabry, Suite 101
Tampa, FL 33618
Phone: (813) 282-0011
Fax: (813) 926-0170
E-mail: HSSHEIDER@aol.com
Web site: http://browser.to/heidersresumecenter
Member: PARW, NRWA
Certification: CPRW
Resume: 6

Illinois

Arlington Heights

Joellyn Wittenstein
A-1 Quality Résumés
2786 N. Buffalo Grove Rd., Unit 206
Arlington Heights, IL 60004
Phone: (847) 255-1686
Fax: (847) 255-7224
E-mail: Joellyn@interaccess.com
Member: NRWA
Certification: CPRW
Resumes: 27, 129

Chicago

Cathleen M. Hunt
Write Works
6645 N. Oliphant Ave., Ste. H
Chicago, IL 60631
Phone: (773) 774-4420
Fax: (773) 774-4602
E-mail: cmhunt@ibm.net
Member: PARW, NRWA, Board of
   Edison Bark C of C
Certification: CPRW
Resume: 171
Cover letter: 2

Glen Carbon

Carla Culp Coury
10 Downing Place
Glen Carbon, IL 62034
Phone: (618) 288-1625
E-mail: ccoury@empowering.com
Certification: CPRW
Resumes: 33, 44, 64, 181, 193, 225
Cover letter: 14

Schaumburg

Steven A. Provenzano
A Advanced Resume Service, Inc.
850 E. Higgins Road, #125-Y
Schaumburg, IL 60173
Phone: (630) 582-1088
Fax: (630) 582-1105
E-mail: Advresumes@aol.com
Web site: www.TopSecretResumes.com
Member: NRWA
Certification: CPRW
Resumes: 29, 102

Indiana

Carmel

Susan K. Schumm
The Printed Page
327 Parkview Place
Carmel, IN 46032
Phone: (317) 581-1057
Fax: (208) 248-6088
E-mail: theprintedpage@email.com
Web site: http://theprintedpage.cjb.net/
Resumes: 120, 121, 158

Indianapolis

Carole Pefley
TESS, Inc.
5661 Madison Avenue
Indianapolis, IN 46227
Phone: (317) 788-8377
Fax: (317) 788-8378
Member: PARW
Certification: CPRW
Resumes: 111, 118

Vincennes

Colleen S. Jaracz
Innovative Computer Concepts
2581 S. Harvest Acres Drive
Vincennes, IN 47591
Phone: (812) 882-2009
Fax: (812) 882-2192
E-mail: kokolar1@hotmail.com
Resumes: 15, 20, 28, 61, 62, 73, 85, 97, 100, 101, 177, 186, 226, 227
Cover letters: 3, 7, 9

Maine

Bangor

Joan M. Roberts
CareerMasters
61 Main Street, Suite 55
Bangor, ME 04401
Phone: (207) 990-2102
Fax: (207) 990-1197
E-mail: MECareerMasters@aol.com
Web site: www.careercounseling.com
Member: NRWA
Certification: MA, CAGS, CPRW
Resumes: 110, 128, 149
Cover letter: 8

Saco

Patricia Martel
Saco Bay Business Services
263 Ferry Road
Saco, ME 04072
Phone: (207) 284-4960
Fax: (207) 284-5937
E-mail: sbbs@ime.net
Web site: http://w3.ime.net/ ~ sbbs
Member: PARW
Resumes: 58, 130

Waterville

Elizabeth (Lisa) M. Carey
Connections Secretarial Services
6 Boutelle Ave.
Waterville, ME 04901
Phone: (207) 872-5999
Fax: (207) 872-5999
E-mail: RezWriter@aol.com
Certification: CPRW
Resumes: 3, 35
Cover letter: 20

Waterville

Becky J. Davis
Connections Secretarial Services
6 Boutelle Ave.
Waterville, ME 04901
Phone: (207) 872-5999
Fax: (207) 872-5999
E-mail: RezWriter@aol.com
Certification: PLS, CPRW
Resumes: 122, 139

Massachusetts

Northampton

Shel Horowitz, Director
D. Dina Friedman, Co-Director
Accurate Writing & More
P.O. Box 1164
Northampton, MA 01061
Phone: (413) 586-2388
Fax: (617) 249-0153
E-mail: shel@frugalfun.com
Web site: www.accuratewritingandmore.com
Resumes: 1, 31, 162, 220, 229

Michigan

Flint

Janet L. Beckstrom
Word Crafter
1717 Montclair Ave.
Flint, MI 48503
Phone: (800) 351-9818
Fax: (810) 232-9257
E-mail: wordcrafter@voyager.net
Member: PARW
Resumes: 77, 86, 151, 190

Fremont

Patricia L. Nieboer
401 Miller Street
Fremont, MI 49412
Phone: (231) 924-0594
E-mail: zemo@ncats.net
Certification: CPS, CPRW
Resumes: 87, 170

Newport

Deborah L. Schuster
The Lettersmith Résumé Service
P.O. Box 202
Newport, MI 48166
Phone: (734) 586-3335
Fax: (734) 586-2766
E-mail: lettersmith@foxberry.net
Web site: www.thelettersmith.com
Member: PARW, CareerMasters
Certification: CPRW
Resumes: 70, 78, 79, 80, 81, 82, 106, 107, 117

Niles

Patricia Strefling
Resume Writing and Design
3130 S. 11th Street, Suite 103
Niles, MI 49120
Phone: (616) 684-4633
Fax: (616) 684-9898
Member: PARW
Certification: CPRW
Resume: 23
Cover letter: 18

Novi

Lorie Lebert
Résumés for Results
P.O. Box 267
Novi, MI 48376
Phone: (248) 380-6101
Fax: (248) 380-0169
E-mail: DoMyResume@aol.com
Web site: www.DoMyResume.com
Member: PARW, CareerMasters
Certification: CPRW, JCTC
Resumes: 12, 14, 56, 132, 135, 147, 163, 189, 203
Cover letters: 22, 27

Minnesota

Rochester

Beverley Drake
CareerVision Resume & Job Search Systems
1816 Baihly Hills Drive SW
Rochester, MN 55902
Phone: (507) 252-9825
Fax: (507) 252-1559
E-mail: bdcprw@aol.com
Member: PARW, AJST
Certification: CPRW, IJCTC
Resumes: 19, 50, 51, 166

Montana

Butte

Kathlene Y. McNamee
The Word Wizard
523 East Front Street
Butte, MT 59701
Phone: (406) 782-1063
Fax: (406) 782-1063
Web site: www.lifepathcreations.com
Member: PARW
Certifications: CPRW, JCTC
Resume: 92

New Hampshire

Exeter

Stephen H. Mazurka
Mazurka Group Resumes & Writing Services
12 Wentworth Street
Exeter, NH 03833
Phone: (603) 772-7087 or (800) 778-7087
E-mail: stevemaz@nh.ultranet.com
Resumes: 4, 53

New Jersey

Fair Lawn

Vivian Belen
The Job Search Specialist
1102 Bellair Ave.
Fair Lawn, NJ 07410
Phone: (201) 797-2883
Fax: (201) 797-5566
E-mail: vivian@jobsearchspecialist.com
Web site: www.jobsearchspecialist.com
Member: NRWA, AJST, Five O'Clock Club Guild
Certification: NCRW, CPRW, JCTC
Resumes: 55, 72

Rochelle Park

Alesia Benedict
Career Objectives
151 W. Passaic St.
Rochelle Park, NJ 07662
Phone: (800) 206-5353
Fax: (800) 206-5454
E-mail: careerobj@aol.com
Web site: www.getinterviews.com
Member: PARW, CMI (Board), AJST
Certification: CPRW, JCTC
Resumes: 25, 40, 49, 173, 207, 217, 222

Toms River

Rhoda Kopy
A HIRE IMAGE™
26 Main Street, Suite E
Toms River, NJ 08753
Phone: (732) 505-9515
Fax: (732) 505-3125
E-mail: ahi@injersey.com
Member: PARW, NRWA, CareerMasters
Certification: CPRW
Resumes: 36, 127, 148, 165
Cover letters: 11, 16, 28, 30

West Paterson

Melanie A. Noonan
Peripheral Pro
560 Lackawanna Ave.
West Paterson, NJ 07424
Phone: (973) 785-3011
Fax: (973) 785-3071
E-mail: PeriPro1@aol.com
Member: PARW, NRWA
Certification: CPS
Resumes: 17, 113, 150, 188, 197
Cover letters: 19, 29

New York

Elmira

Betty Geller
Apple Résumé & Career Services
456 West Water Street
Elmira, NY 14905
Phone: (607) 734-2090
Fax: (607) 734-2090
E-mail: appleresumes@aol.com
Web site: www.accessresumes.com
Member: NRWA
Certification: CPRW, NCRW
Resumes: 2, 10, 13, 16, 30, 32, 46, 60, 74, 84, 153, 160, 211

Elmira Heights

Lynda C. Grier
OMS
2104A College Avenue
Elmira Heights, NY 14903
Phone: (607) 734-3491 or (800) 900-3491
Fax: (607) 734-4099
E-mail: offman@extrope.net
Member: PARW
Resume: 94

New York

Etta R. Barmann
Compu-Craft Business Services, Inc.
124 East 40th St., Suite 403
New York, NY 10016
Phone: (212) 697-4005
Fax: (212) 697-6475
E-mail: erbarmann@aol.com
Member: PARW
Certification: MSW, CSW, CPRW
Resumes: 144, 215

David Feurst
Compu-Craft Business Services, Inc.
124 East 40th St., Suite 403
New York, NY 10016
Phone: (212) 697-4005
Fax: (212) 697-6475
E-mail: erbarmann@aol.com
Member: PARW
Certification: CPRW
Resume: 8

Judith Friedler
CareerPro New York
56 Barrow St., #G-1
New York, NY 10014
Phone: (212) 647-8726
Fax: (646) 349-1563
E-mail: JudyCPro@aol.com
Web site: www.rezcoach.com
Member: NRWA
Certification: CPRW, NCRW, IJCTC, Five O'Clock Club Guild, CareerMasters, CCM
Resumes: 7, 71, 142, 156, 198

Scotia

Barbara M. Beaulieu
Academic Concepts
214 Second St.
Scotia, NY 12302
Phone: (518) 377-1080
Fax: (518) 382-8462
E-mail: barbra2@banet.net
Member: PARW, NRWA
Certification: CPRW
Resume: 185

Wellsville

Catherine Seebald
1904 Riverview Drive
Wellsville, NY 14895
Phone: (716) 593-1981
Fax: (716) 593-1981
E-mail: jcl228hp@aol.com
Resumes: 59, 98, 221, 228
Cover letter: 13

Yorktown Heights

Mark D. Berkowitz
Career Development Resources
1312 Walter Rd.
Yorktown Heights, NY 10598
Phone: (888) 277-9778 or (914) 962-1548
Fax: (914) 962-0325
E-mail: cardevres@aol.com
Web site: CareerDevResources.com
Member: CMI, PARW, NCDA, ACA
Certification: NCC, NCCC, CPRW, JCTC
Resume: 76

North Carolina

Asheville

Dayna J. Feist
Gatehouse Business Services
265 Charlotte St.
Asheville, NC 28801
Phone: (828) 254-7893
Fax: (828) 254-7894
E-mail: Gatehous@aol.com
Member: PARW
Certification: CPRW, JCTC
Resume: 192
Cover letter: 24

Charlotte

Rose Montgomery, Owner
Mail Order Resume Service
P.O. Box 25155
Charlotte, NC 28229
Phone: (704) 366-9749
Fax: (704) 364-2737
E-mail: deskpub@aol.com
Resumes: 43, 67, 202

Wilmington

Sandy Adcox Saburn
Innovative Coaching Group
3608B Oleander Drive, Suite 103
Wilmington, NC 28403
Phone: (910) 251-9598
Fax: (910) 251-9564
E-mail: icoach@bellsouth.net
Web site: www.innovativecoaching.net
Certification: CPRW
Resumes: 24, 68, 88, 183
Cover letter: 17

Ohio

Athens

Melissa L. Kasler
Résumé Impressions
One N. Lancaster St.
Athens, OH 45701
Phone: (740) 592-3993
Fax: (740) 592-1352
E-mail: mkasler2@eurekanet.com
Member: PARW, NRWA
Certification: CPRW
Resumes: 109, 152, 199

Cincinnati

Louise M. Kursmark
Best Impression Career Services, Inc.
9847 Catalpa Woods Court
Cincinnati, OH 45242
Phone: (888) 792-0030
Fax: (513) 792-0961
E-mail: LK@yourbestimpression.com
Web site: http://yourbestimpression.com
Member: PARW, NRWA, AJST
Certification: CPRW, JCTC, CCM
Resume: 141

Oklahoma

Bartlesville

Laura C. Karlak
936 Sandstone Drive
Bartlesville, OK 74006
Phone: (918) 333-5925
Fax: (918) 333-5925
E-mail: lkarlak@aol.com
Certification: CPRW
Resumes: 63, 196
Cover letter: 12

Rhode Island

Cranston

Phyllis Fern
The Write Place
1062 Reservoir Avenue
Cranston, RI 02910
Phone: (401) 944-0470
E-mail: PhylFern@aol.com
Member: PARW
Certification: CPRW
Resume: 172
Cover letter: 15

South Carolina

Clemson

Karen Swann
TypeRight
384-4 College Avenue
Clemson, SC 29631
Phone: (864) 653-7901
Fax: (864) 653-7701
E-mail: karzim@carol.net
Member: PARW
Certification: CPRW
Resumes: 126, 175, 182
Cover letter: 1

Greenwood

Gwen P. Noffz
110 Satcher Dr.
Greenwood, SC 29646
Phone: (864) 227-3771
E-mail: Psomas@greenwood.net
Certification: CPRW
Resumes: 22, 99

Tennessee

Hendersonville

Carolyn S. Braden
Braden Résumé Solutions
108 La Plaza Dr.
Hendersonville, TN 37075
Phone: (615) 822-3317
Fax: (615) 826-9611
E-mail: bradenresume@home.com
Member: PARW
Certification: CPRW
Resume: 103
Cover letter: 25

Texas

Houston

Nell Turk
Superior Systems
7007 Gulf Freeway, Suite 133
Houston, TX 77087
Phone: (713) 645-9609
Fax: (713) 645-6076
E-mail: Nell@resumehound.com
Web site: www.resumehound.com
Member: NRWA
Resume: 112

New Braunfels

P. J. Margraf
The Career Consulting Corner
1492 Cloud Lane
New Braunfels, TX 78130
Phone: (830) 625-9515
E-mail: career30@careercc.com
Web site: www.careercc.com
   or www.careerconsultingcorner.com
Resumes: 146, 179

Tyler

Ann Klint
Ann's Professional Résumé Service
1608 Cimmarron Trail
Tyler, TX 75703
Phone: (903) 509-8333
Fax: (734) 448-1962
E-mail: Resumes-Ann@tyler.net
Member: PARW, NRWA
Certification: CPRW, NCRW
Resume: 145
Cover letter: 26

The Woodlands

Cheryl Ann Harland
Résumés By Design
25227 Grogan's Mill Rd., Suite 125
The Woodlands, TX 77380
Phone: (281) 296-1659
Fax: (281) 296-1601
E-mail: cah@resumesbydesign.com
Web site: www.resumesbydesign.com
Member: PARW
Certification: CPRW
Resumes: 39, 167, 180

Utah

Salt Lake City

Lynn P. Andenoro
My Career Resource
1214 East Fenway Avenue
Salt Lake City, UT 84102
Phone: (801) 883-2011
E-mail: Lynn@MyCareerResource.com
Web site: www.MyCareerResource.com
Member: PARW, NRWA
Certification: CPRW
Resume: 91

Virginia

Blacksburg

Dr. Kathryn Jordan
Employment Counseling Services, Inc.
201 Church Street
Blacksburg, VA 24060
Phone: (540) 552-2562
Fax: (540) 953-0557
Resume: 224

Virginia Beach

Anne G. Kramer
Alpha Bits
4411 Trinity Ct.
Virginia Beach, VA 23455
Phone: (757) 464-1914
E-mail: akramer@livenet.net
Member: PARW
Certification: CPRW
Resume: 134

Washington

Washougal

Janette M. Campbell
Business Assistants
420 K Street
Washougal, WA 98671
Phone: (360) 835-3441
Fax: (360) 835-7671
E-mail: janettec@worldaccessnet.com
Member: NRWA
Certification: CPRW, NCRW
Resumes: 104, 164, 223

Woodinville

Carole S. Barns
A Great Career®, Inc.
17307 139th Ave. NE
Woodinville, WA 98072
Phone: (425) 487-4008 or (800) 501-4008
Fax: (425) 489-1995
E-mail: BarnsAssoc@aol.com
Web site: www.agreatcareer.com
Member: PARW, NRWA
Resumes: 5, 89, 157, 205
Cover letter: 21

West Virginia

Charleston

Barbie Dallmann
Happy Fingers Word Processing & Résumé Service
1205 Wilkie Dr.
Charleston, WV 25314
Phone: (304) 345-4495
Fax: (304) 343-2017
E-mail: BarbieDall@mindspring.com
Web site: www.ibssn.com/happyfingers
Member: NRWA
Certification: CPRW
Resumes: 41, 93, 195
Cover letters: 4, 5

Wisconsin

Appleton

Kathy Keshemberg
A Career Advantage
1615 E. Roeland, #3
Appleton, WI 54915
Phone: (920) 731-5167
Fax: (920) 739-6471
E-mail: kathyKC@aol.com
Web site: www.acareeradvantage.com
Member: NRWA
Certification: NCRW
Resumes: 178, 216

Location Unknown

Betty Callahan, Resumes 57, 105, 138, 214, 218
Randy Clair, Resumes 26, 37, 38, 48, 161, 174, 208
Jennie R. Dowden, Resumes 114, 133
Shari Favela, Resume 52
Robin Folsom, Resumes 184, 212
Leah K. Goodrich, Resume 131
Janet Hanke, Resume 140
Barry Hunt, Resume 219
Terek A. Jabali, Resumes 21, 176
Marie Keenen Mansheim, Resume 95
Kathleen McConnell, Resume 47
Julie R. Marshall, Resumes 115, 124
David Newbold, Resume 143
Annamarie Pawlina, Resume 125
Sharon Payne, Resumes 116, 168
Claudia Stephenson, Resumes 9, 90, 123, 154
Connie S. Stevens, Resumes 119, 136, 137
Bernard Stopfer, Resumes 108, 191
John Suarez, Resumes 34, 45, 75, 206
Georgia Veith, Resumes 11, 155, 169

For those who would like to contact the Professional Association of Résumé Writers, its address is as follows:

Professional Association of Résumé Writers
1388 Brightwaters Blvd., N.E.
St. Petersburg, FL 33704
Phone: (727) 821-2274
Toll-free: (800) 822-7279
Fax: (813) 894-1277
E-mail: parwhq@aol.com
Web site: www.parw.com

For those who would like to contact the National Résumé Writers' Association, write to Ms. Pat Kendall (NRWA President) at reslady@aol.com or call 1-888-NRWA-444. For membership information, contact Tisha Silvers (tmsilvers@yahoo.com).

Occupation Index

Current or Last Position

Note: Numbers are resume numbers in the Gallery, not page numbers.

3-D Product and Tooling Designer, 81

A

Account Executive, 18, 209, 210
Account Representative, 206
Account Specialist Health
   Resources, 126
Accredited Records Technician, 128
Administrative Secretary, 9
Aircraft Overhauler, 61
Art Director, 46
Assistant Clinical Division Officer
   (U.S. Navy), 200
Assistant Manager, 41, 134, 135,
   181, 192
Assistant to Director, 10
Assistant to Mortgage Broker, 155
Auto Body Painter, 197
Auto Part Sales Manager, 202
Auto Race Track Promoter, 20

B

Bake Shop Trainer, 162
Banquet Server, 143
Bookkeeper, 16
Branch Manager, 178
Broiler Cook, 139
Buyer, 45

C

CAD Designer, 87
Carpenter, 72, 164
Case Manager, 104, 125
Cashier Trainer, 122
Cashier, 38, 122
Certified Hospice Nurse, 104
Certified Medical Transcriptionist,
   128
Certified Nursing Assistant, 130
Charge Nurse, 101
City Editor, 199
Clerk, 16
Client Services Supervisor, 181
Collection Manager, 174

Collections Coordinator, 37
Community Health Nurse, 125
Computer Operator and Systems
   Professional, 27
Computer Services Technician, 33
Computer Systems Manager, 34
Concrete Truck Driver, 158
Consultant, 24, 223
Consultant/Owner, 220
Consulting Analyst, Bank, 189
Corporate Risk Management
   Specialist, 179
Credit Manager, 173
Custodian, 65
Customer Service Manager, 40
Customer Service Representative, 1,
   36
Customer Service Support
   Representative, 8

D

Department Manager, 63
Deputy Clerk, 152
Design Engineer, 82
Detective Sergeant, 149
Development Assistant, 226
Development Production Support
   Supervisor, 71
Director of Golf Instruction, 191
Director of Management
   Development, 54
Director of National Sales/Training,
   54
Director of Sales, 215, 216
Director of Store Design, 49

E

Electronics Technician, 70
Emergency Medical Technician,
   148
Emergency Room Registration
   Nurse, 115
Engineering Technician, 31
Environmental Technician, 95

F

Facilities Chef, 144
Field Guide, 94
Field Representative, 193
Field Service Engineer, 56
Financial Consultant, 7
Front End Manager, Marketing, 32
Full-Charge Bookkeeper, 165
Funeral Director Intern, 186
Funeral Home Assistant (Intern), 227

G

Gateway Service Supervisor, 169
General Insurance Agent, 224
General Manager, 182
General Manager, Country Club, 96
General Office Clerk, 13
Golf Course Intern, 97
Golf Course Superintendent, 93
Graphic Artist, 46
Graphic Designer/Artist, 52
Graphics Artist, 50, 51
Graveyard Captain, Hotel and
   Restaurant Service, 143

H

Head Floral Designer, 44
Head Photographer, 22
Home Health Aide, 124
Home Health Care Registered
   Nurse, 112
Hotel General Manager, 140
Human Resource Associate, 147
Human Resources Manager, 145, 146

I

Illustrator, 46
IMG Marketing Specialist, 217
Implementation Manager, 225
Independent Beauty Consultant, 208
Industrial Engineer, 78, 79
Instructor, 24

K

Kitchen Staff Person, 132

L

Labor Relations Representative, 190
Laboratory Technician, 127
Laborer, 89
Lead Technician, 29
Leading Chief Petty Officer (U.S. Navy), 195
Legal Administrative Assistant, 11
Legal Assistant, 156
Library Page, 76
Licensed Vocational Nurse, 116
Lighting Consultant, 175
Litigation Manager, 174
Loan/Service Officer, 6

M

Machine Operator, 161
Machinery Technician (U.S. Coast Guard), 198
Maintenance Mechanic, 75, 159
Maintenance Technician, 160
Manager of Business Operations, 218
Manager of Customer Care, 39
Manager, 26, 219
Manager, Executive Dining Room, 142
Manager, MIS Operations, 25
Marine Patrol Officer, 151
Marine Training Officer, 151
Master Journeyman Automotive Technician, 57
Materials Manager, 99
Mechanic, 59
Mechanical Technician, 68
Medical Assistant, 127
Mental Health Assistant, 103
MIS Coordinator, 30
MRO/Buyer, 73

N

New Car Salesman, 43
Newsletter Editor, 17
Newspaper Typesetter, 154
Not specified, 35, 90, 106, 123
Nurse Coordinator, Radiology, 111
Nurse Technician, 103
Nursing Services Manager, 110
Nursing Supervisor, 105

O

Occupational Therapist Aide, 120, 121
Occupational Therapy Assistant (Intern), 229

Office Manager, 14, 165, 176
Offset Stripper, 48
Operations Control Manager, 168
Operations Manager, 185
Operations Supervisor, 138
Owner of Consulting Firm, 19, 166
Owner, 26
Owner, Catering Service, 133
Owner/Manager of Family-Owned Business, 188
Owner/Manager, 183

P

Paralegal, 156
Parts Manager, 168
Police Sergeant, 150
Police Station Commander, 150
Police Training Officer, 153
Pond Designer, 21
Precision Measurement Equipment Laboratory Supervisor, 194
Prep Cook, 139
Production Manager, 184
Production Operator, 66
Production Supervisor, 77, 91, 211
Production Worker, 91
Professional Sales Representative, 214
Project Coordinator, 187
Project Engineer, 80
Propulsion Maintenance Facility Manager (USAF), 196
Psychiatric Nurse Supervisor, 109
Psychic, 131
Purchasing Manager, 167

Q

Quality Assurance Specialist, 212
Quality Assurance Supervisor, 64

R

Registered Nurse, 107, 108, 112, 117
Rehab Equipment Specialist, 118
Resident Counselor, 228
Respiratory Technician, 113
Restaurant Manager, 136, 137, 141
Restaurant Owner, 141
Roofer, 85

S

Sales Associate, 201, 203
Sales Counselor, 213
Sales Manager, 221
Sales Representative, 204
Secretary, 12, 114
Senior Collector, 206
Senior Credit Manager, 171

Senior Environmental Coordinator, 98
Senior Health Care Consultant, 129
Senior Lab Technician, 84
Senior Methods Analyst, 190
Server, 143
Service Coordinator, 205
Service Manager, 2
Shift Leader, 122
Shop Foreman, 58
Showroom Manager, 175
Site Manager, 42
Sportswriter, 22
Staff Nurse, 110, 119
Staff Nurse, Same Day Surgery, 102
Statehouse Reporter, 199
Stationary Engineer, 161
Store Manager, 163
Substitute Engineer, 92
Substitute Teacher, 53
Supervisor (USAF), 69
Supervisor, 3, 48, 67, 190
Systems Programmer, 23

T

Teacher's Assistant, 55
Team Leader, 41
Team Manager/Installer, 62
Technical Illustrator, 47
Technician Team Leader, 74
Technician, 60
Teller, 23
TQL Coordinator, 30
Training Coordinator, 100
Training Store Manager, 181
Transportation Supervisor, 170
Travel Expense Auditor, 5

U

Underwater Construction Project Manager, 88
Underwriting Representative, 172
Unigraphics Senior Layout Detailer, 86

V

Vice President of Operations, 177
Vice President of Sales, 83
Vice President, 222

W

Waitperson, 132
Warehouse Foreman, 157
Warehouse Worker, 28
Warranty Administrator, 4

Features Index

Note: Numbers are resume numbers in the Gallery, not page numbers.

The following commonly appearing sections are not included in this Features Index: Work Experience, Work History, Professional Experience, Related Experience, Other Experience, Education (by itself), and References. Variations of these sections, however, *are* included if they are distinctive in some way or have combined headings. As you look for features that interest you, be sure to browse through *all* the resumes. Some important information, such as Accomplishments, may not be listed if it is presented as a subsection of an Experience section.

A

About Me, 62
Academic Achievements, 153
Academic Emphasis, 218
Academic Preparation, 17
Accomplishments, 26, 86, 164, 178, 198
Accomplishments and Experience, 19, 166
Achievements, 5, 9, 40, 142, 217. *See also* Relevant Achievements.
Activities, 10, 125
Activities/Interests, 2, 16, 201
Addendum, 19
Additional, 207
Additional Credentials, 197
Additional Data, 209
Additional Design Experience, 52
Additional Experience, 45, 49
Additional Leadership Activities, 196
Additional Skills, 229
Additional Training, 59, 66, 98
Additional Work Experience, 165
Address, 91
Affiliation(s), 20, 111, 155, 184, 203, 212, 215. *See also* Community Affiliations, Professional Affiliations, Certifications and Affiliations.
Areas of Expertise, 23, 77, 207
Areas of Skill & Expertise, 25
Areas of Skills and Strengths, 49
Associations, 174
Associations and Affiliations, 132
Award and Professional Affiliations, 97
Awards, 69, 194
Awards & Memberships, 50

B

Background, 26, 174
Background Highlights, 17
Background Summary, 48
border. *See* page border.
box, 12, 19, 152, 222. *See also* shadowed box. *Compare* 122.
Budgetary Skills, 168
bullet
    italic diamond as separator, 140
bullets (other than filled circles, squares, and hyphens)
    arrow, 38, 77
    asterisk, 94, 143
    check mark, 3, 17, 24, 87, 144
    chevron, 195
    diamond, 22, 25, 28, 39, 40, 49, 62, 89, 101, 120, 121, 125, 129, 153, 158, 167, 171, 173, 180, 184, 188, 198, 207, 213, 214, 217, 226
    em dash, 48, 98
    en dash, 181, 222
    filled concave diamond, 20, 46, 131, 139
    filled cross, 119
    five-point star, 170, 174, 198, 224
    floral, 44
    four-part diamonds, 96, 189
    half-filled pencil, 85
    matching graphic, 227
    pen nib, 41
    pencil, 97
    pointing finger, 150
    silhouette plane, 61
    right-pointing tip, 19, 24, 26, 27, 37, 55, 56, 69, 108, 135, 163, 166, 178, 191, 194, 213

    thick-thin lines segment, 100
    thick-thin octal star, 50, 51
    thickening arrow, 77
    unfilled arrow, 114
    unfilled circle, 12
    unfilled concave diamond, 15, 139, 186
    unfilled diamond, 14, 57, 89, 138
    unfilled square, 132, 197
    unfilled shadowed circle, 122, 188
    unfilled shadowed square, 133, 147, 190, 195, 205
    WP IconicSymbolsB tip, 82, 93, 126, 177

C

Capabilities, 9, 35, 131, 142, 161
Career Experience, 72
Career Focus, 17, 135, 174
Career Goal(s), 81, 207
Career Highlights, 147
Career History, 208
Career Objective, 40, 48, 49, 60, 92, 109, 123, 124, 170, 173, 185, 211, 217
Career Profile, 13, 176, 223. *See also* Profile.
Career Summary, 129
Certificates, 59, 98
Certification(s), 57, 63, 68, 96, 102, 109, 118, 121, 123, 127, 133, 179
Certifications and Affiliations, 19, 166. *See also* Affiliations.
Certifications and Memberships, 95
change in format, 59
Civic Affiliations, 175

columns, 6, 10, 13, 16, 19, 23, 24, 35, 37, 38, 42, 44, 45, 47, 49, 50, 51, 52, 54, 57, 62, 66, 68, 75, 77, 84, 88, 89, 92, 104, 105, 110, 114, 117, 118, 128, 138, 139, 140, 154, 166, 168, 187, 189, 190, 194, 195, 200, 208, 210, 228

combination resume with an addendum, 19

Community Activities, 92, 179

Community Affiliations, 15, 85, 177. *See also* Affiliations.

Community/Area Involvement, 208

Community Involvement, 110

Community Involvement/Volunteer, 174

Community/Professional Activities, 6

Community Service, 1, 17, 26, 43, 221, 228

Competencies, 199

Computer/Equipment/Skills, 12

Computer Experience, 154

Computer Knowledge, 155

Computer Proficiency, 40, 217

Computer Skills, 6, 31, 60, 137, 167, 209

Construction Equipment and Tools, 89

contact information
    also at bottom of second page, 163
    at bottom of page, 20, 100, 226, 227

Continuing Education, 121, 167, 189

Correspondence Courses, 202

Contact, 209

Coursework Experience, 213

Credentials, 74

Current Certification, 112

D

decorative paper, 111

Demonstrated Strengths, 173

Diving Specialties, 89

E

Education/Awards, 100

Education/License, 107

Education/Memberships, 35

Education/Professional Development, 14, 145

Education/Professional Seminars, 15

Education/Professional Training, 185

Education/Seminars, 177, 226

Education/Specialized Training, 75

Education/Training, 16, 159

Education/Certification, 148

Education and Certification, 56

Education and Licenses, 119

Education and Professional Development, 110, 128

Education and Seminars, 37

Education and Training, 86, 91, 116, 122, 140, 174, 195, 199, 206, 208, 228

Educational Background, 27, 40, 129, 173, 214, 217

ellipses, 6, 50, 51, 93, 109, 131, 150, 165, 191

Emphasis, 201

Emphasis, Interests, 208

Employers, 168

Employment, 221

Employment Experience, 223

Employment Highlights, 43, 67, 202

Employment History, 190

Employment Objective, 86, 176. *See also* Objective.

Employment Summary, 147, 201

Experience Highlights, 21

Experience Profile, 219

Experience subheadings, 22

Experience Summary, 194, 209

Expertise, 18, 72, 163

F

Fashion Retail Experience, 15

Focus, 87

font
    Courier, 4
    special use of, 45, 51, 195

functional resume, 1, 16, 22, 35, 157

G

Goal, 150

Goal/Interest, 20

graphic, 41, 44, 70, 79, 93, 116, 117, 139, 170, 206, 227

H

Health Care Experience, 103

Highlights, 49, 72, 149

Highlights of Employment, 150

Highlights of Nursing Experience, 119

Highlights of Qualifications, 2, 86, 91, 108, 125, 140, 145, 159, 171, 190, 191, 206, 208

History, 18

Hobbies, 90

Hobbies/Activities, 37

Honors, 99

Honors and Achievements, 101

Honors and Awards, 9, 193. *See also* Awards.

Human Resource Management Experience, 146

I

Interest(s), 67, 73, 84, 213

Inventory Skills, 168

J

Job Target, 57

K

Key Skills Profile, 219

Keyword Summary, 224

L

Languages, 42, 65, 113

Leadership Training, 194

License and Certification, 101

Licenses, 7, 60, 108, 161

Licensure, 54

Licensure and Professional Affiliation, 170

Limitations, 21

line(s)
    horizontal
        between categories in a section, 3
        between sections, 6, 14, 24, 33, 45, 56, 64, 66, 77, 80, 89, 128, 132, 151, 166, 181, 193, 200, 202
        enclosing information, 10, 35, 38, 42, 54, 64, 68, 72, 83, 84, 94, 99, 100, 109, 114, 132, 147, 159, 163, 165, 172, 174, 180, 181, 210, 218
        enclosing section headings, 125
        partial, with section headings, 190, 222
        special
            in contact information, 12, 23, 25, 30, 35, 39, 79, 82, 90, 92, 131, 134, 149, 156, 178, 179, 180, 181, 188, 192, 193, 201, 213
            with section headings, 19, 192, 203, 214
        with section heading(s), 17, 48, 49, 110, 134, 135, 176, 207. *See also* enclosing section headings.
        with thicker line overlays, 24, 33, 80

vertical
 between graphic and
  information, 44
 between person's name and
  information, 209
 between section headings and
  information, 105, 113
 between testimonials and
  information, 96
 pair of, 168
 with contact information, 5,
  186

M

Major Accomplishments, 129, 207
Major Projects & Accomplishments,
 25
Major Strengths, 6
Managerial Skills, 168
Membership(s), 54, 96, 121. *See also*
 Professional Memberships.
Military, 90, 159, 169, 199, 204
Military Experience, 63, 88, 197
Military Honors & Awards, 199
Military Schools, 202
Military Service, 32, 68

O

Objective, 1, 2, 3, 5, 10, 11, 13, 15,
 16, 21, 22, 23, 28, 29, 36, 38, 55,
 58, 61, 63, 66, 67, 69, 70, 74, 76,
 80, 88, 89, 90, 91, 95, 96, 101, 102,
 103, 107, 108, 113, 114, 119, 120,
 121, 127, 130, 133, 134, 136, 137,
 139, 143, 144, 148, 150, 152, 153,
 154, 157, 158, 160, 165, 181, 184,
 186, 197, 205, 206, 212, 219, 224,
 226, 227. *See also* Career Objective,
 Employment Objective,
 Professional Objective, Work
 Objective.
Objective and Goal, 97
Of Special Note, 203
Office Administration, Including
 Human Resource Issues, 166
Office Management Experience, 15
Other, 224
Other Employment, 188, 197
Other Information, 163
Other Work Experience, 53
Overview, 35, 114
Overview of Qualifications, 66

P

page border, 8, 10, 25, 26, 34, 40,
 46, 49, 76, 119, 123, 145, 173, 201,
 207, 217, 222

Payoffs, 96
Personal, 200
Personal Data, 81
Personal Profile, 186
Personal Qualifications, 161
Personal Qualities, 168
Personnel Skills, 168
Pertinent Skills, 127. *See also* Skills.
Previous Certifications, 112
Previous Experience, 172
Prior Experience, 176
Problem-Solving Expertise, 192
Professional Accomplishments, 223
Professional Achievements, 149
Professional Affiliations, 18, 76, 93,
 128, 145. *See also* Affiliations.
Professional and Community
 Affiliations, 44, 223
Professional Associations, 107
Professional Background, 131
Professional Development, 44
Professional Employment, 49
Professional Employment History,
 108
Professional Goal, 213
Professional Highlights, 39, 214, 224
Professional Memberships, 137,
 217. *See also* Memberships.
Professional Objective, 94, 140, 146,
 159, 179. *See also* Objective.
Professional Organizations, 118, 179
Professional Overview, 14
Professional Profile, 30, 41, 200. *See*
 also Profile.
Professional Safety Work History, 179
Professional Seminars, 97, 186
Professional Skills, 11. *See also* Skills.
Professional Summary, 39, 207
Professional Training, 144
Professional Training and
 Development, 180
Profile, 4, 5, 8, 12, 15, 20, 24, 29,
 33, 37, 44, 46, 47, 61, 62, 72, 73,
 76, 78, 79, 82, 85, 94, 96, 97, 99,
 101, 102, 110, 125, 128, 156, 159,
 167, 169, 172, 175, 177, 178, 180,
 182, 184, 187, 198, 199, 204, 205,
 210, 212, 215, 226, 227. *See also*
 Career Profile, Professional Profile,
 Technical Profile.
Profile of Experience and
 Accomplishments, 174
Profile/Skills, 100
Profile Summary, 40, 211, 217
Project Management Philosophy, 195
Public Office, 221, 228

Q

Qualifications, 31, 32, 44, 56, 80,
 89, 93, 98, 132, 152, 170, 221, 228

Qualifications & Strengths, 57, 105,
 138
Qualifications Summary, 15, 77,
 141, 185, 195
Qualified by, 150

R

Related Activities, 53, 151
Related Background Summary, 170
Related Experiences, Strengths, 201
Related Work History, 170
Relevant Achievements, 32
Relevant Experience, 137, 185
Relevant Professional Experience, 104
Relevant Skills and Experience, 38
Research Experience, 203
Results, 163

S

School and Community Activities, 88
section headings in a box, 86
Selected Achievements, 191
Selected Examples of Success, 96
Selected Specialized Training, 18
Seminars/Training, 48
shading, 147, 203, 217, 222
shadowed box, 19, 166. *See also* box.
Skill Profile, 43
Skill Summary, 186
Skills, 8, 10, 71, 88, 153, 154, 162,
 198. *See also* Computer Skills,
 Pertinent Skills, Professional Skills.
Skills and Abilities, 13, 16, 67, 90, 92
Skills and Accomplishments, 36
Special Projects, 92
Special Skills, 62, 65, 76
Special Training, 33, 88
Specialized Training, 39, 57, 58, 76,
 118, 161
Specialized Training & Education,
 142
Strengths, 26, 28, 107, 117, 118,
 181, 193, 217
Strengths and Skills, 197
Student Experience, 186
Studies, 87
Summary, 7, 70, 71, 88, 133, 143,
 148, 161, 162, 163, 191, 193, 196,
 214, 220
Summary of Experience, 53, 98, 190
Summary of Expertise, 188
Summary of Professional
 Experience, 108
Summary of Qualifications, 3, 12,
 16, 36, 37, 38, 45, 58, 59, 65, 103,
 111, 126, 127, 130, 135, 137, 139,
 144, 146, 157, 164, 179, 183, 210,
 216, 222

Summary of Qualifications and
  Highlights, 189
Summary of Skills, 160
Summary Profile, 208
Supplemental Experience, 55
Synopsis of Personal Attributes, 191

T

table, 12, 13, 19, 57, 203
Technical Coursework, 92
Technical Equipment, 89
Technical Experience, 62
Technical Profile, 25. *See also* Profile.
Technical Skills, 48, 60, 113

Technical Summary, 27
Technical Training, 61, 194
Testimonial(s), 20, 37, 44, 69, 96,
  100, 199
Thumbnail Sketch, 17
Training, 26, 53, 68, 151, 221
Training & Certifications, 24, 64
Training & Education, 111
Training/Education, 171
type
  effective changes, 25

U

United States Navy Experience, 195

V

Volunteer, 21
Volunteer Activities, 150
Volunteer Community Involvement,
  38
Volunteer Experience, 101, 203, 208
Volunteer Work, 67

W

Work Objective, 171
Writing, Editorial, and Desktop
  Publishing Support Services, 19